Lecture Notes in Computer Science 12700

More information about this subseries at http://www.springer.com/series/7407

Steven Derrien · Frank Hannig ·
Pedro C. Diniz · Daniel Chillet (Eds.)

Applied Reconfigurable Computing

Architectures, Tools, and Applications

17th International Symposium, ARC 2021
Virtual Event, June 29–30, 2021
Proceedings

 Springer

Editors
Steven Derrien (iD)
IRISA
University of Rennes 1
Rennes, France

Pedro C. Diniz (iD)
INESC-ID
Lisboa, Portugal

Frank Hannig (iD)
Friedrich-Alexander-Universität
Erlangen-Nürnberg
Erlangen, Germany

Daniel Chillet (iD)
ENSSAT
University of Rennes 1
Lannion, France

ISSN 0302-9743   ISSN 1611-3349   (electronic)
Lecture Notes in Computer Science
ISBN 978-3-030-79024-0   ISBN 978-3-030-79025-7   (eBook)
https://doi.org/10.1007/978-3-030-79025-7

LNCS Sublibrary: SL1 – Theoretical Computer Science and General Issues

This Springer imprint is published by the registered company Springer Nature Switzerland AG
The registered company address is: Gewerbestrasse 11, 6330 Cham, Switzerland

Preface

The 17th International Symposium on Applied Reconfigurable Computing (ARC 2021) was organized by the Université de Rennes 1 and Inria, France, during June 29–30, 2021. Unfortunately, due to the ongoing protective measures resulting from the COVID-19 pandemic and the subsequent travel restrictions, we had to opt for a virtual ARC 2021 symposium meeting.

As with previous years, the ARC 2021 edition covered a broad spectrum of applications of reconfigurable computing, from driving assistance, data and graph processing acceleration, and computer security to the societal topic of supporting early diagnosis of COVID-19 infections. This year's symposium program included 14 regular and 11 short (poster) contributions selected from a total of 36 submissions. The selection process was very competitive with each submission having an average of four reviews. The strong technical program also included a keynote talk on the timely topic of FPGA hardware security in the cloud by Prof. Dirk Koch from the University of Manchester, UK.

This year's successful program was made possible by the contribution of many talented individuals. First and foremost, we would like to thank all the authors who responded to our call for papers and the members of the Program Committee and the additional external reviewers who, with their opinion and expertise, ensured a program of the highest quality. Last but not the least, we would like to thank Angeliki Kritikakou who ensured that publicity and web interactivity remained engaging and responsive.

Thank you all.

June 2021

Daniel Chillet
Frank Hannig
Steven Derrien
Pedro C. Diniz

Organization

General Chair

Daniel Chillet   University of Rennes 1/ENSSAT, France

Program Committee Chairs

Frank Hannig   Friedrich-Alexander University Erlangen-Nürnberg,
           Germany

Steven Derrien   University of Rennes 1, France

Steering Committee

Hideharu Amano	Keio University, Japan
Jürgen Becker	Karlsruhe Institute of Technology, Germany
Mladen Berekovic	Braunschweig University of Technology, Germany
Koen Bertels	QBee.EU, Belgium
João M. P. Cardoso	University of Porto, Portugal
Katherine (Compton) Morrow	University of Wisconsin-Madison, USA
George Constantinides	Imperial College London, UK
Pedro C. Diniz	INESC-ID, Portugal
Philip H. W. Leong	University of Sydney, Australia
Walid Najjar	University of California, Riverside, USA
Roger Woods	Queen's University Belfast, UK

Program Committee

Hideharu Amano	Keio University, Japan
Zachary Baker	Los Alamos National Laboratory, USA
João Bispo	University of Porto, Portugal
Vanderlei Bonato	University of São Paulo Brazil
Marcelo Brandalero	Brandenburg University of Technology, Cottbus, Germany
Christos Bouganis	Imperial College London, UK
João Canas Ferreira	University of Porto, Portugal
João M. P. Cardoso	University of Porto, Portugal
Ray Cheung	City University of Hong Kong, Hong Kong
Daniel Chillet	University of Rennes 1/Inria, France
Steven Derrien	University of Rennes/Inria, France
Pedro C. Diniz	INESC-ID, Portugal
Giorgos Dimitrakopoulos	Democritus University of Thrace, Greece

Additional Reviewers

Muhammad Ali
Anna Drewes
Hassan Ghasemzadeh Mohammadi
Veronia Iskandar
Ahmed Kamaleldin
Farnam Khalili Maybodi
Konstantina Koliogeorgi
Martin Koppehel

Christian Lienen
Daniele Passaretti
Amin Sahebi
Pedro Filipe Silva
Leonardo Solis-Vasquez
Lukas Sommer
Christoph Spang
Ioannis Stamoulias

Contents

Applications

Fast Approximation of the Top-k Items in Data Streams Using a Reconfigurable Accelerator

Ali Ebrahim$^{(\boxtimes)}$ and Jalal Khalifat

University of Bahrain, Sakhir Campus, Bahrain
ahasan@uob.edu.bh

Abstract. This paper presents a novel method for finding the top-k items in data streams using a reconfigurable accelerator. The accelerator is capable of extracting an approximate list of the topmost frequently occurring items in an input stream, which is only scanned once without the need for random-access. The accelerator is based on a hardware architecture that implements the well-known *Probabilistic* sampling algorithm by mapping its main processing stages to two custom systolic arrays. The proposed architecture is the first hardware implementation of this algorithm, which shows better scalability compared to other architectures that are based on other stream algorithms. When implemented on an Intel Arria 10 FPGA (10AX115N2F45E1SG), 50% of the FPGA chip is sufficient for 3000+ Processing Elements (PEs). Experimental results on both synthetic and real input datasets showed very good accuracy and significant throughput gains compared to existing solutions. With achieved throughputs exceeding 300 Million items/s, we report average speedups of 20x compared to typical software implementations, 1.5x compared to GPU-accelerated implementations, and 1.8x compared to the fastest FPGA implementation.

Keywords: Data stream · Probabilistic sampling · Top-k items · FPGA

1 Introduction

Ranking elements or items in data according to their frequency is a fundamental problem in data science. In many applications, a user maybe just interested in finding the top-k most frequent items in input data (k is a positive integer! example: top-100 frequent items). Frequent items of interest could represent popular search queries in a server, frequently visited websites in network traffic, top-selling items in retail data, most active stocks in financial data, etc. In the aforementioned examples, finding an exact list of the top-k items using conventional algorithms is very difficult due to the nature of the data. The data can be either a continuous feed that can't be buffered and processed quickly enough with the available computational resources, or simply, the data is just too large to handle with the available memory.

Such large sources of data are best modeled as a "data stream" [1]. In the data stream model, the data is only allowed to be processed once before deletion. Usually, approximation techniques are used in stream algorithms to meet the time and memory constrains.

© Springer Nature Switzerland AG 2021
S. Derrien et al. (Eds.): ARC 2021, LNCS 12700, pp. 3–17, 2021.
https://doi.org/10.1007/978-3-030-79025-7_1

Many approximate algorithms have been developed to find frequently occurring items in data stream [2, 3]. A distinct class of these algorithms is referred to as "counter-based" algorithms. In general, counter-based algorithms use a fixed number of counters to guess the frequent items in a single pass over the input. The larger the number of counters, the better the accuracy of the results.

With the growing demand for high-throughput stream processing, it is important to explore the use of hardware accelerators to accelerate stream algorithms. While Graphics Processing Units (GPUs) are an excellent choice for applications that require vector processing, Field Programable Gate Arrays (FPGAs) have shown great potential in spatial processing [4, 5]. Custom accelerators tailored for specific applications can be efficiently implemented using the high-density and high-speed FPGA devices available today. In addition, modern FPGAs contains all the necessary optimized hardwired Intellectual Property (IP) cores required for high performance acceleration, examples: high-speed transceivers, PCIe controllers, DDR memory controllers, etc.

This paper presents the architecture and FPGA implementation of a novel accelerator for finding the top-k items in data streams. The presented architecture is the first hardware adaptation of the *Probabilistic* sampling algorithm proposed in [6]. The architecture maps the algorithm to two custom systolic arrays that feed through a standard input FIFO. When implemented on an Intel Arria 10 10AX115N2F45E1SG device, 3000+ PEs consumed less than 50% of this FPGA chip. Furthermore, timing closure was achieved with minimal place-and-route effort for clock frequencies exceeding 250 MHz. Test results on both synthetic and real datasets showed that the FPGA implementation of the accelerator has near-perfect accuracy for naturally skewed input streams. In addition, the test results showed that the effect of data skew is negligible on the accelerator's throughput, which was sustained at an item update per clock cycle in all test runs. This is a significant improvement, compared to other FPGA-based accelerators, GPU-accelerated implementations, and software implementations.

The remainder of this paper is organized as follows: Sect. 2 presents a gentle introduction to the "top-k items" problem and the *Probabilistic* algorithm. Section 3 discusses the related published work on accelerating the top-k problem using FPGAs. Section 4 details the proposed hardware architecture and its operation. Section 5 discusses the FPGA implementation of this architecture using an Intel Arria 10 FPGA. Test results based on synthetic and real datasets are presented in Sect. 6 along with the discussion and evaluation. Finally, conclusions and future work plans are summarized in Sect. 7.

2 Approximate Top-K Items in Data Stream: Probabilistic Sampling

Assume a stream S of size N. A naive exact solution for finding the top-k items in S is to keep a counter that count the number of occurrences of each distinct item when processing S. This requires l distinct counters, where l is the number of distinct items in S. For a general input distribution, finding an exact solution is impractical or even impossible due to the space complexity. An approximate algorithm aims to find an approximate list of the top-k items using m counters, where $m << l$. The *Probabilistic* sampling algorithm in [6] is generally considered fast and efficient for finding the approximate top-k items using m counters. The algorithm divides the input stream into rounds of size r, which are processed using the m counters. At the round boundaries, the algorithm updates a list of the k distinct items with the highest round counts (see Fig. 1).

Algorithm: Probabilistic

---

for *each round of r items in S* **do**
    for *each item in round* **do**
        if *item is stored* **then**
        └ Increment item's count
        else if *stored items* $< m$ **then**
        └ Store item and set its count to 1
    Update a record of k distinct items with highest round counts
    └ Clear all m stored items and counts

Fig. 1. Pseudo code for the *Probabilistic* algorithm

The authors in [6] proved that for an arbitrary distribution, with high probability, the true frequencies of the reported k items are close to the frequencies of the truly most frequent items in N. In fact, any top item with a relative frequency above the threshold of $1/\sqrt{mN}$ is guaranteed, with high probability, to be reported by the algorithm. Of course, the larger m, the more probable that a true top item will not be missed. The best choice of r will depend on whether the size of the stream N is known beforehand or not. For best results, r should be set to $\sqrt{mN}$, if N is known. In case the exact size of the stream is unknown, r is still set to $\sqrt{mN}$, however, the parameter N is dynamically updated as $N = 1, 2, 4, ..., 2^j, ...$ until the stream is exhausted.

3 Related Work

In systolic array architectures, globally clocked PEs can be arranged spatially to execute hundreds, or even thousands of instructions per clock cycle [7]. The idea of pipelining a large number of counting units or PEs using the FPGA reconfigurable resources was explored for accelerating itemset mining of transactional datasets [8–10]. These itemset mining accelerators were designed to find common sets or sequences among a huge number of separate transactions rather than counting items in a data stream. A limited number of systolic array architectures were specifically designed to address stream item counting and the top-k problem. In [11], the authors presented three reconfigurable accelerators, the best out of the three is a systolic array that implements the *Space-Saving* algorithm [12]. Similar to *Probabilistic*, *Space-Saving* uses m counters that monitor the first m distinct items. However, a new incoming item, not in the any of the m counters, replaces the item with the minimum count rather than being discarded. Mapping this behavior to hundreds of sequentially connected PEs is difficult because the position of the PE monitoring the item with the minimum count needs to be known and accessible to be able to place the new item. In [11], the architecture relies on physically re-arranging the items within the array so that the position of the item with the minimum count is fixed. This resulted in a complex array that does not scale well when its size is increased. The authors in [13], presented a similar optimized array with better scalability, however, it can only accept a new item every two clock cycles. The array in [14] is also based on the *Space-Saving* algorithm. It consists of simple PEs with unidirectional data flow. The item with the minimum count is replaced with a new item by stalling the array to feed a special instruction that replaces the item. This array achieved higher average throughput compared to [11] and [13], however, the throughput was significantly affected by the input skew.

Another interesting work is the accelerator presented in [15], which is not based on a systolic array architecture. It implements the *Count-Min* sketch algorithm [16]. The accelerator uses a family of hash functions to update a bucket of count values representing estimates of item counts. The count values are stored in dual-port block RAM to allow for simultaneous read/write operations. Although the *Count-Min* algorithm can be used for the top-k problem, the implemented accelerator was designed so that it requires an item of interest to be queried in order to update and output its estimated count. This does not directly fit into the top-k problem, which assumes no prior knowledge of the items in the stream. Finally, the systems in [17, 18] also utilize block RAM to store the count estimates of frequent items, however, each RAM memory location is shared between an item count register and other fields necessary for computing the frequent items. Both implementations could only fit very small count registers, which are insufficient for any practically sized inputs.

4   The Proposed Accelerator

4.1   Architecture Overview

There are two main operations in the *Probabilistic* algorithm: counting the first m distinct items in each round and updating a list of the top-k items from the m items. We map these two operations to two systolic arrays one with m PEs and the other with k PEs (see Fig. 2). Similar to the works in [11, 13, 14], we model the items as fixed-sized integers, say, 32-bit. We aim for m to be in the range of few thousand PEs and k in the range of few hundred PEs. These ranges are assumed to be practical for a general input distribution, and also feasible for implementation on a med-density FPGA. The input stream is fed into an input FIFO, which interfaces to the first array through some control logic. The control logic generates the necessary control signals to pass the items in rounds. The m PEs are designed to be as small and simple as possible. During a round, each m PE continuously forwards a count update for the item it monitors. These updates are passed to an "Item Filter" when they exit the array. The item filter blocks any update with count less than the minimum count in the current top-k item list. The second array keeps a list of the k distinct items with the highest count updates received from the item filter. This array is more complex than the first array, as it requires stalling and feedback when replacing an existing top-k item with a new item. It also requires a FIFO buffer to account for the stalling operations and to put backpressure on the input stream when needed. Considering the relatively small size of k, readouts of the top-k items can be easily obtained using a parallel-in serial-out shift register.

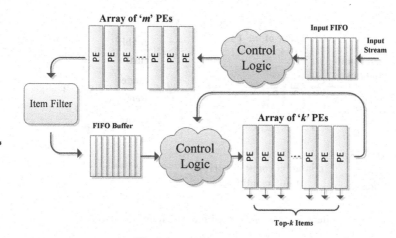

Fig. 2. Architecture overview

4.2 Counting Items in a Round

Whenever data is present in the input FIFO and no backpressure is caused by the internal FIFO buffer, the control logic proceeds with the item counting process, which is performed using the first array in the accelerator. All the PEs in this array are identical and have very simple interconnections as shown in Fig. 3. There are two control signals passed from one PE to the next. A *clock enable* signal is used to turn on/off a PE. A *mode* signal is used to make a PE execute one of two simple procedures. A PE can operate in the following modes: COUNT and FORWARD. There are also two parameters passed between PEs, an "item" parameter, and a "count" parameter. These two parameters are forwarded from one PE to the next as *<item, count>* pairs representing the count updates of the monitored items.

During a round, the array updates the counts of the first m distinct items before all internal registers in the PEs are reset at the boundary with the next round. A simple timeout counter is used to indicate the round boundaries. At each round boundary, the array is stalled for two clock cycles to allow for an asynchronous clear signal to propagate through the array (see Fig. 3). The default mode of the array is the COUNT mode. In this mode, PEs execute the algorithm in Fig. 4. An empty PE enabled in COUNT mode will always store the incoming item and set its count to 1. Whenever this item is encountered again, the count is incremented and the updated *<item, count>* pair is passed to the next PE in the FORWARD mode. PEs enabled in the FORWARD mode, will act like "forwarding circuits" causing the *<item, count>* updates to propagate through the array. When the *<item, count>* updates exit the array, they are received by the item filter. The purpose of this filter is to reduce the load on the second array in the accelerator by filtering out any update with a count value less than the minimum count value in the current top-k item list.

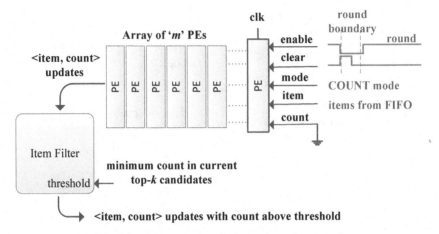

Fig. 3. Counting the first distinct m items in a round

Algorithm: COUNT Mode

```
// Upon receiving a new item in COUNT mode
if PE is empty then
│  Store item and set count to 1
└  Pass <item, count> pair to next PE in FORWARD mode
else if incoming item = stored item then
│  Increment count
└  Pass <item, count> pair to next PE in FORWARD mode
else
└  Pass incoming item to next PE in COUNT mode
```

Fig. 4. COUNT mode

4.3 Maintaining a Record of the Top-k Items

The *<item, count>* updates with counts exceeding the threshold of the filter will pass to the second array through a FIFO buffer. The interconnections of the PEs in the second array are shown in Fig. 5. Opposed to the first array, PEs are not reset between rounds, a global reset signal is only used for resetting the array if the entire system is to be reset. An extra "*min.*" interconnection is used for shifting the minimum count value out of the array. In addition, the current *<item, count>* record of the top-k items can be read through parallel connections. This requires the inclusion of a parallel-in serial-out shift register of size k. PEs in this array operate in two modes: the UPDATE and the REPLACE mode.

Updating Count Values. New *<item, count>* updates are loaded in the array from the FIFO buffer in the UPDATE mode. In this mode, the PEs execute the algorithm in Fig. 6. An empty PE will always store the incoming *<item, count>* pair as a top-k item candidate. A populated PE will evaluate the incoming item with the item it stores, if the items match and the incoming count value is larger than the stored count value, the stored count value is updated. In case of an item mismatch, the incoming <item, count> pair is forwarded to the next PE in the UPDATE mode. At the same time, the incoming value at the *min.* interconnection is compared to the stored count value and the minimum out of the two is forwarded to the next PE. By tying the *min.* input pins of the first PE to a high logic state, the minimum count value in the array will eventually exit the array along with an <item, count> pair if no match is found in any of the *k* populated PEs. This minimum count value is essential for two operations: 1) used as a reference for the item to be replaced according to *Probabilistic*, 2) used as a threshold value for the item filter.

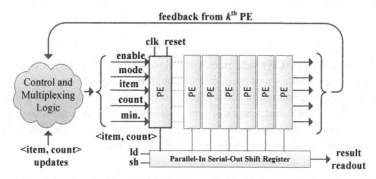

Fig. 5. PEs maintain a record of the top-*k* items

Algorithm: UPDATE Mode

```
// Upon receiving an <item, count> pair and min.  count
   value in UPDATE mode
if PE is empty then
   Store <item, count> pair
else if incoming item = stored item then
   if incoming count > stored count then
      Update stored count

else
   Pass incoming <item, count> pair to next PE in UPDATE mode
   Pass min(stored count, incoming min. count value) to next PE
```

Fig. 6. UPDATE mode

Replacing the Item with Minimum Count. If an <item, count> pair exits the array in the UPDATE mode with a count value larger than the shifted minimum count value, the control logic registers the minimum count value and stalls the array to reload the <item, count> pair along with the minimum count value back to the first PE in the REPLACE mode (see Fig. 7a).

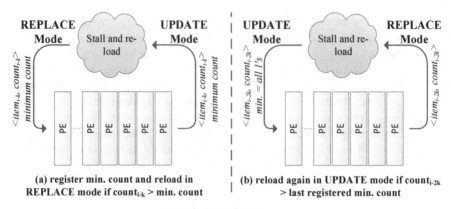

Fig. 7. Stalling the array

The PEs in the REPLACE mode execute the algorithm shown in Fig. 8. In this mode, an incoming *<item, count>* pair propagates through the array until it replaces a stored pair when the incoming minimum count reference value matches the stored count value in a PE. Also, the *<item, count>* pair stops propagating through the array if the incoming item matches a stored item. This situation could occur when consecutive *<item, count>* updates of the same item are reloaded in the REPLACE mode.

Algorithm: REPLACE Mode

```
// Upon receiving an <item, count> pair and min.  count
   value in REPLACE mode
if incoming item = stored item then
   if incoming count > stored count then
      Update stored count

else if incoming min. count value = stored count then
   Replace current <item, count> pair

else
   Pass incoming <item, count> pair to next PE in REPLACE mode
   Pass incoming min. count value to next PE
```

Fig. 8. REPLACE mode

In general, replacing an item from the top-k candidates will only cause a single clock cycle stall. This should not affect the overall throughput of the array because the total number of occurrences of a new top-k candidate should be small compared to the size of a processing round. However, it is possible for an *<item, count>* pair not to replace a stored pair when it is reloaded into the array in the REPLACE mode. This occurs because it is possible for the minimum count value in the array to change by successive updates before it is registered. This situation is detected when an *<item, count>* pair exits the array in the REPLACE mode (see Fig. 7b). If the count value is no longer larger than the last registered minimum count, no further action is needed because the item is no longer considered a top-k candidate. Otherwise, to deal with this unlikely situation, the minimum count value needs to be recalculated by reloading the <*item, count*> pair for another pass through the array in the UPDATE mode.

5 FPGA Implementation

This section evaluates the scalability of the proposed accelerator when implemented on a modern FPGA. The Intel (formerly Altera) Arria 10 10AX115N2F45E1SG FPGA device was chosen as a target device [19]. This is the largest device in the mid-range/mid-density Arria 10 GX family with 427,200 Adaptive Logic Modules (ALMs). This device contains all the necessary features for hardware acceleration: hard Gen3 PCIe IP block, hard DDR4 memory controllers and an extensive range of supported soft IPs.

All the results reported in this section are post-place-and-route results obtained after setting the router effort option in the synthesis tool to normal (balanced between area and speed). Both the "item" and the "count" parameters in the accelerator were fixed at 32-bit similar to the works in [11, 13, 14]. Configurations with array sizes that would result more than 50% chip utilization were not considered. This to account for any required IPs when integrating the accelerator into a larger system: PCIe controller, DDR RAM controller, DMA controller, etc.

Table 1 shows the resource utilization breakdown and the maximum clock frequency (f_{max}) achieved for the first array in the accelerator when configured in different sizes. As expected from a systolic array design, the maximum clock frequency does not drop sharply when increasing the array size from 1000 to 3000 PEs. This was also the case for the more complex second array when increasing the number of PEs from 100 to 300 (see Table 2). It is noted that the results reported in Table 2 are for arrays that include the parallel-in-serial-out shift register required for the result readout. Based on the initial results from Table 1 and Table 2, we implemented three configurations of the full accelerator with m fixed at 3000 to allow for best accuracy within the 50% chip utilization constrain. k was set to 100, 200 and 300, respectively. The FIFOs were implemented using the block RAM resources in the FPGA and the depth of both FIFOs in the accelerator was fixed at 256. For easier synchronization and less complex control logic, we implemented the FIFOs as First World Fall Through (FWFT) FIFOs (known as Show-Ahead FIFOs in Intel FPGAs). The resource utilization and maximum clock frequency of the three accelerator configurations are shown in Table 3. We note that the depth of the FIFO buffer, shown in Fig. 2, should theoretically be at least k to guarantee that the FIFO will never overflow as a result of the array stall situations explained in Fig. 7. The FIFO depth is a little short of k in the third accelerator configuration in Table 3, however, we show later in Sect. 6 that this did not have any impact in practice.

All configurations in Table 3 have more than double the number of PEs compared to the systolic array accelerators presented in Sect. 3. We note that these accelerators are based on a different algorithm implemented on different FPGA families, therefore, comparing the number of PEs is insignificant. A rather more interesting comparison is the number of distinct items and the size of the stream each system can handle. Using 32-bit items, as in the case of all presented accelerators, allows for streams with up to 2^{32}

Table 1. Resource utilization and maximum clock frequency for the first array in the accelerator on an Intel Arria 10 FPGA (10AX115N2F45E1SG)

Array size (m)	ALMs	Registers	f_{max} (MHz)
1 PE	57 (<1%)	132	606
1000	59223 (14%)	138021	359
2000	118231 (28%)	271037	348
3000	177185 (41%)	410128	346

Table 2. Resource utilization and maximum clock frequency for the second array in the accelerator on an Intel Arria 10 FPGA (10AX115N2F45E1SG)

Array Size (k)	ALMs	Registers	f_{max} (MHz)
1 PE	127 (<1%)	227	414
100	13180 (3%)	27218	343
200	26511 (6%)	54820	329
300	39823 (9%)	79284	306

Table 3. Resource utilization and maximum clock frequency for the proposed accelerator on an Intel Arria 10 FPGA (10AX115N2F45E1SG)

Accelerator Size	ALMs	Registers	Block RAM	f_{max} (MHz)
$k = 100, m = 3000$	184056 (43%)	430105	24576 (<1%)	308
$k = 200, m = 3000$	200278 (47%)	456424	24576 (<1%)	290
$k = 300, m = 3000$	216450 (51%)	484125	24576 (<1%)	276

distinct items, which is sufficient for many practical applications. This includes product IDs in market basket data, IPv4 addresses, port numbers in network traffic or hashes of larger data structures. Our accelerator has a clear advantage in the size of streams it can handle. In all previously proposed accelerators, the use of 32-bit count registers imposes that the maximum size of the stream that can be processed safely is 2^{32}. This is because, during streaming activity, the counter values keep growing and never reset until the stream is exhausted. For infinite streams, the counts of frequently occurring items could overflow causing invalid results. In our accelerator, this issue is not present because the count values are reset at the round boundaries according to *Probabilistic*. In fact, our accelerator can handle infinite streams by limiting the size of the round, and this will only cause a degradation of the overall accuracy of the results.

6 Experimental Evaluation

6.1 Throughput

There are two factors that would affect the average throughput in the proposed accelerator: the operating clock frequency and the backpressure on the input stream caused by the array stalls in the accelerator. We use the f_{max} reported in Table 3 as the operating frequency in our experiments. We assume that this choice of operating frequency is reasonable in a production implementation since f_{max} was achieved using minimal place-and-route effort and minimal physical optimizations in the synthesis tool.

There are two sources of stalls in the proposed accelerator, the fixed two clock cycle stall caused by the "clear" process at the beginning of each round (see Fig. 3), and the possible stalls cause by items circulating in the second array of the accelerator to place new top-k candidates (see Fig. 7). To study the effect of the input distribution on the overall throughput, we used four different synthetic datasets as inputs in our simulation testbeds of the three accelerator configurations in Table 3. The datasets were generated as Zipfian distributions [20]. The size of all datasets was fixed at $N = 10^7$ and Zipfian parameter (α) was varied from 1.0 to 2.5 in intervals of 0.5. We performed two simulation runs for each dataset and each accelerator configuration. In the first run the size of N was assumed to be known beforehand, so, the size of r was fixed throughout the test run ($r = \sqrt{mN} = 173205$). In the other run the size of N was assumed to be unknown, so, N was updated dynamically according to *Probabilistic* (see Sect. 2).

Table 4. Throughput comparison of the proposed accelerator with published work when α is varied from 1.0 to 2.5 in intervals of 0.5

Implementation	Algorithm	Throughput (Million item/s)		
		Min.	Max.	Average
Software [2]	SSL	5	22	15
Xilinx Virtex-6 FPGA (1024 PEs) [11]	Space-Saving	95	95	95
Xilinx Virtex-6 FPGA (1024 PEs) [13]	Space-Saving	73	242	152
Intel Arria 10 FPGA (1200 PEs) [14]	Space-Saving	101	200	174
GPU [21]	GSS-Ballot	12	27	18
GPU [22]	GPUSB	207	207	207
Proposed (Top-100)	*Probabilistic*	308	308	308
Proposed (Top-200)	*Probabilistic*	290	290	290
Proposed (Top-300)	*Probabilistic*	279	279	279

In all test runs, the measured throughput was approximately equal to the maximum theoretical throughput of one item update per clock cycle. In fact, most of the back-pressure on the input stream was attributed to the stalls between rounds required for the asynchronous clear process, which caused a negligible effect on the overall throughput. Considering the wide range of data skew evaluated (α), we conclude that the proposed accelerator's throughput is independent of input distribution. According to the f_{max} values reported in Table 3, the throughput of the proposed accelerator will range from 308 to 276 for configurations that consume less than 50% of the target FPGA device. In Table 4, we compare the throughput of our accelerator to other FPGA accelerators, software and GPU-accelerated solutions. We only consider implementations that specifically support the top-k item problem in the data stream model. The throughput values reported in Table 4 for the previously published work were extracted from the figures showing the throughput as a function of α in the relevant publications.

Compared to the fastest software implementation in the comprehensive study of stream algorithms in [2], which uses a 4 Dual Core Intel(R) Xeon(R) 2.66 GHz with 16 GB of RAM, we can see that our accelerator can achieve an average speedup from 18.6× to 20.5× depending on the configuration used. Compared to the fasted FPGA implementation, the achieved average speedup is 1.6×–1.8×, and finally compared to the fastest GPU-accelerated solution, the achieved average speedup is 1.3×–1.5×.

6.2 Accuracy

In FPGA implementations of stream algorithms, the total number of counters we can use is limited by the number of PEs we can fit into the FPGA's reconfigurable resources. Increasing the number of counters is more difficult in FPGA implementations compared to standard von Neumann machines because the reconfigurable resources are much more limited compared to the memory resources in a computer. As the number of counters would affect the overall accuracy of the results, it is important to evaluate the accuracy of our proposed accelerator, or at least show that the proposed accelerator would generate results with acceptable accuracy for most practical cases. In this section, we test the accuracy of the proposed accelerator when streaming naturally skewed data from real datasets.

We select the largest configuration of the accelerator in Table 3 ($m = 3000, k = 300$) as the basis for our accuracy analysis. This configuration supports monitoring up to 300 top items. We use four different real datasets with properties summarized in Table 5. All of these datasets are easily available and widely used by the datamining community for analysis of itemset mining algorithms. *Retail* contains market basket transactions data from an anonymous Belgian retail store [23]. *Kosarak* is a collection of click-stream data from a Hungarian on-line news portal [24]. *Chainstore* contains customer transactions from a major grocery store in California, USA [25]. Finally, *BMS2* contains click-stream data from an anonymous webstore [25].

All of the aforementioned datasets were originally structured as transactional datasets consisting of several separated transactions, each containing a number of integer items. For the purpose of stream item counting, these datasets were pre-processed to merge the transactions into a serial stream of items. The results obtained from simulation were compared to the exact results generated by offline software analysis. We only considered the case of an unknown input size, as this is the more realistic scenario in most data stream applications. Figure 9 shows the accuracy of the accelerator when varying k for the different datasets. We define the accuracy metric as:

$$\text{Accuracy} = \frac{\text{No. of correct top } k \text{ items in the result}}{k} \tag{1}$$

Table 5. Real datasets

Dataset	Distinct Items	Size
Retail	16469	908399
Kosarak	41270	8019015
Chainstore	46086	8042879
BMS2	3340	358278

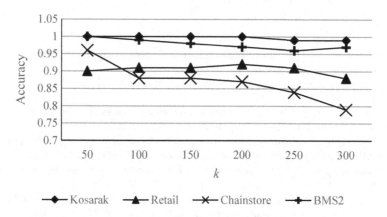

Fig. 9. Accuracy results for real datasets

Overall, the accelerator accuracy averaged at 0.94. We can see that the accuracy is near-perfect for click-stream datasets *Kosarak* and *BMS2*. The average accuracy for market basket datasets *Retail* and *Chainstore* was slightly less, which averaged at 0.91 and 0.87, respectively. The worst case accuracy result was 0.79 for the top-300 items of *Chainstore*.

7 Conclusion

This paper presented a novel reconfigurable accelerator for approximating the top-k items in data streams. The accelerator is based on a novel hardware adaptation of the single-pass *Probabilistic* sampling algorithm. The presented architecture was shown to be practical for implementation in FPGAs. In an Intel Arria 10 10AX115N2F45E1SG

FPGA, 50% of the resources allowed for 3000+ counters, more than double the number of counters in previously proposed architectures that are based on other stream algorithms. This achieved number of hardware counters was enough for approximating the top-k items in real datasets with average accuracy exceeding 90% (k up to 300). Test results on synthetic datasets with a wide range of date skew showed that the throughput of the presented accelerator is independent of the input distribution. With one item updated every clock cycle, the achieved throughputs ranged from 279–300 Million items/s for different configurations of the accelerator ($k = 300, k = 200$ and $k = 100$). This provides significant throughput gains compared to software, GPU-accelerated implementations, and previously proposed reconfigurable accelerators. Furthermore, the proposed accelerator allows for much larger streams to be processed safely using similarly sized count registers compared to previously proposed accelerators. This is an important feature, which is frequently overlooked, especially for streams that can be infinite in size. Future work will focus on optimizations and also exploring architectural modifications to further enhance the scalability of the presented accelerator. This includes exploring the use of hash tables using the memory resources of the FPGA to expand the m hardware counters.

References

1. Muthukrishnan, S.: Data streams: algorithms and applications. Found. Trends® Theor. Comput. Sci. **2**(1), 117–236 (2005)
2. Cormode, G., Hadjieleftheriou, M.: Finding frequent items in data streams. VLDB Endow. **2**(1), 1530–1541 (2008)
3. Manerikar, N., Palpanas, T.: Frequent items in streaming data: an experimental evaluation of the state-of-the-art. Data Knowl. Eng. **4**(68), 415–430 (2009)
4. Biookaghazadeh, S., Zhao, M., Ren, F.: Are FPGAs suitable for edge computing? In: {USENIX} Workshop on Hot Topics in Edge Computing (HotEdge 2018) (2018)
5. Shawahna, A., Sait, S.M., El-Maleh, A.: FPGA-based accelerators of deep learning networks for learning and classification: a review. IEEE Access **7**, 7823–7859 (2018)
6. Demaine, E.D., López-Ortiz, A., Munro, J.I.: Frequency estimation of internet packet streams with limited space. In: European Symposium on Algorithms, pp. 348–360 (2002)
7. Kung, H., Leiserson, C.E.: Systolic arrays (for VLSI). In: Sparse Matrix, pp. 256–282 (1979)
8. Baker, Z.K., Prasanna, V.K.: Efficient hardware data mining with the Apriori algorithm on FPGAs. In: 13th Annual IEEE Symposium on Field-Programmable Custom Computing Machines (FCCM 2005), pp. 3–12 (2005)
9. Prost-Boucle, A., Pétrot, F., Leroy, V., Alemdar, H.: Efficient and versatile FPGA acceleration of support counting for stream mining of sequences and frequent itemsets. ACM Trans. Reconfigurable Technol. Syst. (TRETS) **3**(10), 1–25 (2017)
10. Sun, S., Zambreno, J.: Design and analysis of a reconfigurable platform for frequent pattern mining. IEEE Trans. Parallel Distrib. Syst. **9**(22), 1497–1505 (2011)
11. Teubner, J., Muller, R., Alonso, G.: Frequent item computation on a chip. IEEE Trans. Knowl. Data Eng. **8**(23), 1169–1181 (2010)
12. Metwally, A., Agrawal, D., El Abbadi, A.: Efficient computation of frequent and top-k elements in data streams. In: International Conference on Database Theory, pp. 398–412 (2005)
13. Sun, Y., et al.: Accelerating frequent item counting with FPGA. In: 2014 ACM/SIGDA International Symposium on Field-Programmable Gate Arrays, pp. 109–112 (2014)

14. Ebrahim, A., Khlaifat, J.: An efficient hardware architecture for finding frequent items in data streams. In: 2020 IEEE 38th International Conference on Computer Design (ICCD), pp. 113–119 (2020)
15. Tong, D., Prasanna, V.K.: Sketch acceleration on FPGA and its applications in network anomaly detection. IEEE Trans. Parallel Distrib. Syst. **4**(29), 929–942 (2017)
16. Cormode, G., Muthukrishnan, S.: An improved data stream summary: the count-min sketch and its applications. J. Algorithms **1**(55), 58–75 (2005)
17. Tong, D., Prasanna, V.: Online heavy hitter detector on FPGA. In: 2013 International Conference on Reconfigurable Computing and FPGAs (ReConFig), pp. 1–6 (2013)
18. Zazo, J.F., Lopez-Buedo, S., Ruiz, M., Sutter, G.: A single-FPGA architecture for detecting heavy hitters in 100 gbit/s ethernet links. In: 2017 International Conference on ReConFigurable Computing and FPGAs (ReConFig), pp. 1–6 (2017)
19. Intel Arria 10 Device Overview. https://www.intel.com/content/dam/www/programmable/us/en/pdfs/literature/hb/arria-10/a10_overview.pdf. Accessed 26 Jan 2021
20. Zipf, G.K.: Human behavior and the principle of least effort (1949)
21. Cafaro, M., Epicoco, I., Aloisio, G., Pulimeno, M.: Cuda based parallel implementations of space-saving on a GPU. In: 2017 International Conference on High Performance Computing & Simulation (HPCS), pp. 707–714 (2017)
22. Erra, U., Frola, B.: Frequent items mining acceleration exploiting fast parallel sorting on the GPU. Procedia Comput. Sci. **9**, 86–95 (2012)
23. Brijs, T., Swinnen, G., Vanhoof, K., Wets, G.: Using association rules for product assortment decisions: a case study. In: Fifth ACM SIGKDD International Conference on Knowledge Discovery and Data Mining, pp. 254–260 (1999)
24. Frequent itemset mining dataset repository, University of Helsinki. http://fimi.cs.helsinki.fi/data/. Accessed 26 Jan 2021
25. Fournier-Viger, P., et al.: The SPMF open-source data mining library version 2. In: Berendt, B., Bringmann, B., Fromont, É., Garriga, G., Miettinen, P., Tatti, N., Tresp, V. (eds.) ECML PKDD 2016. LNCS (LNAI), vol. 9853, pp. 36–40. Springer, Cham (2016). https://doi.org/10.1007/978-3-319-46131-1_8

Exploiting 3D Memory for Accelerated In-Network Processing of Hash Joins in Distributed Databases

Johannes Wirth[1]([⊠])(ID), Jaco A. Hofmann[1], Lasse Thostrup[2], Andreas Koch[1](ID), and Carsten Binnig[2]

[1] Embedded Systems and Applications Group, TU Darmstadt, Hochschulstr. 10, 64289 Darmstadt, Germany
{wirth,hofmann,koch}@esa.tu-darmstadt.de
[2] Data Management Lab, TU Darmstadt, Hochschulstr. 10, 64289 Darmstadt, Germany
{lasse.thostrup,carsten.binnig}@cs.tu-darmstadt.de

Abstract. The computing potential of programmable switches with multi-Tbit/s throughput is of increasing interest to the research community and industry alike. Such systems have already been employed in a wide spectrum of applications, including statistics gathering, in-network consensus protocols, or application data caching. Despite their high throughput, most architectures for programmable switches have practical limitations, e.g., with regard to stateful operations.

FPGAs, on the other hand, can be used to flexibly realize switch architectures for far more complex processing operations. Recently, FPGAs have become available that feature 3D-memory, such as HBM stacks, that is tightly integrated with their logic element fabrics. In this paper, we examine the impact of exploiting such HBM to accelerate an inter-server join operation at the switch-level between the servers of a distributed database system. As the hash-join algorithm used for high performance needs to maintain a large state, it would overtax the capabilities of conventional software-programmable switches.

The paper shows that across eight 10G Ethernet ports, the single HBM-FPGA in our prototype can not only keep up with the demands of over 60 Gbit/s of network throughput, but it also beats distributed-join implementations that do not exploit in-network processing.

Keywords: HBM · FPGA · Hash join · INP · In-Network Processing

1 Introduction

Distributed database systems are commonly used to cope with ever-increasing volumes of information. They allow to store and process massive amounts of data

This work was partially funded by the DFG Collaborative Research Center 1053 (MAKI) and by the German Federal Ministry for Education and Research (BMBF) with the funding ID 16ES0999. The authors would like to thank Xilinx Inc. for supporting their work by donations of hard- and software.

S. Derrien et al. (Eds.): ARC 2021, LNCS 12700, pp. 18–32, 2021.
https://doi.org/10.1007/978-3-030-79025-7_2

on multiple servers in parallel. This works especially well for operations which require no communication between the involved servers. For operations which *do* require communication - such as non-colocated SQL joins - sending data between servers can quickly become the performance bottleneck. For these operations, a distributed setup does not always achieve performance improvements, as shown in [11].

Recent papers have suggested the use of In-Network Processing (INP) [2,5, 12] to accelerate distributed computations. INP employs programmable switches to offload processing across multiple servers into the network itself, which reduces the volume of inter-server data transfers. However, the current generation of programmable switches still have some limitations in this scenario. For instance, many current INP solutions are restricted to mostly stateless operations, as they lack large memories. This limits the applicability of these switches for INP, as the aforementioned joins, e.g., cannot be implemented without keeping large state.

As a solution, [8] proposes a new INP-capable switch architecture based on an FPGA, which can be integrated into the Data Processing Interface (DPI) [6] programming framework for INP applications. This architecture provides much more flexibility compared to software-programmable switches and, in addition, is well suited for memory-intensive operations. FPGA based architectures have been show to support hundreds of Gbit/s of network throughput [14], but for stateful operations, such as a database join, memory bandwidth is *still* the limiting factor [8].

Recently, FPGAs using 3D-memory, such as High-Bandwidth-Memory (HBM), have become available. This new memory type allows to perform multiple memory accesses in parallel, resulting in a huge increase in performance compared to traditional DDR memory. However, because multiple parallel accesses are *required* to achieve a performance advantage, the user logic must be adapted in order to actually exploit the potential performance gains.

Our main contribution is to adapt an FPGA-based INP switch architecture [8] to use HBM efficiently. To achieve this, we compare the performance of HBM for different configurations to determine the best solution for our architecture. Finally, in our evaluation we show that our HBM-based version can achieve *more than three times* the throughput of the older DDR3-SDRAM based INP accelerator, and easily outperforms a conventional eight server distributed database setup not using INP.

The remainder of this paper is structured as follows. In Sect. 2 we introduce the organization of HBM on Xilinx FPGAs and analyze its performance for different configurations. Afterwards, Sect. 3 introduces the hash join operation which is used as an example INP operation for our proposed architecture. In Sect. 4 we present a new HBM-based architecture for INP-capable switches. Finally, we report our experimental results in Sect. 5, and discuss some limitations of the current implementation with possible refinements, in Sect. 6.

2   HBM Performance

This section introduces the HBM organization on current Xilinx FPGAs, afterwards the HBM performance for different configurations is analyzed.

2.1   HBM Organization

Selected Xilinx FPGAs include HBM, offering a range of number of logic cells and the available amount of HBM. For the currently available devices, this amount ranges from 4 GB to 16 GB. Independent of the size, the organization of the HBM does *not* differ: The HBM on these devices is split into two *stacks*, which are attached at the bottom edge of the FPGA matrix. Memory access is realized via eight memory channels per stack - each providing two pseudo channels, resulting in a total of 32 pseudo channels over both stacks. Each pseudo channel may only access its associated *section* of memory (1/32 of the available total memory). The programmable logic can access the HBM via 32 AXI3 slave ports. By default, each AXI3 slave port is directly connected to one of the pseudo channels, so each AXI3 port can only access one memory section. Alternatively, an optional AXI *crossbar* can be activated, which allows each AXI3 port to access the *entire* memory space - but at a cost in latency and throughput. In this work, we do *not* use the optional crossbar. Figure 1 shows the organization of one HBM stack.

The 32 AXI3 slave ports are distributed over the entire width of the bottom edge of the FPGA matrix. Each port has a data width of 256 bit and can run at a clock frequency of up to 450 MHz. This results in a theoretical aggregate memory bandwidth of 460 GB/s.

2.2   HBM Performance

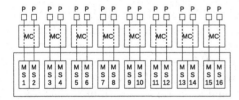

Fig. 1. Organization of a single HBM stack, showing the memory channels (MC), memory sections (MS), and AXI3 slave ports (P). Each line between an AXI3 port and a memory section indicates a pseudo channel. The optional AXI crossbar is not shown.

In many cases, it will not be possible to run the Processing Element (PE) at 450 MHz. Thus, it is either necessary to run the HBM slave ports synchronously at a lower clock frequency, or alternatively, to perform clock domain conversion (CD) by inserting a SmartConnect IP between the PE and HBM. In the latter case, it is also possible to use *different* data-widths and protocols on the PE-side, and also let the SmartConnect perform data-width (DW) and protocol conversion (PV), as required. To assess the performance impact of the different options, we analyze four configurations, ranging from no SmartConnect, to a SmartConnect which performs all three conversions (CD+DW+PV). The four configurations are shown in Fig. 2. Other configurations - for example a

SmartConnect IP with clock domain and protocol conversion - are also possible, but yield no additional performance data as they are covered by the other four options and are thus omitted.

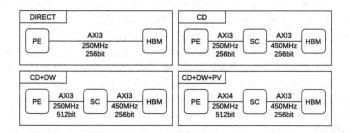

Fig. 2. The four analyzed configurations for connecting the PE with the HBM. The lines represent AXI connections, and are annotated with the protocol version, clock frequency and data width. The configurations are named based on the conversions (CD: clock-domain-, DW: data-width-, PV: protocol-version-) employed.

The rest of this section will compare the performance in various criteria of these four configurations. The goal of this evaluation is to find the best configuration for our specific application scenario. It does *not* strive to be a general evaluation of HBM performance. Thus we focus this evaluation on the *random* access performance, as this is the access pattern used by our hash-join architecture (see Sect. 4). All results shown use only one AXI3 slave port. As we do *not* use the AXI crossbar, the HBM ports are completely independent, and the performance scales *linearly* when using multiple ports in parallel.

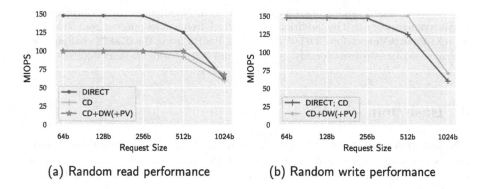

(a) Random read performance   (b) Random write performance

Fig. 3. HBM random access performance in I/O operations per second for the different configurations at a clock frequency of 250 MHz.

Figure 3 shows the random access performance for the different configurations. The results indicate a large performance benefit for small read accesses (up to 256 bit) for the DIRECT configuration, compared to all other configurations. This is likely caused by the additional latency introduced by the SmartConnect as shown in Fig. 4. For small write accesses, all configurations achieve a similar performance, as these are not affected by this additional latency. For wider memory accesses the performance depends less on the latency, but more on the maximum throughput of the AXI connection. Thus, the configurations DIRECT and CD perform worse because in both of the cases where the PE-side has a data-width of 256 bit, and is running at only 250 MHz. Therefore, the maximum throughput is lower than the theoretical maximum of the HBM slave ports.

This shows that for our application, the best solution is omitting the Smart-Connect (DIRECT), as we only use memory accesses with a size of 256 bit (see Sect. 4).

Finally, Fig. 5 shows that for this scenario of small random accesses, the peak performance is reached around 200 MHz. Thus, for our design (see Sect. 4), a clock frequency of 250 MHz suffices to achieve maximum memory performance.

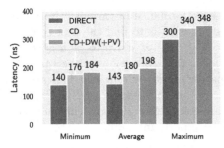

Fig. 4. Read access latency for the different configurations. The addition of an AXI SmartConnect for CD/DW/PV increases the latency considerably.

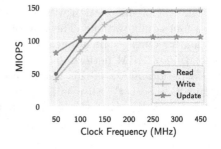

Fig. 5. Random access performance for clock frequencies ranging from 50 MHz to 450 MHz using the DIRECT configuration and 256 bit wide memory accesses.

3   Hash Join

The join operation is common in relational databases for analytical processing, and is frequently used in data warehouses and data centers [3,4]. Its purpose is the merging of two relations into one, based on a shared key (Equi-Join). A database query can include multiple join operations to combine information from multiple tables. Such queries are especially prevalent in Data Warehousing [9], where typical queries join a *fact table* with multiple *dimension tables* in order to compute analytical aggregations. The fact table holds very fine-grained data (e.g., each entry could correspond to one order in a retail store data warehouse), which causes the fact table to typically be orders of magnitude *larger* than the dimension tables. The dimension tables include descriptive attributes of the fact table, and as such need to be joined with the fact table in order to answer analytical queries. While many join implementations exist, we chose to focus on the *no-partition hash join* [1], as this is a commonly used and well understood parallel hash join implementation.

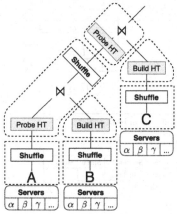

Fig. 6. Traditional distributed database join of the tables A ⋈ B ⋈ C distributed across multiple servers, requiring shuffles

Fundamentally, the join operation consists of two steps: (1) building a hash table on the join key of the smaller *dimension table*, and (2) probing that hash table with the join key of the larger *fact table*. In a query with multiple joins, a hash table is built on each dimension table such that the fact table can be probed into each of the hash tables to produce the query result. On a single-node system this approach works well if the main memory is sufficiently large to hold the database tables, hash tables and intermediate join result. However, for large databases (such as data warehouses), where tables are partitioned across multiple servers in a cluster, the join cannot simply be processed in parallel on each server without network transfers.

Traditionally, for processing such a distributed join, it must be ensured that tuples which share the same join-key from two tables are processed on the *same* server. This step is referred to as *shuffling* (or re-partitioning), and shown in Fig. 6 for three tables partitioned across a number of servers $\alpha, \beta, \gamma, \ldots$. Given the high chance that two tuples with the same join-key do *not* reside on the same server, distributed joins often incur heavy network communication for shuffling, which typically dominates the overall runtime of the join query. The bandwidth requirements for shuffling increase further when the distribution of tuples in the shuffling step is not uniform, as some servers then receive considerably more data than the others [8]. This *skewed* scenario leads to high ingress congestion, which results in low overall system performance and utilization.

As an alternative, we propose to execute the hash join following the *In-Network Processing* (INP) paradigm, for which we realize a high-performance hardware-accelerated INP-capable switch that is able to perform the two steps of the hash join *directly* on data flowing to the switch, without the need for shuffles.

Figure 7 gives a complete example of both the hash join algorithm itself, as well as the INP realization. It also foreshadows some of the design decisions for the microarchitecture of the INP switch, e.g., the use of HBM to hold the hash tables, further described in Sect. 4. Note that, for clarity, we use the foreign keys A.b, A.c, A.d here explicitly in an SQL WHERE clause, instead of employing the

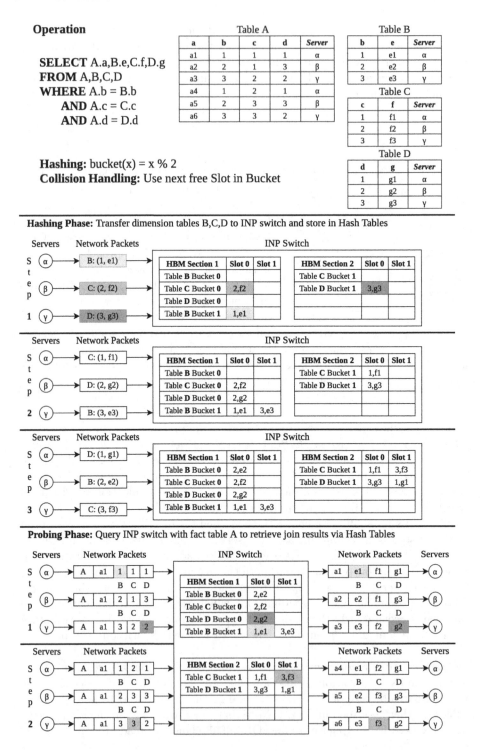

Fig. 7. Sample INP-style hash join over four tables, with data distributed over three servers.

JOIN keyword. In this highly simplified example, we assume that each of the three servers α, β, γ holds just one row for each of the dimension tables, and just two rows of the fact table A.

In the *Hashing Phase*, the three servers α, β, γ transfer the required contents of the tables to-be joined to the switch. This happens in parallel across multiple network ports of the INP switch, and is sensitive neither to the order of the transferred tables, nor to that of the individual tuples. During this transfer, the hash tables are built: For each key value, the hash function determines a *bucket* where that tuple is to be stored in. In the example, the hash function distributes the tuples across just two buckets per database table. The buckets for each table are spread out across multiple memories for better scaling and parallelism (further explained in Sect. 4). Hash collisions are resolved by having multiple *slots* within a bucket, and using the first available slot to hold the incoming tuple. Running out of slots in a bucket is an indicator that the switch memory is insufficient to perform the specific join in INP mode, and a fallback to the traditional join has to be used instead. The issue of these bucket overflows is further discussed in Sect. 4.2 and Sect. 6. In Fig. 7, the buckets and slots used for the tuples incoming over the network are highlighted in the same colors.

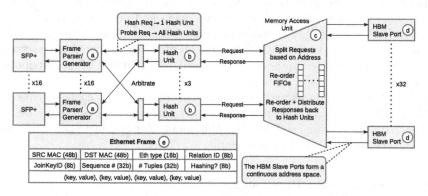

Fig. 8. Full system overview of the proposed INP Hash Join implementation. Hash and probe requests from the 10G Ethernet ports (a) are forwarded to one of the Hash Units (b). Each Hash Unit is responsible for creating one Hash Table. The Hash Units have to access the 32 HBM channels (d), which is realized through specialized arbitration units (c) that ensure routing. The auxiliary units are not shown. For the contents of the Ethernet frame (e), only the relevant parts of the header are shown.

After the hash table has been built in the switch from just the columns of the dimension tables B, C, D required for this specific join, the larger fact table A is streamed in. As it, too, has been distributed over all of the servers $\alpha \ldots \gamma$, this occurs over multiple network ports in parallel. Each of these tuples contains the three foreign keys for selecting the correct rows from the dimension tables. The actual values are then retrieved by using the foreign keys to access the hash table (bucket and slot), and returned by network to the server responsible for this part of the join. Again, we have marked the incoming foreign keys and the outgoing retrieved values in the same colors.

4 Architecture

The architecture presented here is a new design based on an earlier prototype, which was implemented on a Virtex 7 FPGA, attached to two DDR3 SDRAM channels [8]. That older architecture is capable of handling 20 Gbit/s of hash join traffic, but is not able to scale beyond that, as the dual-channel memory can not keep up with the random access demands. We present here a completely new implementation of the same basic concepts, but redesigned to target a newer UltraScale+ FPGA and fully exploit HBM. Figure 8 shows a high-level overview of the system.

The new design can be broken down into four separate parts, which deal with different aspects of the processing flow. Network operations are performed decentralized in network frame parsers (Fig. 8a). The incoming frames are parsed into hash and probe requests, which are then forwarded to the actual hash units (Fig. 8b), where each unit is responsible for managing one hash table. Next in the processing chain is the memory access unit (Fig. 8c), which coordinates the memory accesses coming from the hash units and distributes them to the attached HBMs (Fig. 8d). The results of memory accesses, namely the join tuples in the Probing Phase of the algorithm, are collected, encapsulated into network frames (8a), and returned to the server responsible for that part of the distributed join result.

The Ethernet interfaces and frame parsers (Fig. 8a) run at a clock frequency of 156.25 MHz to achieve 10 Gbit/s line rate per port, while the rest of our design runs at 250 MHz. As discussed in Sect. 2 this is sufficient to achieve the maximum performance for the HBM in our scenario.

4.1 Network Packet Processing

The BittWare XUP-VVH card used in our experiments, contains four QSFP28 connectors, which can provide up to 100 Gbit/s each through four 25 Gbit/s links in one connector. We use these links independently in 10 Gbit/s mode, allowing in a maximum of 16 10 Gbit/s Ethernet connections. The data from each link is transferred over an AXI Stream interface as 64 bit per clock cycle of a 156.25 MHz reference clock. However, the receiving unit must not block. Hence, the units processing the Ethernet data have to be *lock-free*.

To keep things simple in the FPGA, we directly use Ethernet frames and omit higher-level protocols. The frame parsers (Fig. 8a) can parse the frames sequentially without needing any inter-frame state. Each frame starts with the required Ethernet information, source and destination MAC, as well as the Ethernet type, followed by a hash-join specific, custom header. This header contains information to identify the purpose of the frame (hash or probe), the relation the frame belongs to, the number of tuples in the frame, and a sequence number.

The body of the frame contains a number of tuples. For a join with four relations A, B, C and D, each tuple contains eight 32 bit numbers. In the hashing case, the tuple contains only the key and value of the tuple to hash. In the probing case, the first four values indicate the primary key (PK) of A, followed by the foreign keys (FK) of the other relations (three 32b words in total, one for each dimension tables used in this example). The following four values are the corresponding values, which are actually used only in Probe replies. This common structure for both requests and replies, with place holders for the actual result data, was chosen since it keeps the ingress and egress data volumes balanced.

The frame parser retrieves the tuples from the network port and places them in queues to be forwarded to the hashing units. A frame is dropped if the queue is not sufficiently large to hold the entire frame. This avoids a situation where the input channel would block. However, no data is actually lost: The accelerator recognizes this case and explicitly *re-requests* the dropped data from the server, identified by the sequence number and relation ID. When using eight 10G Ethernet connections, about 0.08% of all requests are re-requested in this manner.

In the other direction, probe results are accumulated in a queue and sent back to the source of the request in the same format as described before.

4.2   Hash Table

The hash tables are the core of the algorithm. To keep up with the demands of the network, the hash units (Fig. 8b) are highly throughput optimized. Accordingly, the goal of this implementation is to keep the HBM slave ports as busy as possible, as the random access performance is the limiting factor.

To clarify this, the following section presents a brief introduction to the hash table algorithm employed. The `insert` algorithm requires four steps: (1) find the bucket corresponding to the requested key, (2) request the bucket, (3) update the bucket if an empty slot exists, and (4) write back the updated bucket. Hence, every `insert` requires one bucket read and one bucket write. If the bucket is already full, a bucket overflow occurs, and an extra resolution step is necessary to avoid dropping the data (see below).

The `probe` step is simpler and requires only steps (1) and (2) of the `insert` algorithm, with an additional `retrieve` step which selects the correct value from the slots inside the bucket.

Performance-wise, step (1) is of paramount importance. A poorly chosen mapping between the keys and the values results in lower performance, as either the collision rate increases, or the HBM slave ports are not utilized fully. Fortunately, latency is not critical at this point allowing a fully pipelined design.

Like any hash table implementation, this implementation has to deal with collisions. As each HBM slave port is relatively wide (256 bit for HBM, see Sect. 2) compared to the key and value tuples (32 bit each in our case), the natural collision handling method uses multiple slots per bucket. The number of slots per bucket can be chosen relatively freely, but as the benchmarks performed in Sect. 2 show, a bucket size corresponding to the width of one HBM slave port is optimal.

For the specific case of database joins, it turns out that complicated bucket overflow resolution strategies are not necessary, as the *nature* of the data itself can be exploited instead: The keys used for accessing the hash table are actually the database primary and foreign keys. This means that the keys are usually just numbers ranging from 0 to $N - 1$, with N being the size of the relation. This is especially common in read-only analytical database systems. Accordingly, the values can simply be distributed across the available buckets by using a simple modulo with the hash table size as hash function. For other applications, where this is not the case, and the keys span a larger space, tools such as [13] can be used to generate integer hash functions with good distribution behavior. In our scenario, buckets will only overflow when the entire hash table is already full anyway, resulting in an out-of-memory condition for this specific join.

The hash tables are placed interleaved in memory (see Fig. 7) to let every hash table use all of the available HBM slave ports. The design uses one Hash Unit per hash table in the system, leading to three Hash Units in the system for the proposed evaluation in Sect. 5.

4.3   Memory Access

However, the throughput-optimized spreading of data across all available memory leads to the next problem: The memory accesses from the different hash units have to be routed to the corresponding HBM slave ports (Fig. 8d). Connecting the 32 available HBM slave ports requires additional logic. The naive approach of using the vendor-provided interconnect solutions, which use a crossbar internally, is not feasible. First of all, this approach would *serialize* the majority of requests, making it impossible to fully utilize the HBM slave ports. Secondly, the interconnect has to connect the three master interfaces of the Hash Units with the 32 slave interfaces of the HBM, which results in a large and very spread-out layout, due to the crossbar design of that interconnect. Such a design fails to be routed at the high clock frequencies required to achieve optimal HBM random access performance. Hence, a special unit is needed that arbitrates between the masters, and allows efficient access to all HBM slave ports, while remaining routable.

The proposed design, shown in Fig. 8c, takes memory requests from the hash units and places them in separate queues. The following memory selection step requires two stages to allow routing on the FPGA even with 32 slave ports: The first step splits the incoming requests onto four queues based on their address. Each splitter section handles the access to a sequential section of memory, which corresponds to the placement of the HBM slave ports on the FPGA. The second step then selects a request from the incoming queues using a fair arbiter, and forwards the request to the corresponding HBM slave port.

For the return direction, the out-of-order answers from the HBMs have to be re-ordered, as the Hash Units expect the answers to be in-order with its requests.

This is done by keeping track of the order in which requests have been forwarded to the HBM slave ports. When answers arrive, this queue is then used to ensure that the answers are returned in the same order as they have been requested in.

5   Evaluation

The evaluation of the system focuses on two aspects: (1) The scaling of the system itself across a number of ports, and (2) the performance compared to a classical distributed database hash join system with multiple worker servers.

5.1   System Performance

The proposed system, hereafter referred to as NetJoin, is evaluated using the TaPaSCo [7] FPGA middleware and SoC composition framework to generate bitstreams for the BittWare XUP-VVH board. The Xilinx UltraScale+ VU37P device on the board features 8 GB of HBM and up to 2.8 million "Logic Elements" in a three chiplet design.

Overall, we use only a fraction of the available resources on the VU37P. The biggest contributor is our PE with about 17% of the available CLBs. A detailed list of the resource usage of the PE, HBM, and the SFP+ connections is shown in Table 1.

Table 1. Resource Usage for the PE, HBM and SFP+ controllers. The percentage of the total available resources of this type on the VU37P FPGA is given in parentheses.

	LUTs	Registers	CLBs	BRAMs
NetJoin PE	135k (10.39%)	197k (7.56%)	28k (17.03%)	30 (0.33%)
HBM Controller	1.5k (0.12%)	1.6k (0.06%)	0.5k (0.33%)	0
SFP+ Interface	19k (1.48%)	31k (1.19%)	4.98k (3.05%)	0

The following benchmarks use a three table join scenario, where one fact table A is joined with three dimension tables B, C and D. The first benchmark compares the scaling of the system when varying the number of network interfaces. The size of the dimension tables is kept at 100×10^6 elements, while the fact table has 1.0×10^9 elements. The results, presented in Fig. 9, show that the system scales linearly up to six ports, and slightly less than linearly for seven ports. This indicates that up to six ports, the system is able to fully keep up with the line rate of 60 Gbit/s. Figure 10 shows the scaling for the phases (Hashing and Probing) separately.

5.2   Baseline Comparison

The software baseline not using INP is executed on eight servers, each fitted with an Intel Xeon Gold 5120 CPU @ 2.2 GHz and 384 GB of RAM. The servers are

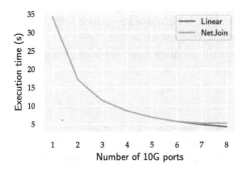

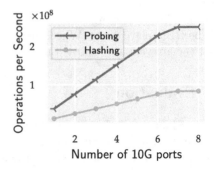

Fig. 9. Scaling of NetJoin performing three joins with table A having 1.0×10^9 and B,C,D having 100×10^6 elements. The system scales linearly up to six ports, and slightly slower up to seven ports, where the memory links become saturated and no further scaling is observed.

Fig. 10. Hashes and probes per second in NetJoin-HBM for the given number of ports. Unsurprisingly, the probe operation is up to three times faster, as it requires only one memory read to perform. Hashing on the other hand, requires one read and one write per operation.

connected via 10G BASE-T using CAT 6 RJ45 cables to a Stordis BF2556X-1T programmable switch. Furthermore, a master server with the same hardware is used to control execution. The baseline system operates with eight SFP+ ports on the switch, for a total maximum bandwidth of 80 Gbit/s.

As before, all the experiments join a fact table A with three dimension tables B, C and D. The first experiment compares the scaling behavior of both approaches for different fact table sizes with fixed dimension tables. The results in Fig. 11a show that even for small sizes of the relation A, the NetJoin approach is already *two times faster* than the software baseline. As the intermediate results are relatively small here, the shuffling step does not incur a big overhead in the software baseline, but is nonetheless noticeable. For larger sizes, however, the advantage of avoiding the shuffling steps by INP becomes more pronounced. In the tested range, NetJoin-HBM is already *three times faster* than the baseline, and its execution time grows slower than the non-INP baseline. Note that these results represent the *optimal* scenario for the software baseline, as the keys are *equally* distributed across all servers. Also, remember that the older DDR3-based INP design from [8] cannot even keep up with the current software baseline, which now uses considerably more powerful hardware than available in the earlier work.

In the skewed case, where only a few servers have to do the majority of the processing, the advantage of the INP approach over the baseline grows, even on the older INP accelerator. In this scenario, one server receives 34.6% of the data, a second server receives 23.1% of the data and the rest receives 15.4%, 10.2%, 6.9%, 4.6%, 3% and 2% respectively. As described in Sect. 3, this leads to high ingress congestion and much sequential processing. The INP approach, on the other hand, does not suffer from this issue, and is able to process the data in the same way as before. The results in Fig. 11b confirm this observation. For very

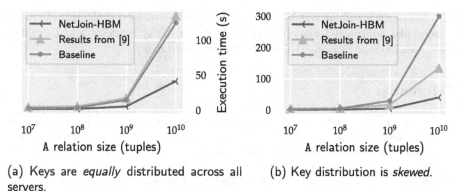

(a) Keys are *equally* distributed across all servers.

(b) Key distribution is *skewed*.

Fig. 11. Comparison of NetJoin-HBM, the baseline running in software on eight servers, and the older DDR3-based architecture from [8] which runs at 20 Gbit/s. Three joins are performed with tables B, C and D at a static size of 100×10^6 tuples. The size of relation A is varied.

small sizes of A, the NetJoin-HBM approach remains about two times faster. Increasing the size of A shows that the skewed case is handled poorly by the software baseline. At the highest tested table size, NetJoin-HBM is already 7.2× faster than the baseline for the skewed scenario. For comparison, the unskewed baseline is about 2.3× faster than its skewed counterpart.

6   Conclusion and Future Work

This work is motivated by the observation that the performance of an existing FPGA-based INP switch architecture is mainly limited by the memory access performance. To overcome this bottleneck, we propose an enhanced architecture, which uses HBM instead of DDR memory. We show that by exploiting HBM, we achieve more than *three times* the throughput of an older DDR3 SDRAM-based INP accelerator for joins [8].

The design is currently limited by the size of the available HBM memory. As most HBM-FPGA boards also still include DDR4-SDRAM, it would be possible to increase the amount of available memory by using *both* memory types. However, this would be a more complex architecture, due to the access differences between HBM and DDR, and the necessity to partition the data between HBM and DDR.

Another issue of our current architecture is the possibility for write after read errors. Considering the average response time of the HBM is 35.75 cycles, there can be cases where a *second* read to the same bucket occurs *before* the earlier write has been completed. The probability of this happening can be calculated based on the probability of a collision happening depending on the number of outstanding requests, which is about 5.45×10^{-6} [10]. For many data-analytics applications, this error rate will be acceptable. However, in applications where this chance for error can not be tolerated, a possible solution is the introduction a cache-like approach for keeping track of the in-flight requests and handling these avoiding the hazards (similar to MSHRs in caches).

References

1. Blanas, S., Li, Y., Patel, J.M.: Design and evaluation of main memory hash join algorithms for multi-core CPUs. In: Proceedings of the ACM SIGMOD International Conference on Management of Data, SIGMOD 2011, Athens, Greece, 12–16 June 2011, pp. 37–48. ACM (2011)
2. Blöcher, M., Ziegler, T., Binnig, C., Eugster, P.: Boosting scalable data analytics with modern programmable networks. In: Proceedings of the 14th International Workshop on Data Management on New Hardware. DAMON 2018. Association for Computing Machinery, New York (2018)
3. DeWitt, D.J., Katz, R.H., et al.: Implementation techniques for main memory database systems. SIGMOD Rec. **14**(2), 1–8 (1984)
4. Dreseler, M., Boissier, M., Rabl, T., Uflacker, M.: Quantifying TPC-H choke points and their optimizations. Proc. VLDB Endow. **13**(8), 1206–1220 (2020)
5. Firestone, D., Putnam, A., et al.: Azure accelerated networking: Smartnics in the public cloud. In: Proceedings of the 15th USENIX Conference on Networked Systems Design and Implementation, NSDI 2018, pp. 51–64. USENIX Association, USA (2018)
6. Gustavo, A., Binnig, C., et al.: DPI: the data processing interface for modern networks. In: Proceedings of CIDR 2019 (2019)
7. Heinz, C., Hofmann, J., Korinth, J., Sommer, L., Weber, L., Koch, A.: The TaPaSCo open-source toolflow. J. Signal Process. Syst. **93**, 1–19 (2021). https://doi.org/10.1007/s11265-021-01640-8
8. Hofmann, J., Thostrup, L., Ziegler, T., Binnig, C., Koch, A.: High-performance in-network data processing. In: International Workshop on Accelerating Analytics and Data Management Systems Using Modern Processor and Storage Architectures, ADMS@VLDB 2019, Los Angeles, United States (2019)
9. Kimball, R., Ross, M.: The Data Warehouse Toolkit: The Complete Guide to Dimensional Modeling, 2nd edn. Wiley, Hoboken (2002)
10. Preshing, J.: Hash collision probabilities (2011). https://preshing.com/20110504/hash-collision-probabilities/
11. Rödiger, W., Mühlbauer, T., Kemper, A., Neumann, T.: High-speed query processing over high-speed networks. Proc. VLDB Endow. **9**(4), 228–239 (2015)
12. Sapio, A., Abdelaziz, I., et al.: In-network computation is a dumb idea whose time has come. In: Proceedings of the 16th ACM Workshop on Hot Topics in Networks, pp. 150–156. HotNets-XVI, Association for Computing Machinery, New York (2017)
13. Wellons, C.: Hash function prospector (2020). https://github.com/skeeto/hash-prospector
14. Zilberman, N., Audzevich, Y., Covington, G.A., Moore, A.W.: NetFPGA SUME: toward 100 Gbps as research commodity. IEEE Micro **34**(5), 32–41 (2014)

Design Tools

Evaluation of Different Manual Placement Strategies to Ensure Uniformity of the V-FPGA

Johannes Pfau[1]([✉])[iD], Peter Wagih Zaki[2][iD], and Jürgen Becker[1][iD]

[1] Institute for Information Processing Technologies, Karlsruhe Institute
for Technology, Karlsruhe, Germany
{pfau,becker}@kit.edu
[2] German University in Cairo, New Cairo City, Egypt
peter.naam@student.guc.edu.eg

Abstract. Virtual FPGA (V-FPGA) architectures are useful as both early prototyping testbeds for custom FPGA architectures, as well as to enable advanced features which may not be available on a given host FPGA. V-FPGAs use standard FPGA synthesis and placement tools, and as a result the maximum application frequency is largely determined by the synthesis of the V-FPGA onto the host FPGA. Minimal net delays in the virtual layer are crucial for applications, but due to increased routing congestion, these delays are often significantly worse for larger than for smaller designs. To counter this effect, we investigate three different placement strategies with varying amounts of manual intervention. Taking the regularity of the V-FPGA architecture into account, a regular placement of tiles can lead to an 37% improvement in the achievable clock frequency. In addition, uniformity of the measured net delays is increased by 39%, which makes implementation of user applications more reproducible. As a trade-off, these manual placement strategies increase area usage of the virtual layer up to 16%.

Keywords: FPGA · EDA · Placement · Virtual FPGA

1 Introduction

In recent years, virtual Field Programmable Gate Arrays (FPGA) architectures (V-FPGAs) have been introduced in academia [2]. Unlike common commercial and academic FPGAs, the V-FPGA is an FPGA architecture layered onto a base FPGA architecture: A commercial host FPGA architecture is synthesized for a silicon chip target, and the V-FPGA layer is synthesized for that host FPGA architecture. The virtual layer is implemented as a bitstream to be programmed onto the host FPGA. User applications are synthesized using a custom toolchain for the V-FPGA layer and the resulting application bitstream is

This work was supported by the German Research Foundation (DFG) within the PAR-FAIT project (DFG 326384402).

S. Derrien et al. (Eds.): ARC 2021, LNCS 12700, pp. 35–49, 2021.
https://doi.org/10.1007/978-3-030-79025-7_3

programmed onto it. V-FPGA architectures have been applied for three main use cases: First, as an abstraction layer, providing a common bitstream format independent of commercial FPGA architectures. This allows using features such as partial dynamic reconfiguration on FPGAs which do not natively support this [6]. Secondly, V-FPGAs can be used for FPGA architecture research: Novel ideas can be integrated in the architecture and tested on a hardware implementation, which can provide additional insight compared to simulation. This becomes especially useful when investigating heterogeneous System-on-Chips (SoCs) solutions, which may combine processing systems and reconfigurable logic [2,4]. Thirdly, using the V-FPGA as a basic FPGA architecture: Here it is realized using standard cell synthesis for silicon targets and can be used to evaluate the usage of different transistor technologies in FPGAs.

Targeting FPGAs instead of silicon, synthesizing and implementing a V-FPGA requires different considerations than normal FPGA architectures. Most notably, whereas FPGAs are usually designed in a custom or semi-custom way based on tiles, V-FPGA architectures are written in standard hardware description language. Usual FPGA synthesis is used, trying to minimize critical path length to meet a target clock frequency. The V-FPGA code introduces a hierarchy of components and supports the concept of tiles. These tiles are a logical representation and used for silicon targets, but are not considered in the synthesis, mapping and placement onto the host FPGA. This leads to various issues:

1. The final target clock frequency must be given without knowing the user application. Usually an "as fast as possible" solution is used, but for common timing driven synthesis and placement, this means manually increasing the frequency until the design fails to synthesize, which is a time-intensive process.
2. The V-FPGA architecture is not uniform: For example, the delay of a connection between two neighboring tiles depends on their location on the FPGA. Whereas the maximum delay can be used to describe the architecture for the synthesis toolchain targeting the virtual layer, this limits the ability to overclock user applications: As routing is not deterministic, a user application may be synthesized to different tiles in different synthesis runs and the real timing slack varies. To achieve deterministic results, the delays of the V-FPGA layer need to be uniform.
3. As any FPGA architecture consists of configurable elements and multiplexers, it is possible to form combinational loops on these architectures. Such loops break timing analysis and need to be marked accordingly using disable timing constraints, otherwise timing analysis obtained from commercial tools is wrong.
4. As the FPGA synthesis tools are not aware of the structure of the V-FPGA architecture, they are essentially just placing a large network. This may increase runtime and we postulate it further leads to worse critical path delay for large designs, as the effort to place the whole design becomes too large to yield results similar to a grid-based layout.

To address these problems, we investigate manual placement strategies forcing the mapped design onto certain locations on the host FPGA. First, we describe metrics measuring the variation in delays of similar V-FPGA nets (uniformity), delay and area. Secondly, we explain three strategies to constrain the tiles in the V-FPGA in a grid-like layout, how the size and form of the tiles has to be determined and how we place cells within the tiles. In the end, we evaluate the results based on the introduced metrics. Results show that the three different strategies increase uniformity and lead to decreased maximum delay, at the cost of slightly increased area.

2 Related Work

For previous research in placement algorithms for FPGA, we can differentiate two research areas: Placement algorithms for generic FPGA applications and manually guided placement for specific applications. Research on generic placement algorithms has largely been conducted using academic open source tools. The most-widely used of these tools is Verilog to Routing (VTR), which consists of three main tools: Odin II for synthesizing circuits designed in Verilog into generic Lookup Table (LUT) resources, ABC for technology-mapping those resources into architecture specific LUTs, and Versatile Place and Route (VPR) for packing, placement, and routing. Research led to the introduction of new techniques and algorithms for placement and packing, focusing on different cost targets such as timing driven, routing-driven or runtime-driven: [7] introduces an algorithm named adaptive range-based Simulated Annealing (ARBSA). It provides an adaptive approach to choose the neighborhood for each block according to the nets it belongs to. The result shows a 1.78X runtime speed up, 10% reduction on wire length and 2% reduction on the critical path with path timing-driven optimization. Research in this area proposes general algorithms, trying to find good solutions regardless of the target application. Results are therefore usually shown relative to the VTR algorithms.

The second group of research uses the concept of manual placement, ranging from guidance to completely manually placed designs. For example, [1] introduced a sea-of-gates architecture called Triptych. It aims to reduce the significant cost paid for routing in standard FPGAs, replacing the logic blocks with Routing and Logic Blocks (RLBs). Routing and Logic Blocks (RLBs) perform both logic and routing tasks, allowing a tradeoff between logic and routing resources on a per mapping basis. Using manual placement made this architecture yield a logic density improvement of up to a factor of 3.5 over commercial FPGA's automatic placement. As another example, Shi et al. analyzed manual placement for their specific FPGA application [5]. It shows that using manual placement leads to a compact and optimized design with shorter nets, reducing propagation delay up to 25%.

Whereas generic algorithms can be used to implement the V-FPGA, they have to be reimplemented in the Vivado synthesis flow, as they originally target VPR. In addition, none of these algorithms takes the regular structure of the V-FPGA into account. The presented application specific manual placement methods on the other hands side, do not directly translate to the V-FPGA structure. They need to be heavily modified to be usable for this use case. In order to improve net delay in the V-FPGA, we therefore investigate specific custom placement methods based on similar ideas, but explicitly considering the V-FPGA architecture and regularity.

3   Background

The placement strategies to be introduced make use of the regular structure of the V-FPGA. As such, they are dependent on both the V-FPGA architecture, as well as on the host FPGA architecture. The strategies have been designed to work with a certain parameter variability in these architectures, but certain assumptions have to be made.

3.1   V-FPGA Architecture

Figure 1a shows the V-FPGA architecture and the arrangement into certain types of tiles. In its simplest configuration, the V-FPGA consists of tiles of configurable Logic Blocks (CLBs), Programmable Switch Matrices (PSMs) and I/O Blocks (IOBs), which are drawn as triangles on the peripheral area. A single tile can contain all of these elements (type 5 and 7), all but the IOB (type 9, the central tiles), PSM and IOB (type 2, 4, 6, 8), PSM and two IOBs (type 1), or only the PSM (type 3). Because of their differences in orientation or structure—and therefore layout —, individual tile types will have to be handled differently. Figure 1a also shows relevant delays for the final architecture: Apart from intra-block delays such as delays in the CLB, these consist of nets

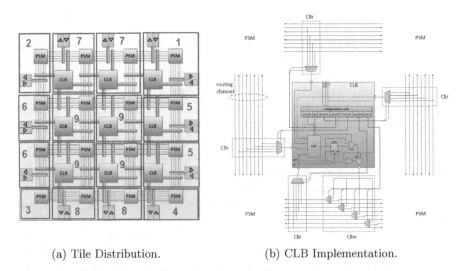

(a) Tile Distribution.   (b) CLB Implementation.

Fig. 1. V-FPGA architecture details: a): Tile Distribution and top-level architecture. b): CLB implementation and routing channels.

in the global interconnect channels. Channel nets can be divided into multiple segments, if they're divided by connection boxes attached to IOB or CLB units (Fig. 1b). Extraction of delays for VPR focuses on these atomic segments, but for assessment of placement results in this publication, we will always consider complete PSM-to-PSM and CLB-to-PSM paths.

3.2 Xilinx 7-Series Architecture

In this work, we primarily target Xilinx 7 Series devices, although the methods are generic and adapt to other host FPGA architectures. For manual placement, the most important aspect of the host FPGA architecture is its uniformity: Placing the V-FPGA in a uniform way is a simple task if the host FPGA is uniform, but this is not the case for recent commercial FPGAs. As an example, consider trying to place the V-FPGA across the whole area of a 7-series device: Delays between two tiles on two sides of a hard IP column will be significantly larger than delays between two tiles not separated by hard IP. Manual placement strategies have to take this effect into account.

3.3 Metrics

To evaluate and assess the results, we first introduce comparison metrics. The commonly used metrics—delays, uniformity and area—have a specific meaning for V-FPGA targets and are crucial for V-FPGA applications.

Uniformity is a measurement of local delay variation across the V-FPGA structure. Placing every tile in the same way, the V-FPGA is a uniform structure, which in theory could be placed uniformly on the host FPGA. In practice, not all tiles have exactly the same internal structure and non-uniformity of the host FPGA architecture will further degrade results. To address this, our definition of uniformity divides the V-FPGA into N_C sets, where each set represents one column. We also group nets into classes, so that the same nets in different tiles are in a class. Uniformity then targets rows within a set, but no uniformity is guaranteed between these sets. This definition is formalized in the following equations:

$$\mu_{c,n} = \frac{1}{N_R} \sum_{r=1}^{N_R} t_{c,r,n} \tag{1}$$

$$\sigma_{c,n}^2 = \frac{1}{N_R} \sum_{r=1}^{N_R} (t_{c,r,n} - \mu_{c,n})^2 \tag{2}$$

$$\bar{\sigma} = \frac{1}{N_C N_N} \sum_{c=1}^{N_C} \sum_{n=1}^{N_N} \sqrt{\sigma_{c,n}^2} \tag{3}$$

$$\overline{c_v} = \frac{1}{N_C N_N} \sum_{c=1}^{N_C} \sum_{n=1}^{N_N} \frac{\sqrt{\sigma_{c,n}^2}}{\mu_{c,n}} \qquad (4)$$

Equation (1) provides the arithmetic mean $\mu_{c,n}$ of the delays (t) of a net class (n) in a column (c), calculated over the V-FPGA rows. $\sigma_{c,n}^2$ then calculates the variance for a net class in a certain column over the rows. This is further used in $\overline{\sigma}$ to calculate the arithmetic mean of the standard deviations of all net classes in all columns. $\overline{c_v}$ provides the arithmetic mean over the coefficient of variation of all net classes in all columns. Whereas the standard deviation is an absolute value and therefore depends on the mean of the delays, the coefficient of variation provides a relative measurement. As the delays in the host FPGA are largely discrete (e.g. fixed delays in LUTs), it is expected that relative delays can not be reduced further at some point. Because of this, we use $\overline{\sigma}$ to guide the design of our strategies and for evaluation of practically achievable uniformity. $\overline{c_v}$ is used to judge the quality of results for V-FPGA: As a smaller delay τ allows to put more logic elements in a path at the same frequency for V-FPGA applications, a constant standard deviation leads to reduced certainty of the number of V-FPGA logic elements in the path. A constant relative value $\overline{c_v}$ signifies unchanged conditions for the V-FPGA application synthesis.

Delay in the V-FPGA is a measurement that determines the final achievable application frequency. Equations to find the maximum delay among the building blocks are given below:

$$\tau_{c,n} = \max_{r \in \{1..N_R\}} t_{c,r,n} \qquad (5)$$

$$\tau = \max_{c \in \{1..N_C\}} \max_{n \in \{1..N_N\}} \tau_{c,n} \qquad (6)$$

$\tau_{c,n}$ selects the worst delay of a net class (n) in a column (c), calculated over the V-FPGA rows. τ uses this to find the absolute maximum delay over all columns and all net classes in the design, providing a single value for evaluation.

Area is measured in number of host FPGA CLBs used by the V-FPGA design. Used CLBs in the design do not solely consist of the V-FPGA building blocks: It also includes CLBs that are constrained to be explicitly not used in placement, optimizing the placement regularity. For partition blocks, their size may need to be slightly more than the minimum required area, as aiming for utilization ratio of 100% may cause routing to fail. 87% utilization rate is the default target chosen by Vivado and is our starting point for manual placement.

3.4 Methodology

Our overall approach to implement and evaluate the custom placement strategies for the V-FPGA consists of three steps: At first, the V-FPGA code is synthesized in Xilinx Vivado. Secondly, we run custom Tool Command Language (TCL) scripts on the synthesized design, adding various timing and location constraints. The third step is needed to evaluate the results and consists of running a custom TCL script to extract timing and area information.

Synthesis. Synthesis largely follows the Vivado default strategy. To ensure proper conditions for the TCL script, some settings are adjusted: The *flatten_hierarchy* option is changed from the default *rebuilt* to *none*. As V-FPGA designs often provide customizable parameters [3], the default option *rebuilt* leads to unpredictable signal names when these parameters change. Changing this setting can also affect optimization across hierarchy levels. To limit the impact of this, the implemented design was analyzed manually and some optimization have been carried out manually in the VHDL source code.

Constraining the Design. As Vivado analyzes every possible path in the design, it will also consider configurations of PSM multiplexers that can create combinational loops. It is therefore not easily possible to constrain the timing of the design by simple definition of the final clock period, as Vivado will break the loops at arbitrary points. This generates long paths through different numbers of CLBs and PSMs, making it further impossible to constrain a path just between two specific PSMs. To solve this problem, these paths are broken manually. The individual atomic nets then have their delay constrained using the *set_max_delay* timing exception, ensuring that the design still meets timing and forcing the timing driving optimization to operate. These constraints will lead to path segmentation, which in this case is the desired outcome. In addition, it will add false path constraints on the original long paths automatically. Path segmentation can affect logic placement and timing results, so special care needs to be taken when examining the Vivado timing reports. In addition to path constraints, we define four clocks for our design: The primary clock as well as three auxiliary clocks used for the configuration of PSM, IOB and CLB elements. The frequency of configuration logic is less important than the application frequency, so configuration clocks will target a lower frequency, avoiding over constraining the design.

Extracting Metrics. The Vivado timing report includes all details to judge how far the design met the timing constraints and usually provides the authoritative source in knowing the delay of all the nets. But in case of the V-FPGA, this report can not be used to extract meaningful data: The combinational loops, path delay constraints and path segmentation hide the important delays of the atomic nets from the timing report. Even though the target value for these nets is given using the path delay constraints, it is still useful to extract the real delays. To remedy this, a TCL script was written to extract the delays manually, using the *get_net_delay* command to get the delays of atomic nets. To get the delay of a whole path consisting of more than one net, a recursive search for nets is done and parts are summed up until the destination of the path is reached.

4   Logic Placement Strategies

In the following, we discuss the three manual placement strategies in detail. We primarily use the uniformity metric to guide development of the strategies, then assess critical path delay and area in the evaluation.

4.1   Basic P-Block Strategy

In the basic P-Block strategy, we contain each tile in a single Partition Block (P-Block): We create a block with suitable size, then use the *add_cells_to_pblock* TCL command to add all cells of a tile to the block. Before a block can be created, the size of the block must be determined. We therefore investigate two options to derive the block size: The first option is to use a size with same width and height for all tiles, resulting in quadratic tiles. The largest tile dimensions are then taken as the unified size for the P-Blocks of all tiles. Alternatively, the size can be chosen according to the required area in each tile. This requires additional rules for tile sizes, to keep the rectangular layout of V-FPGA and avoid irregular layout results. Therefore, the horizontal size for all tiles in the same column and the vertical size for all tiles in the same row have to be identical, leading to rectangular tiles. Figure 2a demonstrates the second option, showing the generated floorplan for a small 3×3 V-FPGA.

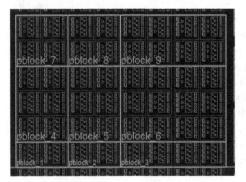
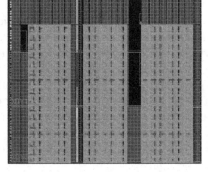

(a) Simple Floorplan.   (b) Split Target Area.

Fig. 2. Floorplanning and P-Blocks: a): Floorplan for 3x3 V-FPGA using individually calculated sizes for each tile. To keep the layout regular, widths and heights of tiles are adjusted accordingly. b): P-Block floor plan demonstrating a larger V-FPGA design. The start point location was forced, so the target area must be split into three smaller areas because of intersecting hard blocks.

Before the V-FPGA can be placed, a suitable host FPGA location and area has to be determined. This step has to consider non-uniformity of the host FPGA: For example, Virtex 7 devices have a rectangular structure with larger gaps (more than 2 columns) and smaller gaps (2 columns) between CLBs. This is caused by I/O banks, clocking and other support logic. In addition, Digital Signal Processor (DSP) and Block RAM (BRAM) blocks are distributed over the chip between CLB columns. In order to reduce net length between placed logic blocks, the largest location with no gaps will be selected. This is supposed to improve net delays and support the rectangular layout of the V-FPGA. Finding the location and area consists of the following steps:

1. Estimate the overall area needed for the design using total CLB count.
2. Create a 2D array which represents available and used CLBs. Then search for the largest possible target area, only considering areas without blockages larger than an accepted gap. A reasonable value for Virtex 7 is two, allowing DSP and BRAM gaps but avoiding larger ones.
3. Calculate tile dimensions, fitting all tiles in square form in the target area.
4. If the previous step fails, set the dimension ratio of all tiles relative to the vertical and horizontal dimensions of the selected target area.
5. If the largest contiguous target area is not large enough to fit the complete design (step three and four failed), the steps are reevaluated. In this reevaluation, multiple disconnected areas are allowed, yielding split target areas as shown in Fig. 2b.
6. Find the vertical and horizontal dimensions of all tiles according to their resource usage.
7. Normalize the dimensions of all tiles in the same column or row.

After the tile sizes, host FPGA location and target area have been determined, the following step completes the basic P-Block placement:

8. Map all V-FPGA cells to the P-Blocks belonging to their tile.

4.2   Nested P-Block Strategy

In addition to the P-Blocks used in the first strategy, this strategy introduces up to two additional P-Blocks within each tile. Logic belonging to the V-FPGA CLBs and IOBs is mapped to these nested P-Blocks accordingly: When defining the P-Blocks, all assigned logic cells are forced into the blocks, but this does not prevent placing any additional unassigned cells into them. Based on this idea, we introduce two more variants in addition to the rectangular vs. quadratic layout distinction: In the partially nested strategy, we use the outer P-Block for the tile and nested blocks for IOB and CLB, but the PSM is only constrained by the outer P-Block. This gives Vivado the freedom to place the PSM in the remaining outer P-Block area, or place part of it inside the nested P-Blocks. In the fully nested strategy, we force Vivado to not place any PSM logic in the nested P-Blocks, prohibiting usage of remaining logic cells in them. Figure 3 demonstrates the concept for a 5×5 CLB V-FPGA.

The placement script is extended with the following steps to create the nested P-Blocks:

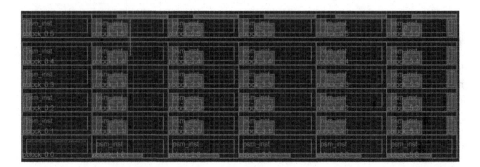

Fig. 3. V-FPGA floorplan with nested P-Blocks. The nested CLB P-Block is divided into two pieces to ensure the minimum possible area is used. The top right corner tile has an extra nested P-Block for its second IOB unit. No internal P-Block was used at all in the bottom left corner tile, as it only contains a PSM.

1. The internal P-Blocks can consist of multiple rectangles. The CLB P-Block is placed at the bottom left corner with height at most equal to the height of the tile minus one. This guarantees some freedom to IOB P-Block and to ensures distribution of the PSM unit over the tile P-Block.
2. The IOB P-Block is placed within the tile P-Block. The side is determined according to the tile type.

4.3   Fine-Grain Manual Placement Strategy

This strategy further constrains logic, directly mapping the relevant LUTs and flipflops to specific LUTs or flipflops in the 7 series host CLB. As there are numerous ways to place the logic within a tile, a manually derived layout is chosen instead of trying to find a fully automated one. The strategy is then made generic to support different V-FPGA parameters, but the layout is fixed to the V-FPGA and therefore cannot be reused for completely different applications. Evaluation of different manual layouts led to a placement as was presented in Fig. 1a: The PSM is located in the upper right corner and the CLB is placed in the lower part of the tile. Figure 4 shows the device view in Vivado after the manual placement strategy has been applied.

The implementation of this strategy operates on two lists for each tile P-Block, an instruction list and a list of the free host FPGA LUTs. The instruction list contains simple V-FPGA logic element place instructions, interleaved with sorting instructions. It is processed element by element, either placing logic elements or resorting the list of free resources. When an element placement instruction is processed, the logic elements are mapped sequentially to the elements in the sorted list of free resources, starting at a specified offset. When a resorting instruction is found, the resorting algorithm sorts the list of remaining available host LUTs. It sorts horizontally or vertically and uses ascending or descending sorting order, depending on the instruction. As an example, the *sort_xy_dd* instruction sorts first based on the x location, and if the x value is

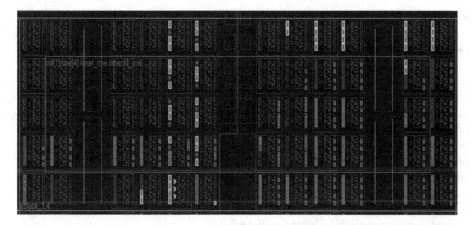

Fig. 4. V-FPGA tile (type 9) placed using the manual placement strategy. Multiplexers of the PSM's top, right, bottom and left side are marked sky blue, green, dark blue and yellow. The CLB is located at the bottom with the LUT, two internal multiplexers and D-flipflop colored in white. Red color represents the configuration units of the tile. Blue blocks at the bottom depict write connection boxes, whereas read connection boxes make up remaining logic around the LUT. (Color figure online)

the same for some CLBs, it uses y as secondary criteria. Descending sorting is applied in both cases. This specific instruction is used to sort the list of available logic elements before placing the right and left multiplexers of the PSM, as they need to be placed vertically from the top right corner. Sorting is always done on the list of free resources, so the length of this list decreases as the placement process proceeds. This makes it possible to reach every single CLB in the P-Block, not just the ones at the borders.

5   Evaluation of the Placement Strategies

To evaluate the different strategies with different V-FPGA parameters, three V-FPGA designs of increasing size have been implemented: A small 2×2 design with 4 CLB tiles total (track width 2), a 5×5 design with 25 CLB tiles (track width 10) and a 8×8 design with 64 CLB tiles (track width 9). The larger track width for the second design has been used to evaluate influence of increasing routing congestion, compared to the influence of the design size. All designs have been evaluated both with fine grain timing constraints and without fine grain timing constraints. We compare the three strategies presented previously, with both quadratic and rectangular tiles for the P-Block strategies. For the manual placement strategy, we use only rectangular blocks, but compare two different placement script variations. In the nested P-Block strategy, we consider both the partially and fully nested variants. Comparisons between the three proposed strategies are held in the previously described metrics of uniformity, worst delay and area. All results are normalized to the Vivado 2019.1 default synthesis results as a baseline.

Uniformity. We assess uniformity as defined in the metrics chapter. Table 1 shows standard deviation $\bar{\sigma}$ for the different designs. In all strategies, for smaller designs, better uniformity is achieved than for larger designs. Also in all strategies, the 5×5 design has worst uniformity when timing constraints are applied. This can be explained by two observations: The 5×5 design uses wide track widths, which increases routing congestion in timing constrained designs and makes it more difficult to reach uniform values. Additionally, in larger designs, non-uniformity of the host FPGA is more prevalent, as the design spans a larger host FPGA area. There is no large difference between uniformity in quadratic or rectangular tile layout, but the rectangular layout performs better or equal to the quadratic layout for all strategies. When comparing the strategies, fully manual placement yields the best uniformity in timing constrained cases and is within 2% of the best results in the other cases. Both variants are similar, but variant 1 provides slightly better uniformity.

Table 1. Standard deviation $\bar{\sigma}$ relative to Vivado standard synthesis results, comparing uniformity. "R" denotes rectangle based strategies.

Timing constraints	Design	Basic	Basic R	Partially nested	Partially nested R	Fully nested	Fully nested R	Manual variant 1	Manual variant 2
No	2×2	0.90	0.95	1.01	0.84	0.89	0.67	0.69	0.83
	5×5	0.82	0.79	0.80	0.80	0.80	0.81	0.81	0.81
	8×8	0.89	0.81	0.93	0.82	0.88	0.82	0.79	0.79
Yes	2×2	0.72	0.71	0.65	0.72	0.65	0.64	0.61	0.75
	5×5	1.04	0.98	1.02	1.02	1.00	1.00	0.90	0.90
	8×8	0.79	0.83	0.82	0.82	0.85	0.82	0.76	0.80

Table 2. Coefficient of variation $\bar{c_v}$ relative to Vivado standard synthesis results, comparing uniformity. "R" denotes rectangle based strategies.

Timing constraints	Design	Basic	Basic R	Partially nested	Partially nested R	Fully nested	Fully nested R	Manual variant 1	Manual variant 2
No	2×2	0.97	1.01	1.03	0.85	0.92	0.71	0.74	0.92
	5×5	0.86	0.83	0.81	0.81	0.81	0.81	0.85	0.83
	8×8	0.93	0.85	0.93	0.82	0.90	0.81	0.83	0.82
Yes	2×2	0.81	0.79	0.72	0.78	0.72	0.68	0.70	0.77
	5×5	0.99	0.97	0.97	0.95	0.96	0.96	0.86	0.87
	8×8	0.88	0.89	0.88	0.87	0.90	0.88	0.78	0.83

Table 2 shows the coefficient of variation $\bar{c_v}$ for the different designs. Overall trends are similar to $\bar{\sigma}$, and for constrained designs, the manual placement variants again yield best results. The reduced standard deviation in delays therefore translates to relative improvements, which can be taken advantage of when synthesizing applications for the V-FPGA.

Delay. Figure 5 shows how these improvements in uniformity translate to improvements in worst-delay τ for the different strategies. Figure 5a demonstrates that results without fine grain timing constraints need to be viewed with some scrutiny: Further analysis showed that without these constraints, Vivado puts little effort into routing optimization. This leads to worse results for most of the strategies, where the fully manual strategies are a notable exception and also yield consistent improvements in the unconstrained case. Interestingly, without these constraints, results of manual strategies get worse for larger designs. As the design is regular, we expected similar or better results for larger designs: The manual placement should be regular, whereas the baseline Vivado synthesis strategy may have to deal with congestion and increasing effort for large designs. Investigating this, we tightly constrained the nets in the design and reevaluated the results, shown in Fig. 5b. In this case, we can see significant improvements for all strategies over the baseline. Furthermore, the advantage of the strategies now increases for larger designs, which we attribute to routing and congestion issues in the Vivado default strategy for larger designs. It can also be seen that in most cases, using a rectangular floorplan leads to less delay than using the simpler square based floorplan. The two variants for manual placement produce the best and similar results, but depending on the size of the design, one may

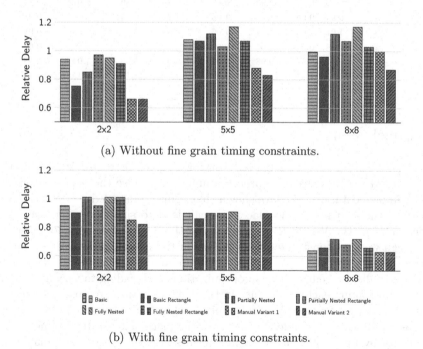

(a) Without fine grain timing constraints.

(b) With fine grain timing constraints.

Fig. 5. Delays τ relative to Vivado standard synthesis results. Of all analyzed atomic needs, the largest increase or the smallest decrease, i.e. the worst case, is shown.

be slightly advantageous. For the largest design, we see an improvement of 37% in the achieved delay.

Area. Table 3 shows how the strategies affect the required host FPGA area. In the case without timing constraints, there is no consistent pattern. This is explained by the fact that the baseline is not timing optimized. For the constrained designs and small designs, most strategies even achieve reduced area usage. As designs get larger, the baseline logic is more localized and the relative overhead of the manual placement strategies increases. Here, worst case overheads of the fully manual strategies are 13% and 16%. We consider this as an acceptable tradeoff, as these strategies also achieve best results in delay reduction for large designs. Rectangular blocks most of the time lead to less used area, which is expected as they can fit the really required tile sizes more closely.

Table 3. Area of used or blocked CLBs relative to Vivado standard synthesis results. "R" denotes rectangle based strategies.

Timing constraints	Design	Basic	Basic R	Partially nested	Partially nested R	Fully nested	Fully nested R	Manual variant 1	Manual variant 2
No	2 × 2	0.89	0.87	0.93	0.85	0.89	0.89	1.07	0.72
	5 × 5	0.99	0.99	1.04	1.00	1.03	1.03	0.99	0.91
	8 × 8	1.01	1.06	1.14	1.06	1.04	1.07	0.99	0.99
Yes	2 × 2	1.05	0.94	1.05	0.95	0.99	0.89	0.86	0.67
	5 × 5	0.93	0.95	0.98	0.92	0.98	0.99	1.04	0.98
	8 × 8	1.03	1.12	1.23	1.13	1.12	1.13	1.16	1.13

6 Conclusion

In this publication, we investigated varying degrees of customization in the Vivado FPGA logic placement process, aiming to reduce the delays in our V-FPGA implementation. We have shown that utilizing knowledge about the regularity of the design in logic placement can lead to significant improvements in net delay of the V-FPGA. Regressions in the delays were only found when the design was not constrained with fine grain timing constraints: Here, due to combinational loops in the V-FPGA, basic timing constraints do not constrain the design fully, preventing certain optimizations and leading to varying results. When constraining each atomic net in the V-FPGA, these regressions will not occur. We further showed that uniformity in the V-FPGA net timing can be used as an indicator to guide the design of the placement strategies: Increasing uniformity by up to 39% in the timing results also lead to reduced maximum delay. Out of the strategies investigated, the most advanced strategy lead to best results. In this strategy, the location of individual CLBs was assigned completely manually using a TCL script and only routing was left to Vivado's automated algorithms. This approach lead to improvements in maximum delay of up to

37% for the largest designs, at increased area costs of up to 16%. Larger designs generally benefit more from the manual placement strategy.

To conclude, these results will allow for higher clock rates in user applications on V-FPGA, lowering the entry barrier for using it in more cases. In addition, the increased uniformity can be used to enable new concepts, such as overclocking of user applications or moving parts of the application dynamically on the V-FPGA. In general, more uniform V-FPGAs also provide more realistic insights for physical FPGA development, as they resemble their uniformity more closely.

References

1. Borriello, G., Ebeling, C., Hauck, S.A., Burns, S.: The triptych FPGA architecture. IEEE Trans. Very Large Scale Integr. (VLSI) Syst. **3**(4), 491–501 (1995)
2. Figuli, P., et al.: A heterogeneous SOC architecture with embedded virtual FPGA cores and runtime core fusion. In: 2011 NASA/ESA Conference on Adaptive Hardware and Systems (AHS), pp. 96–103 (2011)
3. Figuli, P., Ding, W., Figuli, S., Siozios, K., Soudris, D., Becker, J.: Parameter sensitivity in virtual FPGA architectures. In: Wong, S., Beck, A.C., Bertels, K., Carro, L. (eds.) ARC 2017. LNCS, vol. 10216, pp. 141–153. Springer, Cham (2017). https://doi.org/10.1007/978-3-319-56258-2_13
4. Harbaum, T., et al.: Auto-SI: an adaptive reconfigurable processor with run-time loop detection and acceleration. In: 2017 30th IEEE International System-on-Chip Conference (SOCC), pp. 153–158 (2017)
5. Shi, M., Bermak, A., Chandrasekaran, S., Amira, A.: An efficient FPGA implementation of gaussian mixture models-based classifier using distributed arithmetic. In: 2006 13th IEEE International Conference on Electronics, Circuits and Systems, pp. 1276–1279 (2006)
6. Sidiropoulos, H., Figuli, P., Siozios, K., Soudris, D., Becker, J.: A platform-independent runtime methodology for mapping multiple applications onto fpgas through resource virtualization. In: 2013 23rd International Conference on Field programmable Logic and Applications, pp. 1–4 (2013)
7. Yuan, J., Chen, J., Wang, L., Zhou, X., Xia, Y., Hu, J.: ARBSA: adaptive range-based simulated annealing for FPGA placement. IEEE Trans. Comput. Aided Des. Integr. Circuits Syst. **38**(12), 2330–2342 (2019)

Timing Optimization for Virtual FPGA Configurations

Linus Witschen, Tobias Wiersema$^{(\boxtimes)}$, Masood Raeisi Nafchi, Arne Bockhorn,
and Marco Platzner

Computer Science Department, Paderborn University, Paderborn, Germany
{witschen,wiersema,mraeisi,xoar,platzner}@mail.upb.de

Abstract. Fine-grained reconfigurable FPGA overlays, usually called virtual FPGAs, suffer from virtualization costs regarding area requirements and timing performance. Decreasing the area costs of such virtual FPGAs has been the focus of several research efforts over the past years, but adapting the (virtual) timing suffers from the contradiction of having to optimize properties with strong physical ties in an environment that is specifically designed to abstract them away.

This paper explores several methods to optimize the maximum operating frequency of the virtual FPGA ZUMA and its guest circuits despite this conflict using two complementary approaches: fine-tuned physical overlay design optimization through floorplanning in Xilinx' design suite Vivado and delay-optimized virtual synthesis in the VTR tool flow. In our experimental results with virtual benchmark circuits, we respectively improve the operating frequency of a 3×3 or a 5×5 ZUMA architecture of up to 41% and 65% for individual benchmarks, and by 23% and 31% on average. Our results would also scale accordingly should future research uncover new potential to reduce the area cost further.

1 Introduction

Virtualization is a widely used abstraction technique that presents a different view on the resources of a computing system than the physically accurate one by abstracting away from the physical devices' individual details. Lagadec et al. [5] introduced a definition of virtual FPGAs (vFPGAs) as a separate overlay on top of a physical FPGA. The authors discussed the advantages of having an overlay that is not limited by the constraints of the underlying physical FPGA, such as the potential portability of circuits, and providing a means to investigate and experiment with new FPGA architectures. In FPGAs and ASICs alike, an overlay can introduce features that the underlying hardware does not have, most notably fast partial and dynamic reconfiguration. Lagadec et al. also mentioned potential disadvantages of using overlays, namely the area overhead, the reduced clock frequency, and a lack of tool chains for synthesizing to vFPGAs. With ZUMA [3],

This work has been partially supported by the German Research Foundation (DFG) within the CRC901 "On-The-Fly Computing" under the project number 160364472.

© Springer Nature Switzerland AG 2021
S. Derrien et al. (Eds.): ARC 2021, LNCS 12700, pp. 50–64, 2021.
https://doi.org/10.1007/978-3-030-79025-7_4

Brant and Lemieux presented a fine-grained FPGA overlay that improves upon some of these disadvantages by providing a tool chain and lowering the area overhead to a reported 40× through careful architectural choices.

Several objectives have fueled interest in FPGA virtualization in particular over the past decades, which Vaishnav et al. list as follows in their survey [8]: Multi-tenancy, resource management, flexibility, isolation, scalability, performance, security, resilience, and programmer's productivity. Nevertheless, the timing performance of the virtual circuit remains one of the most challenging issues with vFPGAs, i.e., it is hard to perform both an accurate timing analysis and an optimization of the timing. Virtual FPGAs contain a multitude of possible combinational loops because of their programmable interconnection points. As the delay of such loops is potentially infinite, CAD tools need to break them up to at least optimize the timing of the resulting paths that then have distinct (but arbitrary) endpoints. Since the CAD tools lack insight into the structure of the overlay, these artificial breakpoints will be selected effectively at random. As a result, the placement and routing (P&R) step will optimize the timing of a random subpath of each loop of the vFPGA, which can cluster the resources and form the virtual fabric in unexpected ways, likely affecting the timing performance of the overlay negatively.

To tackle the issue of timing optimization for virtual circuits, i.e., to maximize their f_{max}, we propose two approaches. First, we leverage the capabilities of the well-known VPR 8 tool [7] to use back-annotated timing information from the physical implementation to optimize the critical path delay of virtual circuits. Second, we guide the physical design tool – Xilinx' Vivado in this work – to generate improved ZUMA implementations by exploiting our knowledge of the virtual fabric's structure. The introduction and combination of these two approaches ensures that we can harness the full potential of an overlay once its fabric is fully implemented and its timing is analyzed.

The contributions of this paper are thus as follows:

– We introduce a method to map timing information from the physical implementation back to virtual synthesis, thus enabling virtual routing driven by physical timing.
– We present a hierarchical version of the ZUMA overlay description to facilitate floorplanning and show how to convey the structure of the virtual FPGA to physical synthesis.
– We compare and evaluate the performance of our approaches on several virtual benchmark circuits using Xilinx Vivado, in particular its global and out-of-context (OOC) design flows.

The remainder of this paper is structured as follows: We first describe our employed virtual FPGA model in Sect. 2. In Sect. 3 we discuss our new timing-driven tool flow version for virtual synthesis, and in Sect. 4 we propose physical synthesis strategies along with modifications to the fabric of our virtual FPGAs. Section 5 presents the experimental validation of our combined approach, Sect. 6 explores related work, and Sect. 7 concludes the paper.

2   Background: Fine-Grained Virtual FPGA

We base our work on the fine-grained virtual FPGA ZUMA, as introduced by Brant and Lemieux in [3]. ZUMA is a tiled architecture comprising a two-dimensional grid of logic clusters (LCs), input blocks for the LCs, switch boxes, and IO pads. A LC is built of basic logic elements (BLE), each containing a K-LUT, a bypassable FF, and an Input Interconnect Block (IIB) that implements a crossbar connecting the LC inputs and BLE feedback lines to the cluster's BLE inputs. IO pads are placed along the grid perimeter and with two IOs per IO pad, i.e., an $n \times m$ architecture provides $4 \cdot (n + m)$ general purpose IOs that can each be configured as input or output. Figure 1 depicts an example for a 3×3 ZUMA architecture.

By default, ZUMA uses an island style architecture with configuration options for the number of LCs, BLEs per cluster, K, number of connections to and inside the cluster, channel width and wire length. The critical architectural choice that sets ZUMA apart is to store the virtual configuration in distributed RAM, i.e., LUT-based RAM, instead of flip flops. Modern FPGAs allow designs to use LUT-based RAM for both RAM and logic blocks in data paths at the same time, making them ideal building blocks for virtual FPGAs.

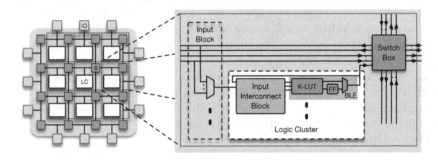

Fig. 1. Exemplary ZUMA vFPGA comprising 3×3 tiles in island style and detailed view of one such tile as introduced in [3].

Brant and Lemieux also addressed the lack of tool chains for virtual FPGAs and employed the open source tool flow VTR [7] and a set of Python scripts to generate both the virtual fabric as configuration for the physical FPGA and the virtual configurations. The tool flow is sketched in Fig. 2, using solid lines to indicate the state of the flow prior to this work, i.e., introduced in [3] and extended in [9]. Starting with a template architecture file that defines the basic ZUMA layout and a file specifying ZUMA architectural parameters, a script generates the architecture description. Then, given a behavioral description of a virtual circuit in Verilog, VTR flow tools (ODIN, ABC and VPR) synthesize, technology map, and pack, place & route the virtual circuit. Additionally, VPR transforms the outer routing resources of the described virtual FPGA architecture into an abstract routing resource graph (RRG), which can be dumped into a file. Based on this abstract routing resource graph and the description of the inner routing resources, i.e., everything inside a LC, a script generates the behavioral description of the virtual FPGA architecture, also in Verilog, ready to be synthesized for a physical host FPGA. The ZUMA script also parses the virtual circuit's netlist and placement & routing files to create the virtual configuration bitstream. Using timing information extracted from a post-implementation timing analysis of the physical synthesis, subsequent runs of the ZUMA flow can furthermore analyze the achievable operating frequency f_{max} of the virtual FPGA for the newly synthesized virtual circuit when using the already implemented and analyzed version of the overlay fabric.

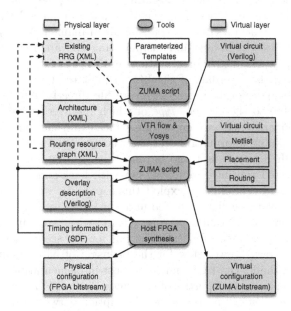

Fig. 2. Physical and virtual ZUMA synthesis flow. Solid outlines represent the state of the art; dashed lines highlight the changes proposed in Sect. 3.

3   Physical Timing-Driven Virtual Routing

In this section, we present how we provide VPR 8 with full timing information for all resources of the virtual FPGA. We achieve that by parsing the Standard Delay Format (SDF) file created by Xilinx' tool flow when synthesizing an overlay into a ZUMA Overlay Description Graph (ODG) and then back-annotating the physical delay information into augmented versions of VPR's input files, as shown in Fig. 2. This allows us to run VPR now not only in the area-driven mode, but also in the timing-driven packing, placement & routing mode. VPR can thus—for the first time—look for an implementation and mapping of the virtual circuit to the virtual resources that minimizes the critical path delay on the host FPGA, thus maximizing f_{max}.

Our work leverages the approach described by Wiersema et al. [9], who presented an SDF file-based method for VPR 7 to extract timing information from a vFPGA after physical synthesis, but extends it by exploiting the new capabilities of VPR 8. The naming scheme of the components in the SDF file allows for a mapping from the physical components back to the virtual ones. To avoid a reduction of timing accuracy, we annotate ZUMA's internal ODG that describes all of the vFPGA's logic and routing resources, so that we can deduce the physically critical path of an overlay configuration, which is not necessarily the longest virtual path. The total propagation delay along the critical path then implies a minimum clock period for the specific overlay configuration on that particular implementation of the fabric. Translating the timing data back into VPR's structures would result in a loss of information, however, since VPR only stores the overlay description in a tileable, coarse-grained manner. VPR generates its RRG at runtime by expanding and instantiating the architecture primitives until it arrives at a detailed representation of all routing resources *outside* of ZUMA's LCs, i.e., the internals of the LCs are not resolved at this level. We would thus have to annotate the architecture file directly, but here the granularity is restricted to the element *type* of which the overlay fabric is built; it describes, e.g., only one master copy of a LC which could thus only be annotated with worst-case timing information over the whole vFPGA.

The new VPR 8 allows us to go beyond this solution, since it can load a previously generated routing resource graph with back-annotated timing into the program at the beginning. To exploit this capability, we have implemented extensions to the synthesis flow depicted in dashed lines in Fig. 2. The extended flow requires to run the virtual synthesis at least twice. The inputs and overall mechanics remain unchanged for the runs, but for the second and subsequent runs for the same overlay we allow for the inclusion of back-annotated timing information from the FPGA back end tools' post-implementation timing analysis. To reflect the physical properties of the synthesized vFPGA within VPR, we propose to significantly extend the stored description between the runs to properly augment it with the timing information. This allows VPR to read-in the timing-annotated vFPGA description in full detail, without having to regenerate the fabric with each run, and to run in timing-driven rather than area-driven mode for the virtual packing, placement & routing.

To facilitate the transfer of the timing information, we split ZUMA's timing-annotated ODG into its extra-LC and intra-LC components and annotate the corresponding VPR storage file for each type with the parsed and aggregated data. For the global, extra-LC resources this is quite straightforward, since we can simply attribute the delay of the physical paths to edges of VPR's RRG. Hence, we take for each ODG node v the worst-case propagation time of a signal from its configured input port I_x to its output port O, add the delay of the virtual wire incident to I_x, and then set this sum as the delay of the RRG edge that corresponds to this wire. This way we only have to take special care of the cases where the ODG is more fine-grained than the RRG, which can happen, for instance, when a RRG node is not k_{host}-feasible. For such nodes we accumulate all delays of the physical path implementing the virtual wire incident to I_x and assign it to the RRG edge incident to I_x, and then add to this the total delay of the singular path between the physical subnodes of v that connects I_x with O. By applying this pattern to the complete graph, we can map all extra-LC overlay delays from the SDF file to edges of the RRG, which will allow us to determine the total delay of the physical paths between two virtual nodes.

For the intra-LC resources the situation is more involved, since VPR instantiates them from only one copy: The pessimistic delay model derived by assuming the worst-case delay for each master resource would not be accurate enough to enable meaningful timing-driven P&R. To overcome this limitation, we propose to push the expansion of the intra-LC resources from the ODG back into the architecture file, by building an augmented architecture that contains individualized LC resources instead of only one singular representative. We prepare this architecture file with empty timing information before even the first run of VPR, to make sure that we only have to add the delay data for subsequent runs and thus preserve the binary compatibility of the architectures with and without timing information.

This preprocessing enables us to later recognize the individual architecture component instances in the generated SDF files and parse their delay data similar to the RRG augmentation described above. On the one hand, we can thus accurately back-annotate the timing information from our ODG into the individualized architecture XML for future runs of VPR, but on the other hand, we cannot avoid one significant downside of this approach with current versions of VTR unless the capabilities of VTR's architecture descriptions would change: VTR models FPGA architectures in a way that considers timing information to be solely tied to logical blocks, while the tiles (i.e., the slots of the grid into which blocks can be placed) remain perfectly homogeneous. To port the timing information back to VTR in a meaningful manner, we thus have to annotate the logical blocks with the delays, instead of attributing it to tiles. This requires us, however, to move away from modeling a generic logic cluster that fits into any tile towards individual logic clusters that have a fixed correspondence to locations in the grid. Obviously this fixed mapping renders the virtual placement step with significantly reduced swapping opportunities that are basically limited to the IO pads, which means that the actual placement will already have been determined by the packing algorithm without chance of further improvement by the placer.

We have attempted to alleviate this issue by declaring all individualized logic clusters interchangeable for the placement step, but this only enables the placer to perform "blind" swaps that it cannot evaluate properly, since VTR will swap the timing information along with the LCs. The results presented in this paper thus all suffer from this severe limitation of their placement and would therefore all benefit from potential future improvements made to VTR's modeling capabilities concerning timing information of grid tiles.

Using the timing-annotated files together, i.e., the individualized architecture file and the RRG, we are then able to provide VPR 8 with accurate information

about the synthesized ZUMA overlay's topology. We want to note that our approach as well as the one in [9] rely on a Linear Delay Model (LDM) instead of
the popular and more accurate Elmore Delay Model (EDM). Betz et al. argue
against the LDM in [1] and strongly favor the EDM instead for their own analysis
within VPR. The EDM requires insights into the resistances and capacitances
of the actual routing resources on the host FPGA. For virtual FPGAs, however,
the graph model in which we perform the routing and timing analysis does not
really reflect a physical reality of the wires by design, which means that even if
we had approximations for the resistance and capacitance of the virtual routing
resources, the differences of the virtual and physical neighborhood of each wire
would defeat the accuracy advantage of the EDM.

4   Physical Design Optimization Through Flooplanning

In this section, we describe how we optimize the physical design through floorplanning on a physical host FPGA using the CAD tools of the device's vendor,
i.e., Xilinx Vivado. We enable floorplanning of the ZUMA overlay by changing
the overlay description from a flat to a hierarchical design. Floorpanning then
allows us to guide Vivado's P&R step to convey the regularity of the fabric to
shorten paths, and thus, reduce delay. We furthermore employ Vivado's out-of-
context (OOC) flow to obtain better results for smaller implementations in most
cases.

When the CAD tools are unaware of the regular structure of the overlay,
they will break up the multitude of combinational loops at arbitrary points,
which will then be subjected to timing optimization during P&R. However, the
involved randomness often leads to a poor timing behavior, thereby increasing
the virtualization costs. The domain knowledge which we leverage to steer the
physical design process of the virtual FPGA fabric to alleviate this issue mostly
follows its hierarchical and regular structure, as depicted in Fig. 1, and comprises
the following elements: The spatial arrangement of the virtual tiles, the similarity
of all tiles except for their connections to IO pads, the regular structure of
the island style with interwoven LCs and routing tracks/switch boxes, the fact
that none of the numerous combinational loops will actually be active unless
the virtual circuit itself contains combinational loops, and the insight that the
distribution logic for the virtual configuration will also require additional space
throughout the fabric but will not affect the f_{max} of the vFPGA.

Originally, ZUMA's overlay was described as a large monolithic design, con-
tained in a single Verilog module. Lavin and Kavini, however, state in [6] that
Vivado often produces better results for small implementations. We therefore
changed ZUMA's Verilog structure from a flat design into a hierarchical one
by encapsulating the logic clusters and their internal components into separate
modules. The hierarchical design is potentially beneficial for two reasons: 1) we
can floorplan the individual modules to provide guidance to Vivado's placer,
and 2) we can initiate Vivado's out-of-context flow, which performs synthesis
and implementation on the standalone modules, i.e., Vivado is processing smaller

implementations before they are integrated into the whole design in a bottom-up flow. For the floorplanning, we investigate two strategies: coarse-grained floorplanning (short: coarse) and fine-grained floorplanning (short: fine). In the coarse strategy, one LC forms one module in the overlay's Verilog description, and in the fine strategy, each LC is further subdivided so that the IIB and each individual BLE also form separate modules.

We use Pblocks that are adjustable by strategy parameters to convey the regularity of the design to Vivado in our fully automated floorplanning, so that we can define location constraints on the physical FPGA for the individual modules defined via the coarse or fine strategy. Completely resembling the regular structure is, however, not feasible, since Xilinx FPGAs provide a column-based architecture, i.e., each component in a column is generally of the same type, e.g., DSP, BRAM, or CLB, but the architectural pattern of the FPGA is not regular, i.e., the column types do not alternate in a specific pattern. CLBs comprise of multiple so-called slices of type SLICEL and/or SLICEM. In the context of our work, CLB columns containing slices of type SLICEM are of particular interest, since these slices implement the distributed LUT-based memory (LUTRAM) that ZUMA overlays are built of. Columns with no LUTRAM cells can thus not be considered in the implementation, causing additional delay due to longer paths spanning over the unused columns.

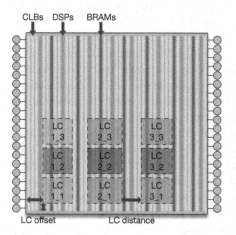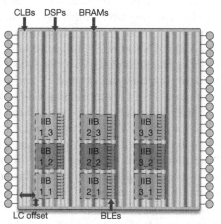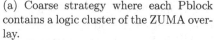

(a) Coarse strategy where each Pblock contains a logic cluster of the ZUMA overlay.

(b) Fine strategy where each logic cluster is further subdivided into their IIB and their, in this case, eight BLEs. Pblocks of the same color belong to the same LC.

Fig. 3. Floorplanning for 3×3 ZUMA overlay. Each colored region with dashed outlines specifies a Pblock on the physical FPGA. Design parameters allow for modifications of the floorplan.

Figure 3a shows a floorplan of a 3×3 ZUMA overlay with the coarse strategy. Each colored box with dashed outlines represents a Pblock for a LC module on the physical design. The design parameters LC offset and LC distance control the offset from the overlay from the lower left corner of the physical device or the distance between the Pblocks of the LCs in x and y direction, respectively. Some parts of the overlay are not location-constrained in the floorplan: the IOs, the virtual-physical interface, the intercluster routing resources, and the input boxes. We allow Vivado to place these components inside Pblocks if resources are free. Since, however, the Pblocks are chosen as tightly as possible for each module to maximize logic density and minimize routing delays, only few resources inside a Pblock remain usable. Thus, introducing space around and between the Pblocks is important to enable Vivado to place the remaining parts of the overlay around and in-between the Pblocks. However, this buffer zone has to be balanced: If too little space is provided, not all components can be placed close to their related parts, causing longer routes, while too much space results in unused area that has to be spanned, which also causes more delay. The width and the height of a Pblock can be controlled via a shape parameter, which constitutes another trade-off parameter accounting for the column-based architecture of the physical FPGA. As discussed, LUTRAM cells are only present in certain columns. Consequently, these columns should be utilized as much as possible, suggesting that a tall and slim shape for the Pblocks would be preferable. However, making the Pblocks too tall results in long vertical routes. On the other hand, Pblocks spanning over multiple columns, may also lead to longer routes due to an increased number of columns inside the Pblocks that cannot contribute to the overlay. This effect is indicated in Fig. 3a where the Pblocks $LC\,2\_i, i \in [1,3]$ are wider than the other Pblocks, since the Pblocks span over unusable columns.

Figure 3b shows an exemplary fine-strategy floorplan for a 3×3 ZUMA overlay where each LC comprises of one IIB and eight BLEs, each encapsulated in separately floorplanned modules. Parameters determine the offset of the overlay on the physical FPGA as well as the distance between IIBs and BLEs. Shape parameters control the height and the width of the IIBs and the BLEs individually. Similar to the coarse strategy, the parameters pose a trade-off. The spacing parameters are used to provide sufficient space for the non-floorplanned components in-between the Pblocks while keeping the space narrow enough to not add extra delay. The shape parameter again seeks to minimize the delay through routes either vertically or over unusable columns.

To enable a feasible implementation of the modules in the Pblocks, the Pblocks have to satisfy the resource requirements of each module. Hence, our automated scripts have to synthesize each module individually to determine the resource requirements. Then, according to the configuration parameters, Pblocks are generated that maximize the logic density to minimize the routing delay while satisfying the resource requirements. In Vivado's OOC flow, the modules are then individually synthesized and implemented for their Pblocks. Since, in the OOC flow, synthesis and implementation is performed on the standalone modules, the individual implementations are smaller. Consequently, Vivado can spend more time on optimizing the design, which may improve the overall outcome. In a bottom-up approach, the implementations are then inserted into their respective Pblocks and the remaining logic is synthesized and implemented. In Vivado's global synthesis flow, the Pblock constraints are respected but all modules are synthesized and implemented as part of the top-level design, which can reduce the quality of the implementation, as Vivado may spend less time on optimizing parts of the design.

At this point we want to stress that our floorplanning approach is somewhat different from the conventional floorplanning for FPGAs. Generally, when floorplanning is performed to achieve timing closure, the critical paths are identified and floorplanning is applied to guide the placer and router. In the context of our work, however, critical paths in the physical domain cannot be identified due to the combinational loops. In fact, a correct timing analysis can only be performed in interplay with the virtual domain when the virtual circuit is known and no combinational loops are present. Then, the path delays from the physical domain can be utilized to perform an exact timing analysis of the design. As a result, the conventional approach in floorplanning to improve the critical paths in the physical domain cannot be performed in our work, making floorplanning more challenging and the effects less predicable.

5   Experimental Results

We performed experiments on a compute system with an Intel Xeon Silver 4208 CPU@2.10 GHz and 187 GiB of main memory, and targeted Xilinx' Zynq Z-7100 with the part number xc7z100ffg900-2 using Vivado 2017.1. Using different configurations for the physical design flow, we generated 3×3 and 5×5 ZUMA overlays. Figure 4 reports the achieved results for seven virtual benchmark circuits, utilizing the vFPGA's IOs from 5% up to 100% and CLBs from 4% up to 78%. In the figure, we distinguish between the original physical design flow, i.e., a monolithic ZUMA description without floorplanning and a global synthesis flow in Vivado, and the coarse or fine physical design flow, i.e., a hierarchical ZUMA description with floorplanning, executed either in a global or OOC fashion.

The figure shows the absolute operating frequency f_{max} for ZUMA's original flow, from [9], with area-driven P&R in VPR (*orig-area*) and our timing-driven flow version (*orig-timing*), both without any floorplanning for the physical flow. The strategy *orig-timing* shows the improvements in the operating frequencies achieved with the original flow but with timing-driven routing in VPR. The coarse and fine strategy are indicated by their names and are followed by whether the flow was carried out globally (*glb*) or OOC (*ooc*). In these experiments, the virtual flow was always performed using timing-driven P&R to investigate whether this timing-augmented flow could be further improved through floorplanning or a different physical synthesis strategy, respectively. As the timing results tend to be rather sensitive to the random nature of VPR's algorithms, we have run the virtual synthesis ten times and report the average f_{max} in the figure, as well as the range into which all runs fell.

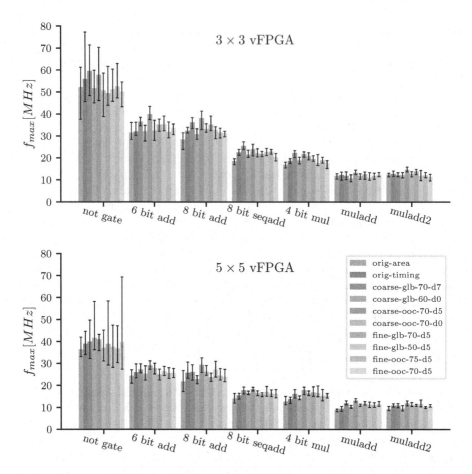

Fig. 4. Operating frequency f_{max} in MHz. Ten runs per benchmark circuit; colored bars show the average result and black lines depict the range of all runs.

Comparison of Area-Driven Versus Timing-Driven P&R. First, we evaluate *orig-area* against its counterpart with timing-driven P&R (*orig-timing*) to investigate the impact on the achievable operating frequency f_{max}. For the 3×3 overlay, the figure shows that exploiting the physical timing information has a positive effect on the frequency, since the averaged operating frequency improved for every benchmark individually and on average by 9% over all benchmarks. In fact, considering all benchmarks, *orig-timing* achieved improvements of up to 32%, while only showing a minor slowdown of 4% for the lowest frequency out of the ten runs for benchmark *muladd* compared to the baseline. At the same time, however, the benchmark improved upon its highest frequency by 5% over the baseline's highest frequency. For the 5×5 overlay, the highest improvement is even slightly better with 35% for the benchmark *8 bit add* and an average improvement of 11% over all benchmarks. Here, only the highest frequency for benchmark 4 *bit mul* showed a minor slowdown of 2%. Thus, we conclude that employing timing-driven P&R is highly beneficial for optimizing the operating frequency of the virtual circuits within a given overlay fabric.

Evaluation of the Impact of the Physical Design Flow Optimizations. For the physical design flow optimizations, we performed experiments in an empirical study using up to 16 different configurations, where an offset in x and y direction was set to enable P&R to utilize the space around the overlay. The coarse strategy offers four and the fine strategy eight design parameters in total. We observed that the most influential parameters for both strategies are the distances between the Pblocks in x direction in combination with different shapes for the LCs in the coarse and the IIB in the fine strategy. The specific parameter value is encoded in the name of the configuration in Fig. 4. The value for the distances range from no distances (suffix *d0*) to large distances (suffix *d7*), and the shapes range from tall and slim (*0*) over squares (*50*) to short and fat (*100*). From the results of our study, we present the best-performing (green tones in Fig. 4) and worst-performing (orange tones) configurations for each strategy here, first for the 3 × 3 overlay, and then for the 5 × 5 overlay using the same configurations. The best-performing configurations are achieving significant improvements over the baseline (up to 41%) as well as over the configuration *orig-timing* (up to 25%) for both overlays. The shape of the Pblocks in these configurations is slightly wider than higher and the space in-between the Pblocks is chosen to just fit the non-floorplanned parts.

Generally, we observe that the coarse strategy leads to higher improvements than the fine strategy. We explain this by the fact that the Pblocks for each module are chosen as tight as possible; hence, leaving little freedom for the placer to investigate different placements in the fine strategy. In other words, in the fine strategy, the information provided through the fine-grained modules and the tight Pblocks are constraining Vivado's P&R too much, in fact hindering its optimizations. The coarse strategy, on the other hand, provides more potential for exploration while still guiding the placement in a sufficient amount to resemble the structure of the virtual FPGA. Furthermore, we observe that *coarse-ooc* performs best overall, which seems to provide Vivado with small enough implementations to produce good results while giving Vivado's P&R enough freedom for optimization. In fact, comparing two identical configurations once synthesized with the global flow and once synthesized OOC, we could observe that OOC generally leads to better results – supporting the observation of Lavin and Kavini that Vivado's results can be improved by synthesizing small parts independently and then stitching them together afterwards. Compared to the original physical design flow, either strategy performs an increased number of synthesis steps. As a result, the runtimes prolong on average from ≈ 2.3×/2.7× (*coarse-glb*) up to ≈ 16.3×/18× (*fine-ooc*) for the 3 × 3/5 × 5 overlay.

We can observe that the worst-performing configurations are nevertheless achieving improvements over our baseline in most cases. Comparing the worst-performing configuration to the configuration *orig-timing*, we can see that for the 3 × 3 overlay only some configurations lead to further improvements. For the 5×5 overlay, however, most configurations even improve upon the configuration *orig-timing*, achieving additional improvements of up to 59%. Overall, we investigated that the configurations that provide little to no space between the Pblocks were belonging to the worst-performing configurations, underlining the importance of providing space for the non-floorplanned parts.

Comparing the two architectures, we observe lower operating frequencies for the 5×5 overlay, which might be against intuition. We attribute this effect to two points of influence: Firstly, the virtual-physical interface for the 5×5 overlay is more complex, since the overlay provides more IOs, and thus, more interconnection points between IOs and logic blocks. Eventually, this results in more logic and longer routes, which affects the delay negatively. Secondly, as discussed in Sect. 3, the current VTR version limits the exploration of placement possibilities to the IO pads, resulting in a potentially non-optimal placement for the logic. The effect becomes more prominent in larger FPGA architectures, since placing logic in the middle, i.e., farther away from the IO pads, can have negative effects on the timing.

6   Related Work

From the virtualization aspects listed in [8] many current publications focus on *multi-tenancy* to facilitate the usage of FPGAs in cloud environments. Knodel et al., for instance, propose in [4] a way to virtualize circuits to achieve good scalability using an FPGA hypervisor that manages several homogeneous vFP-GAs. Much like our floorplanned ZUMA tiles, their vFPGA slots partition the available chip area outside of the hypervisor. Unlike our approach, however, the partitions span over all available columns and are stacked vertically, such that all slots are homogeneous. Just like traditional system virtualization, the guest circuits will then run bare-metal on the FPGA itself, which alleviates most virtualization costs, since it only constricts the implemented circuit to the shape of one or more vFPGA slots and to the provided guest-host interface. Zha and Li follow in [10] the same principle, i.e., partitioning the available space on the FPGA only in row-direction. Where Knodel et al. leverage the capabilities of modern EDA tools to generate a separate configuration for a number of reconfigurable regions, Zha and Li leverage the tool RapidWright [6] instead to rapidly relocate a generically synthesized version of the circuit into the correct slot. This way, they only have to synthesize the circuit with the host FPGA's EDA tools once to obtain a runtime-relocatable version.

The main difference between these and our approach is that they virtualize at the *Multi-Node Level* (cf. [8]), whereas we inherit ZUMA's virtualization at the *Resource Level*, i.e., we actually use a virtualized architecture instead of providing a restricted view on the host FPGA's architecture. Hence, our approach provides an intermediate abstraction level that the other methods do not include, which enables us to, e.g., offer special architectural features to guests even if they are not present in the host, employ custom or open EDA tools for the virtual synthesis, and achieve perfect portability of circuit configurations.

ARGen [2] by Bollengier et al. actually concerns the timing closure of resource-level virtual FPGAs. The authors propose to tackle the issue of the random breaking-up of combinational cycles by the host FPGA's EDA tools not through careful floorplanning, as we do, but by deliberately introducing new registers into each of these paths. However, the inclusion of these new *virtual time propagation registers* (VTPR) prevents a virtual signal from reaching its destination within one physical clock cycle; in fact, the virtual clock has to be tuned to be a multiple of the physical clock, such that the longest virtual path can still propagate the signal over all intermediate VTPRs in that time period. The benefit of this approach is that the resulting virtual fabric constitutes a regular synthesis problem, which is free of combinational loops for the host FPGA's tools, thus enabling designers to reach timing closure for the *physical* synthesis. This does, however, not extend to the *virtual* side, where the authors report that the inclusion of VTPRs brings no improvement in terms of the performance of the synthesized overlay, which is our focus.

7   Conclusion

In this work, we tackled the challenging issue of achieving timing closure for virtual circuits. We proposed to change the virtual FPGA description from a flat design to a hierarchical one. Furthermore, we investigated different floorplanning strategies as well as different design flows in Vivado to implement the overlay on the physical FPGA. To fully exploit the potential of available information, we propagated the results of a static timing analysis of the physical implementation to the virtual design tool to enable timing-driven routing for the virtual circuits. In our experiments, compared to the area-driven baseline implementation, timing-driven routing achieved improvements of up to 32% for a 3×3, and 35% for a 5×5 architecture—on average raising f_{max} by 9% and 11%, respectively. While the timing-driven routing of the virtual circuits already leads to significantly higher f_{max} values, we showed that a well-designed floorplan can yield even further improvements of up to 41% and 65%, while improving the average by 23% and 31% for a 3×3 or a 5×5 architecture, respectively. Overall, we investigated that the design tool Vivado benefits from an out-of-context design flow and a floorplan that resembles the structure of the virtual FPGA, where the imposed constraints leave enough freedom for the placer to allow for exploration.

Our future research focuses on aspects to further improve the timing behavior. While in this paper we presented methods to improve the timing with the application of modularization in the coarse and fine strategies, both in-context and out-of-context, we want to conduct further research on the details of the resulting floorplan, so that we can tap even more of the remaining potential. For individual overlays, we could, for instance, improve on the current results by a further 29%, but translating this into general techniques that work for a wide range of benchmarks remains challenging. Hence, eventually our goal is to formulate clear design rules so that the design tool can automatically generate an optimal floorplan for a given virtual FPGA architecture. Furthermore, should VTR be extended to allow for timing information that is tied to tiles rather than logical blocks, we could model heterogeneous tiles that allow VTR to employ timing-driven placement.

References

1. Betz, V., Rose, J., Marquardt, A.: Architecture and CAD for Deep-Submicron FPGAS. The Springer International Series in Engineering and Computer Science, vol. 497. Kluwer, New York (1999). https://doi.org/10.1007/978-1-4615-5145-4
2. Bollengier, T., Lagadec, L., Najem, M., Le Lann, J.-C., Guilloux, P.: Soft timing closure for soft programmable logic cores: the ARGen approach. In: Wong, S., Beck, A.C., Bertels, K., Carro, L. (eds.) ARC 2017. LNCS, vol. 10216, pp. 93–105. Springer, Cham (2017). https://doi.org/10.1007/978-3-319-56258-2_9
3. Brant, A.D., Lemieux, G.G.F.: ZUMA: an open FPGA overlay architecture. In: International Symposium on Field-Programmable Custom Computing Machines (FCCM), pp. 93–96. IEEE (2012). https://doi.org/10.1109/FCCM.2012.25. https://github.com/adbrant/zuma-fpga
4. Knodel, O., Genssler, P.R., Spallek, R.G.: Virtualizing reconfigurable hardware to provide scalability in cloud architectures. In: Mady, A.E.D., Bostelmann, T., Sawitzki, S. (eds.) The Tenth International Conference on Advances in Circuits, Electronics and Micro-electronics (CENICS), pp. 33–38. IARIA (2017)
5. Lagadec, L., Lavenier, D., Fabiani, E., Pottier, B.: Placing, routing, and editing virtual FPGAs. In: Brebner, G., Woods, R. (eds.) FPL 2001. LNCS, vol. 2147, pp. 357–366. Springer, Heidelberg (2001). https://doi.org/10.1007/3-540-44687-7_37
6. Lavin, C., Kaviani, A.: Build your own domain-specific solutions with RapidWright: invited tutorial. In: Bazargan, K., Neuendorffer, S. (eds.) Proceedings of the 2019 ACM/SIGDA International Symposium on Field-Programmable Gate Arrays, (FPGA), pp. 14–22. ACM (2019). https://doi.org/10.1145/3289602.3293928
7. Murray, K.E., et al.: VTR 8: high performance CAD and customizable FPGA architecture modelling. ACM Trans. Reconfigurable Technol. Syst. 13(2) (2020). https://doi.org/10.1145/3388617. https://verilogtorouting.org
8. Vaishnav, A., Pham, K.D., Koch, D.: A survey on FPGA virtualization. In: Proceedings of the 28th International Conference on Field Programmable Logic and Applications (FPL), pp. 131–138. IEEE (2018). https://doi.org/10.1109/FPL.2018.00031
9. Wiersema, T., Bockhorn, A., Platzner, M.: An architecture and design tool flow for embedding a virtual FPGA into a reconfigurable system-on-chip. Comput. Electr. Eng. 55, 112–122 (2016). https://doi.org/10.1016/j.compeleceng.2016.04.005
10. Zha, Y., Li, J.: Virtualizing FPGAs in the cloud. In: Proceedings of the Twenty-Fifth International Conference on Architectural Support for Programming Languages and Operating Systems (ASPLOS). ACM (2020). https://doi.org/10.1145/3373376.3378491

Hardware Based Loop Optimization
for CGRA Architectures

Chilankamol Sunny[1]([⊠]), Satyajit Das[1][iD], Kevin J. M. Martin[2][iD],
and Philippe Coussy[2][iD]

[1] IIT Palakkad, Palakkad, Kerala, India
112004004@smail.iitpkd.ac.in, satyajitdas@iitpkd.ac.in
[2] Univ. Bretagne-Sud, UMR 6285, Lab-STICC, 56100 Lorient, France
{kevin.martin,philippe.coussy}@univ-ubs.fr

Abstract. With the increasing demand for high performance computing in application domains with stringent power budgets, coarse-grained
reconfigurable array (CGRA) architectures have become a popular choice
among researchers and manufacturers. Loops are the hot-spots of kernels
running on CGRAs and hence several techniques have been devised to
optimize the loop execution. However, works in this direction are predom-
inantly software-based solutions. This paper addresses the optimization
opportunities at a deeper level and introduces a hardware based loop
control mechanism that can support arbitrarily nested loops up to four
levels. Major contributions of this work are, a lightweight Hardware Loop
Block (HLB) for CGRAs that eliminates control instruction overhead of
loops and an acyclic graph transformation that removes loop branches
from the application CDFG. When tested on a set of kernels chosen
from various application domains, the design could achieve a maximum
of $1.9\times$ and an average of $1.5\times$ speed-up against the conventional approach. The total number of instructions executed is reduced to half for
almost all the kernels with an area and power consumption overhead of
2.6% and 0.8% respectively.

Keywords: Coarse grained reconfigurable array (CGRA) · Loop
optimization · Hardware loop · CDFG transformation

1 Introduction

Coarse Grained Reconfigurable Array (CGRA) architectures have proven to be
good targets as specialized hardware in low power embedded applications, such
as Wireless Sensor Networks (WSN), Internet of Things (IoT) and Cyber Physical Systems (CPS). Due to the regular structure with several highly optimized
processing elements (PEs) and simple interconnects, CGRAs provide high performance and energy efficiency. Analyzing the energy consumption of the PEs, it
is inferred that the scope of improvement lies in the control path rather than on
individual units [16]. Since CGRAs are mostly used to accelerate the compute-
intensive portions of an application, specifically the loops, optimizing the control
path for loops will result in significant improvement in energy efficiency.

© Springer Nature Switzerland AG 2021
S. Derrien et al. (Eds.): ARC 2021, LNCS 12700, pp. 65–80, 2021.
https://doi.org/10.1007/978-3-030-79025-7_5

Widely reported works in CGRA implementations [5,11,14] rely on software based loop optimizations to reduce the control flow bottleneck. Popular techniques like loop unrolling [6,16], modulo scheduling [8,13] and polyhedral model based optimizations [10] are broadly used in CGRAs. All these approaches exploit the parallelism available in the innermost loop body and reduce the number of branch execution by transforming the loop to a data flow graph (DFG). However, with the growing complexity of the applications, the loop bounds are becoming larger and number of loop nests as well as total number of loops in an application are increasing. Reducing only the branch instruction in the innermost loop is not sufficient anymore to get high energy efficiency for a whole application. To deal with outer loops, additional instructions to perform iteration counter update, terminating condition checking and branching are required. These additional instructions diminish the overall energy efficiency. Therefore, any effort in the direction of eliminating these non-contributing loop control instructions will aid in optimizing the control path of the whole application and achieving better performance and energy gain.

In this paper, we introduce a novel hardware based loop optimization technique for CGRAs which eliminates the control flow bottleneck in loops. As the target CGRA, we choose the state-of-the-art Integrated Programmable Array (IPA) architecture [3]. In this CGRA, to optimize the loop control bottleneck, loop unrolling is used. On top of this we propose the hardware based loop optimization to enhance the overall performance and energy efficiency. As of now, the optimization is limited to loops with statically known bounds. Experimental results show that the proposed solution reduces the total number of instructions executed to half of that in the baseline software based implementation and achieves a maximum of 1.9× performance gain for a wide range of image and signal processing applications. The first major contribution of this work is a novel lightweight Hardware Loop Block (HLB) for CGRAs which eliminates branch instruction overhead for loop increments or decrements. The second major contribution is in the compilation flow. We propose an acyclic graph transformation in the compilation to transform the software loops in the application CDFG eliminating loop branches. Experiments show that the total number of branch instruction execution is eliminated up to an average of 30× compared to that of the software based approach. Synthesis results show that the added hardware in the baseline architecture brings an area and a power consumption overhead of 2.6% and 0.8% respectively.

The rest of the paper is organized as follows. Section 2 presents the related works on loop optimizations with hardware support, from both general purpose processor and CGRA architectural domains. Section 3 introduces the baseline architecture and loop model and explains the motivation behind this work. Section 4 is dedicated to detail the proposed approach and present the implementation. In Sect. 5 experimental results are discussed and Sect. 6 concludes the paper.

2   Related Works

Hardware based loop optimizations primarily are of two types, zero overhead looping extensions and instruction memory hierarchy optimizations [16]. Zero overhead looping refers to automatically updating the iteration count and taking branch decisions by using dedicated hardware units. One major optimization on instruction memory hierarchy favoring loops is to include loop buffers. Loop buffers cache the instructions that make up the loop body to reduce the instruction fetch cost. We have seen hardware loop support on processors from the early x86 processor, the ISA of which included *loop* instruction and *rep* instruction prefix. The *rep* prefix triggered repeated execution of a single instruction. Many early ISAs included *rep*-like prefixes to support single cycle loops. Program address based and instruction count based zero overhead loop accelerations were proposed for DSP [15] and RISC [9] architectures. They could even provide multi-level loop support by using stack or scratch pad memory. In VLIW architectures [12], a special hardware unit is attached with every issue slot to automatically generate the instruction address. By employing loop buffers, DSP [1] and x86 processors could significantly reduce their energy consumption. The parallel ultra-low power (PULP) cluster architecture [7] is a multi-core platform with hardware support for loops. PULP implemented hardware loop by including an additional controller and a set of registers to store the loop information to its RISC-V cores. By having two sets of dedicated registers, the design could support two level nesting of loops. The instruction pre-fetch-buffer of the architecture acts as a loop cache if the loop body would fit into it, amplifying the effect of the hardware loop.

State-of-the-art CGRA architectures are adopting to implement hardware based loop solutions. Vadivel et al. [16] proposed a zero-overhead loop accelerator (ZOLA) for CGRA architectures. It supports nesting of loops up to four levels. ZOLA is enabled using a custom instruction after configuring all the loop parameters in the configuration register. The configuration of inner loops are kept intact until the outermost loop finishes execution. This prevents the reuse of configuration registers within a nested loop. Hence the total number of loops in a nested structure is limited by the number of configuration registers. For instance, in a ZOLA implementation employing four configuration registers, a nested loop of depth (number of levels) four can have only one loop at each level. In this paper, we propose a hardware based loop implementation which can support up to four levels of nesting and arbitrary number of sibling loops. The term sibling loops refers to loops at the same level or having the same loop as immediate parent. Furthermore, loop configuration is done inline with the execution eliminating the need for an extra configuration phase. ZOLA tries to reduce energy consumption by freeing the extra hardware units its reference architecture employs to implement loop control flow. However, the replacement of units is possible only when they are not used for any other computation. The solution we propose aims to minimize the number of loop control instructions executed by the baseline model, rather than trying to reduce the PE usage.

LASER [2] is another attempt to take hardware support for optimizing the loop execution. It is a hardware-software hybrid solution designed particularly for loops with imperfect nesting and random nesting of conditionals. Nesting of loops is called perfect if all the assignment instructions are inside the innermost loop; otherwise it is called imperfect nesting. In LASER, the compiler flattens

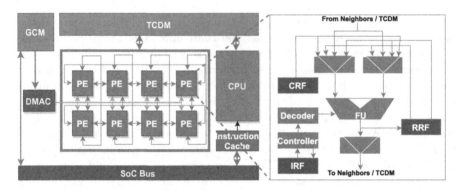

Fig. 1. IPA integrated system

nested loops into a single loop with conditional statements and fuses the true-path and false-path operation nodes. The instruction fetch unit (IFU) is modified to select and execute either the true-path or the false-path instruction based on the branch outcome. By enhancing IFU, LASER tries to better support loops with conditional blocks rather than optimizing the general execution of loops. The basic implementation of looping mechanism remains to be software based. It does not eliminate the condition checking or branch instructions. The solution we propose eliminates those loop control instructions.

3   Background and Motivation

This section gives an introduction to IPA [5], the baseline architecture used to implement our design. The software based loop model of IPA as well as the problem statement is discussed in this section.

3.1   Architecture

The IPA integrated system consists of an array of inter-connected homogeneous processing elements (PEs), a global configuration memory (GCM), and a DMA controller. It is loosely coupled with a host CPU. A multi-banked tightly coupled data memory (TCDM) facilitates data communication between IPA and the CPU. Figure 1 gives the IPA integrated system architecture. Each PE in the PE array houses a functional unit (FU), a controller, a decoder, an instruction register file (IRF), a regular register file (RRF), a constant register file (CRF) and router connections at the input and output. Global configuration memory stores the configurations (instructions and constants) for all the PEs in the PE array, which will be loaded to IRFs and CRFs of individual PEs, prior to execution. At each clock cycle, the PE controller fetches an instruction from IRF and FU executes it to completion.

3.2   Baseline Loop Model

IPA manages loop control flow by supporting branch instructions. The inner-most loop is partially unrolled to exploit instruction and data level parallelism. However, once the loop body completes an iteration, the iteration counter is updated, an unconditional jump to the instruction which checks the terminating condition is performed, the condition check is done and then a conditional jump is performed either to the loop start or to the subsequent instruction in the kernel. Evidently, the counter update, condition checking and branching instructions which contribute only to the loop control mechanism are executed as many times as does the loop body. Performance bottleneck imposed by this overhead can be promptly inferred by comparing the number of loop control instructions against the number of kernel instructions executed. For an imperfectly-nested loop structure of depth d, total number of kernel instructions executed (N_{ke}) can be represented as:

$$N_{ke} = \sum_{i=1}^{d} \sum_{j=1}^{n} p * \prod_{k=1}^{i} q' \tag{1}$$

Total number of loop control instructions executed (N_{lc}) can be computed as:

$$N_{lc} = q * \sum_{i=1}^{d} \sum_{j=1}^{n} \prod_{k=1}^{i} q' \tag{2}$$

where n is the number of loops at level i, p is the number of kernel instructions in j^{th} loop at level i, q' is the loop count of loop at level k and q is the number of loop control instructions executed per iteration. Loop count is the number of times the loop is to be executed. In the proposed design, we target to eliminate the loop control instruction to improve performance and energy efficiency.

4   Proposed Architecture and Compilation Flow

We propose a novel hardware based approach to implement loop control structure on CGRAs. Features which distinguish this design from other solutions are:

 i Support for arbitrarily nested loops: the proposed solution can handle loop nesting up to four levels, which suffices for the studied benchmarks. The loops can be perfectly or imperfectly nested. It can handle arbitrary number of sibling loops.
 ii Synchronous termination of loops at multiple levels: if an instruction happens to be the last instruction of multiple loops in the nested structure, the iteration count of each of those loops are updated in a single cycle in which the innermost loop terminates. If it was the last iteration of those loops, then they all will be terminated instantly.
 iii On the go loop configuration: loop configuration is done inline with the execution. A separate pass through the loop structure is not required to set the configuration registers.

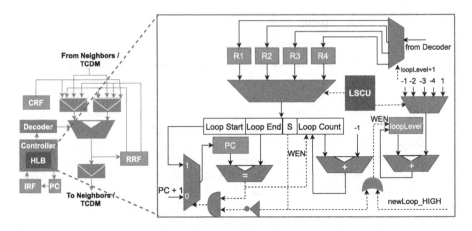

Fig. 2. Baseline PE architecture extended with HLB

The baseline implementation is extended to provide hardware loop support by introducing a Hardware Loop Block (HLB) in the architecture and a pre-mapping CDFG transformation in the compilation flow. Two dedicated instructions, *LOOP_INIT* and *LOOP_CNT* are also provided to initialize and configure the loops. *LOOP_INIT* carries the start and end addresses and *LOOP_CNT* holds the loop iteration count.

4.1   Hardware Loop Block (HLB)

Hardware loop units are incorporated into each PE in the PE array, modifying its architecture as shown in Fig. 2. In the individual PEs, HLB is integrated with the Controller, redefining its branch unit. The branch unit is responsible for updating the program counter (PC), which points to the next instruction to be fetched from the IRF. Loop characteristics such as start address, end address and iteration count are used to configure the loop and need to be stored in registers. To support four levels of nested loop, HLB reserves four configuration registers, one for each level and an extra register for loopLevel which holds the current level number. Each time a new loop is encountered, loopLevel is incremented by one, signifying a move one level deeper and when a loop runs to completion, loopLevel is decremented by one indicating a move up to the parent loop. At each level, the corresponding loop configuration register gets active. This register selection is controlled by the Loop Select Control Unit (LSCU). For instance, when a loop at level 2 is in execution, LSCU chooses the configuration register, R2 (Fig. 2). For every loop that appears at a particular level, the same register is reused to hold the configuration data facilitating the support for arbitrary number of sibling loops at each level.

At each clock cycle, the design compares the current PC value to the configured loop end instruction address to detect the branch-point. Until PC reaches the loop end, execution happens sequentially incrementing PC by one. When the PC and end address values evaluate to be equal, the loop count value is decremented by one and the PC is set to loop start address as long as the loop count is a non-zero value. Loop count becoming zero implies that the current loop has run to its completion and hence it is set as a trigger to decrement loopLevel. Consequently, the parent loop parameters become the current loop configuration, if there is any. PC is updated as PC + 1 which takes the control to its parent loop or to the rest of the kernel as the case may be. If the loop at hand was the outermost loop, then loopLevel will be zero indicating that no loop is in execution.

When a child loop finishes its execution, the design compares PC with the end address of parent loop as well. This is to support synchronous configuration update and/or termination of loops sharing same end address. If the PC value and the parent end address are found to be the same, the loop count of the parent loop is decremented. If the parent loop was in its last iteration, then the loopLevel decrement will be by two. If not, loopLevel will be decremented by one and PC will be updated with the loop start address of the parent loop. This checking repeats for the subsequent levels as well causing loopLevel to be decremented by one, two, three or four depending on the scenario. LSCU facilitates this conditional update on PC and loopLevel. This feature allows the required termination of loops and/or loop count update at multiple levels in a single cycle, benefit of which is particularly evident in the case of perfectly nested loops. It is evident that current PC value and the loop end/start addresses are involved in choosing the next instruction. Since these addresses may vary across PEs, a completely centralized implementation of HLB is not possible. The baseline compilation flow and the required modifications are discussed in the next section.

4.2   Compilation Flow

IPA supports block oriented execution of applications. It implies that the kernel to be accelerated is partitioned into single-entry-single-exit blocks of instructions called basic blocks (BBs) and only one basic block is executed at a time. Therefore the configuration as well as the assembly code are prepared in a block by block fashion. The IPA compiler takes as input the CGRA model and the high level application expressed as a control and data flow graph (CDFG) in which nodes represent BBs and edges represent the control flow between them. Each BB itself is represented as a data flow graph (DFG), BB = (D, O, A) where D is the set of data nodes, O is the set of operation/activity nodes and A is the set of arcs representing data dependencies. PE array (PEA) of the IPA is modelled by a bipartite directed graph of operator nodes and register nodes. CGRA model is the time extended model of PEA in which the timing is represented by connections between registers and operators. It is homomorphic to the basic block DFG and hence the mapping of a DFG onto the PEA is equivalent to finding a DFG in the PEA graph [4].

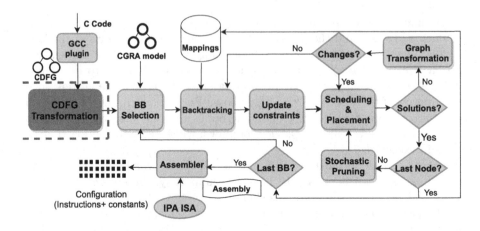

Fig. 3. Baseline compilation flow extended with CDFG transformation

The baseline compilation flow (Fig. 3) starts with generating a CDFG from the application expressed in C language. This is done using GCC 4.8. Next step is to select the BB to be mapped, for which depth first search (DFS) strategy is used. The first BB is mapped without any constraints. However, to map the subsequent BBs, the constraints imposed by the maps of previously mapped BBs are to be considered. For this reason, the first map out of the many mappings generated for the previous BB is chosen as the start point. Constraints from this mapping are inferred and consolidated and this happens in the update constraints phase. To schedule the DFG of each BB, a backward traversal list scheduling algorithm is used. Operation nodes are listed by a priority order based on mobility and fanout. Once the highest priority node is identified, the compiler finds a placement for it in the PEA model and schedules it. If a placement solution could not be found, then the DFG is transformed to improve the placement possibilities. Graph transformations increase the physical or temporal distance between source and sink to keep data dependencies or reduce the node fan outs by operation splitting. The modified DFG then goes into the scheduling and placement phase. If the transformation does not make any change in the DFG, then that calls for a backtracking. Another map from the mapping list is chosen, constraints are updated and the process starts all over again. If the mapping is successful, a stochastic pruning is applied on the partial mapping set to prevent it from growing exponentially. Once the assembly file containing the map for all the BBs is prepared, it is fed to the assembler together with the ISA. Assembler then generates the configuration for the PE array.

In the proposed model, a CDFG transformation phase is introduced as the first step in the compilation flow. Since the transformation is done prior to mapping, it is termed pre-mapping CDFG transformation. Additionally, the priority order in which operations are listed is redefined so that loop activity node would be scheduled to fire as the first activity in the concerned BB. The IPA ISA is extended with two dedicated instructions and the assembler is also modified

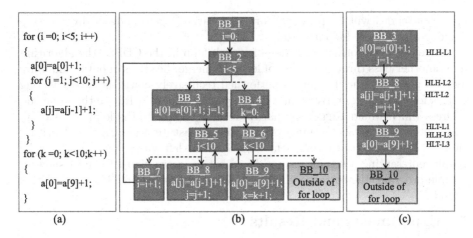

Fig. 4. (a) Sample program; (b) Corresponding CDFG; (c) Transformed CDFG

accordingly. The newly introduced step, CDFG transformation and the modified blocks like Scheduling & Placement, Assembler and IPA ISA are highlighted in Fig. 3. The pre-mapping CDFG transformation is detailed next.

We introduce two new terms, *Hardware Loop Header (HLH)* and *Hardware Loop Terminal (HLT)* to title the entry and exit BBs of the loop. HLH is the BB which dominates all other blocks which constitute the loop body and HLT is last block in that set. Algorithm 1 lists down the steps in transforming the input CDFG. The transformation is applied to loops of depth up to four as the hardware unit is so designed. Iteration count of the loop is computed from the initial and final values of loop control variable and the step by which the variable gets updated in each iteration of the loop. The loop step can be greater than or equal to one and the update can be increment or decrement. The algorithm identifies the first BB in the set of BBs that forms the loop body, which is essentially the true path successor of loop condition checking BB. This BB is designated as the HLH. The last BB in the loop body referred as loop latch in the baseline model is set as the HLT. A loop activity node and a data node holding the loop count value are inserted into the HLH. Address of the last instruction in HLT is the loop end address. As discussed earlier, loop characteristics such as start address, end address and loop count are used to configure the hardware loop and that explains the significance of HLH and HLT. As the next step, the BB that does the condition checking which was the loop header in the baseline model and the back jump from HLT to this BB are eliminated from the CDFG. This essentially does a cyclic to acyclic graph transformation on that part of the CDFG which represents the loop. If the loop control variable is not used as an operand in any of the BBs, then the nodes that correspond to its initialization and increment/decrement operations are removed. If the BB housing those nodes does not include any other node, then that BB as a whole will be pulled out of the CDFG. If the loop control variable is used inside the loop body, then those operation nodes will be preserved and the variable gets updated by the step value, each time the loop iterates.

Once this transformation is done for each loop in the CDFG, the algorithm does another pass through the list of loops to merge the HLTs of outer and inner loops if possible. The merging is performed recursively down the levels as long as it is feasible to do so. By doing this merge, these loops will have the same end address which would trigger the hardware unit to update the loop count of all those loops together as the inner one finishes its last iteration. As the algorithm runs to completion transforming the CDFG, we are left with a very simple acyclic graph representing a significantly reduced set of instructions. Figure 4 shows a sample program, the corresponding CDFG and the transformed version of it.

5   Experiments and Results

5.1   Experimental Setup

In this section, we analyse the implementation results providing performance and area comparison for a set of commonly used DSP applications. To ensure an unbiased evaluation and test the range of applicability, we have chosen a set of loop intensive kernels from various application domains with varying structure of loop nesting. Finite Impulse Response (FIR) filter is included to represent the family of digital filters. By virtue of the four-level nesting of loops, the image processing kernels, 2D convolution, erosion and dilation will aid in a corner case testing of the proposed approach. The kernels, Jacobi-1D and Seidel-2D performing stencil computations are used in several different application domains including data mining and machine learning. Similar is the case with Floyd Warshal kernel which is used for solving all pair shortest path problems. Jacobi-1D performs computations with 3-point stencil pattern over one dimensional data whereas Seidel-2D is a computation over 2 dimensional data with 9-point stencil pattern providing a deeper loop to test with. The generic kernels, matrix multiplication and addition are also included. Altogether the set has a good mix of perfectly and imperfectly nested loops. A detailed characteristics of these kernels is listed in Table 1.

Performance of the hardware loop implementation is compared against that of the baseline IPA architecture that employs only software based loop optimization. The IPA achieves an energy efficiency improvement up to 18×, with an average of 9.23× (as well as a speed-up up to 20.3×, with an average of 9.7×) [5] compared to a RISC-V core [7] specialized for ultra-low power near-sensor processing.

Algorithm 1: Pre-Mapping CDFG Transformation

Result: CDFG'
loopLevel =0; lp=getLoop(CDFG, ++loopLevel); CDFG'=CDFG;
while *lp not NULL* **do**
    if *lp.height > 4* **then**
      | continue;
    else
        loopStartBB=lp.header.truepathSuccessor;
        loopCount=computeLoopCount(lp);
        loopNode=createLoopNodeIn(loopStartBB);
        loopNode.sourceDataNode=createDataNode(loopCount);
        lp.HLH=loopStartBB; lp.HLT=lp.latch;
        lp.HLT.successor=lp.header.falsepathSuccessor;
        lp.header.falsepathSuccessor.predecessor=lp.HLT;
        CDFG'=removeBB(lp.header, CDFG');
        if *isUsedElsewhere(lp.controlVar, CDFG)* **then**
          | continue;
        else
            loopInitBB=loopStartBB.predecessor;
            if *initOnlyBB(loopInitBB, lp.controlVar)* **then**
                loopInitBB.predecessors.successor=loopStartBB;
                loopStartBB.predecessors=loopInitBB.predecessors;
                CDFG'=removeBB(loopInitBB, CDFG');
            else
                removeConstFlag=isConstDataNodeUsedElsewhere (loopInitBB,
                  lp.controlVar);
                removeInitNodes(loopInitBB, lp.controlVar, removeConstFlag);
            end
            removeConstFlag=isConstDataNodeUsedElsewhere(lp.HLT, lp.controlVar);
            removeUpdateNodes(lp.HLT, lp.controlVar, removeConstFlag);
        end
    end
    lp=getLoop(CDFG', ++loopLevel);
end
loopLevel=0; lp=getLoop(CDFG', ++loopLevel);
lpNext=getLoop(CDFG', loopLevel+1);
while *lp not NULL && lpNext not NULL* **do**
    if *(lp.height < 4) && isEmpty(lp.HLT) && (lp.HLT.predecessorList.size==1) &&*
    (lp.HLT.predecessor==lpNext.HLT) **then**
      | lpNext.HLT.successor=lp.HLT.successor;
      | CDFG'=removeBB(lp.HLT, CDFG'); lp.HLT=lpNext.HLT;
    end
    lp=getLoop(CDFG', ++loopLevel); lpNext=getLoop(CDFG', loopLevel+1);
end

5.2   Implementation Results

This section describes the implementation results for the baseline IPA architecture and the proposed design. Both the designs were synthesized with Cadence Genus Synthesis Solution 17.22-s017_1 using 90nm CMOS technology libraries. The IPA implementation on which the experiments are conducted is configured to have a 4×2 PE array with each PE housing a 21×64-bits IRF, a 20×32-bits CRF and a 32×8-bits RRF. On top of this baseline IPA, Hardware Loop Block (HLB) module was integrated to support the proposed optimization. Figure 5 (a) and (b) reports the area and power consumption overhead of the proposed HLB of 2.6% and 0.8% respectively over the baseline architecture.

Table 1. Maximum depth and iteration counts of loops for the listed kernels

Kernel	Depth of nesting	Max. # of loop iterations
Floyd Warshal	3	$60 \times 60 \times 60 = 216,000$
Jacobi-1D	2	$20 \times (28+28) = 1,120$
Seidel-2D	3	$20 \times 38 \times 38 = 28,880$
FIR filter	2	$190 \times 10 = 1,900$
2D Convolution	4	$80 \times 60 \times 3 \times 3 = 43,200$
Erosion	4	$78 \times 58 \times 3 \times 3 = 40,716$
Dilation	4	$78 \times 58 \times 3 \times 3 = 40,716$
Matrix Multiplication	3	$32 \times 32 \times 32 = 32,768$
Matrix Addition	2	$32 \times 32 = 1,024$

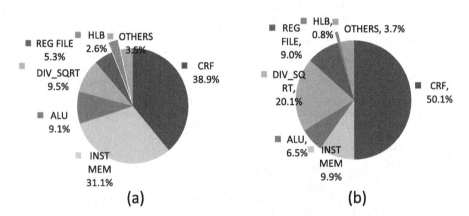

Fig. 5. (a) Area breakdown in PE; (b) Power consumption breakdown in PE

5.3   Performance Analysis

Table 2 presents the comparison of executed instructions in the software based baseline and the proposed hardware based optimization. It is observed that the number of instructions executed is reduced to half for almost all the kernels; achieving an average gain of 2×. The obtained results clearly emphasize that by eliminating loop control instructions, the total number of instructions executed can be greatly reduced. The same is illustrated in Fig. 6 which gives a comparison of the number of instructions executed by accelerating a simple loop on the baseline and proposed models for a 2 × 1 CGRA. The loop control instructions that would be eliminated by the proposed technique are highlighted in red (Fig. 6(b)). Since the loop variable i is used as an operand in the loop body, its initialization and update operations are preserved. By eliminating the highlighted instructions, total number of instructions executed is reduced from 46 to 18 achieving a gain of 2.56× (Fig. 6(e)). It is interesting to note that the gain on reducing the number of branches is 12× ((Fig. 6(d)) which is multiple times

Table 2. Comparison of the total number of instructions executed between the baseline and the proposed models

Kernel	Baseline model	Proposed model	Gain achieved
Floyd Warshal	3,514,585	2,204,373	1.59×
Jacobi-1D	36,525	13,895	2.63×
Seidel-2D	1,627,047	827,389	1.97×
FIR filter	25,858	11,795	2.19×
2D Convolution	1,066,898	1,009,438	1.06×
Erosion	67,379	48,722	1.38×
Dilation	92,379	37,154	2.49×
Matrix Multiplication	410,130	176,399	2.33×
Matrix Addition	12,818	5,391	2.38×
Average			2.00×

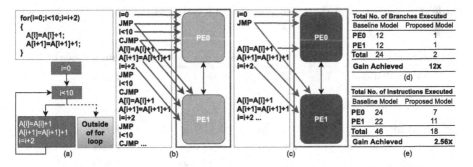

Fig. 6. (a) Partially unrolled kernel and corresponding CDFG; (b) Instructions executed on the baseline model, and (c) proposed model for a 2 × 1 CGRA; (d) Total number of branches executed on baseline vs proposed models; (e) Total number of instructions executed on baseline vs proposed models

of what obtained for the total number of instructions. At any given instant, every PE in the baseline PE array will be executing instructions from the same basic block (BB). To achieve this block-level synchronicity, branch instructions (JMP/CJMP) that govern the control flow between BBs are copied to every PE. Therefore the effect of eliminating one branch instruction from the code will be reflected in the execution profile by many folds. On top of that, more than 50% of the loop control instructions that get eliminated would be branch instructions as can be seen from Fig. 6(b). This explains the huge difference on the gain obtained for branches and total number of instructions. Speed-up or the performance gain achieved by the enhancement over the baseline model is computed as the ratio of execution cycles. As depicted in Table 3, an average gain of 1.5× is recorded for the set of kernels we considered.

Table 4 gives the comparison of the number of branches executed. As expected, the proposed solution outperforms the baseline by a huge margin. An

Table 3. Comparison of latency in terms of execution cycles between the baseline and the proposed models

Kernel	Baseline model	Proposed model	Gain achieved
Floyd Warshal	2,203,210	1,548,434	1.42×
Jacobi-1D	15,197	11,268	1.35×
Seidel-2D	670,945	582,652	1.97×
FIR filter	15,327	9,358	1.64×
2D Convolution	538,623	399,280	1.35×
Erosion	41,726	28,059	1.49×
Dilation	41,750	28,013	1.49×
Matrix Multiplication	271,930	140,713	1.93×
Matrix Addition	9,777	6,569	1.49×
Average			1.50×

Table 4. Comparison of the number of branches executed between the baseline and the proposed models

Kernel	Baseline model	Proposed model	Gain achieved
Floyd Warshal	1,325,288	446,770	2.97×
Jacobi-1D	11,815	164	72.04×
Seidel-2D	487,064	6,248	77.96×
FIR filter	9,126	764	11.95×
2D Convolution	432,646	274,084	1.58×
Erosion	41,661	14,200	2.93×
Dilation	41,661	9,370	4.45×
Matrix Multiplication	139,526	4,164	33.51×
Matrix Addition	4,358	69	63.16×
Average			30.10×

average gain of 30× and a maximum of 78× is recorded. To have the instruction execution on PEs synchronized to the BB boarders, each PE in the PEA would be executing the branch instruction simultaneously. Therefore, eliminating one branch instruction will reduce the number of cycles by one but the reduction on the number of branches will be by the number of PEs. This is the reason why we do not see a direct correlation between the reduction in branches and execution cycles. The total number of basic blocks is also found to be reduced (Table 5) in the proposed solution for all the kernels, effect of which is already seen in the number of branches. It is by the pre-mapping CDFG transformation that the BBs and the branch operations got eliminated. Therefore, the gain in terms of number of BBs and branches acts as an efficiency measure of the CDFG transformation as well. In the next phase, we will explore energy efficiency of the proposed approach.

Table 5. Comparison of the number of basic blocks mapped between the baseline and the proposed compilation flow

Kernel	Baseline model	Proposed model	Gain achieved
Floyd Warshal	16	13	1.23×
Jacobi-1D	14	10	1.40×
Seidel-2D	14	10	1.40×
FIR filter	11	8	1.34×
2D Convolution	24	20	1.20×
Erosion	22	18	1.22×
Dilation	24	20	1.20×
Matrix Multiplication	19	14	1.56×
Matrix Addition	11	7	1.57×
Average			1.40×

6   Conclusion

The performance bottleneck imposed by the overhead of having loop control instructions in kernel execution is often substantial. It is impossible to get rid of all the control bottlenecks with software only loop optimizations. In this paper, we introduced a hardware based loop control mechanism for CGRAs targeted to reduce the number of non-contributing control operations. By moving the loop control to hardware, the proposed model could achieve an average speed-up of 1.5× and reduce the number instructions executed to half, against the baseline CGRA architecture running software based loops. Up to 78× and an average of 30× gain is observed on reducing the number of executed branch instructions with an area and power consumption overhead of 2.6% and 0.8% respectively. The significant improvement noted on a set of kernels with varying loop structure suggests that the discussed design can be presented as a generic loop optimization technique to a wide range of applications.

References

1. Bajwa, R.S., et al.: Instruction buffering to reduce power in processors for signal processing. IEEE Trans. Very Large Scale Integr. (VLSI) Syst. **5**(4), 417–424 (1997)
2. Balasubramanian, M., Dave, S., Shrivastava, A., Jeyapaul, R.: LASER: a hardware/software approach to accelerate complicated loops on CGRAs. In: 2018 Design, Automation & Test in Europe Conference & Exhibition (DATE), pp. 1069–1074. IEEE (2018)
3. Das, S., Martin, K.J., Coussy, P., Rossi, D.: A heterogeneous cluster with reconfigurable accelerator for energy efficient near-sensor data analytics. In: 2018 IEEE International Symposium on Circuits and Systems (ISCAS), pp. 1–5. IEEE (2018)

4. Das, S., Martin, K.J., Coussy, P., Rossi, D., Benini, L.: Efficient mapping of CDFG onto coarse-grained reconfigurable array architectures. In: 2017 22nd Asia and South Pacific Design Automation Conference (ASP-DAC), pp. 127–132. IEEE (2017)

5. Das, S., Martin, K.J., Rossi, D., Coussy, P., Benini, L.: An energy-efficient integrated programmable array accelerator and compilation flow for near-sensor ultralow power processing. IEEE Trans. Comput. Aided Des. Integr. Circuits Syst. **38**(6), 1095–1108 (2018)

6. Dragomir, O.S., Bertels, K.: Extending loop unrolling and shifting for reconfigurable architectures. In: Architectures and Compilers for Embedded Systems (ACES), pp. 61–64 (2010)

7. Gautschi, M., et al.: Near-threshold RISC-V core with DSP extensions for scalable IoT endpoint devices. IEEE Trans. Very Large Scale Integr. (VLSI) Syst. **25**(10), 2700–2713 (2017)

8. Hamzeh, M., Shrivastava, A., Vrudhula, S.: EPIMap: using epimorphism to map applications on CGRAs. In: Proceedings of the 49th Annual Design Automation Conference, pp. 1284–1291 (2012)

9. Kavvadias, N., Nikolaidis, S.: Elimination of overhead operations in complex loop structures for embedded microprocessors. IEEE Trans. Comput. **57**(2), 200–214 (2008)

10. Liu, D., Yin, S., Liu, L., Wei, S.: Polyhedral model based mapping optimization of loop nests for CGRAs. In: Proceedings of the 50th Annual Design Automation Conference, pp. 1–8 (2013)

11. Masuyama, K., Fujita, Y., Okuhara, H., Amano, H.: A 297mops/0.4 mw ultra low power coarse-grained reconfigurable accelerator CMA-SOTB-2. In: 2015 International Conference on ReConFigurable Computing and FPGAs (ReConFig), pp. 1–6. IEEE (2015)

12. Mathew, B., Davis, A.: A loop accelerator for low power embedded VLIW processors. In: Proceedings of the 2nd IEEE/ACM/IFIP International Conference on Hardware/Software Codesign and System Synthesis, pp. 6–11 (2004)

13. Park, H., Fan, K., Mahlke, S.A., Oh, T., Kim, H., Kim, H.S.: Edge-centric modulo scheduling for coarse-grained reconfigurable architectures. In: Proceedings of the 17th International Conference on Parallel Architectures and Compilation Techniques, pp. 166–176 (2008)

14. Prabhakar, R., et al.: Plasticine: a reconfigurable architecture for parallel patterns. In: 2017 ACM/IEEE 44th Annual International Symposium on Computer Architecture (ISCA), pp. 389–402. IEEE (2017)

15. Tsao, Y.L., Chen, W.H., Cheng, W.S., Lin, M.C., Jou, S.J.: Hardware nested looping of parameterized and embedded DSP core. In: Proceedings of IEEE International [Systems-on-Chip] SOC Conference, pp. 49–52. IEEE (2003)

16. Vadivel, K., Wijtvliet, M., Jordans, R., Corporaal, H.: Loop overhead reduction techniques for coarse grained reconfigurable architectures. In: 2017 Euromicro Conference on Digital System Design (DSD), pp. 14–21. IEEE (2017)

Supporting On-Chip Dynamic Parallelism for Task-Based Hardware Accelerators

Carsten Heinz$^{(\boxtimes)}$ and Andreas Koch

Embedded Systems and Applications Group, TU Darmstadt, Darmstadt, Germany
{heinz,koch}@esa.tu-darmstadt.de

Abstract. The open-source hardware/software framework TaPaSCo aims to make reconfigurable computing on FPGAs more accessible to non-experts. To this end, it provides an easily usable task-based programming abstraction, and combines this with powerful tool support to automatically implement the individual hardware accelerators and integrate them into usable system-on-chips. Currently, TaPaSCo relies on the host to manage task parallelism and perform the actual task launches. However, for more expressive parallel programming patterns, such as pipelines of task farms, the round trips from the hardware accelerators back to the host for launching child tasks, especially when exploiting data-dependent execution times, quickly add up. The major contribution of this work is the addition of on-chip task scheduling and launching capabilities to TaPaSCo. This enables not only low-latency *dynamic* task parallelism, it also encompasses the efficient on-chip exchange of parameter values and task results between parent and child accelerator tasks. Our solution is able to handle recursive task structures and is shown to have latency reductions of over 35x compared to the prior approaches.

Keywords: FPGA · Runtime · Task launching · Parallel computing

1 Introduction

FPGAs have become widely available as accelerators in computing systems. As more and larger applications are being offloaded to FPGAs, the required hardware designs are getting more complex. However, applying typical approaches from software engineering, such as divide-and-conquer, or code-reuse, to reduce complexity, is still a challenge. For example, splitting a large application into multiple cooperating smaller accelerators, such as in the well-known *farm* parallel pattern [4], often results in increased communication overhead between the host and the FPGA.

Our work addresses these challenges by adding fine-grained *on-chip* task scheduling to the TaPaSCo framework for reconfigurable computing [6]. This new feature enables low-latency interactions directly between processing elements, without the need for host involvement. It significantly reduces the number of host/accelerator interactions, as shown in Fig. 1. Furthermore, the new capability reduces development effort and the required time for implementing heterogeneous computing systems without sacrificing performance. Our approach

© Springer Nature Switzerland AG 2021
S. Derrien et al. (Eds.): ARC 2021, LNCS 12700, pp. 81–92, 2021.
https://doi.org/10.1007/978-3-030-79025-7_6

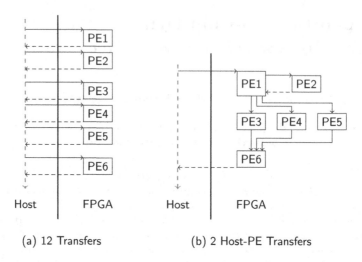

(a) 12 Transfers   (b) 2 Host-PE Transfers

Fig. 1. Host and PE interactions, with (a) the existing host-centric model, and (b) the new on-chip dynamic parallelism.

also enables the use of more expressive computing structures, such as recursion, across resource-shared accelerators.

2   Heterogeneous Computing Architecture

The open-source TaPaSCo framework [6] is a solution to integrate FPGA-based accelerators into a heterogeneous computing system. It addresses the entire development flow by providing an automated toolflow to generate FPGA bit-streams, and a runtime and API for the interaction of a host application with the accelerators on the FPGA. The resulting SoC design consists of the *Processing Elements* (PE) and the required infrastructure, such as interconnect and off-chip interfaces (e.g., host, memory, network). The PEs are instances of the actual hardware accelerators, and can be provided to the system either in an HDL or as C/C++ code for High-Level Synthesis (HLS). TaPaSCo realizes hardware thread pools, each having a set number of PEs to perform the same task. Thus, a human designer or an automated design-space-exploration tool can optimize how many PEs are to be provided for a specific function, optimizing, e.g., for maximum task throughput.

A key feature of TaPaSCo is its support for many different hardware platforms. The first category of platforms are *reconfigurable* system-on-chips with an attached FPGA region. In these architectures, the CPU and the FPGA region share the same address space and both parts have various communication channels for a tight coupling. TaPaSCo supports the older Xilinx Zynq-7000 series and the more recent Zynq UltraScale+ MPSoC (PYNQ-Z1, Ultra96, . . .).

The second category are PCIe-based accelerator cards for compute systems (Xilinx VC709, Alveo U280, . . .). Direct communication between CPU and

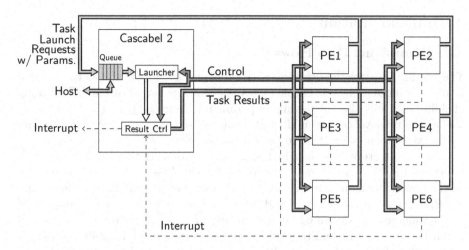

Fig. 2. Cascabel 2 hardware dispatcher/launcher and its AXI Stream connections to the PEs for accepting task requests and distributing task results.

FPGA uses the PCIe-bus. The cards have their own off-chip/on-board memory, thus, a DMA engine handles all memory transfers. This wide range of supported platforms, ranging from small, low-cost FPGAs to high-performance data-center cards, allows a user to select the suitable platform for a given application and enables quickly scaling-up or -down the platform in the development stage or later during deployment. Without any changes to software or the PE implementations, all supported platforms can be utilized. The extension presented in this work also maintains the high portability and thus can be used with all existing platforms.

In its initial version, TaPaSCo employed a software runtime to dispatch a task to a suitable, currently idle PE. Recently, TaPaSCo was sped-up by moving part of this dispatching process from software to hardware. The resulting Cascabel extension [5] employs a hardware queue, which accepts the task requests from the host. The task dispatch (finding a suitable idle PE) and the launch, including the transfer of task parameters and the collection of results to/from the selected PE, is now handled on-chip. This off-loading of the task dispatch decouples the software application on the host side from the PEs on the FPGA. The evaluation has shown that a higher job throughput is achievable, however, with the penalty of an increased latency.

In this work, we present Cascabel 2, which extends the prior version by now allowing the PEs themselves to autonomously launch new tasks without the need for host interaction. This capability is often called *dynamic parallelism*, e.g., in context of GPUs, where threads are able to launch new child threads themselves. The main goal of direct on-chip task launches is to reduce the latency, resulting in task launches with both low latency and high throughput.

3 Implementation

3.1 Control and Data Flows

The on-chip dispatch/launch functionality should be as powerful as the original software solution. Thus, it encompasses not only the actual dispatch/launching of child tasks, but also the passing of parameters from the parent to the child as well as the retrieval of the child result back to the parent task. We thus require bi-directional communication to perform this exchange.

The architecture is shown in Fig. 2. In addition to the regular TaPaSCo interfaces for PE control and interrupt-based signalling, two AXI4 streams are used to enable dynamic parallelism: A 512 bit stream, shown in green, flows from the PEs to the Cascabel 2 unit, and carries new launch requests, including child task parameters. A second 64 bit stream, shown in red, flows from the Cascabel 2 unit back to the PEs and transports the task result, which is generally a single scalar value. Note that these widths are configurable, and can be matched to the application domains, such as a result consisting of a two-element vector of single-precision floats. Also, the Cascabel 2-interface is completely optional. If PEs do not require the dynamic parallelism, no superfluous hardware will be generated.

Cascabel 2 supports the two existing methods of transferring data in TaPaSCo: pass-by-value and pass-by-reference. The former is a parameter with a scalar value, the latter is a parameter containing a reference to a memory location for larger data sizes. The software runtime is responsible for memory management.

3.2 On-chip Dispatch and Launch

Cascabel relies on internal queues for managing incoming tasks and idle/busy PEs and also provides advanced inter-task scheduling operations such as barriers. Adding the dynamic parallelism requires only very few changes here for Cascabel 2. Mainly, the existing memory-mapped interface used by the host to submit tasks for execution into the relevant queues is extended with the stream-based interface used by the PEs to submit task launch requests. For launches, the rest of the operations proceeds as in the initial Cascabel [5].

3.3 Handling Child-Task Return Values

Since tasks in TaPaSCo generally have return values, Cascabel 2 must be able to handle these as well. Compared to the dispatch/launching mechanisms described in the previous section, this requires greater changes in the Cascabel unit and the SoC architecture, especially since different execution paradigms need to be covered by the mechanisms. As shown in Fig. 3, Cascabel 2 supports four ways of handling child task return values, which will be discussed next. Note that for the methods 2) to 4), the launches can occur synchronously (parent task waits for child result to arrive) *or* asynchronously (parent tasks continues after launching child task).

Discard Child Result. Not all PEs actually make use of the return values of child tasks, or require them for synchronization purposes. An example for this would be a PE whose child tasks provide their results elsewhere (e.g., as outgoing packets on a network port).

Return-to-Parent. In general though, parent tasks will be interested in the return values of their child tasks, if only for synchronization purposes ("child task has finished and updated shared state"). As TaPaSCo supports out-of-order completion of tasks, we want to retain this capability for the dynamic inter-PE parallelism. In this mode, the child task's return value is sent back to the PE executing the parent task. As shown in Fig. 4, the return value can be configured to be sent alone (a), accompanied by the producing child's task ID, either in the same (b), or a separate bus transfer beat (c), to support out-of-order completion of child tasks.

Merge/Reduce-to-Parent. For some parallel patterns, such as a task farm, the results of multiple worker PEs must be collected, e.g., in preparation of a reduce operation. To this end, Cascabel 2 provides infrastructure to perform this *merging* in dedicated hardware. When configured, the child task results produced in parallel by multiple worker PEs in the farm will be buffered in BlockRAM, which in turn is then provided to dedicated PEs for performing the reduction/collection operations. Once all merge/reduce tasks have completed, their final result is passed back to the parent task, which in itself may be another merge/reduce PE task.

Return-to-Grandparent. For some parallel patterns, results are not required in the parent of a child task, but higher up in the task hierarchy. Cascabel 2 supports this by allowing a child task to *skip* its parent task when returning results, and instead provide its result to its *grandparent* task. Note that if the grandparent task was also launched in this mode, which can be cascaded in Cascabel 2, yet another level in the task hierarchy will be skipped, quickly propagating the child task's result up even further in the task hierarchy. A practical use for this capability will be demonstrated in Sect. 4.2.

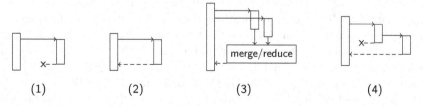

(1)   (2)   (3)   (4)

Fig. 3. Return value handling: (1) Discard, (2) return-to-parent, (3) merge/reduce-to-parent, (4) return-to-grandparent. **x** indicates a discarded result.

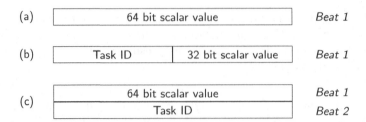

Fig. 4. Stream data formats for child task return values

The logic for realizing the different return actions is implemented in the *Return Ctrl* block (shown in Fig. 2). As new tasks are launched, the *Launcher* block forwards the associated return action to the *Return Ctrl* block, to be performed later upon task completion. When the Cascabel 2 unit receives interrupts from the PEs indicating the completion of a task, it internally looks-up the associated return action provided earlier. In all cases, except for the *discard child result* action, the first step is to read the result value from the PE. Further processing is dependent on the selected action: it either forwards the result to the (grand-)parent, waits for additional return values, or issues a new merge task using the Cascabel 2 unit. Optionally, a task can specify that an interrupt should be raised and sent to the host. This will generally be done only after an entire set of tasks has been successfully completed in hardware.

3.4 Limitations

Cascabel 2 is realized as a custom hardware module and optimized for performance. Thus, even with the provided customization options for each specific PE layout, Cascabel 2 does not reach the complete flexibility of the host-side software-only dispatcher. This section discusses the design decisions and the resulting restrictions.

In terms of arguments, Cascabel 2 by default supports values of 64 bit. This can either be a scalar value, or a pointer to a memory location. Memory management is handled in the TaPaSCo software API on the host side. At this stage, it is thus not possible to dynamically allocate PE-shared memory for on-chip launched tasks. Instead, memory pre-allocated on the host-side could be used. The number of task arguments is currently limited to up to four arguments, which is sufficient for typical applications. Due to the latency optimization, all four arguments are passed in *parallel* in a single beat over the 512 bit-wide launch request interconnect. If more arguments are required, this would either require widening the bus, issuing multiple beats, or passing the arguments via external PE-shared memory, such as on-chip HBM or on-board DDR-SDRAM.

As in all practical implementations (hardware or software), the achievable recursion depth in Cascabel 2 is limited by the capacity of the memory holding the "call stack". Cascabel 2 relies on on-chip BlockRAM to hold the call stack, again aiming for low latencies. The memory capacity used for this purpose can be configured, but will by necessity be much smaller than the DRAM-based main memory call stacks used in software recursion.

In addition, as TaPaSCo PEs are generally not multi-threaded or even re-entrant, a recursive call will always be executed on *another* PE, blocking the calling PE for the duration of the sub-task execution. For example, with recursive task launches following the *Return-to-parent* pattern, each recursion level will lead to one PE becoming blocked, thus limiting the recursion depth to the total number of PEs available on the SoC to execute this task.

4   Evaluation

Our evaluation system is a Xilinx Alveo U280 FPGA card in a server with an AMD Epyc Rome 7302P 16-core CPU with 128 GB of memory. All FPGA bitstreams have a 300 MHz design clock and are synthesized in Vivado 2020.1.

4.1   Latency

The key property when performing on-chip task launches is a low latency. For evaluating this, we use the on-chip launch interface and measure the required clock cycles from writing the task launch command for an immediately returning (NOP) task to the Cascabel 2 launch-command stream, up to when the parent task receives the result value from the child task. This approach follows the con-ventions established in the HPC community for benchmarking task-scheduling systems, e.g., in [3]. This operation takes 62 clock cycles in total, which at the design frequency yields a time of 207 ns for a complete launch-and-return. When performing the same operation with using the host-based software-only sched-uler, it takes 7.41 µs. Using the hardware-assisted software scheduler [5], which is optimized for task throughput instead of task latency, requires 8.96 µs. Thus, Cascabel 2 yields a latency gain of 35x compared to the software-only sched-uler, and a gain of 43x compared to the hardware-assisted Cascabel 1 scheduler. Figure 5 summarizes the measured latencies. In addition to the reduced latency, the on-chip scheduling of tasks avoids the high jitter of both of the software-in-the-loop solutions, caused by the PCIe connection between the host and the FPGA board.

4.2   Recursion

To stress-test the advanced task management capabilities described in Sect. 3.3 on a simple example, we show a *recursion-intensive* approach of computing the Fibonacci sequence, which is defined as

$$f(n) = f(n-1) + f(n-2)$$
$$f(1) = f(2) = 1$$

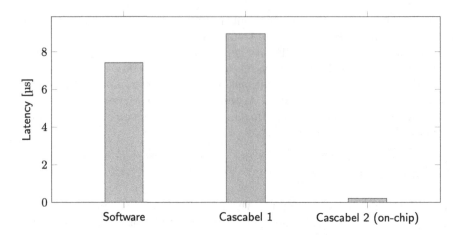

Fig. 5. Comparison of launch latencies: host-side software-only, throughput-oriented hardware-assisted software with Cascabel 1, latency-oriented hardware-only with Cascabel 2

When implementing this computation naively without the merge/reduce support of Cascabel 2, as shown in Fig. 6a, the performance and area efficiency will be very poor, as each of the recursive tasks would wait for a result from their child tasks, which in turn would lead to many occupied, but waiting hardware PEs, and will not scale beyond very small values for n. See Sect. 3.4 for a discussion of this problem.

Using the *Reduce-to-parent* scheme of Sect. 3.3 in a transitive manner, combined with asynchronous (non-blocking) launches of the child tasks, enables the far more efficient execution sketched in Fig. 6b. Here, each task completes immediately after spawning its child tasks with the updated parameters $n - 1$ and $n - 2$. Note that a parent task does not wait for the child tasks' results. Instead, by having *all* of these tasks execute in *Return-to-grandparent* mode, the results of all of the child tasks will propagate up to the outer *reduce* tasks, which actually perform the summing over all of the partial results. That computation has been moved out of the inner nodes of the call graph of Fig. 6b, to the outer reduce nodes. In this manner, the recursion depth is not limited by the PEs available on the chip. The implementation can scale from a single Fibonacci PE, and a single reduce PE for summing, up to many PEs running in parallel. The recursion depth is only limited by the size of the BlockRAM storage used for buffering the recursion results in a call-stack-like manner.

When using two PEs for executing Fibonacci computation tasks, and four PEs for the merge/reduce tasks, computing $f(11)$ as a highly task-intensive stress-test requires just $63.13\,\mu s$, with the bulk of the execution time required for task dispatching/launching (as the computation itself is trivial). When performing host-side scheduling, instead, managing the same parallel structure would require $1.29\,ms$, more than 20x longer. Note again that we have chosen this

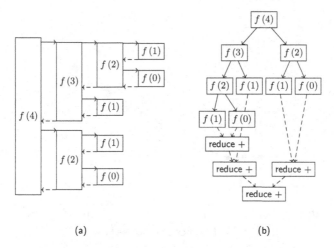

(a)   (b)

Fig. 6. Recursive Fibonacci computation: (a) naive synchronous execution, (b) asynchronous mode with transitive return-to-grandparent value passing and merge/reduce

example to demonstrate the *scheduling* capabilities and speed of the Cascabel 2 system, it is *not* intended to show high-performance computations of Fibonacci numbers.

4.3 Near-Data Processing for Databases

Our second use-case realizes an accelerator for near-data processing, e.g., for use in computational storage [9]. It will examine the performance of Cascabel 2 for less launch-intensive workloads than the previous Fibonacci example. Here, we assume that a database is stored in persistent memory directly attached to the FPGA, and we process aggregation queries on the FPGA near the data (NDP), instead of transferring the data from persistent memory to the host for processing. The sample query we use for this example could be expressed as

```
SELECT avg(age), max(salary), sum(hours)
FROM employees;
```

The database is stored in a format with fixed record size, which allows the use of simple strided offset-based accesses to retrieve the required columns in subsequent rows. On the processing side, we have PEs for the different aggregation tasks (avg, max, sum, etc.) available on the FPGA.

Both the software-scheduled and Cascabel 2 implementations will use these hardware PEs as NDP operations, which compute their results within a *single task each* over an increasing number of records. For each of the aggregations, a separate task will be launched (three in total, for avg/max/sum), either by the TaPaSCo software scheduler, or using Cascabel 2 on-chip. The results are shown in Fig. 7. Obviously, with a larger number of records being processed in each

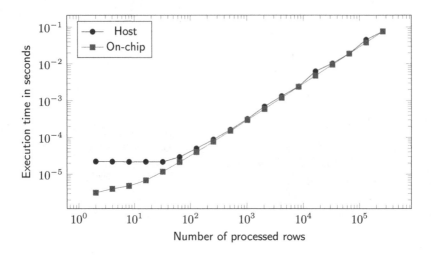

Fig. 7. NDP query runtimes for increasing record numbers

task, the launch overhead per query becomes smaller. However, using Cascabel 2, hardware-accelerated processing remains profitable even for *smaller* numbers of records (e.g., after a narrow selection by a tight WHERE clause). It is faster than software scheduling for fewer than 512 records.

4.4 Resource Utilization and Frequency

The dynamic parallelism features of Cascabel 2 require additional chip resources compared to the initial Cascabel version of [5]. As Cascabel 2 is highly configurable for the needs of a specific application, the actual hardware costs depend on the features enabled. However we can describe some design points here: For the two examples, the merge/reduce buffer was configured to use an extra 32 RAMB36 blocks for buffering intermediate child task results. Also, the Cascabel 2 task launch and result interconnects required just 0.27% extra CLBs compared to the original. In all of our experiments, the absolute resource cost of the Cascabel 2 system was below 2% of the available resources, across all resource types on the Alveo U280 board.

All evaluated designs meet timing closure at the design frequency of 300 MHz. Frequencies of over 500 MHz are achievable [10], but would require increasing the BlockRAM access latency, which we have not done for the examples shown here.

5 Related Work

In contrast to much prior work on HLS that focuses on parallelism *within* a PE [1,8], our focus is parallelism *across* PEs and the required infrastructure to support this. Here, the field of related work is much narrower. One recent example is ParallelXL [2], which also aims for dynamic on-chip parallelism: Their PEs are grouped into tiles, which are attached to two NoCs to perform work-stealing scheduling and argument/task routing. The result is a more distributed system, compared to our centralized Cascabel 2 unit. However, the evaluation of ParallelXL was limited to just a small-scale prototype on a Zynq-7000 device and gem5-based simulations. We believe that our simple n-to-1 and 1-to-n streaming interconnects will scale better than ParallelXL's more expensive NoCs, and still allow performance gains even for highly scheduling intensive workloads, as demonstrated by our task-excessive Fibonacci example. In addition, ParallelXL lacks advanced features such as hardware support for merge/reduce operations and has more limited customizability (e.g., omitting the result interconnect on PEs for void child tasks).

6   Conclusion and Future Work

Our Cascabel 2 system provides high-performance on-chip dynamic parallelism at low resource costs. It extends the scheduling capabilities of prior work (e.g., barriers) with new mechanisms for performing inter-task reduction operations and optimized result passing.

With its short launch latencies, Cascabel 2 could also be employed for hardware-accelerated network processing close to the interface, e.g., as performed in [7] for network security.

Despite its proven advantages, for some applications, the task-based programming model currently at the heart of TaPaSCo is not the optimal one. We are currently working to *combine* task-based reconfigurable computing with self-scheduling streaming operations for use in data-flow applications.

Future performance improvements can be achieved by further enhancing the underlying scheduling method used in Cascabel 2. In particular, for systems with many *different* PE types, the current "FIFO" scheduling may in many cases not reach optimal PE utilization.

Another interesting addition could be the support for communication *across* single FPGA boundaries to scale to larger applications. Specifically, the currently on-chip-only launch/parameter/result interconnects could be extended using direct FPGA-FPGA links in a single server or rack, or even over switchable/routable network protocols in an entire datacenter setting. While such connections carry an additional latency penalty of $\approx 1\,\mu s$, inter-device launch latency would still remain shorter than in the host-based software-only solution initially used for TaPaSCo.

Acknowledgment. This research was funded by the German Federal Ministry for Education and Research (BMBF) in project 01 IS 17091 B.

References

1. Canis, A., et al.: LegUp: high-level synthesis for FPGA-based processor/accelerator systems. In: Proceedings of the 19th ACM/SIGDA International Symposium on Field Programmable Gate Arrays, pp. 33–36 (2011)
2. Chen, T., Srinath, S., Batten, C., Suh, G.E.: An architectural framework for accelerating dynamic parallel algorithms on reconfigurable hardware. In: 2018 51st Annual IEEE/ACM International Symposium on Microarchitecture (MICRO), pp. 55–67. IEEE (2018)
3. Dubucq, T., Forlini, T., Dos Reis, V.L., Santos, I.: Matrix: bench - benchmarking the state-of-the-art task execution frameworks of many-task computing (2015)
4. Ernsting, S., Kuchen, H.: A scalable farm skeleton for hybrid parallel and distributed programming. Int. J. Parallel Program. **42**(6), 968–987 (2014). https://doi.org/10.1007/s10766-013-0269-2
5. Heinz, C., Hofmann, J.A., Sommer, L., Koch, A.: Improving job launch rates in the TaPaSCo FPGA middleware by hardware/software-co-design. In: 2020 IEEE/ACM International Workshop on Runtime and Operating Systems for Supercomputers (ROSS), pp. 22–30 (2020). https://doi.org/10.1109/ROSS51935.2020.00008
6. Heinz, C., Hofmann, J., Korinth, J., Sommer, L., Weber, L., Koch, A.: The TaPaSCo open-source toolflow. J. Signal Process. Syst. (2021). https://doi.org/10.1007/s11265-021-01640-8
7. Mühlbach, S., Brunner, M., Roblee, C., Koch, A.: MalCoBox: designing a 10 Gb/s malware collection honeypot using reconfigurable technology. In: 2010 International Conference on Field Programmable Logic and Applications, pp. 592–595 (2010). https://doi.org/10.1109/FPL.2010.116
8. Prabhakar, R., et al.: Generating configurable hardware from parallel patterns. ACM SIGPLAN Notices **51**(4), 651–665 (2016)
9. Vinçon, T., et al.: nKV in action: accelerating KV-stores on native computation storage with near-data processing. In: Proceedings of the VLDB Endowment, vol. 13 (2020)
10. Xilinx Inc: Performance and resource utilization for axi4-stream interconnect rtl v1.1. https://www.xilinx.com/support/documentation/ip_documentation/ru/axis-interconnect.html#virtexuplus

Combining Design Space Exploration with Task Scheduling of Moldable Streaming Tasks on Reconfigurable Platforms

Jörg Keller[1](✉) ⓘ, Sebastian Litzinger[1] ⓘ, and Christoph Kessler[2] ⓘ

[1] FernUniversität in Hagen, Hagen, Germany
{jorg.keller,sebastian.litzinger}@fernuni-hagen.de
[2] Linköping University, Linköping, Sweden
christoph.kessler@liu.se
https://feu.de/pv/en
http://www.ida.liu.se/~chrke

Abstract. Design space exploration can be used to find a power-efficient architectural design for a given application, such as the best suited configuration of a heterogeneous system from soft cores of different types, given area and throughput constraints. We show how to integrate design space exploration into a static scheduling algorithm for a streaming task graph application with parallelizable tasks and solve the resulting combined optimization problem by an integer linear program (ILP). We demonstrate the improvements by our strategy with ARM big and LITTLE soft cores and synthetic task graphs.

Keywords: Design space exploration · Task scheduling · Energy efficiency

1 Introduction

Data stream processing is an important computation paradigm in embedded (and edge) computing, where a continuous stream of data elements coming from data sensors should, due to its high volume and velocity, be processed as close to the data source as possible. An example is the preprocessing of continuously arriving camera raw data or vehicle sensor data. Such devices are often constrained in power usage (e.g., battery driven and/or using passive cooling only), therefore the throughput requirements often can only be fulfilled by using a heterogeneous multicore platform offering also a type of cores with a special architecture optimized for low power consumption. If the platform is reconfigurable, then also the number of each type of (soft) core must be determined, a phase that is called design space exploration (DSE).

Stream processing programs are usually expressed as a graph of persistent streaming tasks that read in packets of data from their input channels, process one

© Springer Nature Switzerland AG 2021
S. Derrien et al. (Eds.): ARC 2021, LNCS 12700, pp. 93–107, 2021.
https://doi.org/10.1007/978-3-030-79025-7_7

packet at a time, and write a packet of output data to output channels, thus forwarding it to data consumer tasks or to the program's result channel(s). By providing sufficient FIFO buffering capacity along all channels (thus following the Kahn Process Network model [7]), the streaming program execution can be software-pipelined such that all instances of streaming tasks for different data packets in the same *round* in the steady state of the pipeline can execute concurrently (see Fig. 1). On a many-core system, these can then be scheduled to different cores or core groups so that the makespan for one round of the steady-state loop is kept low and the workload is well balanced. Streaming tasks perform a certain amount of work per input packet and can be internally parallel, i.e., run on multiple cores to speed up one instance of their execution. For example, a *moldable* task can use any number of cores that must be determined before the task is executed. *Crown scheduling* [14] is a static scheduling approach for moldable tasks that has been extended to heterogeneous platforms and multiple possible target functions such as maximum throughput for given power budget besides the usual energy minimization per round (thus achieving minimum average power) for given throughput [10]. In all these investigations, the platform was fixed, i.e., the number of cores of each type was given. While the scheduler had the freedom not to use some cores, their chip area could not be used for cores of a different type, which might have been helpful in further optimization, e.g., using more energy-efficient cores instead of high-performance cores if the task structure demands or allows this.

Such tradeoff is possible in a reconfigurable platform such as a field-programmable gate array (FPGA) where multiple soft cores can be implemented and the number of cores of each type is not predetermined (although the maximum combined area of the cores is). To achieve this, we extend the integer linear program (ILP) of the crown scheduler to allow variable core counts of different types. Thus, we integrate design space exploration with the scheduler to generate an energy-optimal configuration of heterogeneous soft cores for an application with given throughput constraints and a platform with a given area.

We evaluate our proposal with a benchmark suite of 40 synthetic task sets and 3 task sets from real-world applications. As core types, we use ARM's big.LITTLE in its original manifestation, i.e. A7 and A15 cores. We use power profiles for different task types and core types derived from measurements on a real platform. We find that our integrated approach improves energy efficiency compared to a fixed platform and that in many cases, the optimal number of LITTLE cores is notably larger than the number of big cores, i.e. different from real platforms. Moreover, our ILP solver is only marginally slower than for a fixed platform, so that we improve DSE time compared to heuristic DSE approaches like steepest descent or tabu search over the configuration space, which call energy computation (which in turn needs at least some approximation to scheduling) at each configuration point considered.

In particular, we make the following contributions:

– We extend crown scheduling from a fixed platform structure to a variable platform structure, i.e. numbers of each type of soft cores in a reconfigurable architecture, in order to find the platform configuration *and* schedule that

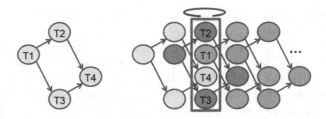

Fig. 1. Left: A streaming task graph with four streaming tasks. Right: The red box shows the steady state of the software-pipelined streaming program execution, where all task instances in one round are independent, i.e. belong to different instances of the streaming task graph or are independent tasks from one task graph instance (Color figure online).

lead in combination to the energy-optimal execution. The presented approach works for any number of different core types.

- We demonstrate the potential for improving energy efficiency over crown-optimal schedules for a fixed platform by evaluation with a multitude of synthetic task sets with realistic task types, several task sets from real-world applications, and power profiles for ARM big.LITTLE types of cores.
- We demonstrate how to generalize this approach to different optimization targets such as minimum area solution for a given power budget and throughput, or a Pareto front of minimum power budgets for different maximum chip sizes of the reconfigurable architecture, given a required throughput.

The remainder of this paper is organized as follows: Sect. 2 introduces the processor, task and power models, and the crown scheduling principle. Sect. 3 explains how to combine the design space exploration for a reconfigurable platform with task scheduling to achieve more accurate predictions. Preliminary results are presented in Sect. 4. Section 5 presents generalizations of our optimization, while related work is discussed in Sect. 6. Section 7 concludes and suggests future work.

2 Background

Architecture Model. We consider a generic multi-/manycore CPU with p cores with dynamic discrete voltage and frequency selection (DVFS). The cores can either be all of the same type (as in standard server multicore CPUs) or of different types (as in ARM big.LITTLE). We assume a configurable platform of a given area, i.e., the cores are soft cores of known area.

A core can execute at most one task (instance) at a time, and can switch the voltage/frequency level between tasks among a given fixed set of K discrete voltage/frequency levels with frequencies f_k, $k = 1, ..., K$, where $f_{\min} = f_1 < f_2 < ... < f_K = f_{\max}$, and the voltage is, for each k, auto-co-scaled to the lowest level still supporting the chosen frequency f_k. For heterogeneous platforms with cores of different types t, the frequencies $f_{k,t}$ and even their number K_t might depend on the core type.

While idle, a core consumes a base-level power $P_{idle,t}$. When executing a task j at some DVFS level k, it consumes a power $\mathrm{power}(t, k, \mathrm{tty}(j))$ that depends on k and on the task type $\mathrm{tty}(j)$, and, in the case of a heterogeneous architecture, also on the core type t. The *task type* $\mathrm{tty}(j)$ of each task j can be roughly characterized by a small number of predefined discrete classes in order to distinguish e.g. computationally intensive from memory-access intensive tasks, as these react differently to frequency scaling. Idle power and task power can, for each DVFS level, task type and core type, either be sampled on the target system using microbenchmarks for the different task types, or be estimated using a theoretical power model. In the following, we will subtract $P_{idle,t}$ from $\mathrm{power}(t, k, \mathrm{tty}(j))$, so that the power drawn by a core of type t executing a task j is

$$\mathrm{power}(t, k, \mathrm{tty}(j)) + P_{idle,t}.$$

Task Model. Each task j, for $j = 1, ..., n$, performs work $\mathrm{work}(j)$, corresponding to the time of executing the task on a single (reference-type) core at unit frequency, i.e., executing the task at frequency f_k results in a runtime $\mathrm{work}(j)/f_k$. This runtime includes the phase where the task writes its output either to a memory shared by all cores, or via an on-chip network to the local memory of the core that runs the follow-up task.

We consider *moldable* parallel tasks, i.e. tasks that can use any number of cores assigned prior to execution, internally employing a parallel algorithm to share the work. We make no assumptions about monotonicity of parallel speedup nor absence of speedup anomalies. Instead, the actual relative speedup $\mathrm{speedup}(j, q)$ of task j with $q > 1$ cores on the target system can, again, be found out by microbenchmarking or be estimated from a theoretical cost model for the deployed parallel algorithm. Obviously, $\mathrm{speedup}(j, 1) = 1$ for all j. Inherently sequential tasks j can be modeled by simply setting $\mathrm{speedup}(j, q) = 1$ for $q > 1$. If a task j has a maximum width or degree of parallelism $W(j)$, then we can e.g. set $\mathrm{speedup}(j, q) = \mathrm{speedup}(j, W(j))$ for $q > W(j)$, i.e. the runtime does not shrink anymore if we use more than $W(j)$ cores. One might even use a lower speedup to account for additional overhead with more cores. For architectures with different core types, we index the tasks' speedup tables also by the core type t, i.e., $\mathrm{speedup}(j, q, t)$, where $\mathrm{speedup}(j, 1, t) = 1$ in general only holds for the reference core type $t = 1$, while for other core types, $\mathrm{speedup}(j, 1, t)$ denotes the relative performance between core type t and the reference core type for the task type of task j.

The time of executing task j at DVFS level k on q cores of core type t is then

$$\mathrm{Time}(j, k, q, t) = \frac{\mathrm{work}(j)}{f_{k,t} \cdot \mathrm{speedup}(j, q, t)}.$$

Crown Scheduling. Crown scheduling [8,14] is a static scheduling technique for the steady state of the software-pipelined streaming task graph where all tasks are active processing data. It considers the subproblems of core allocation to moldable tasks, DVFS level selection, mapping of tasks to specific groups of cores and ordering of task execution in time together, and introduces artificial constraints on core allocation and task sequencing to reduce the integrated optimization problem's complexity without sacrificing significant optimization potential in practice [15].

A key property is the hierarchical organization of the set of p cores by recursive binary partitioning into $2p - 1$ core groups jointly referred to as the *crown*, see Fig. 2 for an example of a balanced binary crown of 8 cores (ignore the colors/shading for now), which consists of 15 core groups in total: The root group of all cores (group 1) is decomposed into two child groups (groups 2 and 3) of half the size each, which are further split into four grandchild groups (groups 4–7) and so on, until we arrive at p leaf groups containing one core each. Note that the crown is exponentially smaller than the power set of p cores with $2^p - 1$ core groups.

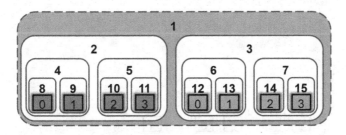

Fig. 2. A heterogeneous crown for a standard big.LITTLE configuration with 4 big cores (orange) and 4 LITTLE cores (green). Note that the root group (1) does not exist, i.e., cannot be assigned (parallel) tasks. (Color figure online)

In a crown schedule, moldable tasks can only be mapped to one of the core groups in the crown. This also implies that the core allocation to each moldable task has to be a power of two. Moreover, a crown schedule is constructed so that each core executes, within each iteration of the steady-state pattern of the software pipeline, the tasks mapped to it in (the same) order of non-increasing core allocation. This allows all cores mapped to a parallel task to simultaneously start their execution, so that the parallel algorithm running in the task does not incur additional delays. Hence, there is no internal fragmentation within the schedule; any idle times due to residual load imbalances only occur at the end of a round. Optimal and heuristic algorithms for crown scheduling have been presented in earlier work [8,14].

Crown scheduling can be generalized [10] to heterogeneous multicore CPUs with different core types such as ARM big.LITTLE, which in our setting combines four A15 ("big") cores with four A7 ("LITTLE") cores. In this case, the top-level subdivision splits the overall heterogeneous core set such that internally homogeneous subsets are obtained as its child groups, and the heterogeneous root group is excluded as a possible mapping target, see Fig. 2. An alternative view, which might be more appropriate for more than two core types, is that each core type has a crown of its own.

3   Combining Design Space Exploration with Scheduling

Up to now, crown scheduling assumes a platform with a fixed number of cores of each core type, and a fixed mapping of core indices and core types. In order to integrate DSE with scheduling, we assume that we can give an upper bound p on the maximum possible number of cores. More exactly, we will set p to be the smallest power of 2 larger than this maximum number. We introduce two integer variables p_1 and p_2 which denote the number of LITTLE and big cores, respectively. In general, we denote the number of cores of type t by p_t. Each core type t gets a crown of its own with groups $i = 1 \ldots, 2p-1$ and cores with indices $l = 0, \ldots, p-1$. For core type t, a group i with maximum core index $\max(i)$ is only existing if $\max(i) < p_t$, cf. Fig. 3.

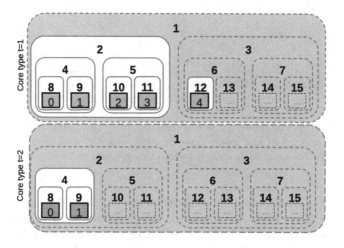

Fig. 3. Crown structures for two different core types. As there are five cores of type 1, core groups 2, 4, 5, 8, 9, 10, 11, 12 exist for $t = 1$ (green, top), and with only two cores of type 2, we have core groups 4, 8, 9 for $t = 2$ (red, bottom). Tasks will only be assigned to the actually instantiated core groups colored in white. (Color figure online)

For fixed values of p_1 and p_2, the ILP below resembles the ILP from [10]. Yet, as p_1 and p_2 are variables, we will define further constraints for them, and minimize the objective function over all possible combinations of these variables.

We use binary variables $x_{i,j,k,t}$ where $x_{i,j,k,t} = 1$ iff task j is mapped to core group i of core type t at frequency $f_{k,t}$. Furthermore, we use binary variables $ex_{i,t}$ where $ex_{i,t} = 1$ iff core group i does not exist for core type t.

We then aim to solve the following optimization problem:

$$\min \quad \sum_{i,j,k,t} x_{i,j,k,t} \cdot \text{time}(i,j,k,t) \cdot \text{power}(t,k,\text{tty}(j)) \cdot \text{size}(i)$$

$$+ \sum_{t} (p_t \cdot P_{idle,t}) \cdot M \tag{1a}$$

$$\text{s.t} \quad \forall j \quad \sum_{i,t} \sum_{k \leq K_t} x_{i,j,k,t} = 1 \tag{1b}$$

$$\forall j \quad \sum_{i,t} \sum_{k > K_t} x_{i,j,k,t} = 0 \tag{1c}$$

$$\forall i,j,t \quad \sum_{k} x_{i,j,k,t} \leq 1 - ex_{i,t} \tag{1d}$$

$$\forall t,l \quad \sum_{i \in G_{l,j,k}} x_{i,j,k,t} \cdot \text{time}(i,j,k,t) \leq M \tag{1e}$$

$$\forall i,t \quad \max(i) - ex_{i,t} \cdot p < p_t \tag{1f}$$

$$\forall i,t \quad \max(i) + (1 - ex_{i,t}) \cdot p \geq p_t \tag{1g}$$

$$\sum_{t} p_t \cdot A_t \leq A_{Total}. \tag{1h}$$

Constraint (1b) ensures that each task j is mapped to exactly one core group of one core type but only to an existing frequency level by (1c), and (1d) guarantees that tasks cannot be mapped to core groups that do not exist. For each core $l = 0, \ldots, p - 1$, let G_l in Constraint (1e) denote the set of all core groups i that comprise l. For the task times $\text{time}(i,j,k,t) := \text{Time}(j,k,\text{size}(i),t)$, Constraint (1e) must hold, i.e., for each core l of each core type t, the total runtime of all tasks mapped to a core group in G_l must not exceed the deadline M. To set variables $ex_{i,t}$, we use the constraints (1f) and (1g). If $\max(i) \geq p_t$, then $ex_{i,t}$ must be 1 because of (1f). By (1g), $ex_{i,t} = 0$ if $\max(i) < p_t$. Besides the obvious non-negativity constraints, the variables p_t need constraint (1h), i.e., the sum of the core areas for the different core types cannot exceed the total FPGA area, where area here also might mean number of CLBs, depending on the FPGA architecture, and the total area might be discounted by a percentage to account for efficiency loss of some kind such as area for wiring. By the choice of p, this also implies $\sum_t p_t \leq p$. The objective function seeks to minimize the sum of the energies needed to execute each task on the core group it is mapped to, plus the power at idle times. While the latter term was a constant for a fixed platform, i.e. not influencing the optimum, it is now variable and must be considered.

Please note that the given ILP can even be helpful for a fixed platform with P_t cores of each core type t, where the cores can be shut down individually if they are not used. If we replace constraint (1h) by $\forall t \; p_t \leq P_t$, then we have an improved variant for crown scheduling with core consolidation, cf. [13].

4   Preliminary Results

The reasoning behind our initial experiments was to facilitate a comparison to the results in [10] in order to assess the additional value of adapting the device's design to the application at hand. To this end, we adopted the experimental setup in [10], in particular: task sets, deadlines, core power consumption values, available core operating frequencies, relative performance figures for big vs. LITTLE cores, and speedup values[1].

We are aware that power consumption and frequencies will not be identical when switching from ASIC cores to soft cores on an FPGA. Still, we assume that the power consumption values (and operating frequencies) of different core types relative to each other might remain as they were.

The original experiments were conducted for 40 task sets with 10, 20, 40, and 80 tasks, respectively (10 task sets of each cardinality). Tasks are of one of five possible types: MEMORY, BRANCH, FMULT, SIMD, or MATMUL. A task's type implies a certain average core power consumption when being executed as well as an affinity to one of the two available core types with regard to its runtime, meaning some task types run faster on LITTLE cores and some on the big ones. All this information is procured from [5]. Furthermore, a task's maximum width is determined by its type in the following manner[2]:

$$W(j) = \begin{cases} 1, & \text{if } j \text{ is of type BRANCH}, \\ w_j \in \{2,4\}, & \text{if } j \text{ is of type MEMORY or FMULT}, \\ 4, & \text{if } j \text{ is of type SIMD or MATMUL}. \end{cases}$$

As before, the operating frequencies to choose from are $\{0.6, 0.8, 1.0, 1.2, 1.4\}$ GHz, the theoretically available 1.6 GHz for the big cores is ignored. Parallel speedups for all tasks, i.e. all task types, on the reference core type (LITTLE) are given by $\text{speedup}(j, 1) = 1$, $\text{speedup}(j, 2) = 1.8$ and $\text{speedup}(j, 4) = 3.44$ and are multiplied by the relative factors from [5, Table 4], to obtain speedups on big cores, cf. [10]. Deadlines are computed as

$$M = 0.6 \cdot \frac{\dfrac{\sum_j \text{work}(j)}{p \cdot f_1} + \dfrac{\sum_j \text{work}(j)}{p \cdot f_K}}{2},$$

with $p = 8$ to obtain deadlines for a platform with 4 big and 4 LITTLE cores.

For further details on the original experimental setup please consult [10]. For these experiments, core idle power was ignored as under fixed round times and fixed core composition, energy consumption caused by idle power is a constant and therefore not relevant with regard to optimization. Now, core composition

---

[1] In [10], we used parallel efficiency, i.e. speedup over core count, and separated the difference in performance between core types from the speedup by using an additional variable $r_{i,j}$.

[2] We did not express the maximum width explicitly in Sect. 2 but included it in the definition of speedup.

can vary, thus idle power must be taken into account, cf. (1a). To enable a meaningful comparison to the results in [10], we added the energy consumption caused by idle power for 4 big and 4 LITTLE cores over a round's duration to the original results.

The Gurobi 8.1.0 solver was employed to obtain ILP solutions. The respective computations were run on an AMD Ryzen 7 2700X with 8 physical cores and SMT under a 5 min (wall clock) timeout. The implementation was carried out in Python utilizing the `gurobipy` module.

Primarily, we are interested in whether a chip of the same size as in [10] can lead to energy savings when altering core composition, i.e., whether jointly optimizing chip design and schedule can lower energy consumption for the execution of the target application. To gain any insight in this regard, we have repeated the original experiments with the ILP from Sect. 3 and the chip's size capped at the value required for the standard configuration of 4 big and 4 LITTLE cores. In the implementation described in [1], a big core occupies an area of $19\,\mathrm{mm}^2$, while a LITTLE core's size is $3.8\,\mathrm{mm}^2$. For the area constraint (1h), we therefore set $A_{Total} = 4 \cdot 19\,\mathrm{mm}^2 + 4 \cdot 3.8\,\mathrm{mm}^2 = 91.2\,\mathrm{mm}^2$. As no more than $\left\lfloor \frac{91.2\,\mathrm{mm}^2}{\min\{19\,\mathrm{mm}^2, 3.8\,\mathrm{mm}^2\}} \right\rfloor = 24$ cores can be placed on the chip, we further set $p = 32$. Also here, the absolute values will not be maintained when going from ASIC to FPGA, yet the relative size of cores, even if measured in configurable blocks (or resources), would rather be the same. Also, we are aware that using a purely additive area model, without consideration of area e.g. for busses, is a simplification, but assume that the majority of the FPGA would be spent for cores, so that the inaccuracy is small.

Table 1. Results for the current experiments in comparison to the original experiments in [10], same chip size

n		10	20	40	80	Total
E_{total} current vs. original experiments	min.	65.2%	70.3%	74.5%	78.5%	65.2%
E_{total} current vs. original experiments	avg.	83.5%	79.2%	80.9%	80.4%	81.0%
E_{total} current vs. original experiments	max.	94.5%	86.4%	86.3%	83.9%	94.5%
#big vs. orig	avg.	−2.2	−2.0	−2.6	−2.3	−2.3
#LITTLE vs. orig	avg.	0.5	−0.6	0.3	−0.3	0.0
E_{idle}/E_{total} current	avg.	0.662	0.642	0.647	0.628	0.645
E_{idle}/E_{total} orig	avg.	0.741	0.770	0.764	0.770	0.761

Table 1 displays the results. It compares energy consumption values E_{total} from the original experiments to those obtained via our current experiments. Depending on task set size, we observe a 16.5–20.8% lower energy consumption on average. For single task sets, energy savings of up to 34.8% are possible. Variance drops with increasing task set size as indicated by growing minimum and decreasing maximum values. All ILPs could be solved either to optimality or solutions are very close to the optimum (the maximum MIPGap value over the 40 experiments is 0.0018).

It becomes clear that a considerable reduction of energy consumption is possible if chip size remains constant while the total number of cores as well as core composition may differ. In particular, the number of big cores was on average 2.3 lower than in the original experiments with fixed values for p_1 and p_2, i.e. the number of LITTLE and big cores, respectively. Interestingly, the total number of LITTLE cores did not change when averaged over all examined task sets. The last two rows in Table 1 contain the fraction of the energy consumption caused by the chip's idle power. For the original experiments, the figures show that idle power[3] is responsible for >75% of the total energy consumption. It is therefore not surprising that significant optimization potential may lie in altering the core composition for a given chip size. In our current experiments, the chip's idle power accounts for 62.8–66.2% of the total energy consumption. Jointly optimizing chip design and the target application's schedule enables a tradeoff between core count on the one hand and higher operating frequencies or heavier parallelization on the other, which proves to be beneficial with regard to energy efficiency.

As unused cores could simply be switched off, eliminating their idle power from the calculation, we scanned the original results from [10] for cores which had no tasks mapped to them. These could then be regarded as switched off, and the energy consumption caused by their idle power deducted from the total energy consumption. As it turned out, all 40 schedules had tasks mapped to each available core, so no cores could be switched off. In a way, this demonstrates the importance of considering chip design at scheduling. After all, our results can not only be employed to prescribe a specific core composition but also increase energy efficiency for a given chip design, where unused cores can be switched off to save energy.

Had our power model not considered a core's idle power, there would be no incentive for the solver to minimize the number of cores when a solution with optimal energy consumption has been reached. Thus, it is conceivable that including the total number of cores in the optimization process might lead to solutions with equally optimal energy consumption but lower core count. By modifying the objective function, energy consumption and core count are jointly minimized:

$$\min \sum_{i,j,k,t} x_{i,j,k,t} \cdot \text{time}(i,j,k,t) \cdot \text{power}(t,k,\text{tty}(j)) \cdot \text{size}(i) + \gamma \cdot (p_b + p_L).$$

Of course, γ must be chosen such that optimality regarding energy consumption is given while core count still makes a relevant difference during optimization.

Beyond scheduling quality we are concerned with the time it takes to compute a schedule (and potentially a core composition) for a given task set. Table 2

---

[3] Please remember that also during task execution, power is composed from "idle" power and power on top, so that idle power mostly indicates static power.

provides information on scheduling times for the original experiments without design space exploration in [10] as well as for our current experiments jointly optimizing chip design and application schedule under an area constraint ($A_{Total} \leq 91.2\,\mathrm{mm}^2$). For small and moderately sized task sets, scheduling times are low throughout. They are notably lower in the original experiments though, which illustrates that considering chip design in the optimization process leads to a higher computational effort than solely optimizing the schedule for low energy consumption. For the larger task sets ($n = 40$, $n = 80$), scheduling times rise significantly in both setups, indicating that the decisive factor is task set size when it comes to problem complexity. Over all task sets examined, the overhead in our current experiments under the area constraint is $\approx$37%. Unsurprisingly, the solver ran into the timeout more often as well (11 timeouts in total vs. 6 in the experiments in [10]). Nevertheless, the largest MIPGap value at timeout was 0.0018, thus we can consider all solutions (near-)optimal.

Table 2. Scheduling times (sums of user and system time) and number of timeouts for the current experiments and for the experiments in [10]

n	Experiments in [10]		Current experiments	
	Avg. scheduling time (s)	#Timeouts	Avg. scheduling time (s)	#Timeouts
10	0.355	0	2.906	0
20	5.175	0	142.798	0
40	1702.486	3	2491.273	5
80	1671.283	3	1984.073	6
Total	844.825	6	1155.262	11

In addition to the synthetic task sets considered in [10], we were interested in whether combined design space exploration and scheduling could offer any benefits when it comes to real applications. Therefore, we have performed the above experiments for three selected applications: H.263 encode detailed in [3], stereo depth estimation (SDE) from [4], and edge detection as described in [11]. The H.263 encode task set is comprised of 9 sequential tasks. SDE features 8 tasks, some of which are sequential while some can be parallelized to an arbitrary degree. This holds true as well for the edge detection application consisting of 6 tasks. Table 3 shows the results for the three applications just presented. It becomes clear that the energy savings are more substantial than for the synthetic task sets, ranging from approximately 35% for the H.263 encode application to 45% for SDE. Optimizing chip design in conjunction with the schedule again pays off as is indicated by the specific chip compositions featuring less than four cores of each type for all three applications. In each case, we chose tight deadlines just about sufficient to produce a feasible schedule. This means that even from a performance-oriented point of view, the chip with four big and four LITTLE cores would not provide any advantages over the individual designs issued by our approach for the respective task sets. Due to the small number of tasks in each application, scheduling times were very low (<1 s) throughout, which is why we will omit any discussion to this effect here.

Table 3. Experimental results for three real-world applications

Application	H.263 encode	SDE	Edge detection
E_{total} design & sched. vs. sched. only	64.9%	55.3%	62.0%
# big cores	3	2	2
# LITTLE cores	1	1	2

5   Generalization

The design space for a streaming application on a reconfigurable platform can be optimized in several dimensions: (1) energy for one round, (2) duration of one round, and (3) number of soft cores of each type (or total area of soft cores). So far, we have given fixed upper bounds for (2) and (3), and minimized the first target under those constraints. However, it is also possible to fix any other two and optimize the third. For (1) and (2), this is explained in [10], where a fixed platform is assumed, i.e., (3) is not a variable.

Here, we can change the optimization goal, e.g. to minimize the duration M of one round, by making M a real-valued variable, using objective function $\min M$, and changing the previous objective function (1a) to a constraint $E \leq P_{bud} \cdot M$, where P_{bud} is a given maximum (average) power budget, and E is a short-hand for the sum in (1a). Similarly, the minimum area for given power budget and throughput can be found by using the left-hand side of (1h) as objective function, using the previous objective function in a constraint as given above, and letting M as a constant as in Sect. 3.

Moreover, it is possible to fix one of those dimensions and produce a Pareto front for the other two. We will exemplify this for the case of determining the minimum (average) power budget vs. chip area for a given throughput, i.e. for a given round length M. This can e.g. be used to find a suitably sized FPGA for a given application.

To do this, we solve a sequence of MILPs, starting with the maximum available chip area A_{max}, and using $A_{Total}(i) = A_{max} - i \cdot A_{LITTLE}$ with $i = 0, 1, 2, \ldots$ until[4] no feasible solution is found. Each solution comprises optimum core counts p_1 and p_2 and the minimum energy E^*, which can be converted into an average power budget by dividing by M. Figure 4 depicts such a Pareto curve for one set of tasks ($n = 20$) with the deadline M from Sect. 4, giving maximum chip area in mm^2 and power in W as the axes, and marking each point in the Pareto curve with (p_2, p_1), i.e. starting with the number of big cores, for that solution. As we

---

[4] A smaller step than the area A_{LITTLE} of the smaller core would not change anything.

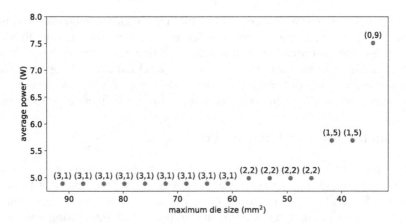

Fig. 4. Pareto curve of power vs. chip area. Each point on the curve is marked with the core counts (p_2, p_1), i.e. with the number of big and LITTLE cores, respectively, for that solution.

can see, for a wide range of the examined maximum die size values, core composition does not change as the most energy-efficient design can be accommodated within the given constraints. Presumably, adding more cores does more damage energy-wise than increasing operating frequencies or extending parallelization, even if there is plenty of unused area left on the chip. When maximum chip size starts to pose an effective limitation, big cores are substituted by one or several LITTLE cores. That way, average power consumption increases but feasible solutions can still be produced down to $34.2\,\text{mm}^2$ die size, when the chip only features LITTLE cores and average power consumption is $\approx 54\%$ higher than for the energy-optimal solution under arbitrary chip size.

6 Related Work

Design space exploration and scheduling have been considered for reconfigurable platforms for decades, cf. e.g. [12] and the references therein, however in largely varying contexts and with widely differing goals.

Holzer et al. [6] and Duhem et al. [2] consider the combination of design space exploration and scheduling in the context of reconfiguration at runtime, while we consider static scheduling. Sarma and Dutt [17] consider design space exploration of heterogeneous chip multiprocessors with a given power or area budget for several given core types, with the goal of optimizing for energy, performance or a combination of these. In contrast to our work, they use sequential tasks with dynamic scheduling by the operating system scheduler, and DVFS is not considered. Uscumlic et al. [19] and Li et al. [9] consider design space exploration and scheduling via ILP and evolutionary computation, respectively, but in the application, i.e. for a fixed platform, while we target an architecture where different numbers and types of soft cores can be used.

The closest related work seems to be [16]. They combine modulo scheduling and design space exploration, and solve for performance and energy efficiency, i.e., they generate a Pareto front of solutions so that the designer has a choice. However, their tasks are instructions in a high-level hardware design language, and their resources are operation units like adders or multipliers, while our tasks are parallelizable programs in itself, and our resources are different types of cores.

7   Conclusion and Future Work

We have presented an approach to integrate design space exploration and static scheduling for executing streaming applications on a heterogeneous reconfigurable platform with a minimum of energy consumption achieving a required throughput. Our preliminary experiments indicate that integrating the design space exploration, i.e. determining the number of soft cores of different core types, with the scheduling does not notably increase scheduling time, and at the same time improves energy efficiency by 19% on average via selecting optimum core counts within a given area available in a reconfigurable architecture.

Moreover, we have exemplified that the approach can be generalized for other targets than energy efficiency, such as minimum area solution for a given power budget and throughput, and to produce a Pareto front relating two optimization goals like minimum power budgets for different areas of the reconfigurable architecture, given a required throughput.

Future work will comprise to evaluate our approach for more than two core types and to validate our experiments on a real configurable platform. Moreover, for core counts that are not powers of 2 we might achieve further improvements by using non-binary or asymmetric binary core groups, e.g. like in [18].

References

1. Lal Shimpi, A.: Samsung Details Exynos 5 Octa Architecture & Power at ISSCC 2013 (2013). https://www.anandtech.com/show/6768/. Accessed 01 Mar 2021
2. Duhem, F., Muller, F., Aubry, W., Le. Gal, B., Négru, D., Lorenzini, P.: Design space exploration for partially reconfigurable architectures in real-time systems. J. Syst. Architect. **59**(8), 571–581 (2013). https://doi.org/10.1016/j.sysarc.2013.06.007
3. Eindhoven Technical University, Electronic Systems: Dataflow Benchmark Suite (DFbench) (2010). http://www.es.ele.tue.nl/dfbench/
4. Hautala, I.: From dataflow models to energy efficient application specific processors. Ph.D. thesis, Oulu University, Finland (2019)
5. Holmbacka, S., Keller, J.: Workload type-aware scheduling on big.LITTLE platforms. In: Ibrahim, S., Choo, K.-K.R., Yan, Z., Pedrycz, W. (eds.) ICA3PP 2017. LNCS, vol. 10393, pp. 3–17. Springer, Cham (2017). https://doi.org/10.1007/978-3-319-65482-9_1
6. Holzer, M., Knerr, B., Rupp, M.: Design space exploration for real-time reconfigurable computing. In: Proceedings of the 41st Asilomar Conference on Signals, Systems and Computers, pp. 1981–1985 (2007). https://doi.org/10.1109/ACSSC.2007.4487583

7. Kahn, G.: The semantics of a simple language for parallel programming. In: Proceedings of the IFIP Congress on Information Processing, pp. 471–475. North-Holland (1974)
8. Kessler, C.W., Melot, N., Eitschberger, P., Keller, J.: Crown scheduling: energy-efficient resource allocation, mapping and discrete frequency scaling for collections of malleable streaming tasks. In: 23rd International Workshop on Power and Timing Modeling, Optimization and Simulation, pp. 215–222 (2013)
9. Li, Z., et al.: Using design space exploration for finding schedules with guaranteed reaction times of synchronous programs on multi-core architecture. J. Syst. Architect. **74**, 30–45 (2017). https://doi.org/10.1016/j.sysarc.2016.12.003
10. Litzinger, S., Keller, J., Kessler, C.: Scheduling moldable parallel streaming tasks on heterogeneous platforms with frequency scaling. In: Proceedings of the 27th European Signal Processing Conference (EUSIPCO 2019), September 2019
11. Litzinger, S., Keller, J.: Code generation for energy-efficient execution of dynamic streaming task graphs on parallel and heterogeneous platforms. Concurrency and Computation: Practice and Experience n/a(n/a), e6072 (2021). https://doi.org/ https://doi.org/10.1002/cpe.6072
12. Maestre, R., Kurdahi, F., Fernandez, M., Hermida, R., Bagherzadeh, N., Singh, H.: Kernel scheduling techniques for efficient solution space exploration in reconfigurable computing. J. Syst. Architect. **47**(3), 277–292 (2001). https://doi.org/10.1016/S1383-7621(00)00050-3
13. Melot, N., Kessler, C., Keller, J.: Improving energy-efficiency of static schedules by core consolidation and switching off unused cores. In: Proceedings of the International Conference on Parallel Computing (ParCo 2015), pp. 285–294. IOS Press (2016). https://doi.org/10.3233/978-1-61499-621-7-285
14. Melot, N., Kessler, C., Keller, J., Eitschberger, P.: Fast Crown scheduling heuristics for energy-efficient mapping and scaling of moldable streaming tasks on manycore systems. ACM Trans. Archit. Code Optim. **11**(4) (2015)
15. Melot, N., Kessler, C., Keller, J., Eitschberger, P.: Co-optimizing core allocation, mapping and dvfs in streaming programs with moldable tasks for energy efficient execution on manycore architectures. In: Proceedings of the 19th International Conference on Application of Concurrency to System Design (ACSD-2019), Aachen, Germany. IEEE, June 2019. https://doi.org/10.1109/ACSD.2019.00011
16. Oppermann, J., Sittel, P., Kumm, M., Reuter-Oppermann, M., Koch, A., Sinnen, O.: Design-space exploration with multi-objective resource-aware modulo scheduling. In: Yahyapour, R. (ed.) Euro-Par 2019. LNCS, vol. 11725, pp. 170–183. Springer, Cham (2019). https://doi.org/10.1007/978-3-030-29400-7_13
17. Sarma, S., Dutt, N.: Cross-layer exploration of heterogeneous multicore processor configurations. In: Proc. 28th International Conference on VLSI Design and 14th International Conference on Embedded Systems. IEEE (2015). https://doi.org/10.1109/VLSID.2015.3
18. Torggler, M., Keller, J., Kessler, C.W.: Asymmetric crown scheduling. In: Kotenko, I.V., Cotronis, Y., Daneshtalab, M. (eds.) 25th Euromicro International Conference on Parallel, Distributed and Network-based Processing, PDP 2017, St. Petersburg, Russia, March 6–8, 2017. pp. 421–425. IEEE Computer Society (2017). https://doi.org/10.1109/PDP.2017.22
19. Uscumlic, B., Enrici, A., Pacalet, R., Gharbi, A., Apvrille, L., Natarianni, L., Roullet, L.: Design space exploration with deterministic latency guarantees for crossbar mpsoc architectures. In: Proc. IEEE International Conference on Communications (ICC). pp. 1–7 (2020). https://doi.org/10.1109/ICC40277.2020.9149076

Task-Based Programming Models for Heterogeneous Recurrent Workloads

Jaume Bosch[1,2](✉) ⓘ, Miquel Vidal[1] ⓘ, Antonio Filgueras[1] ⓘ,
Daniel Jiménez-González[2] ⓘ, Carlos Álvarez[2] ⓘ, Xavier Martorell[2] ⓘ,
and Eduard Ayguadé[1,2] ⓘ

[1] Barcelona Supercomputing Center, 08034 Barcelona, Spain
{jaume.bosch,miquel.vidal,antonio.filgueras,eduard.ayguade}@bsc.es
[2] Universitat Politécnica de Catalunya, 08034 Barcelona, Spain
{djimenez,calvarez,xavim}@ac.upc.edu

Abstract. This paper proposes the extension of task-based programming models with recurrent workloads concepts. The proposal introduces new clauses in the OmpSs task directive to efficiently model recurrent workloads. The clauses define the task period and/or the number of task body repetitions. Despite the new clauses are suitable for any device, their support has been implemented using the capabilities of FPGA devices in embedded systems. These heterogeneous systems are common in industrial applications that usually develop recurrent workloads. The evaluation shows a huge gap in the applications' programmability, saving lines of code, and increasing the code readability. Besides, it shows the efficient management of recurrent tasks when performed in FPGA devices, which can support one order of magnitude finer tasks. All these improvements perfectly suit the needs of cyber-physical heterogeneous systems, which are frequently used in industrial environments to run recurrent workloads.

Keywords: Task-based parallelism · Recurrent workloads ·
Heterogeneous computing · FPGA · OmpSs · OpenMP

1 Introduction

Task-based parallel programming models have demonstrated to be a powerful tool to develop applications targeting heterogeneous platforms [4,12]. There are new parallel programming models with native support for heterogeneous systems (e.g. OpenACC [8] and CUDA [7]). Also, different parallel programming models, which were initially designed for multicore processors, introduced new features to support such heterogeneous systems (e.g. OpenMP [9] and OmpSs [4]).

The importance of heterogeneous systems has grown in last years as co-processors can increase the computational power of systems while keeping the power consumption restricted. The FPGAs are reconfigurable co-processors that allow implementing custom application logic within them. This logic can implement parts of applications, so they are executed faster and with a smaller power consumption than in the general purpose processor of the host.

© Springer Nature Switzerland AG 2021
S. Derrien et al. (Eds.): ARC 2021, LNCS 12700, pp. 108–122, 2021.
https://doi.org/10.1007/978-3-030-79025-7_8

Periodic systems (i.e., recurrent workloads) are a common workload in industrial environments and real-time applications. Those workloads use the task concept to define the different activities that must be executed periodically (after some amount of time). Thereby, task-based parallel programming models are great candidates to support recurrent workloads. We propose extending the current syntax of task-based parallel programming models to define the main recurrent task parameters. Therefore, modeling recurrent workloads can be accomplished efficiently in terms of code lines, and with all parallel capabilities of baseline programming models. Also, we propose using the reconfigurable heterogeneous platforms to efficiently manage these recurrent workloads. These platforms will provide an efficient management of recurrent tasks, keeping the great programmability provided by the parallel programming models.

The remainder of the paper is organized as follows. Section 2 describes the OmpSs@FPGA ecosystem. Section 3 describes the proposed programming model extension. Section 4 describes the implementation developed on top of OmpSs@FPGA to support the proposed extensions directly inside the FPGA co-processors. Section 5 presents the evaluation of the new design in an SoC. Finally, Sect. 6 presents the related work and Sect. 7 concludes.

2   Background

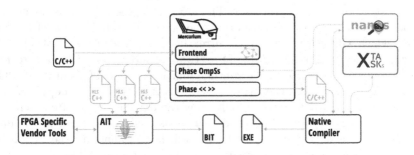

Fig. 1. OmpSs@FPGA compilation process

The OmpSs@FPGA ecosystem is an upgrade of the OmpSs [4] infrastructure (Mercurium source-to-source compiler and Nanos++ runtime) to incorporate FPGA support [2]. OmpSs is a task-based parallel programming model that extends the OpenMP 3.1 syntax and has been an active forerunner of the current tasking capabilities available in OpenMP 5.0. OmpSs@FPGA modifies Mercurium compiler, to support the generation of an independent source code file for each task with the FPGA target; and Nanos++ runtime, to handle the data movements between the host and FPGA memory, and offload the tasks to the device. Moreover, the ecosystem is composed by other tools like AIT (Accelerator Integration Tool), which combines all FPGA files generated by Mercurium and calls specific vendor tools that generate the bitstream; and xTasks library, which provides a common API to Nanos++ for data and task management regardless the communication protocol between the host and the FPGA. The structure of all those tools is shown in Fig. 1.

```
1   #pragma omp target device(fpga) num_instances(2) \
2     copy_inout([BSIZE]buffer, [1]offset)
3   #pragma omp task
4   void read_sensor(float *buffer, unsinged int *offset) {
5     buffer[*offset] = ...;
6     *offset += 1;
7   }
8   int main(...) {
9     float buffer[BSIZE]; unsigned int offset = 0;
10    read_sensor(buffer, &offset);
11    #pragma omp taskwait
12  }
```

Listing 1: OmpSs@FPGA task example

The definition of an FPGA task in the OmpSs programming model can be seen in Listing 1. In contrast to OpenMP, OmpSs supports the annotation of function declarations that result in a task spawn every time the function is called. In Listing 1, we can see that function **read_sensor** is annotated with the task and target directives. The **device(fpga)** clause executes the task in an FPGA device instead of the host processor. The **num_instances(2)** clause defines the number of FPGA task accelerators that should be generated in the FPGA bitstream, which will be available to concurrently execute the instances of this task. The **copy_inout([BSIZE]buffer, [1]offset)** clause defines the data regions accessed by the task body, so the runtime manages a copy of them into FPGA memory before and after each task execution. Also, there are **copy_in(...)** and **copy_out(...)** clauses which only copy the data before or after each task execution respectively. In addition, data regions could be defined in the data dependence clauses (**in**, **inout**, and **out**) which also annotate the regions as task dependences to order the execution of tasks at runtime. The implementation supports task nesting within FPGA tasks. Therefore, FPGA task accelerators may spawn new FPGA/SMP/GPU tasks and synchronize them with the regular taskwait.

For each FPGA task in the application, Mercurium compiler isolates its source code in a separate source file and embeds it in a communication wrapper. This wrapper has a common external interface independent of task arguments, and it provides instrumentation capabilities and data caching optimization. Finally, the generated files are provided to AIT which generates an FPGA bitstream with all task accelerators and the management logic. The IP blocks placed in the FPGA design with their interconnections are shown in Fig. 2.

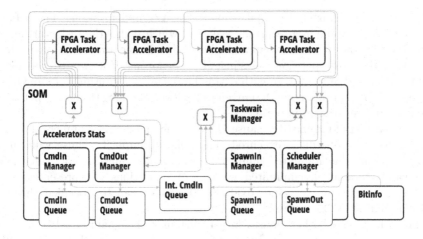

Fig. 2. OmpSs@FPGA bitstream organization

The FPGA task accelerators are connected with input and output streams to the SOM Hardware Runtime (HWR) [3]. The SOM module handles the commands sent by the host runtime and manages the messages sent by the FPGA task accelerators (task execution finished, task spawn, spawned tasks synchronization, etc.). The communication between the host runtime (through xTasks library) and the HWR is done by commands submitted into the 4 queues shown in Fig. 2. Each of the queues is managed by an IP block: CmdIn Manager forwards the commands to the FPGA task accelerators, CmdOut Manager notifies about executed commands, Scheduler Manager forwards the tasks spawned within the FPGA (into Int. CmdIn Queue when the task can be executed directly in the FPGA, into SpawnOut Queue otherwise), SpawinIn Manager handles executed task commands for reverse offloaded tasks, Taskwait Manager counts the tasks executed in each context for later synchronization.

3 Programming Model Extension

The OmpSs programming model has been extended with new clauses to annotate the recurrent tasks information. Although we present the clauses for the OmpSs programming model, they could also be incorporated in the OpenMP standard with the same semantics. The clauses are intended to provide the information of recurrent tasks which are periodically triggered by a timer. We keep as future work the support for recurrent tasks triggered by external events.

The period and num_repetitions clauses have been added to the existing task directive. They are optional and only one of both is needed to create a recurrent task. Both clauses take a single expression, which is evaluated as a 32 bits value at runtime. Therefore, the value may be unknown at compile time.

The period(N) clause defines the minimum amount of time between the beginning of two task executions. By default, the time is expressed in microseconds, but this may be changed at compile time (using a compiler option). The default (implicit) clause value in a recurrent task is 0, which makes the task start again just after it finishes. The same happens when the task execution takes longer than the period: the next repetition starts just after the former. However, this behavior could be changed in the future with extra clauses or by a runtime option. Other approaches could be: aborting the current repetition, aborting the next repetition, schedule both repetitions in parallel.

The num_repetitions(N) clause defines the maximum number of times that the task body will be executed. The default (implicit) clause value in a recurrent task is an unlimited number of repetitions. Since 0 repetitions may be a valid amount, the unlimited number of repetitions is represented with the largest representable value (0xFFFFFFFF) which can be specified through OMP_REPS_UNLIMITED constant.

The semantics of other clauses in a recurrent task remain equal to a regular task. The same criteria apply to other programming model directives, like the taskwait. The recurrent tasks will not become finished until all repetitions have been run. Therefore, a taskwait after a recurrent task will not be accomplished until all task repetitions have been run. Also, the data dependences in a recurrent task only postpone the execution of the first repetition but not the others, and the successor tasks of a recurrent task are not ready until all repetitions are executed. However, a recurrent task can periodically spawn a set of child (nested) tasks with dependences between them. This makes possible having data dependences between periodically executed tasks.

```
1   #pragma omp target device(fpga) num_repetitions(reps) period(1000000) \
2       copy_inout([BSIZE]buffer, [1]offset)
3   #pragma omp task
4   void read_sensor(float *buffer, unsigned int *offset, const int reps);
5
6   int main(...) {
7       read_sensor(buffer, &offset, 10);
8       #pragma omp taskwait
9   }
```

Listing 2: OmpSs example with a recurrent task

Listing 2 shows the example of Listing 1 extended with the new recurrent clauses. The read_sensor task has been annotated with the run_repetitions and period clauses in line 1. Therefore, the task's body will be executed reps times (10 as shown in function call of line 7) every 1 s (1000000 μs in the clause value). The taskwait in line 8 will be accomplished after all task body repetitions have been executed. Similarly, successor tasks that have a common data dependence on the same element (annotated with in, inout, or out clauses) will be ready to execute once recurrent tasks finish.

Two new APIs have been defined in the programming model to control the execution of recurrent tasks. Those APIs must be called within the recurrent tasks and apply to itself.

omp_get_periodic_task_repetition_num returns the current repetition number which is under execution. The first repetition is the number 1, since 0 is returned when the task is non-recurrent.

omp_cancel_periodic_task cancels the remaining repetitions of the current recurrent task. It does not cancel the remaining task code after the API call.

4   Implementation

The programming model extension has been implemented on top of OmpSs@FPGA. This section presents the modifications that we performed in order to support the recurrent tasks management in the FPGA task accelerators. In addition, the support for critical regions between task accelerators inside the same FPGA device has been introduced. This is very useful to coordinate the different accelerators during the execution as the recurrent tasks start their execution autonomously without any synchronization.

4.1   Mercurium Compiler

The OmpSs translation phase has been extended to support the new clauses. The compiler forwards the period and number of repetitions information to the runtime during the task creation if any of the clauses appear. The information is provided using a new runtime API. In contrast, the compiler emits the regular API calls for task creation if the task directive does not contain neither **period** nor **num_repetitions** clauses.

The wrapper generated by the compiler in the C++ HLS intermediate files has been extended. It has to support a new command (similar to the task execution command) with the number of repetitions and period information. The wrapper has to handle the calls to omp_get_periodic_task_repetition_num and omp_cancel_periodic_task APIs which could be called within the task code. Moreover, the support for critical regions in the FPGA task accelerators requires sending a message to the new **Lock Manager** of HWR.

4.2   Nanos++ Runtime and xTasks Library

The Nanos++ runtime has been extended with a new API that is called during the task spawn to set the recurrent information. The API is called **nanos_set-_wd_recurrent** and it takes 3 arguments: the reference/pointer of the task being spawned, the minimum period between task executions, and the number of repetitions.

The xTasks library has been extended to support the new task information. When a task has to be offloaded to the FPGA and it is a recurrent task, the new command is issued instead of the previous task execution command.

4.3 FPGA Design Support

The support of the new features only requires minor changes in the FPGA task accelerators and HWR. The main change is the new command that must be supported by the HLS wrapper (generated by Mercurium) and the HWR. Also, the new Lock Manager has been added inside the HWR to manage exclusive access to critical regions.

The FPGA task accelerators have been extended to support the new capabilities. The wrapper generation has been modified to implement the repetitions management. In addition, two new ports have been added to delay the task body executions the specified amount of time. The ports are used to read a counter that is incremented every clock cycle, and the frequency of such increment. With this information, the wrapper is able to accurately wait the needed amount of time between repetitions.

The lock acquire and release messages, which are sent to support the critical regions on the FPGA task accelerators, are forwarded through the existing interconnections. These interconnections are the ones going between SOM and FPGA task accelerators, and vice-versa.

The Lock Manager is a new IP block developed in C++ using HLS tools and added inside the SOM HWR. It has input and output interfaces to receive and acknowledge the messages sent by the FPGA task accelerators. Those streams are connected like Taskwait Manager or Scheduler Manager, as shown in Fig. 2. The module's purpose is to keep the state of different locks that may be concurrently acquired and released by the FPGA task accelerators. To this end, the module has an internal table with the state of each lock. The module can receive two types of messages in the input stream: acquire messages and release messages. Whenever it receives a new message, it looks for the lock identifier (sent by the FPGA task accelerator) in the internal table and sets or clears the lock state. The response is successful in the acquire messages when the lock was not previously set and fails when the state is unchanged.

The number of entries in the internal lookup table is fixed during the AIT design stage. The current implementation has a direct mapping in the table for each lock ID. However, this could be changed and implement an N-way table. There must be enough entries in the table to ensure that nested locks do not map to the same entry. Otherwise, the system will enter in a deadlock state due to the impossibility of acquiring the inner lock.

The CmdIn Manager has been updated to consider the new command format that xTasks library may send to the FPGA task accelerators. The new command has the same format as the previous execute task command but with an extra word (number of repetitions and period) that also has to be forwarded.

5 Evaluation

The evaluation of the proposed design and implementation of recurrent tasks has been done in terms of programmability and productivity, limitations of tasks management, and power savings. Section 5.1 presents the experimental setup used in the evaluation. Section 5.2 presents the evaluation of the limitations and management overheads of the proposed design using a synthetic benchmark. Section 5.3 shows the results for a sensor monitoring use case in embedded systems. Finally, Sect. 5.4 presents the evaluation of the proposal for a face detection application.

5.1 Experimental Setup

The evaluation of the proposal modifications has been done in a Zedboard with real executions. The board contains a Xilinx Zynq®-7000 All Programmable SoC [1], and it is commonly used in embedded industrial systems as it offers high versatility with reduced power consumption and budget. The SoC is composed of 2 ARM Cortex-A9 cores, that run at 667 MHz, a Xilinx Zynq-7000 FPGA and a main DDR3 memory of 512 MB. The board is booted using the Ubuntu Linux 16.04 operating system. All FPGA bitstreams have been generated and executed at 100 Mhz.

The tools used to generate the application bitstream and binaries are: Vivado Design Suite 2020.1, GNU C/C++ Compiler 6.2.0, and PetaLinux Tools 2019.2. The modifications have been developed on top of OmpSs@FPGA release 2.3.0.

5.2 Synthetic Benchmark

The synthetic benchmark executes a recurrent task NUM_REPS times every PERIOD microseconds. The task, called foo, lasts for duration microseconds. With these parameters, we can explore the runtime limits to manage fine-grain recurrent tasks. The NUM_REPS and PERIOD information can be provided into the programming model using the proposed clauses or handled at application level without the proposal extensions. Listing 3 shows the pseudo-code of benchmark tasks. The foo task is always used, but without the new clauses (num_repetitions and period) in the baseline implementation. The foo_manager task is only needed in the baseline implementation to launch and synchronize the recurrent task every PERIOD microseconds from the SMP host threads. In contrast, the foo_manager task is not needed with the proposed extensions, and foo is directly called.

Implementing the management logic of a recurrent task requires an effort from programmers and additional code. In contrast, the logic can be avoided by just using a couple of programming model clauses. The baseline system requires one extra task of 8 lines for each recurrent task (like foo_manager in Listing 3). During the period wait, the taskyield directive [9] (line 12) is used to avoid blocking the host thread executing the manager task. However, the task consumes resources and adds pressure to the host runtime. In contrast, the proposal moves the management complexity into the FPGA task accelerator, which only needs to receive the task information with the number of repetitions and the period. This has a minimal footprint in the resources used by the FPGA task accelerator as shown in Table 1 (for a 100 Mhz build). In terms of power consumption, the proposal removes the need to use an A9 core for recurrent task management, which consumes 277 mW. Indeed, it only increases the FPGA task

```
1   #pragma omp target device(fpga) /* num_repetitions(NUM_REPS) period(PERIOD) */
2   #pragma omp task
3   void foo(int duration) { usleep(duration); }
4
5   #pragma omp task
6   void foo_manager(int duration) {
7     for (unsigned int rep=0; rep<NUM_REPS; rep++) {
8       double t_ini = wall_time_us();
9       foo(duration);
10      #pragma omp taskwait
11      while ((wall_time_us() - t_ini) < PERIOD && rep < (NUM_REPS - 1)) {
12        #pragma omp taskyield
13  } } }
```

Listing 3: Recurrent synthetic benchmark tasks pseudo-code

accelerator power by 1 mW while doing the same work. Both powers are reported by Vivado in the post-implementation power summary.

Table 1. Vivado resources utilization and power report for Zedboard (100 Mhz)

Name	BRAM	DSP	FF	LUT	Power
Zedboard	280	220	106.400	53.200	–
ARM A9 Core	–	–	–	–	277 mW
foo baseline	0 (0%)	2 (0,9%)	593 (0,6%)	478 (0,9%)	7 mW
foo proposal	0 (0%)	4 (1,8%)	921 (0,9%)	792 (1,5%)	8 mW

The time devoted to each repetition is PERIOD, or duration if the task execution lasts more than the task's period (concurrent repetitions are not allowed). Then, the optimal execution time (Eq. 1) is defined by NUM_REPS multiplied by the time devoted to each repetition, except for the last one that only needs to consider the task execution time (duration) as the benchmark can immediately finish. Moreover, the effectiveness of an execution (Eq. 2) is defined by the ratio between the optimal execution time and the real execution time (100% means optimal).

$$Time_{optimal} = (num\_reps - 1) * max(duration, period) + duration \quad (1)$$

$$Effectiveness_{exec} = Time_{optimal}/Time_{exec} \quad (2)$$

Figure 3 shows the effectiveness (y-axis) of the synthetic benchmark when changing the task period (x-axis). Figure 3a shows the results at nanoseconds scale, and Fig. 3b shows the results at microseconds scale. Each chart has different series that correspond to different task durations. The task durations are labeled in the legend and are only shown for periods equal or larger than them. The number of repetitions is constant in all results at the same scale and proportional between them (10.000.000 in Fig. 3a and 10.000 in Fig. 3b). The FPGA device is configured at 100 Mhz. The blue series show the effectiveness of synthetic benchmark implemented with the proposal enhancements and having the recurrent task management in the FPGA task accelerator. On the other hand, the orange series show the effectiveness of baseline implementation using a manager task in the host threads. These baseline series are labeled in the legend with *(host)*.

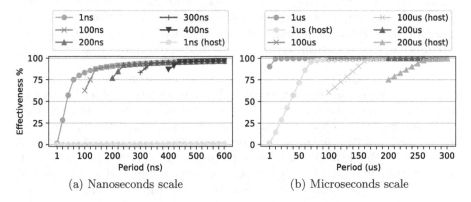

(a) Nanoseconds scale (b) Microseconds scale

Fig. 3. Effectiveness of synthetic benchmark for different task duration values (Color figure online)

The effectiveness results in Fig. 3 show that the proposal implementation always obtains higher effectiveness than the baseline implementation. All series behave similarly, the effectiveness increases the higher the period until the difference between the period and the task duration is at least 60 ns for the proposal and 70 µs for the baseline. After these offsets, the effectiveness stabilizes near to 99%. The 70 µs in the orange series are due to the communication round-trip between the host and the FPGA task accelerator. In contrast, the management inside the FPGA task accelerators (blue series) only needs 60 ns to check the number of remaining repetitions and whether the period has elapsed or not. Therefore, the integrated management of recurrent tasks avoids host-FPGA communications with overheads 1167× smaller than the ones in the baseline.

5.3 Sensors Monitoring

The sensors monitoring is a common workload in industrial environments. Its purpose is collecting information from any kind of sensors with a given frequency to know the elements state and keeping track of it, or even reacting if some irregularity is detected. We developed a benchmark that simulates this behavior based on a real and complex application. We defined a recurrent task for each sensor and one to handle the samples, all of them are FPGA tasks. The first tasks are responsible for retrieving and storing the sensor data into intermediate buffers. The handling task merges all data from sensors into a sample and orchestrates a parallel sample processing. Therefore, the benchmark scalability can be analyzed based on the sensors' reading period and the number of sensors that are being read. We defined 3 different implementations depending on which new capabilities are being used:

- cHost deps. Recurrent tasks managed at application level (without the new clauses) and using data dependences to synchronize the recurrent tasks.
- cHost cri. Recurrent tasks managed at application level (without the new clauses) and using critical regions to synchronize recurrent tasks.
- cFPGA. Recurrent tasks managed by the programming model (with the new clauses) and using critical regions to synchronize recurrent tasks.

The manager task that implements the recurrent support at application level requires a significant amount of extra logic. It has to keep track of the last submit timestamp and the number of repetitions executed for each recurrent task. Also, a finalization condition has to be maintained to know when all recurrent tasks have finished and then break the manager loop. The loop checks if the current timestamp is behind the last start timestamp plus the specified period for each recurrent task. If so, the task is launched, and their state inside the manager is updated. Once all recurrent tasks have been checked, the manager waits for them and yields until more tasks have to be submitted.

The management without the proposed capabilities assumes that the duration of recurrent tasks is smaller than the smallest period or recurrent tasks. This is due to the taskwait after the task spawns (similar to line 6 of Listing 3). For durations longer than the smallest period, the management will delay some task spawns. In contrast, the proposal implementation does not have such limitation as the recurrent tasks are managed independently. Also, the host manager only can ensure the period between task spawns but not task starts, which may be delayed by the runtime when no executors are available or due to runtime overheads. The recurrent tasks management implemented in the proposal has a good period precision as the repetitions management is kept together with the executor (the FPGA task accelerator).

Figure 4a shows the effectiveness (y-axis, computed like in synthetic benchmark) for the 3 implementations among different base periods (x-axis). The number of repetitions for the sensors reading task is fixed to 10, and there are 2 sensors in all executions. The host implementations only maintain the effectiveness above 1 ms base period. In contrast, cFPGA maintains the effectiveness above $10\,\mu s$ base period, which is 100 times smaller. Moreover, the host implementations fail to execute with base periods below $100\,\mu s$ due to an excessive memory consumption generated by the huge number of created tasks in Nanos++ runtime.

Figure 4b shows the effectiveness (y-axis) for the small base periods of Fig. 4a, where effectiveness starts to decay, among different amounts of read sensor tasks. Figure 4b helps to see how the proposal and the baseline behave with different amounts of recurrent tasks (the read sensors in this case). The results confirm the 100x difference between both implementations seen in previous results. The

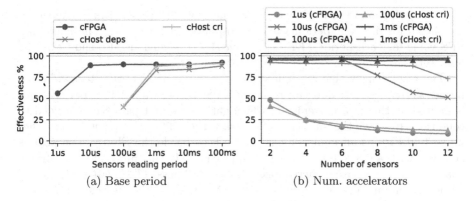

Fig. 4. Effectiveness of sensors monitoring benchmark

proposal implementation effectively handles all amounts of sensors for 1 ms and 100 μs periods. Meanwhile, `cHost cri` loses some effectiveness with 12 sensors for 1 ms period, and it suffers with the 100 μs period regardless of the number of sensors. In contrast, `cFPGA` shows a similar effectiveness decrease with 1 μs period. It keeps the effectiveness for periods above 1 μs.

5.4 Face Detection

The detection of faces on pictures is a common workload in several scenarios. One of them is the analysis of an image stream in real-time, which could benefit from the new FPGA capabilities. The implementation is based on a previous port to OmpSs@FPGA developed in AXIOM project [5]. The application periodically analyzes a frame buffer with 2 sets of filters implemented with FPGA tasks. The first set is performed by blocks (144 × 144 pixels including the needed padding) for all the frame and using 2 instances of the FPGA task accelerator. The second set is only performed to pixels with a minimum score after the first pass using 1 FPGA task accelerator. After the filters and if some face is detected, an SMP task is triggered with the list of coordinates to render the frame as shown in Fig. 5a.

We defined two implementations to compare the management of the application with the new recurrent task capabilities against equivalent management in the baseline. The `cFPGA` implementation, which periodically executes the top-level task in the FPGA using the `period` and `num_repetitions` clauses. The `cHost` implementation, which executes the top-level task in the SMP threads and supports the periodic behavior at application level without using programming model extensions. The number of frames processed (number of repetitions of top-level task) in each execution is 30, and they have been extracted from an input video that contains three people walking in a row. This amount of frames provides long enough executions to gather significant executions for the performance analysis.

Figure 5b shows the FPS (y-axis) handled by cFPGA and cHost. The values are shown for different period values of top-level task (x-axis). The maximum FPS value for each period ($FPS_{max}(period) = 1/period$) is also shown by the Max. series.

The results show that the cHost is not a performant option to handle the frames as the best rate does not reach 0.5 FPS (2 s per frame). The performance is limited by the data movements, which gather the first pass scores needed to conditionally spawn the tail tasks. In contrast, the cFPGA implementation reaches up to 1.79 FPS as all management can be kept inside the FPGA. The peak is achieved with a 0.3 s period, which is approximately the duration of one frame analysis when there are no active pixels for the tail pass. The cFPGA performance is the maximum value for periods above 0.7 s, which is the average duration of the analysis. Between 0.3 and 0.7 s for the period, some frames are processed within the period time and some are not. Therefore, the performance scales but not at the maximum values.

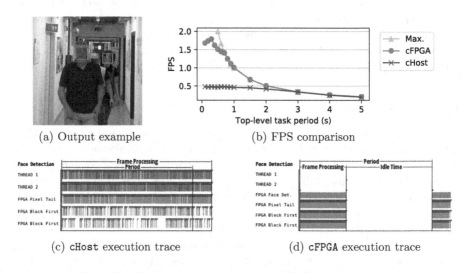

(a) Output example   (b) FPS comparison

(c) cHost execution trace   (d) cFPGA execution trace

Fig. 5. Face Detection execution results (Color figure online)

Figures 5c and 5d show two execution traces of Face Detection (cHost and cFPGA respectively) for a 2 s period. Both have the same elapsed time (x-axes) and show the activities (colors) in the different computing elements (y-axis). The activities shown are: orange for execution of tasks in FPGA task accelerators, red for execution of top-level task, dark-red for task offload from host to FPGA, and white for idle time. Traces clearly show the sparsity of FPGA tasks in cHost and that they are compacted in cFPGA. The baseline implementation takes too long due to the task management which occupies the 2 host threads all the time with the execution of top-level task (red regions) and the offloading of FPGA tasks (dark-red regions). The huge overheads result in an under-utilization of FPGA task accelerators and a poor frame rate. The cHost requires all the trace time (approximately 2.25 s) to handle the frame which is above the desired period of 2 s. In contrast, the cFPGA lasts for 700 ms, and the system remains idle until the next repetition is launched. Therefore, the FPGA management is able to support more frames per second as shown in Fig. 5b chart. Another relevant fact is that the host threads are not needed almost any of the time. That optimizes the power budget of the application without impacting the overall performance as both threads could be switched off and turned on when needed.

6   Related Work

There are previous works that consider extending task-based parallel programming models with real-time system capabilities. Serrano et al. [11] analyze the usage of OpenMP to develop critical real-time systems. They analyze the timing constraints, which are not considered in this thesis but are fully compatible. They briefly introduce an event clause that is used to define when a recurrent task must start executing. Besides, Pop et al. [10] propose an OpenMP extension to define persistent tasks that work in a stream fashion. Those tasks are similar to the recurrent tasks proposed in this paper but they are activated by the availability of input data instead of by a timer. Also, we propose the support of those tasks using the FPGA capabilities to have accurate and low-latency management.

Other previous efforts try to extend the capabilities of accelerators and optimize their usage in heterogeneous systems. CUDA Dynamic Parallelism [7] adds support for nested execution of CUDA kernels. Vesely et al. [13] discuss the support of operating system calls in GPGPUs. Heinz et al. [6] discuss the TaPaSCo runtime optimization to increase the execution rates in FPGA-accelerated jobs. All of them also extend and optimize the heterogeneous systems but without targeting real-time workloads or efficiently allowing their definition.

7   Conclusion

This paper proposes the extension of task-based programming models with recurrent workloads concepts. The proposal introduces new clauses in the task directive to efficiently model recurrent workloads. The clauses have been introduced in the OmpSs programming model but they are suitable for standard task-based parallel programming models like OpenMP. The evaluation of different benchmarks shows a huge gap in the application programmability. Besides, it shows the efficient management of recurrent tasks when performed in FPGA devices, which is able to support one order of magnitude finer tasks. The reduction of management overheads provides big idle gaps during the execution of the application. This allows smaller periods of recurrent tasks than the baseline, or reducing the power consumption as the elements could be switched off. All these improvements perfectly suit the necessities of new cyber-physical and heterogeneous devices when running recurrent workloads.

Acknowledgments. This work is partially supported by the European Union H2020 Research and Innovation Action (project 801051), by the Spanish Government (projects SEV-2015-0493 and PID2019-107255GB, grant BES-2016-078046), and by the Generalitat de Catalunya (contracts 2017-SGR-1414 and 2017-SGR-1328).

References

1. Avnet: ZedBoard Technical Spec. (2020). http://zedboard.org/content/zedboard-0
2. Bosch, J., et al.: Application acceleration on FPGAs with OmpSs@FPGA. In: 2018 International Conference on Field-Programmable Technology (FPT). IEEE, December 2018
3. Bosch, J., et al.: Breaking master-slave model between host and FPGAs. In: Proceedings of the 25th ACM SIGPLAN Symposium on Principles and Practice of Parallel Programming, pp. 419–420, February 2020
4. Duran, A., et al.: OmpSs: a proposal for programming heterogeneous multi-core architectures. Parallel Process. Lett. **21**(02), 173–193 (2011)
5. Filgueras, A., et al.: The AXIOM project: IoT on heterogeneous embedded platforms. IEEE Des. Test **PP**, 1 (2019)
6. Heinz, C., Hofmann, J.A., Sommer, L., Koch, A.: Improving job launch rates in the TaPaSCo FPGA middleware by hardware/software-co-design. In: 2020 IEEE/ACM International Workshop on Runtime and Operating Systems for Supercomputers (ROSS), pp. 22–30 (2020). https://doi.org/10.1109/ROSS51935.2020.00008
7. NVIDIA: CUDA Dynamic Parallelism Programming Guide (2019)
8. OpenACC Consortium: The OpenACC Application Programming Interface (2011)
9. OpenMP ARB: OpenMP API Specification (2018). https://www.openmp.org/spec-html/5.0/openmp.html
10. Pop, A., Cohen, A.: A Stream-Computing Extension to OpenMP, pp. 5–14, January 2011
11. Serrano, M.A., Royuela, S., Quiñones, E.: Towards an OpenMP Specification for Critical Real-Time Systems, pp. 143–159, January 2018
12. Thoman, P., et al.: A taxonomy of task-based parallel programming technologies for high-performance computing. J. Supercomput. **74**(4), 1422–1434 (2018). https://doi.org/10.1007/s11227-018-2238-4
13. Veselý, J., Basu, A., Bhattacharjee, A., Loh, G.H., Oskin, M., Reinhardt, S.K.: Generic system calls for GPUs. In: 2018 ACM/IEEE 45th Annual International Symposium on Computer Architecture (ISCA), pp. 843–856. IEEE (2018)

Architecture

Multi-layered NoCs with Adaptive Routing for Mixed Criticality Systems

Nidhi Anantharajaiah[(✉)], Zhe Zhang, and Juergen Becker

Institute for Information Processing Technologies (ITIV),
Karlsruhe Institue for Technology (KIT), Karlsruhe, Germany
`nidhi@kit.edu`

Abstract. Multiple applications of different criticality are increasingly being executed on the same System-on-Chip (SoC) platform to reduce resource consumption. Communication resources like the Network-on-Chip (NoC) on such platforms can be shared by such applications. Performance can be improved if the NoC is able to adapt at runtime to the requirements of different applications. An important challenge here is guaranteeing Quality of Service (QoS) for critical applications while improving overall performance of critical and non-critical applications. In this paper, we address this challenge by proposing a multi-layered hierarchical NoC which utilizes an adaptive routing algorithm. The proposed routing algorithm determines nodes connecting higher layers at runtime which have a shorter hop count to the destination nodes. Depending on the criticality of the applications, the packets are forwarded on shorter or longer hop paths. An adaptive congestion avoidance feature is integrated. Without congestion awareness, the proposed algorithm which utilizes multiple layers has upto 38% decrease in latency and with congestion awareness has upto 56% decrease in latency compared to the popular XY routing. When comparing algorithms which use different layers, the algorithm with congestion awareness has upto 29% decrease in latency and upto 16% increase in throughput.

Keywords: Network-on-Chip · Multi-Layered Network-on-Chip · Adaptive routing algorithm

1 Introduction

Multiple applications of different criticality are increasingly being executed on the same System-on-Chip (SoC) platform [1]. Such platforms usually contain memory and processor tiles and are interconnected using a Network-on-Chip (NoC) [2]. With the increase in number of processors and memory tiles, performance of the interconnect fabric plays an important role. If the NoC can adapt and address challenges at runtime then the performance of the applications can be improved.

Mesh topology is commonly implemented in a NoC due to its scalability, ease of implementation and uniform nature. A static routing is usually preferred in the

© Springer Nature Switzerland AG 2021
S. Derrien et al. (Eds.): ARC 2021, LNCS 12700, pp. 125–139, 2021.
https://doi.org/10.1007/978-3-030-79025-7_9

NoC when critical applications which require guarantees at design time are using it. Therefore it is challenging to utilize adaptive routing in mixed criticality NoCs.

In this paper, we present design and implementation of a multi-layered NoC with an adaptive routing algorithm designed to be beneficial for mixed criticality systems. The topology is mesh based, multi-layered and hierarchical. The motivation for mesh based topology is to maintain uniformity and ease of implementation. The routing algorithm is adaptive, monitors the environment to identify paths with less traffic to avoid congestion and routes packets accordingly based on the criticality of the packets. The algorithm supports applications which require guarantees by forwarding them on known paths. For packets which do not require guarantees, paths are chosen depending on the availability.

The contributions in this paper are summarized below:

- Design and Implementation of a multi-layered Hierarchical NoC targeting mixed criticality systems.
- A runtime congestion aware adaptive routing algorithm which routes packets on different paths depending on its criticality on such a multi-layered NoC to improve latency and throughput.

2   Motivation and Related Work

Multiple applications of varying criticality can share the same resources on a SoC platform. Applications of different criticality can arrive, occupy resources and finish running at different points in time. Applications can be running on a cluster of tiles or spread across the platform. The mapping can depend on the requirements of the application and resource availability at the time. Some of the applications which are critical can require guarantees at design time. The communication and memory resources are shared by such critical and non-critical applications. Locations of the memory units and IO tiles are usually fixed on SoC platforms. For memory intensive applications high traffic is seen on paths to and from memory tiles.

Critical packets and non-critical packets are sharing the same communication resources like links and routers. It can be beneficial, if the paths of critical and non-critical packets are decoupled. One option is to have dedicated links using virtual channels. In such cases they still share router resources and the arbitration policy on such routers can still have an impact on critical packets due to non-critical packets. Another option is to have dedicated links and routers for the critical packets. That requires a high amount of resources and can require the knowledge of mapping at design time. We aim to combine these approaches by implementing layers in a NoC and having parts of the layers occupied exclusively by critical applications. We also take into account that topologies need to be generic and uniform such that it can be used by a large set of applications and are not customized to a small set of applications.

Related work which address similar challenges are as follows. Though multi-layered topologies have been in existence for NoCs, we focus on NoCs which address improving access at runtime between frequently communicating tiles using links with reduced hop count. A hierarchical NoC in [3] aimed to improve access between communication centric tiles like memory and IO tiles and proposed a hierarchical network built from different types of subnetworks. The topologies here were chosen according to the applications requirements at design time and routing is done using lookup tables in the routers and the performance was compared against 2D mesh. The location of communication centric tiles here should be known at design time in order to choose a suitable topology. In [4,5] authors presented a Skip-Links architecture which dynamically alters the NoC topology at runtime to reduce logical distance between frequently communicating nodes. The aim was to bypass routers to reduce the logical distance. The performance was compared against mesh demonstrating hop count and energy reductions. Certain restrictions are present on the placement of such Skip-Link to decrease complexity in routing.

Some of the NoCs addressing challenges in mixed criticality systems by providing isolation between different criticality packets are as follows. A run-time configurable NoC design enabling throughput guarantees with reduced impact on latency for Best Effort (BE) traffic is presented in [6]. Here the BE traffic is prioritized over the guaranteed throughput (GT) traffic in NoC routers and only switch priorities when required providing sufficient performance isolation among different criticality levels. In [9], time-triggered communication that offers safety by establishing temporal and spatial segregation of the communication channels is described. Adaptivity enables the communication backbone to adapt the injection time of messages according to the real execution time of computational tasks. In [8], authors propose a QoSinNoC framework, a set of QoS-aware NoC architectures. It allows non-critical communication to pass through the critical region, provided they do not utilize common router resources. An extended Logic Based Distributed Routing (LBDR) mechanism is proposed and is implemented using table based routing in each router. Authors in [10] proposed a NoC router to support mixed criticality systems based on an accurate WCCT analysis for high-critical flows. The proposed router jointly uses Wormhole and Store And Forward switching modes for low- and high-critical flows, respectively. The assumption here is that small packets compose the high-critical traffic and the Store And Forward switching mode is used for high-critical flows.

In this paper by using multiple network layers, using an adaptive routing algorithm, we utilize the link and router resources to direct critical and noncritical paths along different paths to reduce influence between critical and noncritical applications. We aim to utilize the base mesh layer for non-critical packets and utilize upper layers with lower hop counts for more critical packets. Some of the distinguishing characteristics are summarized here

- Critical applications implemented on several Tiles spread across the SoC have higher priority and are assigned paths of lesser hop counts across layers to communicate with each other. Non-critical packets share resources when available or are directed on paths with longer hop counts.
- A non table based adaptive routing algorithm is proposed for a multi-layered NoCs which is scalable and flexible.

– Memory and IO Tiles which are generally at fixed locations and are sometimes
  spread across the SoC can benefit from such a NoC by having heavy traffic
  to and from such nodes be restricted to certain paths to reduce congestion.

Such a multi-layered NoC comes with the cost of increase in router resources,
with the increase in links in routers which connect the different layers. So a trade-
off between the resource consumption and benefit in performance is desired.

3   Topology of the Proposed NoC

The topology we are using for our approach is a multi-layered mesh. The basis
for communication is a base mesh layer connecting all of the nodes. Alternating
nodes on this layer are additionally connected using another network with a
mesh topology to create a second layer. And alternating nodes on the second
layer are connected to create the third and so on.

In this paper, to demonstrate the advantages of such a topology and the
supporting routing algorithm we consider an example of a three layers, 5 × 5
variant as illustrated in the Fig. 1. The network interconnects 25 tiles. Meanwhile
the number of ports of a router varies depending on its position in the network.
The minimum number is 4 (example at Tile 1, three in E, S, W direction and a
local port) and the maximum possible number of ports is 9 (example at Tile 12,
2 in each of the cardinal direction, plus 1 local port).

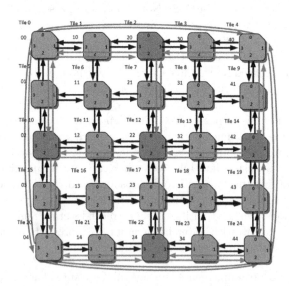

Fig. 1. A 5 × 5 3 layered NoC

In the proposed NoC, priorities are assigned to the layers as shown below.
For dimensions of 5 × 5 and 3 layers, the priority of layers is provided below.

$$Layer_1 > Layer_2 > Layer_3 \tag{1}$$

For a general n-layered network, Layer_n is the base layer which connects all the nodes and Layer_1 is the top most layer.

$$Layer_1 > Layer_2 > ..... > Layer_n \tag{2}$$

In this example the nodes are classified into three classes according to their location.

- Class 1: Routers connected by the highest priority layer (here it is the 2×2 mesh). Highlighted in green.
- Class 2: Routers connected using the intermediate layer (here it is the 3×3 mesh) which do not belong to Class 1. Highlighted in red.
- Class 3: Routers connected using the base layer (here it is the 5×5 mesh), which do not belong to Class 1 and Class 2.

4   Description of the Routing Algorithm Without Congestion Avoidance

We start by explaining the routing algorithm without a congestion avoidance feature. The path with shortest hop count between a source and destination nodes is selected across layers. Since the paths can be computed at design time, one way to implement such an algorithm can be by using a table based routing scheme. For this method the paths are computed at design time for a certain source and destination pair. Routing tables are implemented at each router, which store the output port to be chosen for a certain destination node. The values in the routing tables are fixed. A disadvantage of such an implementation is that tables do not scale well and are not flexible. For a 9×9 mesh, each router needs to store a table containing the output port for the 80 potential destinations. To avoid the implementation of routing tables and to have flexibility we present a routing algorithm which computes the path at run time. This makes the implementation of the algorithm lightweight, flexible and scalable.

The routing algorithm at every router forwards the packets on paths which use the least number of hops. To achieve this, a Near Node (NN) function is designed. That is carried out as follows. Consider a source (x_s, y_s) and destination pair (x_d, y_d). For a node (x, y) the NN function computes the nearest node (x_n, y_n) located between (x_s, y_s) and (x_d, y_d) which connects to the higher layers. The NN function is used to compute nearest nodes for the source and destination nodes. This results in (x_{sn}, y_{sn}) and (x_{dn}, y_{dn}) which are nearest nodes to source and destination nodes respectively and satisfy Eqs. 3 and 4.

$$(x_s < x_{sn} < x_d) \text{ or } (x_s > x_{sn} > x_d) \text{ and } (y_s < y_{sn} < y_d) \text{ or } (y_s > y_{sn} > y_d) \tag{3}$$

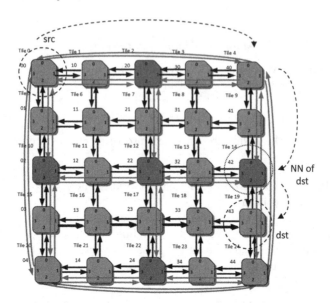

Fig. 2. Example when source is (0, 0), destination is (4, 3) and Nearest Node for destination is computed to be (4, 2).

$$(x_s < x_{dn} < x_d) \text{ or } (x_s > x_{dn} > x_d) \text{ and } (y_s < y_{dn} < y_d) \text{ or } (y_s > y_{dn} > y_d) \quad (4)$$

Now let us use a general example to show how a packet travels between a source (x_s, y_s) and destination node (x_d, y_d) using this NN function. For reference, let us consider the same for XY routing and only consider the base layer. A packet first travels in the X direction towards the destination and then the Y direction. It utilizes the links only in the base layer.

The proposed routing algorithm now seeks to utilize the links in the higher layers which have shorter hop counts. The NN function determines the nearest node to the source (x_{sn}, y_{sn}) and nearest node to the destination node (x_{dn}, y_{dn}). The entire path between the source and destination node is now divided into three sub-paths due to these nodes. Now the packets travel as shown in Eq. 5.

$$(x_s, y_s) \rightarrow (x_{sn}, y_{sn}) \rightarrow (x_{dn}, y_{dn}) \rightarrow (x_d, y_d) \quad (5)$$

Within each of the sub-paths, the XY routing algorithm is utilized to travel between nodes. For example, between (x_s, y_s) and (x_{sn}, y_{sn}), multiple paths are possible, but to achieve minimal routing between these nodes and to keep the algorithm simple, XY routing is used. Similarly between (x_{sn}, y_{sn}) and (x_{dn}, y_{dn}), XY routing is used to transport the packets.

Let us explain this by using an example. A packet is transported from $(0, 0)$ to $(4, 3)$. The destination node is $(4, 3)$, its possible nearby nodes are $(4, 2)$ and $(4, 4)$. This is illustrated in Fig. 2. The NN function always selects a node, which is located between the source and destination node. In this example, the near node of $(4, 3)$ is $(4, 2)$. It is located on a higher layer and is located between source and destination node, and thus will be chosen as near node of the destination node. Since the source node already connects the highest layer, the nearest node of the source node is the source node itself. Now the packet travels using the path $(0, 0) \rightarrow (4, 0) \rightarrow (4, 2) \rightarrow (4, 3)$. Between $(0, 0)$ and $(4, 0)$ a layer 1 link is used. Between $(4, 0)$ and $(4, 2)$ a layer 2 link is used. And between $(4, 2)$ and $(4, 3)$ the layer 3 link is used.

In general, to summarize, the routing algorithm prioritizes higher layers to forward the packet. The NN function is used to determine intermediate nodes and the path is broken into sub-paths. The general rules the NN function follows are as follows for the example of the 5×5 three layer network:

– Routers of Class 1 don't use the NN function, because they are already on the Layer with highest priority.
– The nearby node that is computed by the NN function for routers of Class 2 are members of Class 1, and the nearby node for routers of Class 3 belong to Class 1 or 2.

5   Description of the Routing Algorithm with Congestion Avoidance

The algorithm described in Sect. 4 is a static algorithm, the packets are always routed on the same paths for a certain pair of source and destination nodes. The paths do not change even if there is less or more traffic on those paths. In this algorithm, paths with low hop count are desired by packets generated by all nodes. When there is high traffic, there is a high possibility that the nodes connecting the higher layers experience more traffic since all packets are attempting to travel on the paths with the shortest hop count. The resulting delay increases with the increase in injection rate of each node due to the increase in the waiting times within the router. To solve this issue, a congestion awareness feature is integrated into the algorithm. The algorithm reads the input buffer status of the downstream routers and makes a decision among the possible output ports. In the results section we present latency and throughput results of the algorithm with and without the congestion avoidance feature to present the difference in performance. The results show improvement when the congestion avoidance feature is integrated in the algorithm.

In this section we elaborate the congestion avoidance feature. Let us take an example, consider a packet from node $(0, 0)$ to $(3, 0)$ as shown in Fig. 3. Here only a section of the network is shown for ease of explaining. There are multiple paths possible across the layers. The first path uses only the top layer (one hop), the second path uses the intermediate layer and base layer (2 hops) and the third path uses only the base layer (3 hops).

At router $(0, 0)$, three output ports are possible to reach the destination. The path with the shortest hop count is using the port connecting the top layer. The next shortest path is using the port connecting layer 2 and the longest is the

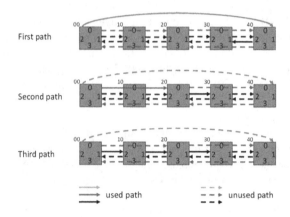

Fig. 3. Possible paths from node 00 to 30

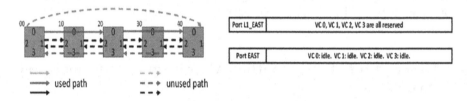

Fig. 4. Virtual Channel Status

port connecting the base layer. In the version without congestion avoidance, the packets always chose the port connecting the top layer which results in the lowest hop count. In the second version, with congestion avoidance, the router reads the input buffer status of the downstream routers and makes a choice according to the priority of the ports. The priority of the ports are as follows:

$$port_{layer1} > port_{layer2} > port_{layer3} \qquad (6)$$

When the input buffer in the downstream router via port $port_{layer1}$ is full then the port $port_{layer2}$ is considered. If this input buffer is full as well then port $port_{layer3}$ is considered. When this is full as well the process repeats until space is available in any of the downstream input buffers. This results in less congestion around the routers connecting higher layers and also uses the base and lower layers more efficiently. This aims to evenly distribute packets across layers.

An example to demonstrate the working of the congestion aware routing is presented in Fig. 4 when the source node is $(0, 0)$ and destination is $(4, 0)$. There are two ports possible to choose from at the source and depending on the virtual channel status in the downstream route, an output port is chosen.

In version 1 of the algorithm, critical and non-critical packets are treated the same by the routing algorithm. In version 2, critical packets are always routed on the paths with the shortest hop counts and the non-critical packets can be routed on paths with the shortest or longer hop counts. In high traffic scenarios, to avoid influence of non-critical packets on congestion of critical packets, non critical packets are routed across higher hop count paths. A field in the header flit of the packet is reserved to identify if a packet is critical or not, and the router processes the packet and computed the output port accordingly.

6   Router Architecture

The router architecture used is based on the router in [7] and is shown in Fig. 5 for 'n' number of ports. Number of ports range from 4 to 9 depending on the router's position in the network. As an example, a router at location $(0, 0)$ is shown in Fig. 6. There are input buffers which are of depth 4 and four virtual channels are implemented in the router. Occurrence of deadlocks can be mitigated with the help of virtual channels. Certain forbidden turns by the routing algorithm can be allocated to specific virtual channels to break the dependency loop. A Routing Unit (RU) is present at each port to process the packet. Arbitration used here is Round Robin. The router supports both Guaranteed Service(GS) and BE communication. Wormhole switching is used to forward the packets. Link width implemented is 32 bits and example of a packet format for a header flit is shown in Fig. 7. The header flit comprises of source and destination address along with a service level field to indicate BE or GS. A one bit field (adapt) is assigned in the header to inform the router if it is a critical packet or not. For critical applications which require guarantees this field is set to 0. This ensures that paths which the packets follow do not change at runtime. If an application does not require guarantees then this field is set to 1 indicating that the paths can be changed at runtime depending on the traffic.

It can be observed that with an increasing number of ports, there is an increase in the input buffers and the crossbar resources also increase. One of the motivations of just connecting the alternate nodes in the higher levels of the network was to reduce the number of high port routers. For the proposed algorithms, the one bit adapt field implemented in the header is used to indicate if the packet is critical or not, and the packet is forwarded accordingly.

7   Results and Analysis

The routers are designed using System Verilog and results are generated using HDL simulator Modelsim. We present the results on a 5×5 three layer NoC. The results of the proposed congestion aware algorithm are compared against the popular XY routing, a modified XY routing for layered mesh and the static algorithm without congestion algorithm described in Sect. 4. A uniform random traffic is generated to test the algorithms. In this traffic case, each node has equal

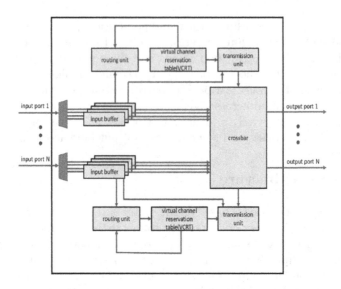

Fig. 5. Architecture of the used router

probability to send packets to every other node. Thus all pairs of source destination pairs are considered here. The packet length is also varied to show the
influence on congestion and how the proposed algorithm with congestion avoidance performs better with increasing packet length. We use an FPGA platform
to obtain resource utilization for the approach.

A summary of the algorithms used is shown below:

– XY Routing: Traditional XY Routing utilizing only 2D mesh (only the base
  5×5 layer)
– Layered XY routing: Modified version of the XY routing which functions as
  follows. If the source and destination nodes are on the same layer then XY
  routing is used to transport the packet using the routers on same layer. For
  example if the source and destination nodes are on a Layer 2, then a packet
  is transported only on routers on layer 2. If the source and destination belong
  to different layers, regular XY routing is used utilizing only routers on the
  base layer.
– Near Node Function without Congestion Avoidance (NN without CA)
– Near Node Function using Congestion Avoidance (NN with CA)

Throughput and latency results when the packet length is 10 is shown in
Figs. 8 and 9 respectively. With the integration of congestion avoidance there
is an improvement of upto 16% in throughput. For latency, the algorithm with
congestion avoidance has a decrease of upto 56% in latency compared to XY
routing and decrease in upto 29% in latency when compared against the algorithm without congestion avoidance. In this packet length, the throughput of
XY, Layer XY and NN are comparable. The NN algorithm, always transports

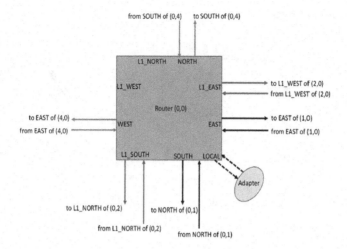

Fig. 6. Router at location (0, 0) showing all of the connected ports with indices

Fig. 7. Packet format as is used for the algorithm with congestion avoidance

packets on paths with the shortest hop counts. This can lead to creation of hotspots in the network which is eased by directing packets on longer hop paths when available. This results in increase in throughput of NN with CA algorithm when compared with the other algorithms with the increase in injection rate. With the increase in packet length, we can see in Figs. 10 and 11 the algorithm without CA increasingly performs better than traditional XY routing. There is an improvement in the results of the algorithm with congestion avoidance when compared with the rest.

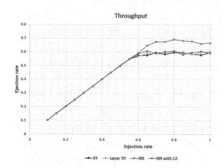

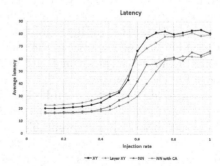

Fig. 8. Throughput   **Fig. 9.** Latency in cycles

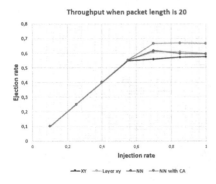

Fig. 10. Comparison of throughput

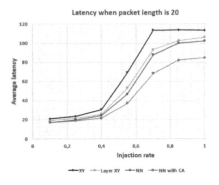

Fig. 11. Comparison of latency

The effect of packet length on latency is presented in detail by showing a comparison under different packet lengths in Fig. 12. It is seen that with increase in the injection rate, saturation value of the latency is lesser for the NN with CA. For packets of length 5 for example, the improvement is less when compared against longer packet lengths of 10 and 20 as is shown. With the presence of longer packets, number of occupied routers increases for a single packet thereby increasing the possibility of hotspot when there is a high injection rate. Using congestion avoidance the packets are more evenly distributed across layers. The packets are forwarded towards less frequently used paths (long hop) thereby decreasing overall latency.

An important drawback in such a multi-layered NoC implementation is resource utilization. The increase in different parts of the routers is discussed here, one is an increase of resources when routers of high port count are used and another is resource increase in the routing unit when adaptive routing is implemented. Resource utilization of a routing unit is presented in Table 1 for the different algorithms. Target Platform is Virtex-7 FPGA (7vx485tffg1761-2) and tool used is Xilinx Vivado 18.3. Resources utilized by the routing unit for different algorithms is shown and it can be seen that the proposed routing algorithm uses more resources, which is expected when compared with XY routing. Such a routing unit is present at each port of the router. Even with increase in complexity of the routing algorithm and the number of ports, the resources utilized by the routing units in the router is considerably lesser than rest of the router resources as shown in Fig. 13. The input buffers here occupy a major portion of the resources.

Multi-layered networks can be beneficial for large scale networks. For small scale networks and in situations where severe resources constraints are present, the proposed NoC is not profitable due to its high port count routers which occupy more resources than a router in a regular mesh topology. But with increasing number of tiles being utilized in SoC platforms, the network size

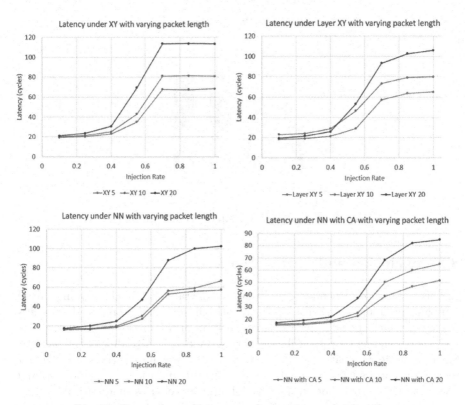

Fig. 12. Comparison of latency under varying packet lengths

growing, the presence of layers and adaptive algorithms can yield benefits as can be seen in terms of latency and throughput here. At the expense of fraction of more resources, the improvement seen in latency and throughput is profitable in such circumstances.

Table 1. Resource utilization of one routing unit. For comparison, percentage of resource consumed by one routing unit in a 5-port router is also shown.

Resource	XY (%)	LayerXY (%)	NN (%)	NN with CA (%)
Slice LUTs	6 (0.094%)	6 (0.094%)	93 (1.46%)	305 (4.8%)
Slice Reg	0	0	4 (0.1%)	4 (0.1%)

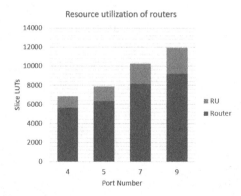

Fig. 13. Comparison of router resource utilization

8   Conclusion and Future Work

In this paper, we presented a multi-layered hierarchical NoC targeting mixed criticality systems with an adaptive algorithm. The NoC comprised of multiple layers which the adaptive routing algorithm utilized to evenly distribute the packets depending on the availability of the links and criticality of the packets. Since multiple applications of varying criticality are sharing the same communication resources like routers and links, critical applications are prioritized and assigned the shortest hop paths. In high traffic scenarios, non-critical packets are assigned paths with longer hop counts to decrease influence over critical packets. Thus decreasing the congestion scenarios for critical applications and improving overall performance. The algorithms were tested in random uniform traffic scenarios with multiple packet lengths. Improvements could be observed in latency and throughput. Even without congestion avoidance the proposed algorithm which utilizes multiple layers to reach the destination has upto 38% decrease in latency and with congestion avoidance has upto 56% decrease in latency compared to XY routing. When comparing algorithms which use different layers, the algorithm with congestion avoidance has upto 29% decrease in latency and 16% increase in throughput. Since the proposed routing algorithm utilizes upto 30% percentage of the router resources, such a network is more suitable for large scale NoCs which can benefit from the presence of multiple layers. For future work, for routers with high port counts, the possibility of clock gating for unused resources is planned to decrease power consumption.

Acknowledgements. This work was funded by the Deutsche Forschungsgemeinschaft (DFG, German Research Foundation) - project number 146371743 - TRR 89: Invasive Computing.

References

1. Burns, A., Davis, R.I.: A survey of research into mixed criticality systems. ACM Comput. Surv. **50**, 6 (2017). Article 82 (January 2018), 37 pages
2. Benini, L., Micheli, G.D.: Networks on chips: a new SOC paradigm. Computer **35**, 70–78 (2002)
3. Lankes, A., Wild, T., Herkersdorf, A.: Hierarchical NoCs for optimized access to shared memory and IO resources. In: 2009 12th Euromicro Conference on Digital System Design, Architectures, Methods and Tools, Patras, Greece, pp. 255–262 (2009)
4. Hollis, S.J., Jackson, C.: Skip the analysis: self-optimising networks-on-chip (Invited Paper). In: 2010 International Symposium on Electronic System Design, Bhubaneswar, India, pp. 14–19 (2010)
5. Hollis, S.J., Jackson, C., Bogdan, P., Marculescu, R.: Exploiting emergence in on-chip interconnects. IEEE Trans. Comput. **63**(3), 570–582 (2014). https://doi.org/ 10.1109/TC.2012.273
6. Tobuschat, S., Ernst, R.: Providing throughput guarantees in mixed-criticality networks-on-chip. In: 2017 30th IEEE International System-on-Chip Conference (SOCC), Munich, pp. 292–297 (2017)
7. Heisswolf, J., Bischof, S., Rückauer, M., Becker, J.: Efficient memory access in 2D Mesh NoC architectures using high bandwidth routers. In: 2013 26th Symposium on Integrated Circuits and Systems Design (SBCCI), Curitiba, Brazil, pp. 1–6 (2013)
8. Avramenko, S., et al.: QoSinNoC: analysis of QoS-aware NoC architectures for mixed-criticality applications. In: 2018 IEEE 21st International Symposium on Design and Diagnostics of Electronic Circuits & Systems (DDECS), Budapest, pp. 67–72 (2018)
9. Maleki, A., Ahmadian, H., Obermaisser, R.: Fault-tolerant and energy-efficient communication in mixed-criticality networks-on-chips. In: 2018 IEEE Nordic Circuits and Systems Conference (NORCAS): NORCHIP and International Symposium of System-on-Chip (SoC), Tallinn, pp. 1–7 (2018)
10. Dridi, M., Rubini, S., Lallali, M., Flórez, M.J.S., Singhoff, F., Diguet, J.-P.: Design and Multi-Abstraction-Level Evaluation of a NoC Router for Mixed-Criticality Real-Time Systems. J. Emerg. Technol. Comput. Syst. 15, 1 (2019). Article 2 (February 2019), 37 pages

PDU Normalizer Engine for Heterogeneous In-Vehicle Networks in Automotive Gateways

Angela Gonzalez Mariño[1]([✉]), Francesc Fons[1], Li Ming[1],
and Juan Manuel Moreno Arostegui[2]

[1] Huawei Technologies Duesseldorf Gmbh, Munich, Germany
{angela.gonzalez.marino,francesc.fons,li.ming}@huawei.com
[2] Technical University of Catalunya, Barcelona, Spain
joan.manuel.moreno@upc.edu

Abstract. In this work, authors propose the concept of Protocol Data Unit (PDU) normalization for heterogeneous In-Vehicle Networks (IVN) in automotive gateways (GW). Through the development of the so-called PDU Normalizer Engine (PDUNE), it is possible to create a novel protocol-agnostic frame abstraction layer for PDU and signal gatewaying functions. It consists of normalizing the format of the frames present in the GW ingress ports of any kind (e.g. CAN, LIN, FlexRay or Ethernet). That is, the PDUNE transforms the ingress frames into new refactored frames which are independent of their original network protocol, and this occurs in an early stage before being processed across the different stages of the GW controller till reaching the egress ports, optimizing thus not only the processing itself but also the resources and latencies involved. The hardware (HW) implementation of the PDUNE exploits Software Defined Networking (SDN) architectural concepts by decomposing each ingress frame in two streams: a data frame moving across the data plane and an instruction frame provided with all the necessary metadata that –in parallel and synchronously to the data frame– evolves through the different processing stages of the GW controller performed directly in HW from the control plane. The PDUNE has been synthesized as a coarse-grain configurable HW accelerator (HWA) or co-processor attachable to the system CPU of the GW controller, aimed at contributing towards future automotive zonal GW solutions targeting heterogeneous IVNs with stringent real-time routing and tunneling functional constraints.

Keywords: In-Vehicle Network · Gateway · Protocol Data Unit · Frame normalization · HW Accelerator · Software Defined Networking

1 Introduction

Today's automotive In-Vehicle Networks (IVNs) integrate many different technologies and communication protocols. Although Ethernet is becoming more and more used for IVNs, this heterogeneity will continue to exist in the following years due to two main factors [1]. The first one is backward compatibility, since sensors and actuators in the market today use legacy buses such as CAN, LIN or FlexRay as interface and will

© Springer Nature Switzerland AG 2021
S. Derrien et al. (Eds.): ARC 2021, LNCS 12700, pp. 140–155, 2021.
https://doi.org/10.1007/978-3-030-79025-7_10

continue to do so in the near future. Introduction of new technologies will be gradual, so the coexistence of legacy and new technologies is mandatory. The second one is the fact that there is no alternative that can cover all the use cases of IVNs. Nowadays, the universal bus covering from high-speed to low-speed at a reasonable cost does not exist. Therefore, in future automotive platforms, there is a need to efficiently handle this heterogeneity and, as in existing architectures, the component that enables the translation between different protocols is the Gateway (GW).

Current state-of-the-art GWs are micro-controller (MCU) based software (SW) centric solutions, mainly following the AUTOSAR standard software architecture (Fig. 1 [2]), but this is not enough to support future IVN requirements. Timing and safety requirements make hardware (HW) implementations – in the way of new hardware accelerators (HWA) or peripherals seamlessly integrated into those MCUs or Network/System-on-Chip (NoC/SoC) devices – a need for many compute-intensive and time-consuming functionalities, and heterogeneous protocol handling is one of them. Therefore, there is a clear need to design HW and SW in combination in order to deploy the GW of the future. This HW/SW codesign enables a wide range of possibilities in terms of computation by designing specific HWA to offload the CPU of the GW controller and significantly increase the performance without a very high impact on cost.

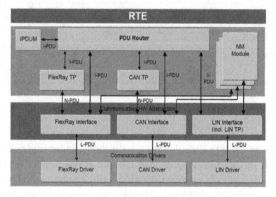

Fig. 1. AUTOSAR software architecture (Source: AUTOSAR)

The work described in this paper provides advances towards management of heterogeneity of protocols present in IVNs by designing a HWA or co-processor named PDUNE that allows to abstract the differences between communication protocols and adapt whatever network OSI layer 2 frame to internal processing, independently of its protocol. For the proposed HW co-processor, a Proof of Concept (PoC) has been developed and several tests have been conducted in order to determine advantages and disadvantages of the innovation proposed in this work.

The remainder of this paper is structured as follows. Section 2 provides an overview of the related art. In Sect. 3, we highlight the differentiation features of the newly proposed concept. Next, we describe the system architecture and low level design in Sect. 4. The developed PoC is presented in Sect. 5 and afterwards the experimental results obtained are exposed in Sect. 6. Finally, we conclude the work in Sect. 7.

2   Related Art

Today's automotive IVNs handle the technologies and communication protocols heterogeneity via SW, mainly following the AUTOSAR standard. As illustrated in Fig. 1, different protocols are handled with dedicated communication drivers and the differences between them are abstracted in SW within the micro-controller abstraction layer (MCAL) [3]. This abstraction addresses the most widely used IVN protocols in the automotive industry, i.e. LIN [4], CAN [5], CAN FD [6], FlexRay [7] and Automotive Ethernet [8]. When looking closely at these protocols, we realize that they share many characteristics. To start with, all of them are composed of a header, payload and tail, as depicted in Fig. 2. Additionally, all of them have some rules to determine frame integrity based on frame size and a specific field for error detection. These protocol characteristics are what the AUTOSAR SW stack exploits, providing an abstraction layer to extract the information embedded in the different frames coming from specific HW PHYs or transceivers for each protocol. Authors in [9] also exploit these protocol characteristics and provide a Software Defined Networking framework for interoperability.

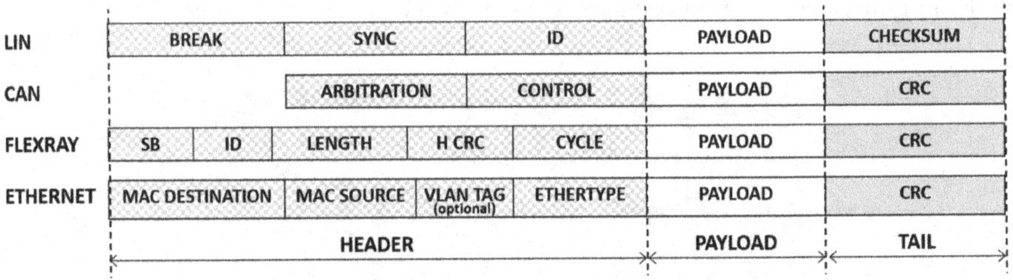

LIN	BREAK	SYNC		ID	PAYLOAD	CHECKSUM
CAN		ARBITRATION		CONTROL	PAYLOAD	CRC
FLEXRAY	SB	ID	LENGTH	H CRC	CYCLE	PAYLOAD	CRC
ETHERNET	MAC DESTINATION	MAC SOURCE	VLAN TAG (optional)	ETHERTYPE	PAYLOAD	CRC
	HEADER				PAYLOAD	TAIL

Fig. 2. IVN protocols frame format

As explained above, most state-of-the-art solutions handle this network heterogeneity via SW although in the most recent years, some HWA specialized in one network protocol have been introduced. As examples of the most advanced HW network processors in the market, there are the Enhanced Data Engine concept from Bosch [10, 11], and the S32G Vehicle Network Processor from NXP [12], where we see that they include HW communication controllers for each protocol (e.g. CAN or LIN). However, these controllers are independent, disconnected from each other, and the management of different protocols still happens at SW level. For the NXP Vehicle Network Processor, we show the architecture block diagram as a reference of the most novel HW architecture in the state of the art. As seen in Fig. 3, the proposal to provide support for heterogeneous IVN communication protocols is to include one dedicated HW controller per interface. Note that in this architecture there are separate controllers for Ethernet, CAN, FlexRay, LIN, etc. Regarding this topic, the "COPA" framework presented by Intel [13] supports the tendency towards using HWA for network processing. However, as the previous examples, it is focused on one single network protocol.

It is within this landscape that we identify the gap of heterogeneous network protocol management in HW. Our proposal is to communalize the HW needed to process all the communication protocols in one single architecture that can abstract the differences between protocols by providing the required configuration parameters. This proposal is based on the fact that differences between protocols (at OSI model layer 2) from a structural perspective are mainly a matter of size, adjacent bit fields and how the frame integrity must be calculated (refer to Fig. 2). These differences can be abstracted by configuration parameters determining which rules must be applied to calculate frame integrity. From a functional perspective, the differences are based on what information is stored where, but this can be abstracted as well. To the best of the authors' knowledge, such a HW solution does not exist in today's related art and this represents the main contribution of the research pursued in this work.

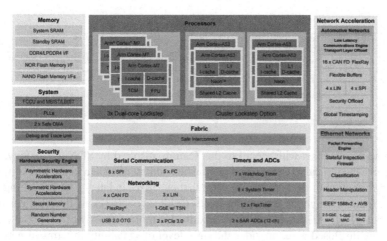

Fig. 3. SG32 block diagram (Source: NXP)

3 Differentiation and New Features

In this paper, we present PDUNE, a PDU Normalizer Engine for heterogeneous in-vehicle networks in automotive GWs, which is an innovative protocol-agnostic frame abstraction layer for PDU and signal gatewaying functions. In essence, it is a HWA that permits to manage the heterogeneity present in automotive networks via configuration registers written by the system CPU to achieve thus a single and common frame processing path along the GW controller for any ingress frame, independently of the nature or network type of its ingress port. By defining the correct level of granularity required for this application, it is possible to select the configuration parameters needed to achieve the protocol agnostic processing. This provides a new level of abstraction for handling heterogeneous networks while reducing system complexity. As a secondary objective, PDUNE maximizes QoS and usability of resources by optimizing the frame normalization concept and providing a common HW architecture to process any type of frame protocol at OSI layer 2 or higher.

The generic architecture of a GW consists of an ingress stage, a processing stage and an egress stage, where the ingress stage accommodates the frame to the internal architecture, the processing stage performs the processing required for the specific frame, and the egress stage shapes the output traffic according to specific rules. Figure 4 depicts the described High Level Design (HLD) of a GW controller. As seen in this block diagram, PDUNE is covering the frame normalization stage within the ingress stage. One of the novelties introduced at system level is the transport of an internal instruction or metadata in parallel with the data frame itself in order to encode the information needed in other GW stages to process such data frame.

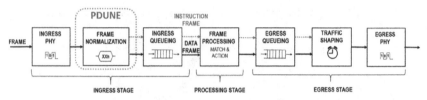

Fig. 4. Gateway diagram architecture (HLD)

The approach taken with regard to this feature, inspired by SDN technology, aims to minimize the typical overhead generated when adding metadata in the way of further header information of the data frame, a fact that penalizes in latency when shifting such resultant frame through the processing stages inside any networking device (i.e. switch, router or gateway). All these aspects are described in more detail in Sect. 3.1. The system architecture disclosed here, provides the right level of scalability in terms of networks and ports and defines an open and extendable instruction set able to encode any kind of frame processing function needed in next-generation automotive GWs. In this sense, this work aims at contributing to the standardization of network-agnostic frame processing and interfacing. The architecture of PDUNE disclosed in this paper is currently patent pending.

3.1 Software Defined Networking Approach

Traditional frame normalization consists of adding a new layer to transmission protocols by inserting a new header and a new tail that embed the required metadata for normalization purposes. While this approach allows reusing the original transmission media by adding coders/decoders in a layered manner, it affects the frame transmission latency by increasing the amount of data to be transmitted. Designing our PDUNE HWA from scratch gives the opportunity to rethink this model and optimize it for the specific GW architecture in which PDUNE is envisioned (Fig. 4). The optimization proposed in this work is to split the normalized frame into two buses, one being the original data frame bus, and a new one consisting of the generated metadata which constitutes the control bus. Following the SDN concept of separating data plane and control plane, we keep the data frame in the data plane, and introduce a new bus in the control plane to transport the information or related metadata needed across the gateway in order to process that data frame going through the data plane. This information is transported in parallel, at frame rate, adding zero latency to the frame internal transport.

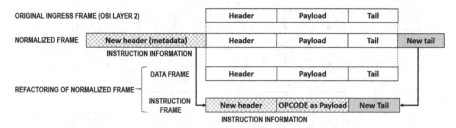

Fig. 5. SDN-based optimization of frame normalization

The new control bus is conceived as a frame of a new protocol in itself, with its own header, payload and tail. The header consists of information related to the frame that might be necessary across different stages of the architecture while the payload consists of information, which is specifically sent from one stage to the next one. Finally, the tail introduces an integrity check to the control frame itself to guarantee robustness in the transport. This approach is graphically illustrated in Fig. 5.

Since PDUNE is the first functional block within the full GW architecture, it is where this control bus is originated, creating the native GW instruction frame. At this stage, the header is composed of information related to the ingress port and fields related to the frame processing are initialized with default values. It will be afterwards, when going through the GW that these fields will be updated accordingly to the frame processing result (e.g. frames of a given port start with a default priority, and this will be updated after performing match and action over the frame in order to determine the priority that corresponds to that specific frame). The introduction of this native GW instruction frame, allows not only to process different types of protocols, but also to simplify the gateway design by providing a common format for frame processing across the different gateway stages (see Fig. 4).

4   System Architecture and Design

In this section, the architecture of PDUNE is described in detail. First, an overview of the main blocks that compose PDUNE and its interfaces is presented. Second, control plane functional blocks are described, covering the main aspects of the system configuration and the generation of the instruction frame. Finally, the data plane architecture is described as well.

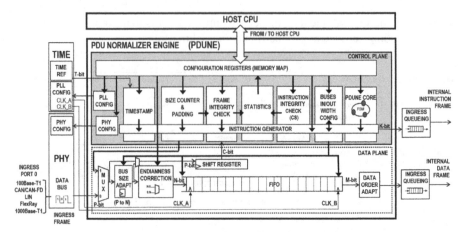

Fig. 6. High level PDUNE block diagram

As described in the previous section, PDUNE is located within the ingress stage of a GW, in between the physical layer (PHY) and the ingress queueing (refer to Fig. 4). The block diagram in Fig. 6 shows the internal architecture of PDUNE together with its external interfaces. A division between control plane and data plane is shown in this diagram on the first level. Then, internal blocks of both the control plane and the data plane are depicted on the second level. The details of both the control plane and the data plane internal blocks are explained later in this section. With regard to interfaces, apart from the ones which are also depicted in Fig. 4, corresponding to the PHY and ingress queueing, there are two more interfaces: one is the interface connecting PDUNE to the system CPU that is used for control and monitoring, and the other one is the interface with the system clock, which is connected to both the control plane and the data plane to provide independent timing control in each block.

4.1 Control Plane Architecture

The control plane consists of a set of configuration registers in the form of a memory map accessible by the system CPU in order to configure PDUNE parameters and collect performance information at run-time, together with several functional blocks that allow to compose the instruction frame and to accommodate the data path to the configured protocol. There is also a Finite State Machine (FSM) that acts as flow controller, orchestrating the operation of the independent blocks and determining when the instruction and data frames must be sent out. At PDUNE level, only the structural differences across protocols need to be taken into account (Fig. 2), and the information related to the protocol itself can be embedded in the instruction frame in order to be known and used by the following GW processing stages. Of course, something that cannot be standardized across protocols is the interface between layer 2 and layer 1 of OSI Model [14], since physical layer and transceiver configuration is absolutely protocol dependent. As an outcome of this analysis, the functional blocks that compose PDUNE control plane specified in Fig. 6, are described below:

- **PHY configuration:** As explained above, the PHY configuration is protocol dependent. This block is in charge of configuring the PHY transceiver according to protocol requirements that will be specified in the control plane memory map.
- **Phase Locked Loop (PLL) configuration:** One of the configuration parameters that are required by PDUNE is the capability to select operating frequency for data path interfaces (both input and output). Therefore, it is necessary to configure the external system PLL that is providing the clock according to the selected frequency.
- **Timestamp**: For internal processing, it is required to know in which moment a frame was received through the ingress port. For this, the timestamp of reception is sampled by this block making use of the information received via the timer interface.
- **Size counter and padding strategy**: both for frame integrity check and for internal frame processing, it is needed to know the size of the incoming frame. Therefore, this block counts the received data (in bytes or bits, depending on configuration) and accommodates the frame size to the internal architecture data buses by adding padding data when needed. Padding is not only inserted according to in/out data buses of PDUNE but also according to the whole system data buses used in order to avoid conflicts in later stages.
- **Frame integrity check**: As explained before, from a structural point of view, it is needed that PDUNE determines whether received frames are valid or not. This is done according to configuration parameters determining the acceptable minimum and maximum frame sizes, the result of the size counter module, and the selected integrity check algorithm to apply to the frame (e.g. CRC or checksum (CS)). One important aspect to take into account with regard to integrity check is the operation mode in which PDUNE is configured. GW processing usually performs according to two operation modes: store&forward or cut-through. In store&forward mode, first the frame is stored, then the integrity of the frame is checked, and finally if it is a good frame, it is transmitted. In cut-through mode, as soon as some portion of the frame is received, the transmission begins, without checking if it is a good one or not. With regard to this, PDUNE also provides the two options. When operating in store&forward mode, PDUNE stores the frame internally until it is fully received. While receiving the frame, it calculates the integrity check and, at the end, if the frame is good, it sends it to the next stage indicating in the instruction frame that this frame is correct. On the contrary, if the frame is bad, it sends the frame to the next stage as well, but indicating that this frame is incorrect and must be dropped. When operating in cut-through mode, PDUNE does not store the frame internally, it starts the transmission as soon as possible. In this case, the instruction indicates that the operation mode is cut-through.
- **Instruction generator**: the instruction frame explained in Fig. 5 is generated in parallel with the result of all blocks that intervene in its computation. The instruction format and how fields are configured/computed is depicted in Fig. 7. Note that the instruction described here has been defined for the specific use case of IVNs and the protocols required in them. However the PDUNE concept can be extended to support any other protocol and the instruction can be modified accordingly, in terms of format, number of fields, types and/or sizes, by redesigning the instruction generator.

  As seen in the figure, the instruction is composed of a six-field header, a payload and a tail. The information inserted in the header is information that will be needed by

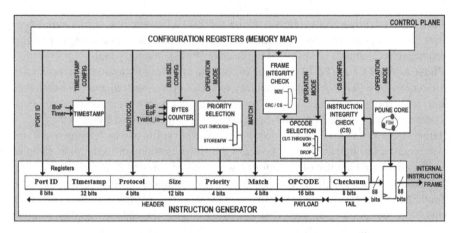

Fig. 7. Instruction generator block diagram and instruction frame format

later stages related to the frame or port configuration. Some fields in the header are configured directly by a register in the control plane memory map like both Port ID and Protocol fields. These fields are fixed for each configuration and need no computation. Other fields like Timestamp or Size are computed at run-time by the functional blocks described above. The priority field is fixed but dependent on the operation mode configuration (store&forward or cut-through). The Match field is used to indicate to the following processing stage if the frame matches any of the filtering rules, and if there are actions pending for the frame. Since it is not related to PDUNE but to later processing stages, at PDUNE level it is fixed to a value meaning "Pending Matching". The payload consists of an Operation Code (OPCODE) that indicates the next stage what action must be done with the frame. At PDUNE level, i.e. frame normalization stage of Fig. 4, there are only three possible OPCODEs: CUT-THROUGH, NOP (no operation) or DROP. The OPCODE is selected according to the operation mode of the port and the result of the frame integrity check. The processing stage overwrites OPCODE field with the corresponding instruction to the performed matching. Finally, the tail consists of the integrity check result for the instruction. PDUNE core FSM decides when to sample the instruction.

- **Instruction integrity check**: In order to guarantee the correct transmission of the instruction across the GW, an integrity check is appended in the tail. The instruction integrity check is calculated in parallel with the instruction register values adding no latency to the frame generation. The algorithm used is the 8-bits CS.
- **PDUNE core FSM**: The core FSM provides flow control over PDUNE operation. It detects Begin of Frame (BoF) and End of Frame (EoF) and provides information to control plane and data plane on when to send out both the data frame and the instruction frame. According to the operation mode (store&forward or cut-through) the flow will be different. For cut-through it will be right at the beginning (size won't be updated, but it must still be calculated for padding generation). For store&forward, instruction will be sampled after receiving the complete frame, and the correct frame size will

be embedded in instruction. A small pseudo code summarizing the functionality of PDUNE core is shown next.

```
switch(OPERATION_MODE):
    case(STORE_AND_FORWARD):
        if(EoF=1) then
            INSTRUCTION_FRAME_OUT<=INSTRUCTION_FRAME;
            FIFO_READ_EN<=not(FIFO_EMPTY);
        elsif (FIFO_READ_EN=1) then
            FIFO_READ_EN<=not(FIFO_EMPTY);
        else
            FIFO_READ_EN<=0;
        end if;
    break;
    case(CUT_THROUGH):
        INSTRUCTION_FRAME_OUT<=INSTRUCTION_FRAME;
        FIFO_READ_EN<=not(FIFO_EMPTY);
    break;
```

Code 1. PDUNE core FSM

- **Control plane memory map**: Since PDUNE is designed as a HWA attached to the system CPU, its configuration registers are part of the system memory map. Thus, the access by the CPU would be done as in a regular CPU peripheral, by assigning PDUNE a base address and using an offset address to access each specific register, i.e. REGISTER_ADDRESS = BASE_ADDRESS + OFFSET_ADDRESS. The definition of PDUNE memory map is exposed in Table 1, using 16-bit registers as a valid size to distribute all the parameters defined. All configuration registers are writable by the CPU while statistics registers are readable and resettable from CPU.
- **Statistics**: The statistics block collects information on how many frames have been received, how many of them are correct, etc. It also collects information about the generated instructions and provides information to the CPU about the link status.

Table 1. PDUNE memory map

Offset	Reg. Name	Function	Offset	Reg. Name	Function
0x1X	INTERFACES CONFIGURATION		0x2X	PORT CONFIGURATION	
0x10	DATA_BUS_WIDTH	Data bus width (in/out)	0x20	PORT_CONFIG	Port parameters
0x12	CTRL_BUS_WIDTH	Control bus width (in/out)	0x22	OPERATION_MODE	Operation mode & priority
0x14	TIMESTAMP_WIDTH	Input Timer bus width	0x4X	INSTRUCTION FIELDS CONFIGURATION	
0x16	FIFO_BUS_WIDTH	FIFO buses width (R/W)	0x40	INST_FIELD_SIZE0	Size of Port ID & Protocol
0x18	GCD_SBUS_WIDTH	System bus width (Greatest Common Divisor)	0x42	INST_FIELD_SIZE1	Size of Priority & Matching
0x3x	STATISTICS		0x44	INST_FIELD_SIZE2	Size of OPCODE and CS
0x30	LINK_STATUS	Link status information	0x46	DEF_OPCODE	Default instr. OPCODE
0x32	RX_COUNT	Received frames count	0x48	DROP_OPCODE	OPCODE for a frame drop
0x34	DROP_COUNT	Invalid received frames count	0x4A	SIZE_COUNT	Data size count parameters
0x36	INST_COUNT	Generated instructions count	0x4C	PADDING	Padding pattern
0X38	INST_FAIL_COUNT	Invalid instructions count	0x4E	MATCH	Match counter
0x5X	PHY INTERFACE CONFIGURATION		0x6X	FRAME INTEGRITY CHECK CONFIGURATION	
0x5X	RESERVED	HW dependent	0x60	INTEGRITY_CHECK	Integrity check method

4.2 Data Plane Architecture

As depicted in Fig. 6, the data plane consists mainly of a First-In First-Out (FIFO) memory and several functional blocks that accommodate the input frame to the internal data path. The PDUNE data plane functional blocks –which are configured by the control plane according to the memory map detailed above– are described below:

- **Padding Multiplexer**: At PDUNE data plane input a multiplexer allows to add the required padding data according to the padding strategy managed by control plane.
- **Bus size adapter**: Each PHY delivers input data in different manners, and with a different bus data width. This block adapts the input size to the size selected to store the frame in the internal FIFO configured by control plane.
- **Shift register for Frame Integrity Check calculation**: Each protocol computes an integrity check not only with a different algorithm, but also over a different amount of data. This block adapts the input data bus width to the width needed for frame integrity check calculation. The parameters required for this adaptation are configured by the control plane. Note that if the width needed for this calculation is the same as the internal FIFO write interface width, this block is not needed, and bus size adapter output can be directly connected to the Frame Integrity Check block.
- **Endianness correction**: Each protocol might deliver input data with different endianness, therefore, it is needed to have the option to adapt to the internal convention. After bus size adaptation, input frame goes through the Endianness correction block, which adapts data endianness according to the configuration set by the control plane.
- **FIFO memory**: The core of the data plane is the internal FIFO memory that allows storing the frame while the control plane is making the decision of when to send it out, and building the instruction frame. Input/output data bus width is configured by control plane and each interface can run with different clock domains.
- **Data order adapter**: Finally, depending on the FIFO in/out bus width configuration data might need reordering. This reordering is provided by the data order adapter block which is also configured by the control plane to deliver data in the adequate order for the internal architecture application.

5 Proof of Concept

In order to test and validate the PDUNE concept proposed in this work, a HW implementation with Hardware Description Language (HDL) has been developed and simulation tests have been performed. The target platform for the design is the Xilinx Zynq UltraScale+ MPSoC XCZU19EG [15].

The key concept behind PDUNE is the HW reconfiguration capability to normalize any network protocol using the pre-defined configuration registers. Therefore, the test consists in several use cases, using different protocols and configuration options (operation mode, data bus sizes, etc.) in order to prove that all of them are possible with the same underlying hardware, and that performance is not affected.

As seen in Fig. 8, for each of the use cases, an external stimulus is generated according to the use case configuration, and the obtained normalized frame (internal instruction +

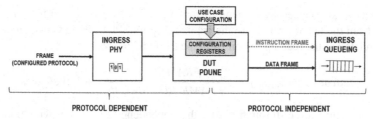

Fig. 8. PoC system architecture

data frames) is analyzed. In order to verify performance and flexibility of PDUNE, several realistic use cases are selected for validation.

Two of the most widely used protocols are selected, Ethernet and CAN, and both of them are tested in different operation modes (cut-through or store&forward) with different frame sizes, in order to see the impact in performance of the different design parameters. Other design parameters are fixed across experiments in order to be able to properly evaluate and compare results. In Table 2, the specific configuration of PDUNE memory map (see Table 1) used in our tests is presented.

Table 2. PoC PDUNE registers configuration

Register Name	Configuration in PoC	Register Name	Configuration in PoC
INTERFACES CONFIGURATION		PORT CONFIGURATION	
DATA_BUS_WIDTH	Input: ETH 4 bits / CAN 1 bit Output: 8/32 bits	PORT_CONFIG	Port ID: 0 Protocol: ETH / CAN
CTRL_BUS_WIDTH	96 bits	OPERATION_MODE	CUT-THROUGH / STORE&FORWARD
FIFO_BUS_WIDTH	FIFO input bus: 8 bits FIFO output bus: 8/32 bits	INSTRUCTION FIELDS CONFIGURATION *Instruction configured according to instruction format proposed in this work. See **Fig. 7.**	
TIMESTAMP_WIDTH	32 bits	FRAME INTEGRITY CHECK CONFIGURATION	
GCD_SBUS_WIDTH	96 bits	INTEGRITY_CHECK	Checksum

In this PoC, FIFO size is fixed at 2048 bytes because this allows accommodating the maximum frame size of the considered protocols. The number of positions in the FIFO is adjusted internally depending on configured FIFO input bus size.

Finally, the main metrics used to evaluate the performance of PDUNE are:

- **Latency**: One critical aspect of switching and gatewaying devices is the end to end latency. Therefore, it is also a key metric of PDUNE as one common step of the gatewaying path for every single ingress frame in the GW. Latency is measured as the difference between begin of frame reception in PDUNE input, and begin of frame transmission in PDUNE output. Like this, when analyzing the latency introduced by PDUNE we identify two differentiated performance modes, related to the operation mode selected. When operating in store&forward mode, latency is impacted by the frame size, and therefore unpredictable between consequent frames. This is inherent to store&forward operation mode where a frame must be received completely before continuing to traverse the system in order to check its consistency. Equation 1 describes the latency experienced by a frame traversing PDUNE in store and forward mode. Apart from the latency related to the frame reception, PDUNE adds one clock cycle delay related to the read operation from the FIFO memory.

$$Latency_{Store\&Forward} = \lceil \frac{FRAME\ SIZE}{FRAME\ BUS\ SIZE\ IN} \rceil + 1 \text{ clk cycles} \qquad (1)$$

When operating in cut-through mode, the dependency of latency with frame size disappears, since frames are transmitted as soon as possible. Equation 2 describes latency experienced by a frame traversing PDUNE in cut-through mode. In this case, latency is constant (hence, predictable) among frames of different sizes and depends on the relationship between in/out interface sizes. An additional clock cycle related to the read operation from FIFO memory is present as in the previous case.

$$Latency_{Cut-Through} = \lceil \frac{FRAME\ BUS\ SIZE\ OUT}{FRAME\ BUS\ SIZE\ IN} \rceil + 1 \text{ clk cycles} \qquad (2)$$

Note that because of PDUNE architecture, latency is protocol independent and no other parameters than the ones mentioned affect latency of frames across PDUNE.

- **HW resources**: In order to evaluate the cost in terms of silicon area of the proposed HWA, the HW resources required in our PoC are exposed for the different use cases.

6   Experimental Results

In this section, a summary of the results obtained with the PoC is exposed and the performance according to the relevant metrics defined in Sect. 5 is evaluated. Table 3 shows the latency measurements obtained for all use cases both in clk cycles and nanoseconds. Note that frame size refers to the full frame size, not only payload. The experiments were run with a base clk period of 6 ns since this allows to process data coming from a 1Gbit Ethernet transceiver. For simplicity, the same clk frequency is used in the CAN use case. As seen in Table 3, simulation results correlate with the expected theoretical values (Eqs. 1 and 2).

With the objective of providing a better understanding of PDUNE performance, Fig. 9 depicts the test results for Ethernet use cases. The difference in behavior between store& forward and cut-through can be observed (the first one waiting for the full frame before starting transmission, and the second one starting as soon as possible). Also, the impact of different bus sizes in PDUNE output is shown in the same Figure.

For instance, the store&forward mode when going from 4 bits input data bus to 32 bits output data bus is able to transport the full frame in a shorter time than it is received due to higher output bus bandwidth (note that Tvalid out is shorter in time than Tvalid in for this use case). This does not impact latency in PDUNE itself, but allows to speed up the transport of the frame internally across the other gatewaying stages (see Fig. 4), improving the overall system latency.

Table 3. Experiment results - latency

PROTOCOL	BUS SIZE (bits)		OPERATION MODE	FRAME SIZE	LATENCY (clk cycles)	LATENCY (ns)
	In	Out				
ETH	4	8	STORE&FORWARD	86 Bytes	173	1038
ETH	4	8	CUT-THROUGH	86 Bytes	3	18
ETH	4	32	STORE&FORWARD	86 Bytes	173	1038
ETH	4	32	CUT-THROUGH	86 Bytes	9	54
ETH	4	32	STORE&FORWARD	1522 Bytes	3045	18270
ETH	4	32	CUT-THROUGH	1522 Bytes	9	54
CAN	1	8	STORE&FORWARD	96 bits	97	582
CAN	1	8	CUT-THROUGH	96 bits	9	54
CAN	1	32	STORE&FORWARD	96 bits	97	582
CAN	1	32	CUT-THROUGH	96 bits	33	198

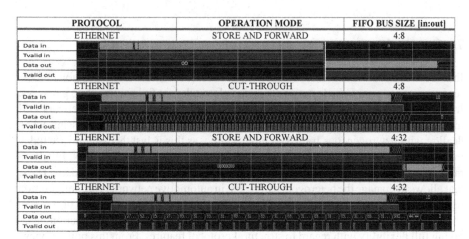

Fig. 9. Experiment results – simulation waveforms (Ethernet use case)

The cut-through operation in that same configuration starts transmission after 9 clk cycles (32/4 + 1 (Eq. 2)), but it is not continuous because input rate is lower than output rate (note that Tvalid out is not asserted continuously). Therefore the output interface clock (CLK_B in Fig. 6) can be reduced by a factor of 8 (output width/input width) and not impact the system latency, achieving benefits associated with clk frequency reduction e.g. lower power consumption or lower silicon heating. In Table 4 a summary of the HW resources used by PDUNE implementation is presented. Results are given in absolute numbers in order to assess the impact of PDUNE integration in a GW chipset design. As it can be seen from the table, HW resources used by PDUNE are very little, meaning that the integration of this new HWA in a full GW controller design using the target platform [15] will not have a big impact on the full system design. Note that in all use cases, total BRAM used is half a BRAM tile. This is due to the fact that the amount of memory used by PDUNE is fixed at 2048 bytes, which is half of the minimum BRAM tile in UltraScale + devices (4kB). Also note that both in Ethernet and CAN use cases, when going from 8 to 32 bits output bus, CLB LUTs and CLB REGs used are reduced. This is due to the fact that internal BRAM blocks in UltraScale + devices (BRAMB18E2 primitive [16]) use 32 bit wide positions. Therefore, when using a different data bus width, additional logic and registers are needed to perform the size adaptation.

Table 4. Experiments results – HW resources

PROTOCOL	BUS SIZE (bits)		HW RESOURCES		
	In	Out	BRAM kB	CLB LUTs	CLB REGs
ETH	4	8	2	300	313
ETH	4	32	2	296	309
CAN	1	8	2	291	293
CAN	1	32	2	282	289

7   Conclusions

In this work, authors disclose the new PDUNE conception, a new normalization process for heterogeneous in-vehicle networks with a clear relevant fit in automotive gateways. It consists of a new abstraction layer similar and fully compatible with the network OSI model but intended to provide protocol agnostic frame gatewaying processing when dealing with heterogeneous frames as input source, as this is just the natural case today in automotive IVN field where legacy network technologies (e.g. LIN, CAN, FlexRay) must coexist with new ones (e.g. Ethernet, PCIe, MIPI). PDUNE is conceived as a HWA that allows to manage the heterogeneity present in automotive networks via configuration registers written by the system CPU, all integrated into the NoC/SoC device of our GW controller. We defined the set of parameters that allow providing this abstraction layer, giving full flexibility with regard to structural protocol features. From this point of view, PDUNE keeps all protocol definition parameters configurable and sizeable.

We developed a PoC in order to validate the fact that it is possible to achieve such intended abstraction layer driven by coarse-grain configurable parameters that allow the system to extract the frame information required for gatewaying processing independently of the input frame protocol, and successfully proved the viability of this concept. From our results, we can realize that this new normalization concept is fully scalable and not limited by latency, allowing to keep performance always under control and compliant, moreover, with SDN. As shown in the experimental results, PDUNE introduces only 1 additional clock cycle in terms of latency when comparing to normal gatewaying frame reception latency. We also presented the number of resources needed to implement the new HWA, considering this very useful information to estimate the cost and viability of porting this normalization concept to the next generation of NoC/SoC devices of future zonal GW controllers to be plugged into the autonomous, connected, electric and shared vehicles of tomorrow.

References

1. Zeng, W., Khalid, M.A., Chowdhury, S.: In-vehicle networks outlook: achievements and challenges. IEEE Commun. Surv. Tutor. **18**(3), 1552–1571 (2016)
2. AUTOSAR. Layered Software architecture (2017). https://www.autosar.org/fileadmin/user_u pload/standards/classic/4-3/AUTOSAR_EXP_LayeredSoftwareArchitecture.pdf
3. Gosda, J.: AUTOSAR - Communication stack. AUTOSAR (2009). https://hpi.de/fileadmin/ user_upload/fachgebiete/giese/Ausarbeitungen_AUTOSAR0809/CommunicationStack_ gosda.pdf
4. LIN Consortium. LIN Specification Package - Revision 2.2A (2010). https://www.cs-group. de/wp-content/uploads/2016/11/LIN_Specification_Package_2.2A.pdf
5. International Organization for Standardization (ISO). ISO 11898 - Road vehicles - Controller Area Network (CAN) (2015). https://www.iso.org/standard/63648.html
6. BOSCH Gmbh. CAN with Flexible Data-Rate - Specification version 1.0 (2012). https:// web.archive.org/web/20151211125301/http://www.bosch-semiconductors.de/media/ubk_ semiconductors/pdf_1/canliteratur/can_fd_spec.pdf
7. FlexRay consortium. FlexRay Communications System - Protocol Specification version 3.0.1 (2010). https://svn.ipd.kit.edu/nlrp/public/FlexRay/FlexRay%E2%84%A2%20P rotocol%20Specification%20Version%203.0.1.pdf
8. OPEN Alliance. Automotive Ethernet Specifications. http://opensig.org/about/specifications/
9. Halba, K., Mahmoudi, C.: National Institute of Standards and Technology. Gaithersburg, Maryland, USA. In-Vehicle Software Defined Networking: An Enabler for Data Interoperability, Lakeland (2018)
10. Dr. Andreas Lock, Robert Bosch Gmbh. Trends for future in-vehicle communication (2020)
11. Crepin, B.T.J.: Intelligente Hardware beschleunigt Ethernet - Data Engine für schnelle Ethernet-Architekturen im Fahrzeug. Automobil Elektronik, no. 4 (2013)
12. NXP. S32G safe and secure vehicle network processors (2020). https://www.nxp.com/docs/ en/fact-sheet/S32G-VEHICLE-NW-FS.pdf
13. Krishnan, V., Serres, O., Blocksome, M.: Intel Corporation. Configurable Network Protocol Accelerator (2021)
14. International Organization for Standardization (ISO). ISO-IEC 7498 - Information technology — Open Systems Interconnection — Basic Reference Model (1994). https://www.iso.org/sta ndard/20269.html
15. Xilinx.DS891-zynq-ultrascale-plus-overview. https://www.xilinx.com/support/documenta tion/data_sheets/ds891-zynq-ultrascale-plus-overview.pdf
16. Xilinx. UG573 - UltraScale Architecture Memory Resources User Guide (2020). https://www. xilinx.com/support/documentation/user_guides/ug573-ultrascale-memory-resources.pdf

StreamGrid - An AXI-Stream-Compliant Overlay Architecture

Christopher Blochwitz[1]([✉]), León Philipp[1], Mladen Berekovic[1],
and Thilo Pionteck[2]

[1] University of Lübeck, Lübeck, Germany
{blochwitz,berekovic}@iti.uni-luebeck.de
[2] Otto von Guericke University, Magdeburg, Germany
thilo.pionteck@ovgu.de

Abstract. FPGAs are part of a modern data-centre and are used as hardware accelerators, which allows to accelerate applications and adapting to the current compute requirements dynamically. Overlay architectures provide a flexible system, which enables the hardware accelerator to adapt its applications by exchanging (sub-)functions on run-time. Such overlay architectures usually consist of multiple run-time reconfigurable tiles. Multiple tiles can be connected to form an application-specific accelerator. In this paper, we present an AXI-Stream-compliant overlay architecture – called *StreamGrid* with advanced multi-stream routing architecture, memory (DDR4, HBM) access for the application, and a configuration and monitoring system. Furthermore, the impact of buffering strategies, grid-size, and data width of the AXI-Stream interface is explored in terms of resource utilization and the achievable clock frequency. The fastest configuration of the overlay architecture has a maximum clock frequency of 752 MHz on a Xilinx Alveo U280 FPGA Card. Furthermore, a case study of a database query engine is evaluated and compared to a static design with the same functionality. The raw execution performance is comparable for both design, but the set up times is now drastically reduced from several 10 min to less than 3 ms, efficiently enabling hardware-accelerated queries.

Keywords: AXI-Stream · FPGA · Data-flow graph · Overlay · Semantic web

1 Introduction

From IoT to the cloud: high performance for computational-intensive applications is achieved through the extensive use of parallelism as it is provided by FPGAs. In order for alternative hardware to become established in data centres, high computing power and power efficiency, as well as easy and fast programmability, are essential. Especially hardware designs for FPGAs have a long development time, and the synthesis of such a design often takes several hours. To accelerated this process, a lot of development work is currently being done on new methods that can efficiently map abstract descriptions into hardware. The best-known example is OpenCL, which can use massive parallelism of various computing devices such as CPUs, GPUs, or FPGAs. However, OpenCL synthesis does not fully exploit the computing capabilities of FPGAs, because they provide

© Springer Nature Switzerland AG 2021
S. Derrien et al. (Eds.): ARC 2021, LNCS 12700, pp. 156–170, 2021.
https://doi.org/10.1007/978-3-030-79025-7_11

a software-centric model, which calls single hardware-accelerated function-by-function on the FPGA [17]. For maximum application performance and simplified programming experience, so-called *overlay architectures* are used.

Overlay architectures are typically stream-centric: The idea behind these is to break down an application into its data-flow graph and map this graph onto interconnected functional units. Instead of synthesizing this data-flow graph and its corresponding functional units and interconnection, which would be as time-intense as conventional hardware design flow, instead, the FPGA resources are partitioned into a coarse-grained grid-like structure which can be dynamically configured in a modular fashion with functional units being supplied as pre-synthesized library elements. For the remainder of this paper, the following terminology will be used: A grid element is called reconfigurable partition (RP). A single grid holds the so-called functional unit (FU) and according to connection to neighbouring RPs. The entirety of all RPs, external communication interfaces (e.g. PCIe), memory controller, and communication & control API forms the overlay architecture.

The presented overlay architecture utilizes the AXI-Stream interface [1, 16], which belongs to the standard interfaces of ARM and Xilinx. The use of this interface enables fast integration of AXI-Stream-based FUs as intellectual property modules (e.g. Vivado IP Catalog), modules from high-level synthesis, or own RTL designs. The aim is maximum compatibility for as many applications as possible. For this purpose, we examined the influence of various design parameters (buffer-strategy, grid-size, and data width) of our overlay architecture concerning resource utilization and maximum clock frequency on a Xilinx Alveo U280 Card with a Virtex Ultrascale+ FPGA.

This paper is structured as follows: First, we give a short introduction to data-flow graphs and the induce for execution on an overlay architecture. Next, we provide an overview of the related work, focusing on overlay architectures at the application level. Third, we present our overlay architecture *StreamGrid* in detail and the possibilities for parameterization and configuration. Afterwards, we explore the design space of the system targeting resource utilization and clock frequency for the mentioned parameters. Finally, a case studies of an advanced DFG-based application – Semantic Web Query Engine – including a comparison to the original static design is shown.

1.1 Data-Flow Graph

In order to be applicable to overlay architectures, the to-be-accelerated application must be representable by a data-flow graph (DFG). In Fig. 1, is shown an example of a DFG, which consists of nodes and edges, with the nodes representing operators of an application or task. The directed edges representing the flow of data from node to node. The overlay architecture supports two types of operators: unary operators (blue node) (e.g. negation) and binary operators (red node) (e.g. add, mult).

DFGs are widely used in parallel processing such as Digital Signal Processing (DSP) [2] or streaming applications [5]. In the commercial area, Maxeler can be mentioned whose *MaxCompiler* identifies and analyzes data flows within the source code and then outputs a synthesized FPGA design [6]. Prabhaler et al. [10] present a programming model, which is able to map a DFG on an overlay architecture. The overlay architecture presented there is optimized to enable a high degree of parallelism and

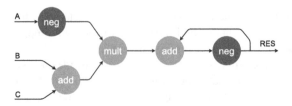

Fig. 1. Data-Flow Graph consisting of 5 nodes and directed edges. Unary nodes (blue) – 1 input-stream, binary nodes (red) – 2 input-streams. (Color figure online)

throughput by enabling the mapping of the entire DFG on the overlay architecture and allows both maximum data and pipeline parallelism.

2 Related Work

The *StreamGrid* overlay architecture addresses applications, which are compliant with the AXI-Stream interface. To the best of our knowledge, there is no work that supports the AXI-Stream interface, because most of the overlay architectures are developed for a specific application. Furthermore, the overlay architectures cannot be configured in such a flexible way as the presented one, because of the missing advanced routing mechanism and the degree of parameterization. In order to never the less allow a comparison to the state of the art, we hence focus on application-specific overlay architectures targeting stream-data processing. FPGA-on-FPGA architectures are not specifically covered for not addressing the application layer.

Capalija et al. [4] address applications that can be represented by a DFG. In contrast to our approach, the DFG is mapped in many elementary basic operations, such as add, sub, and so on. They present a 355 MHz 24 × 16 integer core and a 312 MHz 18 × 16 floating point core overlay architecture on an Altera Stratix IV FPGA, which have been tested with 15 different applications confirming the good performance of the architecture. Ma et al. present [7] a framework that enables software developers to compile HLS-functions on run-time and execute them on an FPGA. For this, an overlay architecture is used, which consisting of multiple partially reconfigurable areas and providing a network of FIFOs between them. The design is evaluated for different applications and shows that functional units of a high-level synthesis using the overlay architecture and framework can perform similar to pure hardware modules.

FLexi TASK [8] by Mbongue et al. introduces an overlay architecture that combines point-to-point communication between direct neighbours and a network-on-chip (NoC) architecture. Depending on the distance between two communication partners (PE), the direct connection (short distance), or the NoC (long-distance) is used. The authors test different applications on a 10 × 10 overlay architecture on an Altera Cyclone V FPGA and compare the execution time with the native execution time on an ARM Cortex A9. A maximum acceleration of 195× is achieved. The architecture used is suitable for task-based applications with one or two operands.

Mueller et al. [9], and Werner et al. [12] speed-up database queries by running them on an FPGA. For this, one large reconfigurable area on an FPGA is reserved, a hardware model of the query is created using macros and is synthesized. The synthesis takes between 20 and 30 min, depending on the query. The processing of the query on the FPGA is 31× faster than a software implementation. Werner et al. [13] introduce a second version in which several smaller reconfigurable areas were created and linked to a tree structure. Pre-synthesized FUs can now be combined and mapped on run-time.

Wilson et al. [14] present a recurrently generated Overlay Architecture for application development. They use High-Level Synthesis to compile the application into an intermediate representation and afterwards generates an overlay architecture, which fulfills the requirements of the application. The subsequent versions of the application than only has to be composed to the overlay architecture's tiles. If the application is not executable on the overlay architecture, a new version of the overlay architecture is generated. This accelerates the development process up to 100 000×.

3 *StreamGrid* – **An AXI-Stream-Compliant Overlay Architecture**

The *StreamGrid* overlay architecture is based on the AXI-Stream interface, which allows the use a wide range of IPs, HLS modules, and RTL designs. Furthermore, it implements an advanced routing mechanism enabling double/triple use of each tile. The grid size, buffer-strategy, and also data width for the AXI-Stream interfaces are parameterizable and are, therefore, adaptable to different FPGAs and use cases. The overlay has a rectangular structure with $n \times m$ tiles, each containing a functional unit (FU). A tile does not necessarily contain an FU, but can also be used to just forward or redirect data to one of its neighbours, which increases overall system flexibility. An FU is mapped to a reconfigurable partition (RP) and can be assigned by any pre-synthesized operator/function at run-time. By connecting multiple tiles, the DFG of the application is assembled.

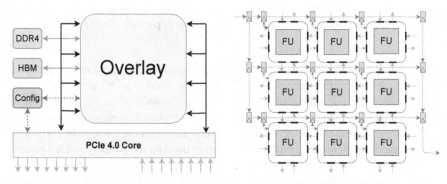

(a) System Overview – Overlay architecture (gray), memory subsystem (green) configuration system (red), and PCIe core (yellow).

(b) Overlay Architecture Grid of 3×3 – partial reconfigurable functional unit (FU) (blue), configuration network (red).

Fig. 2. Overview of the *StreamGrid* overlay architecture. (Color figure online)

3.1   Overlay-Grid

The design overview can be seen in Fig. 2a. It consists of the overlay, configuration and monitoring components, and a memory AXI4 based interconnect for the FUs. At the edge of the grid, AXI-Stream-compatible modules can be connected, which provide communication to other modules or a host system, in our case a PCIe 4.0 core [3]. The overlay architecture depicted in Fig. 2b. It consists of several identical tiles, placed next to each other. Each tile is connected to its direct neighbours at their edges, which is called a 4-neighbourhood. Each communication direction (tx, rx) of every edge has its own interface. All interfaces of a tile correspond to the AXI-Stream standard and thus support a wide range of existing applications and intellectual property cores.

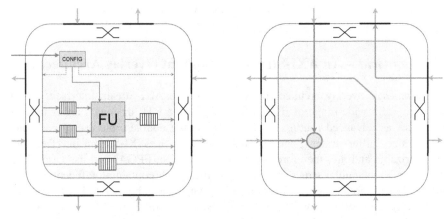

(a) Inner tile architecture – partial reconfigurable functional unit (FU) (blue), configuration network (red), forwarding (green).

(b) Example configuration of the advanced routing mechanism. Path 1 with binary FU (blue), Path 2 & Path 3 forwarding (green).

Fig. 3. Overview of a single tile, including the interfaces to the 4-neighbourhood, the crossbar (outer ring), and the advanced routing with double/triple use in parallel. (Color figure online)

Figure 2b also shows the FU, which is placed into an RP by partial reconfiguration. Figure 3a shows the architecture of a single tile of the overlay architecture. Within the cell, two inputs and one output of each direction are connected to a crossbar system (outer white ring). In the centre of the tile, the FU is placed, which correspondingly implements the two input and one output interfaces. Between the FU and the respective crossbar, there are synchronous buffers, which store the data temporarily and are parameterizable as well. A tile can also be used for forwarding from an input to an output. Therefore additional buffers are implemented and connected to the crossbar (cf. Fig. 3a – green). This allows using the tile in parallel two/three-times for different DFGs, by establishing multiple independent connections inside the tile. In Fig. 3b is shown an example of such a possible tile routing. The blue arrows connect a binary FU with two inputs (north and west) and forward the result to the south. A second and third stream (green) are established for forwarding-only from south-to-west, respectively east-to-north. This advanced routing feature enables a more flexible mapping of operators and reduces fragmentation during the lifetime of the overlay. During the crossbar's reconfiguration, the streams to/from the buffers are stopped for one clock-cycle to be sure, that there is no interrupted data routing. Because of the integrated buffers, the FU can still work during this process. The connection of each FU to the memory subsystem can also be parameterized during synthesis. This feature allows a heterogeneous grid for applications with mixed FU requirements.

3.2 Configuration and Monitoring

The configuration and monitoring modules (red, shown in Fig. 2 and Fig. 3) are responsible for configuring FU and tile. Therefore, control packets (32 bit) are transmitted from the host to the tiles via cascaded shift registers. Each packet contains the destination address for the routing and a bit to identify tile or FU. The configuration-package for the tile contains the switching-data of each crossbar, which is applied to their configuration register. The package addressing the FUs have unused bits, which are for custom-use for the FU application developer. Furthermore, the configuration network also provides an upstream to the host system, enabling monitoring of tiles and FUs. For example, the FUs can signal *computation finished* to the host system, which in return can reconfigure the RP with a new FU.

3.3 Partial Reconfiguration

The partial reconfiguration of the FPGA allows exchanging the functionality on runtime by changing the FU. Depending on the application, these partitions can be larger or smaller and thus implicitly specify the grid size of the specific overlay architecture. Besides, FPGA-specific limits exist for the RP size and placement. For Xilinx devices, the reconfigurable frames are one element (CLB, BRAM, DSP) wide and one clock region high. For example, the Xilinx Virtex Ultrascale+ XCU280 FPGA used in this paper is divided into 12 lines of configuration frames [19, p. 165]. Therefore, it is theoretically possible to implement about 230 RPs per line. The FU's requirements of LUTs, Flip-Flops, BRAM, DSP implies the size, shape, and placement of the RP. Thus, from a practical point of view, up to 32 RP are possible per line. The partial reconfiguration of the FUs is realized by the internal ICAP interface, which is connected to the host system via a dedicated PCIe stream. The ICAP has a bus width of 32 bit and is driven by a 100 MHz clock. This results in a throughput of 3.2 Gbps [19].

4   Evaluation – Impact of Design-Parameters

In this section, the overlay architecture is evaluated in terms of utilization and the maximum achievable clock frequency by analyzing different design parameters (buffer-strategy, grid sizes, data width). For the evaluation a server system with Ubuntu 20.04 LTS is used, which consists of an AMD EPYC 7402P 24-Core Processor, 256 GB DDR4 memory, and a Xilinx Alveo U280 Card [18, 20]. The hardware design is implemented in VHDL using Xilinx Vivado 2020.1.

Default Design Parameter. As mentioned, the *StreamGrid* overlay architecture is parameterizable for different design parameters. Also, the reconfigurable partitions, which implements the FU can be defined by the overlay designer. To have a fair comparison between the values for each design parameter, we defined default values (see Table 1), which are motivated by the application requirements of the *Case Study* Section.

Table 1. Default parameter for the evaluation

Parameter	Default value
Buffer-strategy	Register
Grid-size	4×4
Data width	256 bit

4.1 Buffer-Strategy

The evaluation of the buffer-strategies focus on three different implementations: register (REG), FIFO implemented in Distributed RAM ($FIFO_{dist}$), and FIFO using the FPGA's BRAM ($FIFO_{BRAM}$). All buffer-strategies are realized by Intellectual Property cores provided in Vivado. For Distributed RAM implementations, the smallest possible depth of 32 elements is selected to minimize resource utilization. The BRAM versions have a depth of 512, which corresponds to the maximum depth of a single dual-port BRAM. Using a smaller depth will not result in less utilization of BRAM units. All other IP settings are identical for better comparability and using the clock of the overlay architecture. For our analysis, we use a 4×4 overlay architecture, and an AXI-Stream data-width of 256 bit (cf. *Default Design Parameter*). Table 2 shows utilization and maximum clock frequency for the buffer-strategies. The REG implementation requires between 2.5/3.2 times fewer LUTs and 2.2/2.8 times fewer Flip-Flops. The maximum possible clock for the REG (645 MHz) and $FIFO_{dist}$ (655 MHz) versions are on a similar level and are 37% faster compared to the BRAM version (470 MHz). For a bus width of 256 bit, 8 BRAM modules have to be combined. The linear placing of the BRAMs units on the FPGA leads to stretched placing and therefore result in lower

Table 2. Utilization of the overlay architecture for different buffer-strategies without FUs and PCIe (AXI-stream bus width of 256 bit, size of grid 4×4).

Total	LUT	Flip-Flop	BRAM	f_{max}
	1 303 680	2 607 360	2 016	(MHz)
REG	9 552	19 552	0	645
FIFO dist. RAM	32 078	53 858	0	655
FIFO BRAM	25 636	43 194	192	470

clock-frequency. For applications, which have to accumulate data for further processing a FIFO is required to benefit from pipeline parallelism. For short time intervals, bursts could be also compensated by a $FIFO_{dist}$, for a longer burst the $FIFO_{BRAM}$ should be used. Depending on the application's internal data management, the REG version is most suitable for date-by-date transfers due to its lower resource consumption. For more complex or burst transfers the $FIFO_{dist}$ buffer-strategy should be used because it provides similar performance as the REG version. Both recommended configurations achieve a high clock frequency above 640 MHz. Furthermore, the resource utilization is very low with <1%, respectively 1.9% of the total resources available, providing a maximum on user-accessible resources.

4.2 Grid-Size

The size of the grid is limited by the resource utilization of the FU and the limitations of the configuration frame of the FPGA (cf. Sect. 3.3). The largest possible grid on the Alveo U280 would consist of 12 × 32 elements (384 in total), but due to the resources required by the PCIe core, DDR4 core, and other static components, this is not possible. Therefore, our test-set consists of six implementations for different square grid sizes of the overlay architectures ranging from 2 × 2 up to 7 × 7. As shown in Table 3, the resource consumption of LUTs and Flip-Flops increase super-linearly from a small to a large overlay architecture. Linearity is not possible due to the grid's boundary phenomena, where not all ports are fully connected, as given in the column *per tile*. In this case, the unconnected ports (south and north edge of the grid, cf. Figure 2a) are removed during synthesis. In relative numbers, the resource consumption of the overlay architectures is very low. Only 2.4% of the LUTs and 2.5% of Flip-Flops (without PCIe and Memory core) of the FPGA resources are required for a large 7 × 7 grid. The maximum achievable clock frequency for all implementations is at a similarly high level, ranging from 635 MHz to 684 MHz. Thus, the choice of an optimal overlay architecture can be made based solely on the required number of FUs and available resources. The deviation of the maximum achievable clock frequency is due to the influences of the PCIe core and the Place & Route of Xilinx Vivado. The grid size evaluation shows

Table 3. Resource requirements of the overlay architecture for different sizes of the grid (buffer-strategy REG, AXI-Stream bus width of 256 bit, without FUs).

Total	LUT		Flip-flop		f_{max}
	1 303 680	Per tile	2 607 360	Per tile	(MHz)
2 × 2	2 125	531	4 053	1 013	683
3 × 3	5 097	566	10 354	1 150	635
4 × 4	9 552	597	19 552	1 222	645
5 × 5	15 420	617	31 694	1 268	640
6 × 6	22 733	631	46 758	1 299	640
7 × 7	31 433	641	64 748	1 321	684

that the overlay architecture for each grid-size configuration offers suitable and high-performance implementations and at the same time low resource utilization.

4.3   Data-Width

In this section, the influence of different bus widths of the AXI-Stream interface is investigated. As in the previous evaluation set, REG is used as a buffer-strategy and a grid size of 4 × 4. For the busses, widths of 2^n ranging from 32 to 512 bit are evaluated. As can be seen in Table 4, the resource consumption of a tile increases sub-linearly with the bus width of the AXI-Stream interface. This correlation is because the tile also comprises additional logic for configuration besides the AXI-Stream interfaces. The proportion of resource utilization for the total overlay design of size 4 × 4 is, even in the case of a maximum bus width of 512 bit less than 1.4% of the total resources available. The maximum possible clock frequency is highest at 752 MHz with a bus width of 32 bit and drops to 630 MHz with increasing bus width. The difference between the fastest and slowest design is, therefore, about 19%. The overlay architecture is suitable for a variety of applications due to its low resource consumption and the high maximum clock frequency for all bus widths. The bus width can, therefore, be selected on the basis of the characteristics of the application data.

Table 4. Resource requirements of the overlay architecture for different sizes of the AXI-Stream interface (buffer-strategy REG, size of grid 4 × 4, without FUs).

Total	LUT		Flip-Flop		f_{max}
	1 303 680	Per tile	2 607 360	Per tile	(MHz)
32	2 131	133	4 848	303	752
64	3 194	200	6 997	437	687
128	5 327	333	11 165	698	697
256	9 552	597	19 552	1 222	645
512	18 612	1 163	40 618	2 538	630

The evaluation of the maximum clock frequency for the overlay architecture shows consistently high values of far above 640 MHz, independent of the selected buffer-strategy, grid size, or AXI stream bus width. Furthermore, the low resource utilization for a large grid of 7 × 7 is even about 2.5%. The good results confirm the good suitability of the overlay architecture for a variety of different applications and the good scalability of the grid.

5   Case Study

The aim of this case study is to map applications on the overlay architecture and find optimal design parameter. Therefore, we want to analyse if the overlay architecture fulfils the requirements of the respective application and if the flexibility of the overlay architectures has drawbacks in terms of performance and utilization compared to a static design with the same functionality. In order to properly evaluate the overlay architecture's performance independent of mapping/design software, FUs are mapped manually to the RP.

1	#Get all articles with title, no. of pages and creator.
2	SELECT ?article ?title ?pages ?creator WHERE {
3	?article rdf:type bench:Article .
4	?article dc:title ?title .
5	?article swrc:pages ?pages .
6	?article dc:creator ?creator .
7	}

1	#Get all articles with titles, no. of pages, creator, journal and pub. month.
2	SELECT ?article ?title ?pages ?creator ?journal ? month WHERE {
3	?article rdf:type bench:Article .
4	?article dc:title ?title .
5	?article swrc:pages ?pages .
6	?article dc:creator ?creator .
7	?article swrc:journal ?journal .
8	?article swrc:month ?month .
9	}

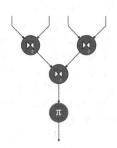

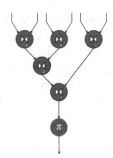

(a) SP^2B-Q3 – SPARQL request and graph.   (b) SP^2B-Q5 – SPARQL request and graph.

Fig. 4. SPARQL request and the corresponding graph of the two evaluation queries SP^2B-Q3 and SP^2B-Q5 of Werner et al. [11].

As the first proof of concept, we used two IP cores of the Vivado IP Catalog: First, Video Processing Subsystem [15], which provides different transforming operations for video streams. The overlay architecture achieved the IP's required clock frequency of 300 MHz and a single FU can be reconfigured in about 3 ms. Second, CORDIC IP core provides trigonometric functions and the conversion of coordinate systems (e.g. arc tangent, sine and cosine, polar to rectangular conversion, and vice versa). The IP is a binary operator with a bus width of 32 bit and a maximum clock frequency of 719 MHz, which is also covered by the overlay architecture (cf. Table 4), without any loss of performance. For this application, the set up time for a single FU is about 1 ms. In the following section, we want to present and analyse a database query engine as a more advanced application in detail.

5.1   Database Queries

The use case of our application is based on a software-centric engine for Semantic Web Databases [11, 13], which offloads database queries to an FPGA. The hardware-factory of the database engine analyses the query and breaks down the DFG of the database-operator into partial operators (projection and join). A corresponding hardware model is composed in VHDL by using macros. Afterwards, the model is synthesized into a static design taking between 20 and 30 min, depending on the query used. This long time for setting up the query in hardware is not acceptable for a database application. In general, the expected response time for a database system is a few seconds or less. For the overlay architecture, we migrated the VHDL-operators of the static design [11, 12] to FUs for our overlay architecture. Both designs (static design and overlay architecture) use two queries examples of the work of Werner et al. [11] (SP^{2}B-Q3 and SP^{2}B-Q5) for evaluation. At the top of Fig. 4 the SPARQL queries are shown. At the bottom, the corresponding data-flow/operator graphs are shown. Each line of the query starting with *?article* corresponds to one input stream of the graph, e.g. Q5 has six input stream, which results in five join operators. The *SELECT* corresponds to the last node of the graph – the projection. The mapping of both graphs into the overlay architecture is shown in Fig. 5.

Clock Frequency. To determine the most suitable buffer-strategy for the presented use case, the maximum clock frequency of the individual operators is required. The projection operator consumes and generates a data value in each clock cycle and can be operated at up to 764 MHz. The join operator can produce data in each clock cycle, too, and can be clocked at 560 MHz maximum. As stated in Sect. 4, the maximum clock frequency for the 4 × 4 REG-based overlay architecture is 645 MHz. Resulting, a synchronous REG-based overlay architecture, is chosen and implemented. Due to the continuous data processing, no FIFOs are required to compensate for any bursts. The resulting clock rate is defined by the slowest of the two FUs, the join, and is 560 MHz. In comparison, the static system achieves a slightly higher clock frequency of 586 MHz/634 MHz (see Table 5), because of the unconstrained placing of the FUs.

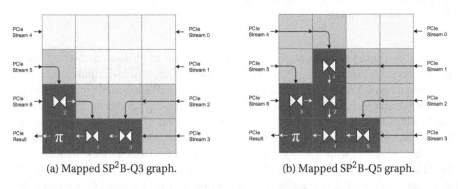

(a) Mapped SP^{2}B-Q3 graph.   (b) Mapped SP^{2}B-Q5 graph.

Fig. 5. DFG mapped on a 4 × 4 overlay grid, including forwarding tiles and external PCIe connection. Dark blue – operator; green – forwarding tile; grey – unused. (Color figure online)

While the estimated raw execution time of the Database Queries are about 8% slower compared to the static design, the set up times for each query are now drastically reduced from several 10 minutes to less than 3 ms as shown in Table 6, efficiently enabling hardware-accelerated queries.

Reconfigurable Partition. As mentioned before, the evaluated queries consist of two different operations: join and projection. In the first step, we have to analyze which of both has a higher utilization of resources (per resource type, cf. Table 5). This defines the required size of the reconfigurable partition on the FPGA. As can be seen in Table 5, the resource requirement of the join is significantly higher compared to the projection. Therefore, it is the limiting operator for the RP. The 8 BRAM blocks of the join are decisive for the minimum size of the block. The x-dimension of the partition reaches the next BRAM column and result in an RP, which offers nearly two times more LUT and four times more Flip-Flops than required for the largest operator (join). A smaller RP leads to a poor synthesis, which is why several sizes of the partition may have to be evaluated. The time to set up the hardware systems is shown in Table 6. The synthesis times for the query Q3 and Q5 of static design is 21:43 min respectively 30:29 min. In contrast, the partial reconfiguration and configuration of the overlay architecture of both queries is 1.79 ms/2.69 ms.

Table 5. Resource requirements and maximal clock frequency of the RP and the semantic web FUs.

Total	LUT	Flip-Flop	BRAM	f_{max}
	1 303 680	2 607 360	2 016	(MHz)
MergeJoin	1 230	1 440	8	560
Projection	91	294	0	764
RP	2 880	5 760	8	–

Table 6. Utilization of the Radix-Tree-Engine of different values of the maximum length m. Furthermore, the clock frequency and the estimated execution time for the btc dataset are shown

	Total	LUT	Flip-Flop	BRAM	f_{max}	Setup time
		1 303 680	2 607 360	2 016	(MHz)	
Q3	Static	4 846	13 054	36	634	21:43 min
	Overlay	16 841	32 608	24	560	1.79 ms
Q5	Static	7 699	19 104	60	586	30:29 min
	Overlay	19 301	35 488	40	560	2.69 ms

Execution Time. In this section, we evaluate the raw execution time of the static and the overlay system for the database query application. Therefore, we tested three data sets (66, 131, 262 Million entries) for each of the two presented queries. The time and the throughput are measured for both systems, which can be seen in Table 7 – column *measured execution time*. As can be seen, the throughput of test runs is in the range of 3.11 GB/s to 3.18 GB/s, which is due to the limitation of the PCIe connection. In order to determine the theoretical maximum execution time (e.g., if direct-attached memory is used), the performance was determined both for the static design and for the overlay architecture by a behavioural simulation. As can be seen in Table 7, the queries can theoretically be accelerated by a factor between 19.4 to 26.7 for the static design, respectively 17.3 to 25.5 for the overlay architecture compared to the PCIe limited execution. The throughput increases to up to 82.7 GB/s analogous to the execution time, which is decreasing with the same ratio. In column – *Theoretical maximal Execution Time*, it can also be seen that the maximum throughput increases with the size of the graph (Q5 – 4 nodes over Q3 – 6 nodes) due to the inherent parallelism of the FPGA. The performance of the overlay architecture is slightly lower compared to the static design, because of the lower clock frequency.

Table 7. Comparison of measured and theoretical max execution time (respectively throughput) on FPGA [11].

	Data set		Measured execution time				Theoretical max execution time			
	[M]	[MB]	Static design		Overlay		Static design		Overlay	
			Time	Throu.	Time	Throu.	Time	Throu.	Time	Throu.
			[ms]	[GB/s]	[ms]	[GB/s]	[ms]	[GB/s]	[ms]	[GB/s]
Q3	66	801	258	3.11	258	3.11	27.8	59.2	31.5	52.2
	131	1 578	501	3.15	501	3.15	47.6	68.2	53.8	60.2
	262	3 096	973	3.18	973	3.18	85.1	74.7	96.4	66.0
Q5	66	838	268	3.12	268	3.12	26.7	64.5	27.8	61.8
	131	1 637	517	3.16	517	3.16	44.7	75.4	46.7	72.1
	262	3 198	1 006	3.18	1 006	3.18	79.3	82.7	83.1	79.0

In this case study, we proved, that the overlay architecture is very suitable for a dynamic database query application. While the resource utilization is about two to four times higher compared to the static system, resulting from the whole RP being taken into account, the maximum clock frequency is similar, so that the raw execution is nearly the same. Now the set up time of less than 3 ms enables fast response times of query request to the database engine.

6 Conclusion

This paper presents *StreamGrid*, our AXI-Stream-compliant overlay architecture. It not only features dynamic FU exchange on run-time by partial reconfiguration of the PR, but furthermore implements an advanced multi-stream routing architecture, memory (DDR4, HBM) access for the application running in hardware, and a configuration and monitoring system. The overlay architecture is parameterizable in terms of buffering strategies, grid-size, and data width of the AXI-Stream interface. We evaluated these parameter sets by implementing the design on a Xilinx Alveo U280 Card using a Virtex Ultrascale+ FPGA. With the exception of BRAM-FIFO buffering, we achieved a constant high clock frequency of more than 630 MHz for all parameters. The linear scaling and the overall low resource utilization ($<2.5\%$) of the FPGA allows a maximum availability of hardware resources for the application itself. Furthermore, we provide a case study to show the suitability of the overlay architecture. The database query engine is evaluated and compared to a static design. The overlay based design achieves a similar performance for the raw execution of the queries but has a much faster set up time, which efficiently enables the hardware-accelerated query engine.

References

1. arm Inc.: AMBA 4 AXI4-Stream Protocol Specification (2010). https://developer.arm.com/documentation/ihi0051/a/Introduction/About-the-AXI4-Stream-protocol
2. Bhattacharyya, S.S., Murthy, P.K., Lee, E.A.: Synthesis of embedded software from synchronous dataflow specifications. J. VLSI Signal Process. **21**(2), 151–166 (1999). https://doi.org/10.1023/A:1008052406396. http://link.springer.com/10.1023/A:1008052406396
3. Billauer, E.: Xillybus PCIe Core (2017). http://xillybus.com/downloads/xillybus_product_brief.pdf
4. Capalija, D., Abdelrahman, T.S.: A high-performance overlay architecture for pipelined execution of data flow graphs. In: 2013 23rd International Conference on Field programmable Logic and Applications, pp. 1–8. IEEE (2013). https://doi.org/10.1109/FPL.2013.6645515. http://ieeexplore.ieee.org/document/6645515/
5. Kudlur, M., Mahlke, S., Kudlur, M., Mahlke, S.: Orchestrating the execution of stream programs on multicore platforms. In: Proceedings of the 2008 ACM SIGPLAN conference on Programming language design and implementation - PLDI 2008, New York, New York, USA, vol. 43, p. 114. ACM Press (2008). https://doi.org/10.1145/1375581.1375596. http://portal.acm.org/citation.cfm?doid=1375581.1375596
6. Lindtjorn, O., Clapp, R., Pell, O., Fu, H., Flynn, M., Mencer, O.: Beyond traditional microprocessors for geoscience high-performance computing applications. IEEE Micro **31**(2), 41–49 (2011). https://doi.org/10.1109/MM.2011.17. http://ieeexplore.ieee.org/document/5719584/
7. Ma, S., Aklah, Z., Andrews, D.: A run time interpretation approach for creating custom accelerators. In: 2015 25th International Conference on Field Programmable Logic and Applications (FPL), pp. 1–4. IEEE (2015). https://doi.org/10.1109/FPL.2015.7293996. http://ieeexplore.ieee.org/document/7293996/
8. Mandebi Mbongue, J., Tchuinkou Kwadjo, D., Bobda, C.: FLexiTASK. In: Proceedings of the 2018 on Great Lakes Symposium on VLSI - GLSVLSI 2018, New York, New York, USA, pp. 483–486. ACM Press (2018). https://doi.org/10.1145/3194554.3194644. http://dl.acm.org/citation.cfm?doid=3194554.3194644

9. Mueller, R., Teubner, J., Alonso, G.: Streams on wires. Proc. VLDB Endow. **2**(1), 229–240 (2014). https://doi.org/10.14778/1687627.1687654. http://dl.acm.org/citation.cfm? doid=1687627.1687654

10. Prabhakar, R., et al.: Plasticine: a reconfigurable architecture for parallel patterns. In: Proceedings - International Symposium on Computer Architecture, vol. 17 (2017). https://doi.org/10.1145/3079856.3080256. https://doi.org/10.1145/3079856.3080256

11. Werner, S.: Hybrid architecture for hardware-accelerated query processing in semantic web databases based on runtime reconfigurable FPGAs. Ph.D. thesis, e University of Lübeck, Lübeck (2016). https://www.zhb.uni-luebeck.de/epubs/ediss1886.pdf

12. Werner, S., et al.: Automated composition and execution of hardware-Accelerated operator graphs. In: 10th International Symposium on Reconfigurable and Communication-centric Systems-on-Chip, ReCoSoC 2015 (2015). https://doi.org/10.1109/ReCoSoC.2015.7238078

13. Werner, S., Heinrich, D., Pionteck, T., Groppe, S.: Semi-static operator graphs for accelerated query execution on FPGAs. Microprocess. Microsyst. **53**, 178–189 (2017). https://doi.org/10.1016/J.MICPRO.2017.07.010. https://www.sciencedirect.com/science/article/abs/pii/S0141933117303757?via%3Dihub

14. Wilson, D., Stitt, G., Coole, J.: A recurrently generated overlay architecture for rapid FPGA application development (2018). https://doi.org/10.1145/3241793.3241797. https://doi.org/10.1145/3241793.3241797

15. Xilinx Inc: Video Processing Subsystem v2.0 LogiCORE IP Product Guide Vivado Design Suite. Technical report, Xilinx Inc., San Jose, California (2021). https://www.xilinx.com/products/intellectual-property/video-processing-subsystem.html

16. Xilinx Inc.: Vivado AXI Reference Guide. Technical report, Xilinx Inc., San Jose, California (2017). https://www.xilinx.com/support/documentation/ip_documentation/axi_ref_guide/latest/ug1037-vivado-axi-reference-guide.pdf

17. Xilinx Inc.: SDAccel Environment Profiling and Optimization Guide. Technical report, Xilinx Inc., San Jose, California (2018). https://www.xilinx.com/support/documentation/sw_manuals/xilinx2018_2/ug1207-sdaccel-optimization-guide.pdf

18. Xilinx Inc.: Adaptable Accelerator Cards for Data Center Workloads. Technical report, Xilinx Inc., San Jose, California (2019). www.xilinx.com/u280

19. Xilinx Inc.: Vivado Design Suite User Guide Dynamic Function eXchange. Technical report, Xilinx Inc., San Jose, California (2020). https://www.xilinx.com/support/documentation/sw_manuals/xilinx2019_2/ug909-vivado-partial-reconfiguration.pdf

20. Xilinx Inc.: UltraScale+ FPGA Product Tables and Product Selection Guide. Technical report, Xilinx Inc., San Jose, California (2021). https://www.xilinx.com/support/documentation/selection-guides/ultrascale-plus-fpga-product-selection-guide.pdf

Security

Increasing Side-Channel Resistance by Netlist Randomization and FPGA-Based Reconfiguration

Ali Asghar[1]([✉]), Benjamin Hettwer[2], Emil Karimov[3], and Daniel Ziener[1]

[1] RAES, Technische Universität Ilmenau, Ilmenau, Germany
{ali.asghar,daniel.ziener}@tu-ilmenau.de
[2] Robert Bosch GmbH, Corporate Sector Research, Stuttgart, Germany
benjamin.hettwer@de.bosch.com
[3] ESAT-INSYS, KU Leuven, Leuven, Belgium
emil.karimov@kuleuven.be

Abstract. Modern FPGAs are equipped with the possibility of Partial Reconfiguration (PR) which along with other benefits can be used to enhance the security of cryptographic implementations. This feature requires development of alternative designs to be exchanged during runtime. In this work, we propose dynamically alterable circuits by exploring netlist randomization which can be utilized with PR as a countermeasure against physical attacks, in particular side-channel attacks. The proposed approach involves modification of an AES implementation at the netlist level in order to create circuit variants which are functionally identical but structurally different. In preliminary experiments, power traces of these variants have been shuffled to replicate the effect of partial reconfiguration. With these dynamic circuits, our experimental results show an increase in the resistance against power side-channel attacks by a factor of ~12.6 on a Xilinx ZYNQ UltraScale+ device.

Keywords: Side-channel attacks · Power analysis attacks · Partial reconfiguration · FPGAs

1 Introduction

The suitability of FPGAs for streaming-based applications make them an efficient hardware platform to host cryptographic implementations like AES or RSA. Also, the reconfigurable nature of FPGAs permits a designer to update an implementation after detecting a security flaw. However, hardware running cryptographic implementations is not always located in a secure environment and hence, is susceptible to physical attacks such as: Side-Channel Analysis (SCA) or Fault Injection Attacks (FIA).

SCA is a pertinent threat for hardware cryptographic implementations. These attacks fall into the category of passive attacks, where the device operation and specifications remain unmodified. The attacker tries to exploit the information leakages from various cryptographic operations running on an electronic device,

© Springer Nature Switzerland AG 2021
S. Derrien et al. (Eds.): ARC 2021, LNCS 12700, pp. 173–187, 2021.
https://doi.org/10.1007/978-3-030-79025-7_12

with an eventual goal to extract the secret key. Some well-known side-channels are power [1], timing [2], and electromagnetic radiation [11].

Since their introduction in 1998 by Kocher et al. [1], power analysis attacks have gained the most attention among all attacks on cryptographic devices. They have now been successfully used against various encryption algorithms [3]. The relative ease with which these attacks can be applied makes them extremely powerful.

The power analysis attacks can either exploit the relationship between the measured power and the operations executed by the device known as Simple Power Analysis (SPA) [1] or by understanding the correlation between the processed data and the measured power called the Correlation Power Analysis (CPA) [1].

Analyzing the basic problem of physical attacks in detail, it becomes clear that the basic principle of cryptography (confidentiality) cannot be applied to the underlying circuit realization of a cryptographic algorithm. An attacker with physical access to the device has no technical and time limits to identify and characterize the security functions and used cryptographic circuits. This is favored by the fact that cryptographic hardware implementations are present as static circuits and can, therefore, be systematically measured and manipulated. However, it is possible to continually change such a hardware configuration by means of reconfigurable technology in an invariable and dynamic manner at run time, the static attack principles of SCA and FIA would certainly render a physical characterization by an attacker difficult or even impossible. Due to their ability to dynamically reconfigure, FPGAs provide an ideal platform to realize this dynamic behavior. Using the *Partial Reconfiguration* (PR) feature of modern FPGAs, parts of a cryptographic circuit can be modified dynamically, without interrupting the remaining logic.

In this work, we explore this idea in detail and analyze whether the dynamic restructuring of a cryptographic circuit serve as a countermeasure against power analysis attacks. The implementation of these dynamic circuits requires a two-step approach. First there is a requirement to create a set of polymorphic realizations of the entire (or parts of) cryptoraphic algorithm. These realizations which are functionally identical but structurally different can then be dynamically shuffled using the Partial Reconfiguration feature of modern FPGAs. This work focuses on the earlier part. Specifically, starting from a single *Register Transfer Level* (RTL) description of the *Advanced Encryption Standard* (AES), we create diversified implementations (netlists) called 'variants', which can be exchanged dynamically using PR.

The remainder of the paper is organized as follows: Sect. 2 covers the literature related to countermeasures against power attacks. Section 3 explains the concept of dynamic circuits and how they can protect a cryptographic implementation. Section 4 provides the details for generating netlist-level variants. Section 5 describes the measurement setup. In Sect. 6, we present a discussion on the results, while Sect. 7 highlights the conclusion and the future work.

2   Background and Previous Work

The main objective of the SCA countermeasures in general is to reduce the relation between the processed data at an intermediate stage of the algorithm (which could be used in an adversarial model), and the actual power consumption of the device. To achieve this goal, the work in [4] proposes a number of countermeasures which are specially suited to FPGA-based cryptographic implementations. Also, Sasdrich et al. presented the use of CFGLUTs [5] for the randomization of AES switch boxes.

The first approach in the direction of using PR to replace parts of a cryptographic implementation at run time was proposed in [6]. The work utilizes a serial-based AES architecture with registers to store intermediate results. The registers are connected to a switch-matrix which can be dynamically reconfigured to randomly change the position of registers between different AES rounds. The additional delay (at different stages) introduced by the registers reduces the correlation between intermediate values and power consumption.

Recently, an alternative method to create variants of a cryptographic circuit was proposed in [7]. The work explores the idea of implementation diversity as a countermeasure by targeting the placement stage of the FPGA CAD flow. A single synthesized netlist of a serial AES implementation is placed with different constraints. The approach results in a number of diversified implementations (configurations) which are functionally similar but physically different, i.e., having different placement and routing on the fabric and consequently, a varying dynamic power consumption. The authors propose that constant shuffling between these configurations using PR will reduce the correlation between the hypothetical intermediate values and the observed power, thus making the power analysis more difficult

The approach in [7] which protects a cryptographic circuit by changing the location during run time has been demonstrated to be a promising method. However, by only modifying the placement and routing, the number of distinct power profiles is limited. In this paper, we explore the idea of implementation diversity from a different perspective. In a standard FPGA CAD flow, a circuit description is first synthesized into a netlist, after which elements get mapped and then placed onto the resources available in the target architecture. If we modify the synthesis step by introducing additional parameters which produce different netlists with the same functionality as the HDL description, then a multitude of implementation variants of the same circuit can be created (see left hand side of Fig. 1). Compared to the approach in [7] where the circuit structure is fixed, we have much more freedom to change the structure of the circuit. A detailed summary of the PR-based countermeasures has been provided in [3].

3   Concept of Dynamic Circuits

As mentioned in Sect. 1, the implementation of dynamic circuits is a two step approach. After the successful realization of different variants of a cryptographic algorithm, we envision a *dynamic reconfigurable system*, where these implementation variants can be loaded/moved during run time at/to different locations.

The variants are partial bitfiles which are generated from different netlists with the same functionality. The constantly changing FPGA configuration is controlled by a hardware-based reconfiguration manager (see Fig. 1). A *True Random Number Generator* (TRNG) is used for the randomized triggering of the loading and the selection of the next variant which shall be loaded into the system. The possibility to load the same partial bitfile at different locations by using a sophisticated design flow [14], further increases the number of different power profiles.

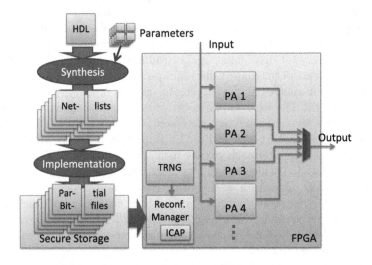

Fig. 1. On the left hand side, our design flow is depicted. From an HDL description, different variants are generated during synthesis by using different (random) parameters and implemented by an own tool flow into partial bitfiles. These partial bitfiles are stored into a secure storage and can by loaded on the different FPGA locations by using a reconfiguration manager which is triggered by a TRNG (right hand side).

In order to generate different netlists from a single HDL description, we are introducing additional parameters which control the synthesis step in a way that different circuit structures are generated by preserving the functionality. Later on in Sect. 4, we propose different methods with different parameters to produce a variety of netlists variants. These variants are implemented in partial bitfiles by using design flow from the tool *GoAhead* [14]. This allows us to load and relocate the same bitfile at different FPGA locations.

Furthermore, to explore the effectiveness of different variants of a cryptographic algorithm, an architecture with only one partial area would be sufficient. However, this approach would suffer from stalling the encryption process during the reconfiguration. To avoid this, a double buffer approach with two partial areas can be used. During the processing on one partial area, the next variant can already be loaded on the other partial area. The switch from one partial area to another can then be done in only a single clock cycle. The drawback is the high area overhead. However, if the cryptographic algorithm is used in a larger system with more partial areas and different modules and sub systems, the non-occupied partial areas can be used for the other modules. One can imagine a streaming hardware accelerator with en- and decryption (see [15] for an example) or a cloud-based FPGA server with multi-tenancy. Recent studies [17,18] have demonstrated the feasibility of launching remote power side-channel attacks on FPGAs in a cloud computing environment, where the fabric can be shared among multiple users or programs. In the proposed *dynamic reconfigurable system*, random selection of a variant and also its target location results in a variety of different configurations which can make successful attacks harder.

One example architecture with multiple partial areas is depicted on the right hand side in Fig. 1. During run time, the reconfiguration manager will be triggered by a TRNG and loads at random time points a randomly chosen variant from a secure storage on a random location on the FPGA over the internal ICAP interface. In Fig. 1, there are four partial areas (PA 1–4) depicted where every partial area can hold a variant implementation. Since only one output of the partial area can be selected by the output multiplexer, only one partial area can be used for calculating the output of the system. However, the other areas could also be loaded with other variants and be active, increasing the noise to make side-channel attacks even harder. Furthermore, special noise generator modules can also be used.

In this paper, we focused on the novel aspects of the generation of variants and the evaluation of the degree of protection against power side-channel analysis. The implementation of the self-configurable system itself is left for future work.

4 Variants Generation

To create variants at the synthesis level, access to the underlying details of a synthesis tool is needed. Unfortunately, most of the commercial tools like *Xilinx Vivado* do not reveal the details of their synthesis process. However, it should be mentioned that Vivado does allow some control over the synthesis stage by setting parameters such as limiting the fan-out of lookup tables or register retiming.

Therefore, to circumvent this problem, we make use of an open-source synthesis tool called *Yosys* [9] to perform modifications at the netlist level. In Subsect. 4.2, we introduce different approaches for netlist randomization. Yosys has been utilized to perform fine-grained changes and alter the mapping of the design and produce a synthesized netlist. Moreover, the list of presented modifications is not exhaustive and serves the purpose of demonstrating the flexibility of netlist manipulation.

4.1 Serial-Based AES Architecture

As a case study, we use a serial-based AES architecture (see Fig. 2) as the reference cryptographic implementation. The serial-based implementation of AES has been optimized for resource usage and requires 570 Look-up Tables (LUTs) and 268 registers. The overall encryption process requires 210 clock cycles. The implementation consists of a *Control Logic* module, *Round Function* module, and *Key Scheduling* module. All of these modules are instantiated in a *Core* entity as shown in Fig. 2. The controller is a finite state machine that determines the next mode of operation, such as initialization state, intermediate or the last round, output available, etc. *Key Schedule* is a module that expands and generates keys for each round based on the given secret key. The *Round Function* module is comprised of the main subfunctions of AES – *AddRoundKey*, *SubBytes*, *ShiftRows*, and *MixColumns*. Additionally, in the *Round* and *Key Scheduling* modules, there is a sub-module called *Cell*, which is a two-input 8-bit register that includes a multiplexer with a selector signal generated by the controller. All of the sub-functions of AES operate on the instances of the *Cell* module storing intermediate state values.

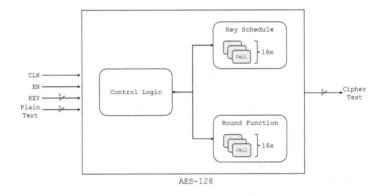

Fig. 2. The used serial-based AES architecture with modules and control signals

4.2 Synthesis Level Changes Using Yosys

Yosys [9] is an open-source synthesis framework supporting Verilog (and VHDL in the commercial edition). Yosys transforms input HDL to internal objects of certain types that allow it to easily manipulate the design at coarse or fine-grain levels. Once all transformations are completed, ABC [10] is used for mapping and final logic optimizations. The design can then be exported as an EDIF or BLIF netlist and used for placement and routing flow.

  With the power analysis side-channel attacks in mind, three classes of variations of the serial-based AES implementation were designed. These variant classes include data hiding, dummy logic generation, and sub-par mapping to influence the power consumption by introducing background noise or data manipulation. Figure 3 illustrates the proposed modifications to generate variants of the serial-based AES architecture. Short description of each variant class is given below:

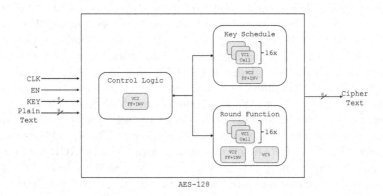

Fig. 3. The modified serial-based AES architecture with modules, control signals, and injected variant classes.

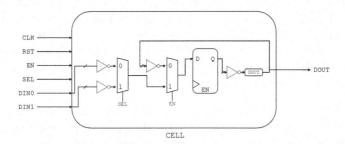

Fig. 4. The modified sub-module *Cell* with additional logic (Color figure online)

1. **Variant Class 1:** We introduce a lightweight hiding approach by applying a Boolean transformation to the value stored in the *Cell* sub-module (see Fig. 4). This entity is used to store intermediate values of the *Round Function* and *Key Schedule* modules of the Serial AES (32 instances as two 128-bit registers, one for each module). The *Cell* sub-module works as a multiplexed 8-bit register that facilitates movement of the intermediate data between sub-functions of the module in which it is included. One of the two inputs (DIN0 and DIN1) is selected and stored in an 8-bit register, which retains this value when the module is not enabled. To create variations in the power profile, we add logic to the *Cell* module that transforms the intermediate values. Logic

for transformation (e.g. inverters shown in red) is injected into the regular data-path (shown in black). This transformation has an effect of introducing noise in the power consumption by causing additional bit switching and avoids storing the true intermediate value in the register. Due to its large presence within the design, the *Cell* sub-module affects all sensitive data in the Serial AES.

2. **Variant Class 2:** For the second variant, we introduce register chains (see Fig. 5), which are dummy chains of cascaded inverters and flip-flops. These run in parallel to the main design and contribute to the noise in power consumption. The chain is randomly inserted into at least one of the three main modules of the Serial AES design (see Fig. 5) and its length is also randomized when the design is modified in Yosys. The input value is either an external signal or the output from the last stage of the chain that is fed back. The external input signal is also used to generate the selector for the input multiplexer, as well as the enable signal for the flip-flops. The signal goes through a *Reduced XOR (RXOR)* function which performs bitwise XOR operation on the multi-bit input and produces a single bit used as the selector signal. For every module, the external input and enable signals are different and change their value during runtime (e.g. Sbox input in *Round Function*). This allows the chain to change its switching profile from round to round and not exhibit a repeating pattern.

3. **Variant Class 3:** We modify the mapping process by restricting selected functions of an AES round to LUT-4 during synthesis. The rest of the design is mapped and synthesized with all regular optimizations. Sub-par mapping (instead of LUT-6 mapping) results in a circuit with a different power consumption profile than the original with minimal changes. We have created a configuration by performing sub-par mapping of *SubBytes*, *Round Function* and *MixColumns* modules.

The extra cells such as the flip-flops, inverters, and multiplexers that are not present in the original design and its HDL description are inserted using the Yosys synthesis tool. By following internal scripting syntax, necessary cells are added to the desired modules before the design goes through the resource mapping process. The design is loaded and synthesized in Yosys by following a script that performs its internal transformations and optimizations, followed by invoking ABC mapping tool and then generating an output netlist.

In order to constrain LUT mapping, as in the Variant Class 3, this script is modified. Before invoking the ABC tool, entities to be constrained are selected and mapped with a modified command that specifies desired LUT sizes, after which the rest of the design is mapped with the unrestricted command. The scripts to introduce a large number of dummy flip-flops are generated using a short C program including randomization of the chain lengths. Overall, complete Yosys scripts are produced from parametrized C programs, that list all of the commands to automate generation of each of a variant as a synthesized netlist ready for placement and routing.

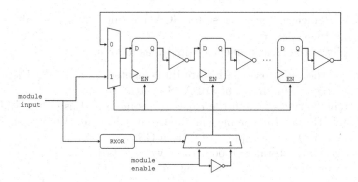

Fig. 5. Proposed *Register Chains*; register-inverter cascades of varying lengths

4.3 Randomness to Generate More Variants

In this work, we generate a limited number of variants to evaluate the effectiveness of netlist level changes as countermeasures against SCA. However, the ideas proposed in Sects. 4.2 could be extended to generate more configurations. As mentioned earlier, for the synthesis level changes, there is more flexibility to introduce randomness in variants generation. This flexibility is explored when the Yosys scripts are generated from a C program. Tuning the parameters in this program allows to generate multiple variations of the same approach or combine different ones. The modifications can be introduced in all or some of the modules of the Serial AES-128 design.

For instance, structure of Variant Class 1 is based on transforming some or all bits of an 8-bit register. This effect also extends to the entire 128-bit state value and introduces non-uniformity in the bit pattern. Additional configurations can be realized by randomizing the Boolean operation applied to the data (instead of only inversion). Variant Class 2 could be randomized by varying the register width (single bit or more), length of the *register chains*, and the modules in which the chains are inserted. These chains also have inherent randomness due to the ability to choose between two inputs. A selector signal dependent on a non-static module input is generated to choose either module input or the last stage output of the chain as the seed value for the chain. For Variant Class 3, it is possible to randomize which modules will get sub-par mapping and the degree of limiting LUT sizes.

5 Measurement Setup

As discussed in Sect. 1, to launch a power analysis attack, a power consumption profile of the cryptographic implementation is needed. We collect the power traces of the serial-based AES by measuring the current through a decoupling capacitor of the FPGA's power supply as proposed in [12].

This measurement setup is better suited for power attacks than the conventional voltage drop over a shunt resistor, as only sharp changes in the power consumption (which are of interest for SCAs) result in a measurable current change across the capacitor.

The details of the measurement setup are as follows:

1. Variants of the serial-based AES are implemented on a ZYNQ UltraScale+ device. The operating frequency of AES is 30 MHz.
2. The current flowing through the capacitor is measured using the EM probe Langer ICR HV500-75. The measured current values are then captured using Picoscope 6404D at a sample rate of 1.25 GS/s.
3. For each variant, a total of 10000 traces were recorded.
4. For recording the traces, an averaging factor of 250 is used, i.e., each trace is an average of 250 traces obtained using the same plain text. This is done to increase the Signal-to-Noise Ratio (SnR).
5. The clock frequency has been set to 30 MHz to have an optimal condition from an attacker's perspective. Setting the frequency to a lower value or the averaging of traces, creates an advantage for the adversary, which in turn leads to a worst-case evaluation of the countermeasure. The max reported and tested frequency of the same AES core is 400 MHz.
6. To emulate the effect of dynamic reconfiguration of circuits using PR, we combine and shuffle the traces of proposed variants. This procedure will have the same effect as shuffling between different configuration using partial reconfiguration using the *reconfiguration manager*. Furthermore, we only analyze the impact of the variants themselves without taking different locations into account.

6   Results

6.1   Attack Model

As mentioned in the earlier sections, power attacks exploit the relationship between the instantaneous power consumption and an intermediate result of the cryptographic algorithm executed by the target device at that time instant. Hence, for a successful attack an effective model is necessary to estimate the power consumption of intermediate results. The authors in [13] recommend the *Hamming Distance* (HD) as a suitable power model (as it can better represent the power consumption in CMOS circuits) for attacking hardware-based cryptographic implementations.

To evaluate the performance of our proposed variants, we have adopted the same evaluation approach as [7]. To estimate the power consumption of an intermediate result, we calculate the HD by finding the *Hamming Weight* (HW) between two consecutive S-box outputs during the first round and then perform a CPA with the measured power traces. The attack model can be represented by Eq. (1):

$$
\begin{aligned}
Hypothetical\_Power = HW[Sbox[Key[i][j] \oplus \\
PT[i][j]] \oplus Sbox[Key[i+4][j] \oplus \\
PT[i+4][j]]]
\end{aligned} \tag{1}
$$

where, PT is the abbreviation for *Plain Text*. *Sbox* represents the switch-box look-up operation. *Key[i][j]* and *PT[i][j]* represents the ith key and plain text bytes corresponding to the jth encryption.

6.2 Evaluation of Yosys Variants

To illustrate the effect of variants developed for the PR-based countermeasure against power attacks, we compare the results from two configurations namely: *Static* and *Protected*. The static configuration represents the original baseline serial AES implementation without any modifications, while the protected configuration has been created by combining and shuffling the traces of the variants (see Sect. 5). In this work, we have created and randomly selected a subset of different configurations of the serial AES design belonging to the 3 variant classes. Choosing a smaller number (8, in this work) of individual variants allows for faster evaluation of the proposed methodology and to determine if further investigation is warranted. The variants named CellOnly, RandMod0, and LutOnly belong to variant classes 1, 2, and 3, respectively. Then, there are variants which are a combination of 2 or more variant classes, such as: CellMod1, CellMod3, CellMod4, and CellMod6 which have been created by combining the modifications of variant classes 1 and 2, while the variant LutMod7 is a hybrid of all the three variant classes. The CPA values for the mentioned variants range from 0.18 to 0.55, with only one design (CellOnly) higher than the baseline value of 0.48. This anomaly could possibly have resulted from the bit switching introduced in Variant Class 1, which has negative impact as it introduces a clear spike into the power profile, leading to a significant increase in the CPA value.

To evaluate the results, we used the attack model described in the previous section with the maximum CPA value serving as an evaluation metric. According to the authors of [13], the complexity of a power attack is proportional to the number of traces required to successfully extract the secret key, which in turn depends inversely on the maximum CPA values. Therefore, a decrease in the observed correlation values increases the difficulty of an attack, as more traces are required for the key extraction.

The results of an attack on the static and protected AES implementation are shown in Fig. 6a and 6b, respectively. The protected implementation has been created by mixing the traces of 9 configurations in total (8 variants + Original Serial AES). Figures 6a and 6b show the maximum CPA values for both implementations as a function of time (sampling points). For both plots, a total of 10000 traces were used. In case of the protected implementation, 1111 traces from each of the 9 configurations (8 variants + Original Serial AES) were combined and shuffled. The results show a significant decrease in the maximum correlation value from ~0.482 for the static design to ~0.136 for the protected configuration, a factor of ~3.54×. Consequently, the number of required traces for key extraction increases from ~120 to ~1513, this change increases the resistance against a power attack by a factor of ~12.6x. The values for required traces were calculated from the rule, given in [13]. Figures 7a and 7b depict the effect of increasing the number of traces on the maximum CPA values for all possible key-byte guesses

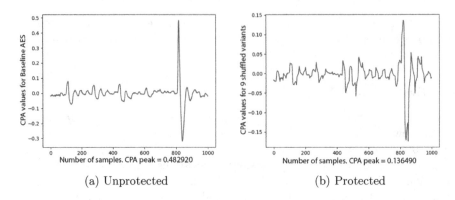

(a) Unprotected   (b) Protected

Fig. 6. CPA Values for Unprotected and Protected AES Implementation

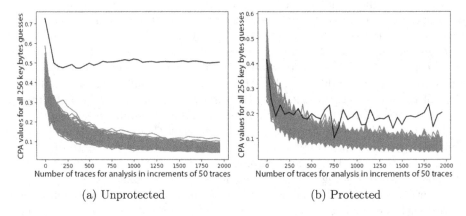

(a) Unprotected   (b) Protected

Fig. 7. Effect of number of traces on max CPA values for AES (correct key guess shown in black)

(0x00 to 0xFF). The correct key-byte is shown in black. From the plot shown in Fig. 7a, it can be observed that the unprotected (baseline) implementation is broken with <50 traces. While for the protected implementation ∼500 traces were needed, as shown in Fig. 7b. The results do not completely agree with the values given by the rule of thumb in [13] but still show a significant improvement in the protection against SCA.

We compare our results with the work in [7], since it also focuses on implementation diversity and utilizes PR as a countermeasure against SCA. The results in [7] show a decrease in the maximum CPA value by a factor of ∼2.2x for 128 configurations. In comparison, the netlist-level variations proposed in this work exhibit a decrease in the maximum CPA by a factor of ∼3.54x, for only nine configurations. This shows that the idea of netlist-level variations is an effective countermeasure against SCA. Furthermore, the work in [7] employs a *Partial Reconfiguration Controller (PRC)*, that acts as a reconfiguration manager, to switch between different configurations and locations. A PRC would generate

Table 1. Resource Utilization of variants.

Design	Utilization		Overhead (x)
Baseline	LUT	570	–
	FF	268	–
Cellonly	LUT	822	252 (1.44x)
	FF	268	–
Randmod0	LUT	1722	1152 (3.02x)
	FF	1404	1136 (5.23x)
LutOnly	LUT	721	151 (1.26x)
	FF	268	–
Cellmod1	LUT	1892	1322 (3.31x)
	FF	1332	1064 (4.97x)
Cellmod3	LUT	2172	1602 (3.81x)
	FF	1724	1456 (6.43x)
Cellmod4	LUT	1800	1230 (3.15x)
	FF	1300	1032 (4.85x)
Cellmod6	LUT	2312	1742 (4.05x)
	FF	1844	1576 (6.88x)
Lutmod7	LUT	2285	1715 (4x)
	FF	1820	1552 (6.80x)

additional noise, decreasing the SnR ratio. Especially when the reconfiguration is done in parallel with the encryption. Thus, we can expect even better results with a PRC included.

It should be noted that the total number of traces to get the key is still pretty low (only 500). Thus, a combination of the proposed technique with a sound masking scheme (embedded into the cryptographic application itself) is advisable and currently under consideration for the future work.

The resource utilization overhead for the variants is given in Table 1. Since the variants were synthesized by Yosys, the utilization overhead is compared with the original (baseline) design which was synthesized using Yosys and implemented in Vivado. Variant Class 2 (Randmod0) shows the highest overhead due to the lengths of dummy chains and control logic inserted into the design. Variant Classes 1 and 3 show a modest overhead of ∼44% and ∼26%, respectively.

7   Conclusion and Future Work

This work introduces the novel concept of netlist randomization as a counter-measure against side-channel analysis. A variety of possible implementations (variants) were explored by modifying the netlist of a serial-based AES archi-tecture. The proposed changes in the netlist were implemented using an open source synthesis tool *Yosys*. Physical measurements on a ZYNQ UltraScale+ device show a significant improvement ~12.6x in the resistance against power attacks. Compared to related work [7], we achieved a much higher degree of protection with only a fraction of generated configurations. Our protection per configuration is ~23x more effective than the approach in [7].

The future work involves three main tasks: firstly, we intend to explore and extend the parameterized variant generation which is expected to produce a larger number of randomized variants. The proposed approach enhances the security of an unprotected AES implementation and hence would be interesting to evaluate its impact on an AES implementation with robust masking scheme such as [16]. Furthermore, our improved circuit variants can be combined with other methods, such as [7], for an even higher degree of implementation diversity. Lastly, we intend to implement a standalone partially reconfigurable system, which can dynamically exchange the variants and their locations on an FPGA. We expect all enhancements to significantly contribute to an increase in the degree of protection against side-channel analysis.

Acknowledgement. This work has been supported by the German Federal Ministry for Eduction and Research (BMBF) within the collaborative research project "SecRec" (16KIS0609).

References

1. Kocher, P., Jaffe, J., Jun, B.: Differential power analysis. In: Wiener, M. (ed.) CRYPTO 1999. LNCS, vol. 1666, pp. 388–397. Springer, Heidelberg (1999). https://doi.org/10.1007/3-540-48405-1_25
2. Kocher, P.C.: Timing attacks on implementations of Diffie-Hellman, RSA, DSS, and other systems. In: Koblitz, N. (ed.) CRYPTO 1996. LNCS, vol. 1109, pp. 104–113. Springer, Heidelberg (1996). https://doi.org/10.1007/3-540-68697-5_9
3. Mentens, N.: Hiding side-channel leakage through hardware randomization: a comprehensive overview. In: 2017 International Conference on Embedded Computer Systems: Architectures, Modeling, and Simulation (SAMOS), Pythagorion, pp. 269–272 (2017)
4. Güneysu, T., Moradi, A.: Generic side-channel countermeasures for reconfigurable devices. In: Preneel, B., Takagi, T. (eds.) CHES 2011. LNCS, vol. 6917, pp. 33–48. Springer, Heidelberg (2011). https://doi.org/10.1007/978-3-642-23951-9_3
5. Sasdrich, P., Moradi, A., Mischke, O., Güneysu, T.: Achieving side-channel protection with dynamic logic reconfiguration on modern FPGAs. In: International Symposium on Hardware Oriented Security and Trust (HOST), pp. 130–136 (2015)
6. Mentens, N., Gierlichs, B., Verbauwhede, I.: Power and fault analysis resistance in hardware through dynamic reconfiguration. In: Oswald, E., Rohatgi, P. (eds.) CHES 2008. LNCS, vol. 5154, pp. 346–362. Springer, Heidelberg (2008). https://doi.org/10.1007/978-3-540-85053-3_22
7. Hettwer, B., Petersen, J., Gehrer, S., Neumann, H., Güneysu, T.: Securing cryptographic circuits by exploiting implementation diversity and partial reconfiguration on FPGAs. In: Design, Automation & Test in Europe Conference & Exhibition (DATE), Florence, Italy 2019, pp. 260–263 (2019)

8. Lavin, C., Kaviani, A.: RapidWright: enabling custom crafted implementations for FPGAs. In: 2018 IEEE 26th Annual International Symposium on Field-Programmable Custom Computing Machines (FCCM) (2018), pp. 133–140 (2018)
9. Wolf, C.: Yosys manual (2013). www.clifford.at/yosys/files/yosys_manual.pdf. Accessed 02 Apr 2020
10. Berkeley Logic Synthesis and Verification Group, ABC: System for Sequential Synthesis and Verification. https://github.com/berkeley-abc/abc
11. Agrawal, D., Archambeault, B., Rao, J.R., Rohatgi, P.: The EM side—channel(s). In: Kaliski, B.S., Koç, K., Paar, C. (eds.) CHES 2002. LNCS, vol. 2523, pp. 29–45. Springer, Heidelberg (2003). https://doi.org/10.1007/3-540-36400-5_4
12. O'Flynn, C., Chen, Z.: A case study of side-channel analysis using decoupling capacitor power measurement with the OpenADC. In: Garcia-Alfaro, J., Cuppens, F., Cuppens-Boulahia, N., Miri, A., Tawbi, N. (eds.) FPS 2012. LNCS, vol. 7743, pp. 341–356. Springer, Heidelberg (2013). https://doi.org/10.1007/978-3-642-37119-6_22
13. Mangard, S., Oswald, E., Popp, T.: Power Analysis Attacks: Revealing the Secrets of Smart Cards. Advances in Information Security, Springer, Heidelberg (2007). https://doi.org/10.1007/978-0-387-38162-6
14. Beckhoff, C., Koch, D., Torresen, J.: Go ahead: a partial reconfiguration framework. In: IEEE 20th International Symposium on Field-Programmable Custom Computing Machines, Toronto, ON, pp. 37–44 (2012)
15. Ziener, D., et al.: FPGA-based dynamically reconfigurable SQL query processing. ACM Trans. Reconfigurable Technol. Syst. **9**, 4 (2016). https://doi.org/10.1145/2845087. Article 25 24 pages
16. Gross, H., Mangard, S., Korak, T.: Domain-oriented masking: compact masked hardware implementations with arbitrary protection order. Cryptology ePrint Archive, Report 2016/486 (2016). https://eprint.iacr.org/2016/486
17. Zhao, M., Suh, G.E.: FPGA-based remote power side-channel attacks. In: IEEE S&P, pp. 229–244 (2018)
18. Krautter, J., Gnad, D., Tahoori, M.: CPAmap: on the complexity of secure FPGA virtualization, multi-tenancy, and physical design. IACR Trans. Cryptogr. Hardw. Embedd. Syst. **2020**(3), 121–146 (2020)

Moving Target and Implementation Diversity Based Countermeasures Against Side-Channel Attacks

Nadir Khan[1]([envelope]) [ID], Benjamin Hettwer[3] [ID], and Jürgen Becker[1,2] [ID]

[1] FZI Research Center for Information Technology, Karlsruhe, Germany
khan@fzi.de
[2] Institute for Information Processing Technology (ITIV), KIT, Karlsruhe, Germany
[3] Robert Bosch GmbH, Corporate Sector Research, Stuttgart, Germany

Abstract. Side-channel attacks (SCAs) are among the major threats to embedded systems' security, where implementation characteristics of cryptographic algorithms are exploited to extract secret parameters. The most common SCAs take advantage of electromagnetic (EM) leakage or power consumption recorded during device operation by placing an EM probe over the chip or measuring the voltage drop across an internal resistor, respectively. In this work, two SCA countermeasures are presented which address these two types of leakage vectors. The first countermeasure supports implementation diversity and moving target defense, while the second one generates random algorithmic noise. These concepts are implemented using the dynamic partial reconfiguration (DPR) feature of modern FPGA devices. Both of the countermeasures are easily scalable, and the effect of scalability on the area overhead and security strength is presented. We evaluate our design by measuring EM emanations from a state-of-the-art System-on-Chip (SoC) with 16 nm production technology. With the most secure variant, we are able to increase the resistance against Correlation Power Analysis (CPA) by a factor of 95 compared to an unprotected AES implementation.

Keywords: Side-channel attacks · Partial reconfiguration · FPGAs · Implementation diversity · Moving target

1 Introduction

Security of microelectronic systems is paramount because of their usage in defense, industrial control systems, communications, data centers, healthcare and automotive. In these systems, security is achieved by utilizing standardized cryptographic algorithms that are considered mathematically secure. However, their respective implementations may leak secret information about their internal state via side-channels such as power consumption [9], electromagnetic (EM) emission [1] and execution time [4]. Once side-channel information is collected, an adversary can run statistical methods on it to extract the cryptographic keys.

© Springer Nature Switzerland AG 2021
S. Derrien et al. (Eds.): ARC 2021, LNCS 12700, pp. 188–202, 2021.
https://doi.org/10.1007/978-3-030-79025-7_13

The statistical analysis method can be differential power analysis (DPA) [2] and correlation power analysis (CPA) [3].

Over the years, researchers and industry developed several methods to counteract side-channel attacks (SCAs). For instance, *masking* aims to randomize intermediate values that are internally processed by the cryptographic device to break the connection between the secret (respectively some intermediate value that depends on the secret) and its power footprint [9]. In contrast, *hiding* countermeasures are different from masking because their goal is to change the power characteristics directly and thus reduce the signal-to-noise ratio (SNR). There is a particular class of hiding techniques that use dynamic partial reconfiguration (DPR) available on modern FPGAs to increase the SCA resistance of cryptographic systems [10].

These methods aim for randomizing the structure and execution process of a cryptographic hardware implementation while maintaining functional correctness. DPR-based SCA countermeasures often create only moderate overhead because the employed reconfiguration infrastructure can be reused for other purposes as well, e.g., to build a fault-tolerant system [11,12].

This paper presents two countermeasures against SCAs. The first, target function relocation (TFR), relocates the target function using DPR. Furthermore, the target-function is implemented using different algorithms with varying power consumption. The selection of the target function's implementation, its location on the chip, and the time interval between DPR operations are made using the outputs of random number generators (RNGs). The moving target approach serves as a countermeasure against EM-based measurement setups while the implementation diversity approach counters power analysis based attacks (DPA and CPA). The second countermeasure is a noise generator (NG), where different noise modules are implemented at an algorithmic-level and are configured on a single location. Here, the selection process is also random.

The proposed countermeasures are scalable, which means the number of locations and implementations can be increased or decreased depending on the use-case. Furthermore, several versions of each countermeasure are implemented and evaluated to show the relationship between resource overhead and achieved security. The main contributions of this paper are:

- DPR is used in several use cases (e.g., accelerators, communication systems), and its support requires additional logic such as a reconfiguration controller. This work proposes to utilize these additional resources to strengthen the security of these systems.
- A complete implementation of both countermeasures is done and presented. An automated flow is implemented that generates different scaled variants of the countermeasures. Furthermore, the implementation-diversity part of the countermeasures can be scaled up/down dynamically (see Sect. 4.7). This makes the design easily adaptable to different scenarios and is a major improvement compared to other similar work.

– The implementation is realized and evaluated on the Xilinx Zynq UltraScale+ MPSoC ZCU102, a state-of-the-art platform for advanced automotive and Internet of Things (IoT) applications based on 16 nm production technology.
– Scaled variants of both countermeasures are evaluated individually and combined to create a more secure system. Furthermore, the effect of scalability on the resource overhead and security strength is presented.

The rest of the paper is organized as follows: Sect. 2 provides state-of-the-art countermeasures against SCAs. The proposed countermeasures and their implementations are discussed in Sects. 3 and 4, respectively. Afterward, the evaluation and discussion are presented in Sect. 5. The paper concludes with Sect. 6.

2   Related Work

The first DPR-based countermeasure against physical attacks has been presented by Mentens et al. [13]. DPR was used to introduce temporal jitter by adding or removing registers between subfunctions of an implementation of the advanced encryption standard (AES). Additionally, spatial jitter could be generated by relocating the subfunctions to four different positions on the chip. However, the number of different configurations that were achieved in that specific approach was comparably low (maximum ten) and thus increased the complexity for a skilled adversary only marginally. Furthermore, the evaluation was only done on paper without performing any power or EM measurements.

In 2011, Güneysu and Moradi exploited the dynamic reconfigurability of selected FPGA components to build a set of generic SCA countermeasures [14]. First, Gaussian noise was generated using lookup tables (LUTs) in shift register mode. Second, a substitute byte (SBOX) scrambling scheme was suggested using the dual-port feature of block RAM (BRAM). Third, several digital clock managers (DCMs) were stacked together to create a randomized clock for the cryptographic core. The proposed countermeasures can be easily combined with arbitrary cryptographic implementations.

Sasdrich et al. employed fine-grained reconfiguration of LUTs (i.e., CFG-LUTs) to randomize the SBOX of a PRESENT implementation [15]. This was achieved by splitting up the (masked) SBOX in two parts with a register in between during runtime. Additionally, the register was pre-charged with the content of a dummy encryption to avoid a hamming distance leakage. However, the scheme is only practical for cryptographic schemes with smaller (e.g., 4×4) SBOXs, but not for ciphers with a larger SBOX such as AES.

Hettwer et al. proposed implementation diversity in combination with DPR to protect cryptographic circuits [6]. From a single netlist of an AES implementation, a number of functionally-invariant physically-different circuits were created by randomizing the placement and routing process. The generated configurations are dynamically exchanged during runtime using DPR. However, since the complete AES was reconfigured, the resource and memory overhead is quite large while achieving only an increased SCA resistance of factor three.

The work proposed in [5] is similar to ours; however, they did not implement most of their claims. For example, like our proposed work, they claimed to use DPR for the configuration of SBOX regions and randomized the selection of location for the target function, its implementation, and the time interval between DPR operations (i.e., between consecutive relocations). Instead, they used twelve static versions of the AES engine, i.e., did not implement and evaluate the stated claims. Furthermore, they discussed the usage of relocatable partial bitstreams, which means single SBOX's partial bitstream can be relocated on any location by changing the frame addresses (FAs) of the bitstreams. However, it was mentioned that this feature is only part of their future work. In order to simulate the effect of DPR, they mixed-up traces from different configurations. The results indicate that it can improve CPA resistance by more than two orders of magnitude. However, the authors stress that a fully operational system is required to determine the actual number of traces needed to break the system, which is not available up to now.

3   Proposed Countermeasures

In this work, two DPR based countermeasures are proposed that utilizes the concepts of moving target (relocating target function) and implementation diversity. Sections 3.1 and 3.2 introduce these countermeasures, respectively, while Sect. 4 discusses their implementation in detail.

3.1   Target Function Relocation (TFR)

The relocation part of the TFR countermeasure is achieved by having multiple reconfigurable regions (RRs) for the target function of an encryption algorithm. This serves as a countermeasure against location-based SCAs such as EM attacks. The term target function here refers to the operation(s) of a cryptographic implementation, which are typically attacked by an adversary (e.g., the SBOX of an AES in our case). The target function is the main cryptographic operation in the power leakage model of the attacked device (see Eq. (2)), which is assumed to have a measurable influence on the deterministic part of power or EM traces [9]. Localized EM-based attacks are usually conducted with small probes having a diameter smaller than one millimeter. The probe is moved over the chip using a spot size smaller than the probe diameter and a certain number of traces are acquired from every position. An individual attack is then performed for all positions to find the most suitable probe position. Moving the target function randomly to different positions on the chip using DPR makes EM attacks substantially harder as the traces for a single location are mixed up with EM radiations from different logical elements of the cryptographic circuit. In general, if there are l different locations for the target function, it can be expected that at least l times more EM traces are needed to successfully recover the secret key [6].

In order to achieve implementation diversity, the target function is implemented in several ways, where each implementation generates a different power footprint. The underlying motivation is that the distinct physical layout (placement and routing) of each target function implementation induces a varying charging capacitance when the implementation is continuously replaced using DPR. This affects the dynamic power consumption of the target function and connected resources (e.g., registers) and helps as a countermeasure against power measurement-based SCAs. These implementations will be referred to as reconfigurable modules (RMs). Random number generators (RNGs) are used for the selection of location (i.e., RR), target function implementation (i.e., RM), and the time interval between DPR operations. These issues are discussed in detail in Sect. 4.

3.2   Noise Generation (NG)

For this countermeasure, the noise generation module can be implemented in several ways and is configured on an RR. In this work, hardware description language (HDL) implementations of a Gaussian noise generator [19], three pseudo RNGs [20,23,24] and two sine wave generators [21,22] are used as basic noise sources, which are taken from open sources. All noise modules are scaled by cascading several of their instances in series so that they have a significant influence on power consumption. Afterward, all possible combinations of the six basic noises are generated that resulted in 63 different noises, which can be calculated using Eq. (1):

$$C = \sum_{r=1}^{n} \frac{n!}{k!(n-k)!} \tag{1}$$

C represents the total possible combinations, and n is the number of noises among which k noises are chosen for a specific combination.

Like the TFR countermeasure, the selection of a noise RM for configuration and the time interval between DPR operations are made randomly. Both countermeasures are general and can be implemented for any encryption algorithm. Implementation differences of the RMs for the target function and noise modules can be at an algorithm-, synthesis- and/or circuit-level. Algorithm-level differences among RMs mean that the RMs are implemented using different algorithms, e.g., an AES SBOX implemented using LUTs and combinational logic. Synthesis-level differences would be changes in the logic structure, placement, and routing. Circuit-level would be fine-grained changes to specific paths such as clock inputs of flip-flops. The two latter cases are discussed in detail by Bow et al. in [5]. In this work, RMs differ on the algorithmic level that creates variants with a more distinct power footprint than only changing placement and routing. The number of RMs can be easily increased by combining algorithmic, synthesis- and circuit-level methods.

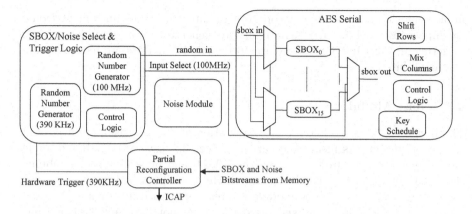

Fig. 1. Block diagram of the SCA-resistant AES.

4 Implementation

The baseline design used for implementing the countermeasures is an 8-bit serial AES-128 encryption core, which requires 264 LUTs and 253 registers. The target board used in the measurement setup is a Xilinx ZYNQ UltraScale+ System-on-Chip (SoC) evaluation board. Since the processing system (PS) of the board is used to deliver plain-text data and key to the core, it is interfaced with the PS using Advanced eXtensible Interface 4 (AXI4). It is also assumed that the target system has a Partial Reconfiguration Controller (PRC) module, which can be used for the configuration of other logic. Therefore, the AXI-interfaced AES and PRC, along with AXI interconnect blocks, are considered the reference design for this work, which requires 3317 LUTs, 4014 registers and 922 CLBs.

The implementation takes 210 clock cycles for single encryption, where each round of AES is computed in 21 cycles. For TFR, SBOX is selected as the target function, as discussed in Sect. 3.1. The reference AES design uses only one SBOX for computing substitute byte functionality for each byte in all the rounds and key scheduling. The block diagram of the SCA-resistant AES is shown in Fig. 1. The functionality of the sub-modules is presented in the following sections.

4.1 AES Serial

AES Serial is a modified version of the reference design. It has 16 SBOXs instead of one and for each SBOX, an RR is created so that they can be placed on different locations of the programmable logic (PL). However, at any clock cycle, only one of the 16 SBOXs will be used during the operation of an AES encryption. Therefore, multiplexers are added at the inputs and outputs (IOs) of the SBOXs, as shown in Fig. 1. More details about the selection of an SBOX and its IOs are discussed in Sect. 4.4.

Four different HDL implementations of the AES SBOX are used in this work: a LUT-based implementation, an inverse LUT-based, inverse on Gallois field implementation taken from opencores.org [18] and Canright's implementation of a compact SBOX [17]. Partial bitstreams are generated for each implementation targeting all the RRs. Since there are 16 RRs and four RMs, we have a total of 64 partial bitstreams.

4.2   Noise Module

The purpose of this module is the contribution of power consumption noise to the overall design. As mentioned earlier in Sect. 3.2, several HDL-based implementations are taken from open sources [19–24] and by scaling and combining them, 63 different versions are generated. Here, scaling a noise module means using several instances of the module to create its scaled-up version. An extra RM for the noise module is generated that does not have any design, which makes a total of 64 RMs. An RR is created for the noise module and partial bitstreams specific to that RR for all 64 versions are generated.

4.3   Partial Reconfiguration Controller (PRC)

Xilinx's PRC is used for the configuration process, which is activated by a hardware trigger. The configuration is done using the internal configuration access port (ICAP). Further details about the usage of dynamic partial reconfiguration (DPR) and PRC can be found in [7] and [8], respectively.

4.4   SBOX Noise Select and Trigger Logic (SNTL)

SNTL is the central controller, which applies countermeasures to the AES module. It chooses values for all the parameters of the countermeasures, and afterward, sends necessary control signals to other modules, e.g., hardware trigger to the PRC. This is done using a control logic and two RNGs, namely $RNG_{390\,KHz}$ and $RNG_{100\,MHz}$. Three random values from the $RNG_{390\,KHz}$, namely *SBOX-Impl*, *TargetLocation*, and *TriggerTime*, are used by the control logic for the TFR countermeasure. The control logic uses *SBOXImpl* to select an SBOX bitstream (RM) and configures it on the location indicated by *TargetLocation* value. The configuration process is triggered when a counter inside the control logic reaches the $TriggerTime_{TRF}$ value. For the NG countermeasure, two random values (*NoiseImpl* and $TriggerTime_{NG}$) are taken from $RNG_{390\,KHz}$. The control logic uses *NoiseImpl* value to select a noise implementation and $TriggerTime_{NG}$ to generate a hardware trigger to start the (re)-configuration.

Since the configuration process runs in parallel with AES encryption, SNTL is also equipped with the functionality to select an SBOX that should be used by the AES design during the encryption process. As stated earlier, an AES encryption takes 210 clock cycles. For each clock cycle, a different SBOX is selected and is provided with the correct input value (i.e., sbox_in in Fig. 1). The rest of the SBOXs are given a random value to further reduce the SNR of the correct SBOX calculation. These random values ($SBOXInput_J$) are taken from

$RNG_{100\,MHz}$. The SBOX selection is also made using a random value (*SBOXSelect*) from $RNG_{100\,MHz}$. Since the AES design is running at 100 MHz frequency, an RNG running at the same frequency is used for the SBOX's IO selection and delivering random values to the inputs of all other SBOXes. Also, the PRC may be currently reconfiguring the selected SBOX. In that case, a complement of the *SBOXSelect* value is used for the selection process because the output of the selected SBOX will be invalid.

The SBOX's IO selection and providing random values at the input of non-selected SBOXes happen in a single clock and for each of the 210 clock cycles. In other words, our AES design, including the countermeasures, has the same latency and takes the same number of clock cycles as the reference design.

4.5   Bare-Metal Application

A bare-metal application running on the PS moves all the partial bitstreams (RMs) from the non-volatile memory (NVM) to the RAM. Afterward, PRC's registers are updated with the memory location and size of the RMs. AES Serial is then continuously provided with plain-text and key values and reading the ciphertext once encryption is completed. A self-test has been implemented to ensure that the AES core works correctly.

4.6   Configuration Times

Since all RRs of the TFR countermeasure are equal in size, the bitstreams generated for them will have the same size, which is 179.5 KB. As mentioned earlier, PRC does the configuration of the bitstreams using ICAP. The bandwidth of ICAP is 3.2 Gb/s at 100 MHz [8], which means PRC will reconfigure SBOX in 0.488 ms. For the NG countermeasure, there are 64 RMs generated for the same RR, where each is 203.7 KB in size. Consequently, the configuration time for the noise module is 0.509 ms.

4.7   Scalability—Variants Generation and Deployment

Both the countermeasures can be implemented in several configurations to generate different variants. Variants can differ based on the number of reconfigurable regions ($\#RRs$), reconfigurable modules ($\#RMs$) or a combination of both that are used in the design. Variants that differ in terms of $\#RRs$ require changes to the design flow. This is mainly because for each RR, a dummy design with interface definition needs to be instantiated in the system while connecting it with other sub-designs. Furthermore, a constraint file is required, which provides information about the physical location of the RR. This file can be generated by doing floorplanning of the RRs manually. For further details about these steps or Xilinx's DPR flow, please see [8].

The other case is where variants differ only in terms of $\#RMs$, i.e., the number of $\#RRs$ is fixed. This scenario can fully take advantage of the proposed work's scalability feature because the design flow needs to be run only once. The deployed countermeasure can be scaled up or down in run-time, i.e., the rest of the system does not require resetting. For scaling up the countermeasure, only additional partial bitstreams for the additional RMs need to provided to the device using a non-volatile memory (e.g., flash). Afterward, PRC's registers need to be updated to support more $#RMs$. For example, if $#RRs$ is fixed to two and $#RMs$ is initially set to four. The design flow will be run to generate full and partial bitstreams. For each RR, four partial bitstreams will be generated, making a total of eight. This cryptographic design, including the countermeasure, can be configured and activated on the device. In this example, we suppose that the design needs to be updated with another variant with the same $#RRs$ and eight RMs. As stated earlier, only new RMs' partial bitstreams need to be generated and provided to the device. This means the additional eight partial bitstreams are provided to the device. Furthermore, PRC's registers need to be updated for the newer variant to take effect. Similarly, if the countermeasure needs to be down-scaled to four RMs, only PRC's registers need to be updated to support fewer $#RMs$.

The purpose of scaling up the countermeasures is to provide higher security, which leads to higher resource consumption. The resource overhead caused by scaling is discussed in the following section, and its impact on the security strength is presented in Sect. 5.

4.8   Scalability—Resource Overhead

As mentioned in the last section, several variants of the countermeasures can be generated by using different values for $#RRs$ and $#RMs$. Using variable values for both parameters will lead to a high number of variants. To have a reasonable number of variants, one of the parameters is set to a fixed value while the other is kept variable. This way, the effect of each parameter can be evaluated individually for both resource overhead and security.

For the first countermeasure, TFR, variants are generated by setting $#RRs = \{2, 4, 8, 16\}$ and $#RMs = 4$. Table 1 shows the resources consumed by each variant in comparison to the reference design. For the second countermeasure, NG, variants are generated by setting $#RRs = 4$ and $#RMs = \{8, 16, 32, 64\}$. The resource overhead for each variant for the latter case is shown in Table 2.

The presented results show that the proposed countermeasures have a different impact on resource consumption. For example, only 7% of extra resources are required by the TFR countermeasure with 2 RRs, and as the $#RRs$ grow, the resource overhead also grows linearly. In the case of NG, the resource overhead is 18% for 8 RMs case. However, the NG countermeasure overhead does not grow linearly with the number of noise modules, e.g., 25% for 64 RMs. The results show that the number of $#RMs$ has a comparatively smaller effect on the resource overhead; however, the same is not valid in the case of memory consumption (see Table 2).

Both countermeasures can be easily combined and its resource overhead will be the sum of their respective overheads. For example, the Look-up Tables

Table 1. Resource consumption overhead and memory requirement with TFR (4 RMs)

Designs	LUT	FF	CLB	Overhead (CLB)	Memory (MB)
AES-Reference	3317	4014	922	–	0
AES-TFR (2 RRs)	3626	4172	991	1.07×	1.43
AES-TFR (4 RRs)	3898	4357	1089	1.18×	2.87
AES-TFR (8 RRs)	4447	4655	1247	1.35×	5.74
AES-TFR (16 RRs)	5556	5252	1422	1.54×	11.48

Table 2. Resource consumption overhead and memory requirement with NG (1 RR)

Designs	LUT	FF	CLB	Overhead (CLB)	Memory (MB)
AES-Reference	3317	4014	922	–	0
AES-NG (8 RMs)	4597	6337	1089	1.18×	1.63
AES-NG (16 RMs)	4662	6398	1098	1.19×	3.26
AES-NG (32 RMs)	4680	6482	1113	1.21×	6.51
AES-NG (64 RMs)	4803	6651	1157	1.25×	13.03

(LUTs), Flip-Flops (FFs) and Configurable Logic Blocks (CLBs) consumed by combining AES-TFR (16 RRs, 4 RMs) and AES-NG (1 RR, 64 RMs) are 7042, 7889 and 1657, respectively. This is an 80% increase of CLB resources as compared to the reference design.

As stated earlier, all the partial bitstreams generated for the TFR countermeasure have the same size, which is 179.5 KB. As the countermeasure is scaled, more partial bitstreams will be required, which will lead to higher memory. Similarly, all the partial bitstream generated for NG countermeasure have the same size that is 203.7 KB. The memory requirements for all the variants of TFR and NG countermeasures are shown in Table 1 and 2, respectively.

4.9   Throughput Overhead

As mentioned in Sect. 4.4, AES with TFR countermeasure has 16 SBOXs, and for each of the 210 clock cycles of the AES encryption, the output value of a randomly selected SBOX is used for the computation. It is also ensured that if an SBOX is being configured, it is not chosen as its output will be invalid. This whole selection process happens in a single clock without any latency. Furthermore, PRC's configuration process and the selection process runs parallel to the AES encryption, which means that the TFR countermeasure does not affect the throughput of the AES encryption.

Similarly, in the case of NG countermeasure, the selection and configuration of noise's partial bitstream happen in parallel to the encryption process. Therefore, the NG countermeasure also does not have any throughput overhead. Finally, the combination of both countermeasures also does not affect the throughput of the encryption process.

5   Evaluation

To evaluate the security gain of TFR and NG countermeasures, EM measurements from a Xilinx ZYNQ Ultrascale+ MPSoC have been acquired. The EM traces have been collected by measuring the current through a decoupling capacitor of the power supply of the FPGA as initially proposed by O'Flynn and Chen [16]. The signal was captured using an ICR HV500-75 near-field probe by Langer EMV and a Picoscope 6404D oscilloscope with an anti-aliasing low-pass filter. We have not used an external amplifier besides the one that is integrated in the probe. The sampling rate of the oscilloscope has been set to 1250 MS/s using a bandwidth of 500 MHz. 100,000 traces have been recorded for several configurations of the design. In order to increase the SNR, an averaging factor of 250 has been applied to each trace. This means that an encryption with a certain plain-text has been repeated 250 times and the average trace of all these encryptions have been saved for analysis. Please note that averaging is a common technique to lower the effect of noise-generating countermeasures such as TFR and NG proposed in this paper.

After pre-processing, we have calculated the Pearson correlation coefficient between the traces and a register transition (hamming distance power leakage) that occurs during the first round in the serialized AES calculation. The hypothetical (power) leakage l model can be represented as:

$$l = HW(SBOX(PT[0] \oplus K[0]) \oplus SBOX(PT[4] \oplus K[4])) \qquad (2)$$

where, HW, PT, K are the abbreviations for Hamming weight, plain-text and AES key, respectively. $SBOX$ represents the sub bytes operation in the AES calculation. Please note that we have chosen the SBOX as the target function due to its non-linearity property. This is beneficial for SCAs as it introduces many bit-flips in the AES state and thus significantly affects the overall power consumption of the circuit. The registers which hold the AES state are placed directly after the SBOX in our design. State transitions of registers (respectively flip-flops) cause the highest instantaneous power leakage in a cryptographic hardware implementation. The leakage of the combinatorial logics (e.g., *AddRoundKey*) is much lower. From an attacker's perspective, it would also be possible to target the mix columns operation. However, this would require to guess 64 bits of the key instead of 16. Such an attack would take much more time (up to several months) and traces compared to an attack against the SBOX output, even in a fully unprotected setting. That is why the SBOX is the main target in SCAs, which is protected by the TFR countermeasure in our approach.

Table 3. Attack results for different configurations

Design	Security (g_{sec})
AES-Reference	1.0
AES-TFR (2 RRs)	4.53
AES-TFR (4 RRs)	11.45
AES-TFR (8 RRs)	14.26
AES-TFR (16 RRs)	17.95
AES-NG (8 RMs)	6.73
AES-NG (16 RMs)	7.25
AES-NG (32 RMs)	12.11
AES-NG (64 RMs)	40.02
AES-TFR (16 RRs) + NG (64 RMs)	94.9

Having the results of the correlation analysis, the required number of traces to break the design n_A can be derived by:

$$n_A \approx \frac{28}{\rho^2}. \tag{3}$$

where ρ is the maximum correlation value for the correct leakage hypothesis [9]. Using that number, we define the security gain g_{sec} as the ratio between the number of traces needed to break a protected design and the number of traces needed to break the unprotected reference design:

$$g_{sec} = \frac{\#\ traces\ protected}{\#\ traces\ unprotected} \tag{4}$$

The results for the corresponding designs can be found in Table 3. From there, we can make several observations. The protection level increases with the number of configurations used for both countermeasures. For instance, for AES-TFR with two reconfigurable regions, 4.53 times more traces are needed to break the design compared to the reference AES, while almost 18 times more traces are needed when 16 placement locations (RRs) are used for the target function. The NG countermeasure also benefits from a higher number of configurations, although all partial bitstreams are placed in the same RR. When all 64 available noise RMs are used, the number of traces needed to extract the correct key (byte) is almost 40 times the traces required for the reference design and approximately 36 times more than that required for the design with 8 RMs. As discussed earlier, the resource overhead (in terms of CLBs) only increases by seven percent when scaling from eight RMs to 64 RMs. Combining the fully-fledged versions of TFR and NG (i.e., with 16 RRs and 64 noise modules) gives a security gain of factor 95. This number is much higher than for all other configurations of the proposed design. A reason for this security gain is that the reconfiguration of the target

Table 4. Comparison of TFR and NG countermeasure with related works

	# Configurations	Resources[1]			Throughput[1]	Memory[1]
		LUT	FF	BRAM		
[13]	10	N/A	N/A	0	6.66×	91 kB
[14][2]	N/A	1706	1169	8	0	N/A
[15]	N/A	1236	388	0	3.03×	N/A
[6]	128	5270	3986	0	N/A	788.48 MB
[5]	12	N/A	N/A	N/A	N/A	N/A
Proposed[3]	128	3725	3875	0	0	24.51 MB

[1] Overhead compared to unprotected design
[2] S-Box Scrambling (i.e., Masking)
[3] AES-TFR (16 RRs) + NG (64 RMs)

function and NG module is done in parallel with the encryption, which again is a source of noise and makes SCAs harder.

Our measurement setup requires 120 traces to recover the encryption key from the reference design. However, when both the countermeasures are added, this number increases to 11 200. Although this boundary is still low, we stress that the countermeasures can be easily scaled to a higher number of configurations (e.g., by exploiting implementation diversity as proposed in [6]). Since we can break the reference design with such few traces, our measurement setup can be considered of high quality. Thus, we can assume our evaluation results as a worst-case scenario.

The TFR scheme can also be applied to masked S-Box designs to achieve a higher level of protection. Suppose a first-order masking scheme would give resistance against one million power traces. Then, the TFR and NG countermeasures would require the adversary to acquire probably more than 100 million traces. We expect that such a system composed of masking and hiding would also be resistant against second-order attacks, as it has been shown in related work [25], especially with a higher number of reconfigurable modules.

The resource overhead of the proposed design compared to related work is illustrated in Table 4. In contrast to the work of Hettwer et al. [6], our countermeasures achieve a much higher security gain (i.e., 3 vs. 95) while having the same number of configurations. Furthermore, memory and resource overhead is lower, and there is no throughput penalty. Other works based on partial reconfiguration have either no experimental results [13] or are not fully implemented [5]. The masking approaches presented in [14,15] have theoretically an unlimited number of configurations (depending on the entropy of the RNG), thus achieving a high level of randomization and protection. However, as mentioned before, scaling improves the security strength of our countermeasures.

6   Conclusion

This work presents two countermeasures against SCAs. The first one utilizes the moving target and implementation diversity approaches that are implemented using the DPR feature. In this countermeasure, multiple implementations of an encryption algorithm's target function are reconfigured on different locations of the PL of an FPGA. The second countermeasure is only implementation diversity-based, where random noise is added to the device's overall power consumption. The decisions of triggering a reconfiguration, location selection for the target function, and selecting the implementation for both cases are performed based on random values. Furthermore, the configuration process and encryption algorithm execute in parallel. The power consumed by the configuration process also acts as noise to the overall power consumption. The countermeasures can be easily scaled and merged. All these features provide a substantial resistance against SCAs when power is either recorded using an EM probe over the chip or by measuring the voltage drop across an internal resistor.

Acknowledgements. This work was supported by the German Federal Ministry of Education and Research (BMBF) under Grant 16KIS0610.

References

1. Gandolfi, K., Mourtel, C., Olivier, F.: Electromagnetic analysis: concrete results. In: Koç, Ç.K., Naccache, D., Paar, C. (eds.) CHES 2001. LNCS, vol. 2162, pp. 251–261. Springer, Heidelberg (2001). https://doi.org/10.1007/3-540-44709-1_21
2. Kocher, P., Jaffe, J., Jun, B.: Differential power analysis. In: Wiener, M. (ed.) CRYPTO 1999. LNCS, vol. 1666, pp. 388–397. Springer, Heidelberg (1999). https://doi.org/10.1007/3-540-48405-1_25
3. Brier, E., Clavier, C., Olivier, F.: Correlation power analysis with a leakage model. In: Joye, M., Quisquater, J.-J. (eds.) CHES 2004. LNCS, vol. 3156, pp. 16–29. Springer, Heidelberg (2004). https://doi.org/10.1007/978-3-540-28632-5_2
4. Kocher, P.C.: Timing attacks on implementations of Diffie-Hellman, RSA, DSS, and other systems. In: Koblitz, N. (ed.) CRYPTO 1996. LNCS, vol. 1109, pp. 104–113. Springer, Heidelberg (1996). https://doi.org/10.1007/3-540-68697-5_9
5. Bow, I., et al.: Side-channel power resistance for encryption algorithms using implementation diversity. Cryptography 4(2), 13 (2020)
6. Hettwer, B., Petersen, J., Gehrer, S., Neumann, H., Güneysu, T.: Securing cryptographic circuits by exploiting implementation diversity and partial reconfiguration on FPGAs. In: Design, Automation Test in Europe Conference Exhibition (DATE), Florence, Italy, vol. 2019, pp. 260–263 (2019). https://doi.org/10.23919/DATE.2019.8714801
7. Xilinx, Partial Reconfiguration Controller v1.3, LogiCORE IP Product Guide, Xilinx, April 2018, vivado Design Suite PG193
8. Xilinx, Vivado Design Suite User Guide: Partial Reconfiguration, Xilinx, 27 April 2018
9. Mangard, S., Oswald, E., Popp, T.: Power Analysis Attacks. Springer, Boston (2007). https://doi.org/10.1007/978-0-387-38162-6

10. Mentens, N.: Hiding side-channel leakage through hardware randomization: a comprehensive overview. In: 2017 International Conference on Embedded Computer Systems: Architectures, Modeling, and Simulation (SAMOS), Pythagorion, pp. 269–272 (2017). https://doi.org/10.1109/SAMOS.2017.8344639

11. Nguyen, T.T., Thevenin, M., Mouraud, A., Corre, G., Pasquier, O., Pillement, S.: High-level reliability evaluation of reconfiguration-based fault tolerance techniques. In: IEEE International Parallel and Distributed Processing Symposium Workshops (IPDPSW). Vancouver, BC, vol. 2018, pp. 202–205 (2018). https://doi.org/10.1109/IPDPSW.2018.00038

12. Reorda, M.S., Sterpone, L., Ullah, A.: An error-detection and self-repairing method for dynamically and partially reconfigurable systems. IEEE Trans. Comput. **66**(6), 1022–1033 (2017). https://doi.org/10.1109/TC.2016.2607749

13. Mentens, N., Gierlichs, B., Verbauwhede, I.: Power and fault analysis resistance in hardware through dynamic reconfiguration. In: Oswald, E., Rohatgi, P. (eds.) CHES 2008. LNCS, vol. 5154, pp. 346–362. Springer, Heidelberg (2008). https://doi.org/10.1007/978-3-540-85053-3_22

14. Güneysu, T., Moradi, A.: Generic side-channel countermeasures for reconfigurable devices. In: Preneel, B., Takagi, T. (eds.) CHES 2011. LNCS, vol. 6917, pp. 33–48. Springer, Heidelberg (2011). https://doi.org/10.1007/978-3-642-23951-9_3

15. Sasdrich, P., Moradi, A., Mischke, O., Güneysu, T.: Achieving side-channel protection with dynamic logic reconfiguration on modern FPGAs. In: IEEE International Symposium on Hardware Oriented Security and Trust (HOST). Washington, DC, pp. 130–136 (2015). https://doi.org/10.1109/HST.2015.7140251

16. O'Flynn, C., Chen, Z.: A case study of side-channel analysis using decoupling capacitor power measurement with the OpenADC. In: Garcia-Alfaro, J., Cuppens, F., Cuppens-Boulahia, N., Miri, A., Tawbi, N. (eds.) FPS 2012. LNCS, vol. 7743, pp. 341–356. Springer, Heidelberg (2013). https://doi.org/10.1007/978-3-642-37119-6_22

17. Canright, D.: A very compact Rijndael S-box, September 2004. https://www.researchgate.net/publication/235155631_A_Very_Compact_Rijndael_S-box

18. Villar, J.C.: Opencores 128/192 AES. Accessed 16 Mar 2019. https://opencores.org/projects/systemcaes

19. Liu, G.: Gaussian Noise Generator (GNG) Verilog IP Core. Accessed 16 Mar 2019. https://github.com/liuguangxi/gng

20. Lal, V.: LFSR-Random number generator. Accessed 16 Mar 2019. https://opencores.org/projects/lfsr_randgen

21. verilog code for SINE PWM. Accessed 16 Mar 2019. https://community.intel.com/t5/Intel-Quartus-Prime-Software/verilog-code-for-SINE-PWM/td-p/144210

22. Simple sine wave generator in VHDL. Accessed 16 Mar 2019. https://vhdlguru.blogspot.com/2010/03/simple-sine-wave-generator-in-vhdl.html

23. Chami, C.A.: Pseudo random generator Tutorial. Accessed 16 Mar 2019. https://fpgasite.wordpress.com/2016/08/09/pseudo-random-generator-tutorial/

24. Pseudo random number generator Tutorial. Accessed 16 Mar 2019. http://fpgasite.blogspot.com/2017/04/pseudo-random-generator-tutorial.html

25. Sasdrich, P., Moradi, A., Güneysu, T.: Hiding higher-order side-channel leakage. In: Handschuh, H. (ed.) CT-RSA 2017. LNCS, vol. 10159, pp. 131–146. Springer, Cham (2017). https://doi.org/10.1007/978-3-319-52153-4_8

Clone-Resistant Secured Booting Based on Unknown Hashing Created in Self-Reconfigurable Platform

Randa Zarrouk[1]($\boxtimes$), Saleh Mulhem[2], Weal Adi[1], and Mladen Berekovic[2]

[1] Institute of Computer and Network Engineering, Technical University of Braunschweig, 38106 Braunschweig, Germany
{randa.zarrouk,w.adi}@tu-bs.de
[2] Institute of Computer Engineering, University of Lübeck, 23562 Lübeck, Germany
{mulhem,berekovic}@iti.uni-luebeck.de

Abstract. Deploying a physically unclonable trusted anchor is required for securing software running on embedded systems. Common mechanisms combine secure boot with either stored secret keys or keys extracted from a Physical Unclonable Function (PUF). We propose a new secure boot mechanism that is hardware-based, individual to each device, and keyless to prohibit any unauthorized alteration of the software running on a particular device. Our solution is based on the so-called Secret Unknown Hash (SUH), a self-created random secret unknown hardwired hash function residing as a permanent digital hardware-module in the device's physical layout. It is initiated in the device in a post-manufacturing, unpredictable single event process in self-reconfigurable non-volatile SoC FPGAs. In this work, we explain the SUH creation process and its integration for a device-specific secure boot. The SUH is shown to be lightweight when implemented in a sample scenario as a DM-PRESENT-based hash function. A security analysis is also presented, highlighting the different proposed sample SUH-class entropies.

Keywords: Self-reconfigurable environment · SoC FPGA · Secure-boot · Physically Unclonable Function · Unknown secret

1 Introduction

Our trust in electronic systems depends on trusting that the physical electronic platforms' software executes all and only the intended operations. Rigorous trustworthiness starts from the foundation and expands through the system software stacks [1]. After power-on and before executing the end-application software, the bootstrap process should ensure that no software component has been modified in an unauthorized manner. Thus, a secure boot becomes an essential requirement for ensuring a bootstrap secure and robust against possible severe attacks [2, 3]. In addition to software integrity, some secure boot variants

R. Zarrouk—Supported by a research grant from the German Academic Exchange Service (DAAD).

ensure software authenticity by deploying a key provisioned by the manufacturer of the System on Chip (SoC). Unfortunately, if the key is not unique to each device, then if one device's secure boot's key is compromised, the secure boot of all the other devices using that same key is also compromised. Thus, establishing a device-specific secure boot eliminates such risk. However, provisioning a unique key for every device can be a logistically demanding task, and even if it is uniquely generated, when stored in a Non-Volatile Memory (NVM), reconfigurable, or One-Time Programmable (OTP), the key is prone to some read-back attacks [4].

An alternative device-specific secure boot solution is to derive a device-unique key from a Physical Unclonable Function (PUF). However, despite what PUF technology promises, additional mechanisms are required to ensure the consistency of PUF's response reproducibility over time. Moreover, a non-protected strong PUF falls 2short against modeling attack.

This paper proposes using a self-created random hardwired cryptographic function, so-called Secret Unknown Hash (SUH), to establish a device-specific secure boot for an SoC environment equipped with reconfigurable hardware fabric. SUH's digital nature makes its responses inherently reproducible over time without the need for additional countermeasures, as in the PUF case. The proposed boot mechanism requires SoC with a self-reconfigurable non-volatile (embedded) Field-Programmable Gate Array ((e)FPGA) fabric as a suitable platform for the SUH creation. SUH can be created during a post-manufacturing unpredictable single event process within the device itself, eliminating the need to trust the SoC manufacturer for provisioning a device-unique secret. The self-created SUH hardware module is distributed in the unoccupied FPGA fabric areas, making it harder for adversary reach. The self-reconfigurable property is still not existent in the non-volatile FPGA landscape, but it is expected to submerge soon due to its demanded properties.

2 Summary of Contributions

In this work:

- We first introduce SUH-based secure boot (Table 1, Fig. 1), and we show state-of-the-art secure boot hardware-based solutions such as PUF-based secure boot.
- We enumerate the PUF limitation (Sect. 3).
- We show how self-reconfigurable non-volatile SoC FPGA enables SUH creation and explain how SUH ensures a device-specific secure boot. (Section 4)
- As proof of the concept, we present a possible sample implementation variant of a SUH based on a lightweight DM-PRESENT and evaluate its security. (Section 5)
- We introduce a generalized comparison between two cases of the class entropy of SUH. (Table 4)

Motivation: SUH vs. PUF Secure Boot. To highlight the importance of the proposed secure-boot mechanism, we summarize the difference between the state-of-the-art PUF-based secure boot with the proposed SUH-secure boot. We propose Table 1 and Fig. 1 to show the characteristics, similarities, and differences of every solution. The hash-based secure boot is to be noted as a reference point since it is the most trivial secure boot

Table 1. Characteristics, similarities, and differences between SUH-based secure boot (our work), hash-based secure boot, and PUF-based secure boot.

Characteristics	Secure boot based on:		
	A hardwired traditional hash function alone	PUF + A hardwired traditional hash function (Fig. 1(a))	**SUH** *(introduced in this work)* (Fig. 1(b))
Offers data integrity	Yes	Yes	**Yes**
Offers data authentication	No	Yes	**Yes**
Offers device authentication	No	Yes	**Yes**
Requires additional measurements for a consistent response reproducibility	No	Yes	**No**
Uses a key	No	Yes	**No**
Created in Post-manufacturing setting	No	No	**Yes**

mechanism. As we show in Table 1, both PUF-based and SUH-based ensure software integrity and authentication along with electronic device authentication. Meanwhile, unlike PUF, our proposal using SUH has the advantage of providing a consistent response reproducibility without additional measures, being keyless, and being created in a post-manufacturing setting.

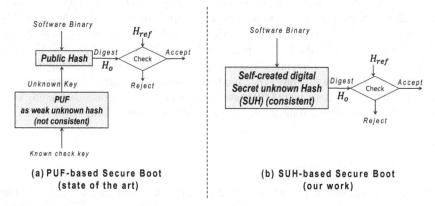

Fig. 1. (a) state of the art of device-specific secure boot and (b) the proposed concept of the device-specific secure boot.

Figure 1 shows how the proposed SUH-based solution replaces the PUF and the hash function while providing a software executable's digest that is unique and individual to the electronic device where the SUH is self-created.

3   Background and Related Work

3.1   Secure Boot

Secure boot is one of the Trusted Computing (TC) mechanisms used to establish a chain-of-trust that starts from a root-of-trust and ends with the last executed software. There are a variety of authentication schemes to establish a secure boot: hash-based, Message Authentication Code (MAC)-based, and signature-based [5, 6]. In this work, we refer to a device as an electronic unit. Two devices with identical models, identical brands, and identically produced are considered two different electronic units.

Device-Specific Secure-Boot. A software digest is unique to the device if a unique device Identity (ID) is included in the hash computation [5, 6]. By generating a device-specific hash value (digest) of the software binary to be authenticated during the boot process, the secure boot is made unique to that device. The benefit is that if the adversary could determine a different pre-image for that device's authentic software digest to use it as malicious software, it does not affect the secure boot of other devices running the same authentic software.

PUF-Based Secure Boot. Several secure boot scenarios utilizing PUF as a key source exist. Some aim to secure the volatile SoC FPGA bitstream, and others aim to secure the processor. The used key is unknown as it is extracted from the PUF and links the software or the bitstream to that specific device. For instance, in [7], Twisted Bistable Ring PUF (TBR-PUF) generates system keys to protect and authenticate the firmware and the operating system using the Advanced Encryption Standard (AES) cipher in a Galois/Counter Mode (GCM). In [8], a diode-connected nMOS transistors PUF generates a 128-bit unique key to be used with the PRESENT cipher and the MAC algorithm to ensure the firmware's confidentiality, authenticity, and integrity. In [9], a Hardware-Embedded Delay PUF (HELP) is implemented into a Xilinx Zynq 7020 SoC FPGA fabric to generate a key encrypting/decrypting a second bitstream containing the programmable logic and the software to be executed. In [10], a Configurable response-length Linear Feedback Shift Register (LFSR) based PUF (CoLPUF) generates the signing keys for a proposed secure boot framework in a RISC-V SoC environment.

3.2   PUFs and Their Limits

PUF can be considered the physical equivalent of a one-way hash function [11, 12]. The significant random physical components constituting the PUF make it inherently unclonable. Several designs of PUF were proposed, and based on their Challenge Responses Pairs (CRP), researchers have classified them into two categories; *Strong PUF* supports a large number CRPs with a space that scales exponentially relatively to the PUF size and *Weak PUF*, which is, on the contrary, supports a limited number of CRPs in a polynomial or a linear space growth [13]. Although PUF can be a compelling solution for device-specific security, not all PUF are "good enough" for some applications' required security level. A PUF should be selected carefully based on some criteria such as uniqueness, randomness, and diffuseness, besides the limits enumerated below:

Predictability. *"An unprotected strong PUF able to resist modeling would be a real breakthrough"* [13]. Strong PUFs are prone to modeling attacks [14]. Thus, they need protection by integrating additional cryptographic primitives [13]. Nevertheless, some protected, strong PUFs still fail against different types of modeling attacks. For example, the Bistable Ring (BR) PUF was improved twice and still exhibits vulnerabilities against modeling attacks. As a first improvement, the TBR-PUF was proposed [15]. The second amelioration suggests XORing at least 4 BRs, which has shown the BR is immune against only one type of modeling attack: the Support-Vector Machines (SVM ML) attack [16].

Response Reproducibility. PUF being an analog function, its responses are not accurately reproducible due to aging, wear out, voltage variation, and environmental conditions such as temperature and noise. An adversary can take advantage of this vulnerability to attack the PUF [17]. A post-processing function must condition the raw PUF responses into high-quality cryptographic keys and ensure their reproducibility. Such functions can be Error Correction Code (ECC), Fuzzy Extractor (FE), or Helper data [13]. Besides the additional implementation costs of such functions, some FE are risky to use when the PUF response entropy is low [18].

Response Length Expansion. Some PUFs provide a small response space of a few bits or, most likely one-bit length [13]. If a PUF is used to generate a key for an encryption algorithm, then the required key length n should exceed $n = 128$ bits. Therefore, such PUFs require additional methods for expanding the response space.

3.3   Clone-Resistant Random Secret Unknown Hardwired Crypto-Functions

PUF became a famous example of exploiting the differences in electronic devices' physical properties to serve as a physical-based security solution. Alternatively, the authors in [4] proposed using uncontrollable permanent differences created within the device after manufacturing as a bio-inspired electronic DNA (e-DNA). The e-DNA is self-created, non-repeatable, hard to clone, and easily provable with the ability to evolve during the device's lifetime and spread all along in the device's hardware. Subsequently, a clone-resistant random secret unknown hardwired dynamic/evolving cryptographic functions were proposed in [19] as a device's e-DNA.

In our work, we exploit the concept of the clone-resistant self-created random hardwired cryptographic function, being a hash function, in a reconfigurable environment focusing on its creation and deployment without covering the additional sophisticated characteristics such as the evolving property and the diffusion of the e-DNA in the whole device's body.

4 SUH-Based Device-Specific Secure Boot

The proposed secure boot mechanism relies on a self-created SUH-hardware module in a post-manufacturing single even process. A hash function is chosen as a building block for the proposed mechanism since its output is an integrity token used in the secure boot process. This hash function is randomly selected from a huge class of hash functions such that the probability of guessing which hash has been selected is negligible—and this hash is secretly self-implemented in the reconfigurable hardware's fabric in hard to predict areas, making it a digital unknown secret for that unique device. PUF itself can be regarded as an unpredictable and unknown physical one-way function [12]. Thus, SUH can be considered as a possible digital replacement to PUF technology.

4.1 SUH Creation

A dedicated temporary software package, so-called Genie-H, generates the SUH within the device in a secure environment. Genie-H is then eliminated irreversibly after its task completion, ensuring that the SUH is an unknown secret since its creator has disappeared. The SUH-generation requires an in-device True Random Number Generator (TRNG). The creation steps are depicted in Fig. 2 as follows: A Trusted Authority (TA_1) injects the temporal Genie-H into the SoC FPGA device SoC_u, during a one-time random single event operation. A huge class of hash functions $\{H_1, H_2, .., H_t\}$ of size t is generated, where $t \rightarrow \infty$ in the best case. Genie-H using a TRNG randomly selects one hash function H_j from $\{H_1, H_2, ..., H_t\}$. Finally, Genie-H is completely and irreversibly deleted. What remains in the SoC FPGA is a SUH-choice that nobody knows. A TA_2, which can be different from TA_1, enrolls the SUH in a secure environment. The TA_2 stimulates the SUH by a set of challenges, Messages (M), and stores the corresponding responses Digests (D) as CRPs of the enrolled device in a secret M_i/D_i record.

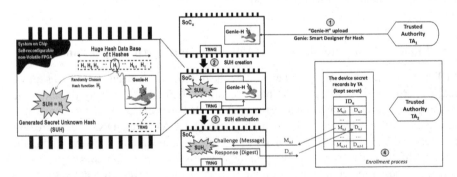

Fig. 2. Creation Steps of SUH on a self-reconfigurable non-volatile SoC FPGA.

Eventually, the only one who knows about which SUH is selected is the already vanished Genie-H. In this setting, nobody knows about the selected SUH even though the hash generation method may be known or published. This creation process exempts the manufacture from provisioning and knowing anything about the device-specific secret for secure boot. It is hard to clone a device whose secret is unknown. The self-created SUH hardwired module is programmed in the FPGA fabric such that it is randomly distributed on the *leftover areas*. Finally, any further reconfiguration/modification is hard-locked forever by burning some *"last fuse"*. We refer leftover areas to the FPGA fabric spaces that remain free after primary programming it with the main intended/commercial applications (e.g., video & image processing, medical, telecom, cloud computing). On the contrary of storing a key in non-volatile memory or storing a design in a well-known FPGA fabric location, SUH is diffused in the leftover areas, which can be disjointed, making it harder to recover SUH by some physical probing points attacks [20].

SUH as a Unique Device ID. Aside from the secure boot authentication, SUH is also used for the device's ID verification via the deployment of the device's corresponding stored M_i/D_i: The verifier asks TA_2 for a M_i/D_i pair from the device's secret record. Then stimulates the device with M_i, and the SUH responds with D_i'. If $D_i' = D_i$, the verifier considers the device as authentic.

4.2 System Model

The SUH creation requires a platform equipped with SoC and a non-volatile (e) FPGA fabric. The FPGA fabric should be able to be self-reconfigurable to enable in-device post-manufacturing secret creation. While non-volatile SoC FPGAs exist, the option of internally self-reconfiguring the non-volatile FPGA fabric is still a futuristic feature. Meanwhile, we implement a SUH candidate on the flash-based SoC FPGA SmartFusion2 since it provides the non-volatility trait and incorporates Differential Power Analysis (DPA) countermeasures to protect the bitstream key(s) to be discovered using side-channel analysis [21]. The generic boot sequence of the SmartFusion2 is shown in Fig. 3. The first piece of code that boots after power-on is the Boot-ROM code defined by the manufacturer and stored as a Metal-Read Only Memory (ROM). The reference digests and executables can be stored in the embedded NVM's reconfigurable ROM sections. In our work, we assume that during the secure boot authentication, after digest generation, the computed digest with the reference digest is compared either within: a protected processor or the FPGA Fabric. In an environment equipped with an OTP memory, the user bootloader code can replace the Boot-ROM code to ensure that the SoC FPGA boot sequence is fully user-defined.

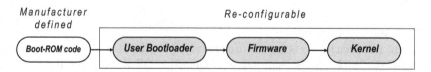

Fig. 3. A generic boot-sequence on the SmartFusion2 SoC FPGA

4.3 Secure Boot Operational Scenario

Setting up the SoC FPGA requires an already in-device self-created SUH, as previously depicted in Fig. 2.

System Set-up. Figure 4(A) demonstrates the system set-up phase. The user needs to upload the different software executables such as the user bootloader, the firmware, and the kernel. Next, the user bootloader runs in a *Set-Up Mode* to generate the firmware's reference digests (D_F) and the kernel's reference digest (D_K). The storage act can be done internally by the bootloader in a self-reconfigurable device since internal reconfiguration is expected from such technology. After the set-up phase, the system is ready to be used.

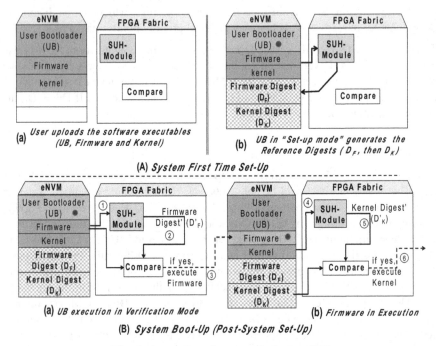

Fig. 4. Secure Boot Sequence deploying SUH

Secure Boot in Action. Figure 4(B) illustrates the steps after power-on, and after that, the Boot-ROM has passed the system's control to the user bootloader. The steps are as follows:

a) The bootloader in execution:
   (1) The firmware binary is fetched from the eNVM to the SUH to generate firmware digest' (D_F'). (2) DF' is compared with DF. (3) If DF = DF', then inputs of the SUH are also equal, and thus the firmware's binary has not been altered. Then, the bootloader passes the system's control to the firmware.

b) The firmware in execution:
   (4) The kernel binary is fetched to the SUH input, and the correspondent digest' (DK') is generated. (5) DK' is compared with the reference digest DK. (6) If DK = DK', the firmware passes the system's control to the kernel to boot.

The chain-of-trust can be further extended due to many possible SUH digests ($2^{n/2}$). Therefore, SUH-CRPs can support the OS kernel to authenticate system services, device drivers, and other applications.

4.4 Adversary Model

The same system can be a target to different attacks with different aims. Some adversaries may try to replace the authentic software, while others may try to impersonate/clone the device ID. In this section, we consider two attack scenarios, the first, where the adversary aims to run an unauthorized version of the software executable, and the second is where the adversary aims to impersonate the device.

Unauthorized Modification of the Software Executable. An adversary seeks that the chain-of-trust does not detect the maliciously modified version of the original software. This goal can be reached either by exploiting the hardware's storage units or exploiting the hash function's limitations. In the first case, the adversary should replace both the software and its digest successfully. Such attacks are not considered in this work because the verification digest is always stored in a tamper-resistant memory in the secure boot context. It is assumed hard for the adversary to change such memory's content. In the second case, the adversary makes sure to find a modified software version that corresponds to the authentic reference digest; the adversary should find a pre-image of the reference digest, which is different from the authentic software executable. Such attacks can be performed based on the hash function limitations. We consider this case in our model through two adversaries with different capabilities:

Unbounded Adversary (UA): can read the eNVM content and challenge the embedded SUH with chosen inputs and observe the output/digest. In this case, the adversary can consider the SUH as a black box.

Bounded Adversary (BA): can read the eNVM content. However, BA can only observe the SUH input and output without challenging the SUH.

Cloning Attack. An adversary tries to clone the device ID to impersonate that device using the authentic ID on a fraud device. The impersonation attack on a device with integrated SUH means that the adversary can somehow identify the SUH. In this adversary model, we suppose that the SUH creation is maintained in a secure environment. Any attempt to clone the SUH is conducted after its creation, implying that the adversary has no access or knowledge of the TRNG-value chosen by Genie-H to the SUH's random selection. The cloning complexity is then proportional to the number of possible hash functions t if the Genie-H is published. If the Genie-H is not published, then the cloning complexity is proportional to all possible hash functions. In our particular sample example, when using an n-to-n bit cipher for constructing the hash function, the choice space becomes $2^n!$.

5 SUH-Sample Implementation and Variants

Designing a cryptographic hash function is challenging, let alone constructing a huge class of hash functions. Meanwhile, a practical approach to generate such a class is by utilizing a block cipher-based iterated hash function [22, 23]. In the following, we introduce one possible variant of a SUH implementation, see Fig. 5, where a PRESENT-like cipher is deployed as a building block of an iterated hash function.

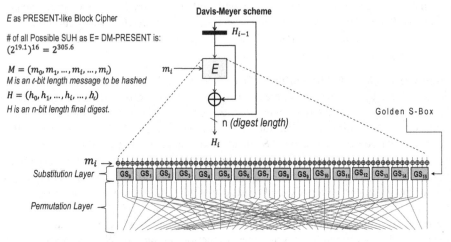

Fig. 5. A sample of a SUH construction based on Davies-Meyer Scheme

5.1 PRESENT-Like Based SUH

PRESENT is a lightweight 64-bit iterated block cipher with two key-length possibilities: an 80-bit key (PRESENT-80) and a 128-bit key (PRESENT-128). The cipher is composed of an adding key, a substitution layer, and a permutation layer [24]. The substitution layer, a nonlinear transformation, is performed via 16 Substitution Boxes (S-Boxes) which are mappings of a 4-bit to 4-bit. A Golden S-boxes (GS) is an S-box exhibiting ideal cryptographic properties [25]: **(1)** Differential Characteristic probability $DC = \frac{1}{4}$, **(2)** Linear approximation probability $LC = \frac{1}{4}$, **(3)** Branch Number $BN = 3$. PRESENT's S-box has these properties; thus, replacing the PRESENT's S-box with any GS maintains the PRESENT cipher's same security level. We exploit this property to define a SUH variant as a PRESENT-like based hash function using randomly selected GSs. Different compact PRESENT-based hash functions were introduced in [26]: **(1)** DM-PRESENT-80 and DM-PRESENT-128: deploying a single block cipher to obtain a 64-bit digest. **(2)** H-PRESENT-128: is a double-block-length hash function for a 128-bit digest. **(3)** C-PRESENT-192: is a triple-block-length hash function for a 192-bit digest. For instance, a SUH variant can be a DM-PRESENT where the S-box is preplaced with randomly chosen GS. Genie-H is responsible for randomly choosing 16 GS to populate the S-box layer. Genie-H can distribute the chosen GS in a random order within the S-Box layer and can, in addition, randomly select one of the secure 12 schemes of the block cipher-based hash construction schemes analyzed in [27].

5.2 DM-PRESENT-Like Hash Implementation

SmartFusion2 SoC FPGA fabric logic elements have 4-input LUTs [28] convenient to the 4-bit to 4-bit S-boxes of the PRESENT-like based SUH variant. Our sample implementation of DM-PRESENT-80-like has consumed in a SmartFusion2 FPGA 526 LUTs and 331 Flip-Flops. Table 2 shows the relatively low percentage of the consumed resources on the different SmartFusion2 SoC FPGAs. The security measures must be implemented, consuming as little hardware as possible since it is usually a protection measure that accompanies the main application.

Table 2. Hardware resource consumption of SUH-PRESENT-80-LIKE based on SmartFusion2 Soc FPGA family

SmartFusion®2 SoC FPGA family	4-input LUTs	Flip-Flops
M2S005	8.67%	5.46%
M2S010	4.35%	2.73%
M2S025	1.89%	1.19%
M2S050/M2S060	0.93%	0.58%
M2S090	0.61%	0.38%
M2S150	0.35%	0.22%

5.3 Security Analysis

We discuss the efforts required for an adversary to clone SUH and to defeat its digest. Every electronic device is susceptible to side-channel attacks if no countermeasure is applied. A detailed evaluation of the side-channel attack on our design is out of the scope of this paper. We assume that the emerging self-reconfiguring mechanisms in "non-volatile" FPGA technologies would offer physical properties prohibiting reaching the bitstream after irreversibly locking the reconfiguration process. Physical side-channel attacks can only be fruitfully discussed first after the self-reconfiguration infrastructure is implemented and exists in future practical devices.

Clone-resistant Device ID. For example, let us consider that the SUH is constructed based on a DM-PRESENT-80-like:

- If 16 GS-Boxes are selected randomly out of $2^{19.1}$ [25], it results in $(2^{19.1})^{16} = 2^{305.6}$ SUHs.

- If, in addition, an iterative hash's compression function is selected randomly out of $12 \approx 2^{3.5}$ [27], then the hash class cardinality is $t = 2^{305.6} \cdot 2^{3.5} \approx 2^{309}$ SUHs. 2^{309} presents the computational cloning attack complexity of a DM-PRESENT-like based SUH.

The attack complexity on cloning the other possible PRESENT-like-based SUH is presented in Table 3.

Table 3. Computational cloning attack complexity of the PRESENT-like based SUH

SUH type	Number of used Golden S-Boxes	Computational cloning attack complexity (# Operations)
DM-PRESENT-80-like DM-PRESENT-128-like	16	$(21^{9.1})^{16} = 2^{305.6} \cdot 2^{3.5} \approx 2^{309}$
H-PRESENT-128-like	32	$(2^{19.1})^{32} = 2^{611.2} \cdot 2^{3.5} \approx 2^{614}$
C-PRESENT-192-Like	96	$(2^{19.1})^{96} = 2^{1833.6} \cdot 2^{3.5} \approx 2^{1837}$

The Entropy of SUH Class. Table 4 addresses the entropy differences that a SUH can offer depending on whether Genie-H is publically known or not. When the Genie-H is not public, all possible hash mappings for a hash function with an m-bit input and an n-bit output are $|H| = 2^{m2^n}$, thus the upper bound of the entropy of |H| in this case, is $m2^n$. In the case that the Genie-H is known, the entropy of |H| is $log_2(t)$, where t is the cardinality of the huge hash class, for instance, in the proposed sample case PRESENT-based SUH variant, $|H| \geq 309$.

Table 4. The entropy of possible SUHs as a clone-resistant identities for different devices

SUH class entropy	Genie-H is public	Genie-H is not public
SUH $\xrightarrow{m}$ SUH $\xrightarrow{n}$	$log_2 t$	$m2^n$

Authentic Software Digest Protection. Let us again consider the case that the SUH is constructed based on a DM-PRESENT-80-like which produces 64-bit digest length; the computational security on the hash digest is as follow:

Case of Unbounded-Adversary Model. The UA can examine the SUH variant as a black box to conduct an online guessing attack. While under such a model, the SUH security level is equivalent to a traditional hash function, SUH still offers a clone-resistant device ID and a device-specific secure boot which, in the worst-case scenario, where one specific device's hash function is defeated, not all devices secure boot would be defeated.

Case of a Bounded-Adversary Model. To defeat the hash function, BA should first determine which SUH is randomly implemented, and this is equivalent to cloning the SUH. The results from Table 4 imply that SUH's successful prediction on DM-PRESENT-80-like construction requires 2^{309} search cycles. In this case, the required computation attack complexity on SUH's digest additionally demands

- $2^{309}.2^{64} = 2^{373}$ computations for a successful pre-image attack,
- $2^{309}.2^{32} = 2^{341}$ computations for a successful collision attack,
- and $2^{309}.2^{64} = 2^{373}$ computations for a successful second pre-image attack.

Under a BA model, for the same hash-bit length, in this example, 64-bit, the SUH's security level is way beyond the traditional hash function's security. The attack complexity on the software's digest of other possible PRESENT-like-based SUH is presented in Table 5. The defined UA- and BA-based attack scenarios are only possible online since the electronic device's SUH is unknown. It is only when an adversary succeeds in cloning the SUH that these attacks are possible offline.

Table 5. Evaluation of the computational security on the digest of PRESENT-like-based SUHs

SUH type	Hash (bit)	Number of used Golden S-Boxes	UA-Attack [29]			BA-Attack		
			Pre.	Coll.	2nd Pre.	Pre.	Coll.	2nd Pre.
DM-PRESENT-80-like DM-PRESENT-128-like	64	16	2^{64}	2^{32}	2^{64}	2^{373}	2^{341}	2^{373}
H-PRESENT-128-like	128	32	2^{128}	2^{64}	2^{64}	2^{742}	2^{678}	2^{678}
C-PRESENT-192-Like	192	96	2^{192}	2^{96}	2^{192}	2^{2029}	2^{1933}	2^{2029}

6   Conclusion

This paper introduces a new device-specific/unit-individual secure boot mechanism for SoC equipped with self-reconfigurable non-volatile (e) FPGA providing a hardware-based trusted foundation for software execution in electronic devices. The introduced approach deploys an in-device self-created Secret Unknown Hash (SUH) that generates a unique software binary digest for each individual electronic device. We showed that SUH being keyless, hardwired, unknown, randomly generated, can replace other solutions to generate device-specific software digests such as using a PUF and a traditional hash function. SUH has the advantage over PUF of ensuring a consistent response reproducibility without additional error correction codes. Comparing to the traditional hash function, SUH has the advantage of providing a clone-resistant unique device ID. We explained how to construct a SUH using a cipher-based hash function such as the PRESENT-like cipher as proof of concept. We showed a SUH sample implementation to be relatively lightweight. Finally, we proved that the proposed SUH offers a high clone-resistance entropy and a high device-specific digest computational security. These particular findings are further beneficial for remote authentication of a fully user-controlled secure booting of devices deploying unknown secrets. The user is responsible for individualizing the device's clone-resistant unknown secret after its manufacturing instead of trusting the manufacturer for exclusively provisioning it, which motivates using on a large scale the hopefully emerging SoC non-volatile (e) FPGAs with the enabled option of self-reconfigurability.

References

1. Arbaugh, W.A., Farber, D.J., Smith, J.M.: A secure and reliable bootstrap architecture. In: Proceedings of the IEEE Computer Society Symposium on Research in Security and Privacy, pp. 65–71. IEEE (1997). https://doi.org/10.1109/secpri.1997.601317
2. Langner, R.: Stuxnet: dissecting a cyberwarfare weapon. IEEE Secur. Priv. **9**, 49–51 (2011). https://doi.org/10.1109/MSP.2011.67
3. Quarta, D., Pogliani, M., Polino, M., Maggi, F., Zanchettin, A.M., Zanero, S.: An experimental security analysis of an industrial robot controller. In: Proceedings - IEEE Symposium on Security and Privacy, pp. 268–285. IEEE (2017). https://doi.org/10.1109/SP.2017.20
4. Skorobogatov, S.P.: Semi-invasive attacks - a new approach to hardware security analysis. Cambridge (2005)
5. Sanwald, S., Kaneti, L., St, M., Martin, B.: Secure boot revisited : challenges for secure implementations in the automotive domain. In: 17th Escar Europe: Embedded Security in Cars, pp. 113–127. Ruhr-Universität Bochum, Universitätsbibliothek (2019). https://doi.org/10.13154/294-6662
6. Bhat, A.: Secure boot, chain of trust and data protection. In: Embedded World Conference 2019 (2019)
7. Jacob, N., et al.: Securing FPGA SoC configurations independent of their manufacturers. In: 30th IEEE International System-on-Chip Conference (SOCC), pp. 114–119. IEEE (2017). https://doi.org/10.1109/SOCC.2017.8226019
8. Muller, K.U., Ulrich, R., Stanitzki, A., Kokozinski, R.: Enabling secure boot functionality by using physical unclonable functions. In: PRIME 2018 - 14th Conference on Ph.D. Research in Microelectronics and Electronics, pp. 81–84. IEEE, Prague, Czech Republic (2018). https://doi.org/10.1109/PRIME.2018.8430370
9. Owen Jr., D., et al.: An autonomous, self-authenticating, and self-contained secure boot process for field-programmable gate arrays. Cryptography **2**, 15 (2018). https://doi.org/10.3390/cryptography2030015
10. Haj-Yahya, J., Wong, M.M., Pudi, V., Bhasin, S., Chattopadhyay, A.: Lightweight secure-boot architecture for RISC-V system-on-chip. In: 20th International Symposium on Quality Electronic Design (ISQED), pp. 216–223. IEEE, Santa Clara, CA, USA (2019). https://doi.org/10.1109/ISQED.2019.8697657
11. Guajardo, J.: Physical Unclonable Functions (PUFs). In: Encyclopedia of Cryptography and Security. Springer, Boston, MA (2011). https://doi.org/10.1007/978-1-4419-5906-5
12. Pappu, R., Recht, B., Taylor, J., Gershenfeld, N.: Physical one-way functions. Science **297**(5589), 2026–2030 (2002). https://doi.org/10.1126/science.1074376
13. Delvaux, J., Peeters, R., Gu, D., Verbauwhede, I.: A survey on lightweight entity authentication with strong pufs. ACM Comput. Surv. **48**, 1–42 (2015). https://doi.org/10.1145/2818186

14. Rührmair, U., Sölter, J.: PUF modeling attacks: an introduction and overview. In: 2014 Design, Automation & Test in Europe Conference & Exhibition (DATE), pp. 1–6. IEEE, Dresden, Germany (2014). https://doi.org/10.7873/DATE2014.361
15. Schuster, D., Hesselbarth, R.: Evaluation of bistable ring PUFs using single layer neural networks. In: Holz, T., Ioannidis, S. (eds.) Trust 2014. LNCS, vol. 8564, pp. 101–109. Springer, Cham (2014). https://doi.org/10.1007/978-3-319-08593-7_7
16. Xu, X., Rührmair, U., Holcomb, D.E., Burleson, W.: Security evaluation and enhancement of bistable ring PUFs. In: Mangard, S., Schaumont, P. (eds.) RFIDSec 2015. LNCS, vol. 9440, pp. 3–16. Springer, Cham (2015). https://doi.org/10.1007/978-3-319-24837-0_1
17. Roelke, A., Stan, M.R.: Attacking an SRAM-Based PUF through wearout. In: 2016 IEEE Computer Society Annual Symposium on VLSI (ISVLSI), pp. 206–211. IEEE, Pittsburgh, PA, USA (2016). https://doi.org/10.1109/ISVLSI.2016.68
18. Koeberl, P., Li, J., Rajan, A., Wu, W.: Entropy loss in PUF-based key generation schemes: the repetition code pitfall. In: 2014 IEEE International Symposium on Hardware-Oriented Security and Trust (HOST), pp. 44–49. IEEE, Arlington, VA, USA (2014). https://doi.org/10.1109/HST.2014.6855566
19. Adi, W.: Autonomous physical secret functions and clone-resistant identification. International Journal of Advanced Science and Technology, vol. 14 (2010)
20. Wollinger, T., Paar, C., Guajardo, J.: Security on FPGAs: state-of-the-art implementations and attacks. ACM Trans. Embed. Comput. Syst. 3, 534–574 (2004). https://doi.org/10.1145/1015047.1015052
21. Microsemi: User Guide SmartFusion2 and IGLOO2 FPGA Security and Best Practices (2017)
22. Lai, X., Massey, J.L.: Hash functions based on block ciphers. In: Rueppel, R.A. (ed.) EUROCRYPT 1992. LNCS, vol. 658, pp. 55–70. Springer, Heidelberg (1993). https://doi.org/10.1007/3-540-47555-9_5
23. Schläffer, M.: Cryptanalysis of AES-Based Hash Functions (2011)
24. Bogdanov, A., et al.: PRESENT: an ultra-lightweight block cipher. In: Paillier, P., Verbauwhede, I. (eds.) CHES 2007. LNCS, vol. 4727, pp. 450–466. Springer, Heidelberg (2007). https://doi.org/10.1007/978-3-540-74735-2_31
25. Saarinen, M.-J.O.: Cryptographic analysis of All 4 × 4-Bit S-Boxes. In: Miri, A., Vaudenay, S. (eds.) SAC 2011. LNCS, vol. 7118, pp. 118–133. Springer, Heidelberg (2012). https://doi.org/10.1007/978-3-642-28496-0_7
26. Bogdanov, A., Leander, G., Paar, C., Poschmann, A., Robshaw, M.J.B., Seurin, Y.: Hash functions and RFID tags: mind the gap. In: Oswald, E., Rohatgi, P. (eds.) CHES 2008. LNCS, vol. 5154, pp. 283–299. Springer, Heidelberg (2008). https://doi.org/10.1007/978-3-540-85053-3_18
27. Preneel, B., Govaerts, R., Vandewalle, J.: Hash functions based on block ciphers: a synthetic approach. In: Stinson, D.R. (ed.) CRYPTO 1993. LNCS, vol. 773, pp. 368–378. Springer, Heidelberg (1994). https://doi.org/10.1007/3-540-48329-2_31
28. Microsemi: SmartFusion2 SoC FPGA Fabric User's Guide (2017)
29. Bogdanov, A., Knežević, M., Leander, G., Toz, D., Varıcı, K., Verbauwhede, I.: spongent: a lightweight hash function. In: Preneel, B., Takagi, T. (eds.) CHES 2011. LNCS, vol. 6917, pp. 312–325. Springer, Heidelberg (2011). https://doi.org/10.1007/978-3-642-23951-9_21

Posters

Transparent Near-Memory Computing with a Reconfigurable Processor

Fabian Lesniak$^{(\boxtimes)}$ [ID], Fabian Kreß [ID], and Jürgen Becker [ID]

Karlsruhe Institute of Technology, Karlsruhe, Germany
Fabian.Lesniak@kit.edu

Abstract. Data intensive applications like machine learning or big data analysis have stressed the requirements on memory subsystems. They involve computational kernels whose performance is not limited by the algorithmic complexity, but by the large amount of data they need to process. To counteract the growing gap between computing power and memory bandwidth, near-memory processing techniques have been addressed to improve the performance in such applications significantly. In this paper, we leverage a general purpose processor extended with a reconfigurable framework to execute hardware-accelerated instructions. This framework features a high-bandwidth memory interface to the nearest memory controller, allowing for greatly increased bandwidth compared to the standard system bus. We introduce region-based data processing, which allows to trigger operations by merely storing data and is especially suitable for large many-core designs. We show two different approaches to trigger the architecture for near-memory operations, one using interrupts for software-assisted processing and one directly interfacing with the hardware accelerator. Our evaluations show a performance gain of 72% on SAD kernels, with memory performance improved by 48%. Benchmarking AES encryption, we can show a speed up of 70%.

1 Introduction

The demands on processor architectures are constantly increasing and one of the major trends of the industry to meet these increasing requirements is the further development and integration of application-specific circuits. Several accelerators for all types of applications are integrated on a single chip. Recent developments in data-centric applications (e.g. large data, AI, media) have shifted the focus to efficient data processing. Improvements in industry include the implementation of SIMD instructions into the instruction set, as the SSE and AVX extensions do, and developments in memory technology increasing data rates as demonstrated with High-Bandwidth Memory (HBM) and Hybrid Memory Cubes (HMCs). Even though these improvements increased processing power and bandwidth, many workloads still saturate available memory bandwidth. This especially becomes important in large-scale systems, where memory transfers span longer distances and multiple levels of hierarchy. Moving processing elements closer to memory is one common approach to overcome these bandwidth limits.

© Springer Nature Switzerland AG 2021
S. Derrien et al. (Eds.): ARC 2021, LNCS 12700, pp. 221–231, 2021.
https://doi.org/10.1007/978-3-030-79025-7_15

Choosing the basic architecture comes down to a trade-off between flexibility and performance. While using a processor brings high flexibility, its performance is considerably lower than a hardware implementation. Alternatively, a specialized ASIC implementation is inherently immutable but provides highest performance. Reconfigurable hardware tries to combine the best of both worlds, typically reaching higher performance than CPU-based solutions and allowing reconfiguration. However, the performance of an ASIC can't be matched and FPGA designs are generally more difficult to build than a software solution. The approach presented in this paper features a combination of a CPU with a reconfigurable FPGA partition, to support execution of control-flow heavy software as well as high performance RTL accelerators close to memory.

2   Related Work

Near-memory computing (NMC) is a common approach to improve performance of data-centric workloads. As many different approaches have already been published, this section classifies some of these approaches and compares them to our design.

An important property of NMC implementations is the type of memory the system is working on. Depending on the workload it can be feasible to place accelerators close to bulk storage, as shown with *Summarizer* [6]. The authors provide interfaces to offload work from the host processor to a SSD controller. In contrast, in-memory approaches like *iPIM* [4], which features an in-memory image processing accelerator, profit from very high memory bandwidth while waiving flexibility.

Apart from the memory target, the fundamental design of the accelerator itself can be distinguished. Several approaches, as previously mentioned *Summarizer*, use CPUs which are placed close to memory to perform operations. The benefits are high flexibility as software can easily be exchanged and low hardware costs due to the broad availability of processors. However, some approaches chose FPGA or ASIC based accelerators for even higher processing power. Corda et al. [1] demonstrated large performance benefits when using FPGAs with direct memory access for fast fourier transform, outperforming both CPU and GPU based approaches.

Reconfigurable processors [2] try to bridge the gap between the flexibility of processor-based approaches and the processing power of specialized hardware. They allow to use special instructions (SIs) to make use of the reconfigurable framework, resulting in faster execution compared to a pure software-based implementation. Previous work also shows how to detect code suitable for SI-based acceleration and generate RTL code for appropriate accelerators automatically [5], reducing hardware design efforts.

In our design, we use such a reconfigurable processor and investigate the advantages of placing it close to memory. This provides a dedicated, high-bandwidth memory interface, but retains the performance and flexibility of a monolithic processor.

3   Concept

This section will first introduce the architecture of our near-memory accelerator (NMA) containing a reconfigurable processor. Afterwards, our region-based approach for transparent operation on the memory bus is discussed and its advantages are highlighted.

3.1   Accelerator Architecture

The core component is a reconfigurable processor which is placed close to memory. Figure 1 shows a high-level view of an example system containing multiple general purpose CPUs, peripherals and memory. The memory has a high-bandwidth connection to the NMA, which consists of a processor core and a reconfigurable framework. Processor and FPGA framework are connected to allow SIs to be executed in the reconfigurable partition.

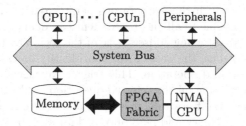

Fig. 1. Near-memory accelerator consisting of processor and FPGA framework in a multi-processor system

By containing a standard CPU core, it can directly execute code without requiring RTL design. The key advantage is the low barrier for porting an existing algorithm to the accelerator: software can easily be adapted to run on the NMA. Even without using the reconfigurable portion of the accelerator, the software can benefit from improved memory performance. The generic concept does not require a specific processor architecture, thus allowing the designer to choose one matching the design constraints. The processor however needs to provide an interface for the reconfigurable framework, allowing custom instructions to call the hardware accelerator.

The reconfigurable framework is an FPGA-based hardware accelerator. It allows to take over computationally intensive tasks from the near-memory processor, thus further boosting performance of the NMA. Implementing an entire algorithm in HDL is often a very time-consuming task. Our approach allows to make use of the interaction between processor and hardware accelerator, as merely the expensive parts of an algorithm have to be implemented in hardware to achieve significant performance gains. Other work, such as initialization and control flow tasks, can still be fulfilled in software. Compared to memory-mapped accelerator interfaces, the close coupling between processor and reconfigurable framework allows to easily engage the accelerator by using an appropriate special instruction.

Reconfiguration features enable to use the accelerator framework for varying tasks. The required accelerator configuration can be loaded when required, falling back to a software implementation if the accelerator is shared and other tasks have higher priority. Additionally, the NMA can adapt to unprecedented use cases in the future, still allowing acceleration of updated software where non-reconfigurable approaches need to fall back to software-only processing.

3.2   Region-Based Near-Memory Computing

The reconfigurable framework is primarily controlled by software, as it requires a special instruction to operate. Typical schemes for sending a command to the NMA are remote procedure calls (RPCs), requiring a communication channel to be set up before. To simplify and reduce communication effort between client and accelerator, we propose to make the accelerator transparent to memory access: The memory, which the accelerator operates on, is fully accessible via the bus and thus accessible to all clients. A client can define regions within that memory, consisting of a starting address, size of the region and an operation. By watching the memory bus, the accelerator can identify access to such a region and trigger the associated operation. This trigger can decide whether enough data is available, depending on the selected operation, and start executing that operation automatically. Afterwards, it is sufficient to stream input data to the respective address in memory and read output data after processing is done.

As in our concept the NMA contains both a CPU core and an accelerator framework, this yields two possibilities for the NMA to be triggered:

Interrupt-Based Trigger. The processor core receives an interrupt after a region received enough data. The NMA starts processing in software and can use the hardware accelerator if suitable. We call this the *software-assisted mode*, as algorithms can be partly accelerated by hardware and run the remaining operations in software.

Direct Hardware Trigger. The hardware accelerator is directly started without software intervention. As no software overhead occurs, this approach allows very low latencies. The NMA processor can execute other code in parallel, as the hardware accelerator does not interfere with the processor resources. However, the respective operation needs to be fully implemented in hardware.

3.3   Software Interface

The region-based concept simplifies the steps necessary in software to use the NMA. Traditional approaches use remote procedure calls (RPCs) or memory-mapped control registers to configure the accelerator and fine-grained execution control is handled by a driver in software. In contrast, our approach requires configuration once, afterwards data transfer to the configured region is sufficient. Figure 2 shows the interaction between client, NMA and memory.

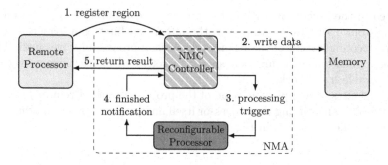

1. register region

Remote Processor

5. return result

NMC Controller

2. write data

Memory

4. finished notification

3. processing trigger

Reconfigurable Processor

NMA

Fig. 2. Configuring regions and using the NMA

The steps required to use the accelerator can be described as follows:

1. The client registers a region for use, including size and an associated operation. Region conflicts with other users need to be avoided, however, the memory management of the operating system can be used to guarantee unique buffer allocation.
2. Payload data is now written directly to memory, a call to `memcpy` or using DMA is sufficient.
3. The NMA observes memory writes and triggers the reconfigurable processor as soon as its processing condition is met. Either the reconfigurable framework is started directly or the software-assisted mode is used, depending on the selected operation.
4. The reconfigurable processor notifies the controller when it has finished processing the region.
5. A result is returned to the client, if necessary.

Interaction with software on the client takes place in steps 1, 2 and 5 only. Steps 2 and 5 can be repeated arbitrarily to process further data. The client thus does not need to send any control commands after setting up the region, reducing communication with the NMA to a minimum.

4 Implementation

After introducing the key aspects of our concept, this section provides the hardware mechanisms that were implemented to evaluate the proposed architecture.

4.1 Overview

The *i*-Core platform [2] is used as framework of the implementation as it already offers some features that match our concept. It provides a reconfigurable processor consisting of a LEON3 core and a reconfigurable framework which is connected to the internal Scratchpad Memory (SPM). Since this framework is attached to the execution stage of the processor, computations can be initiated using custom instructions. Moreover, the integrated bitstream loader allows for runtime reconfiguration of the framework. This approach improves flexibility as various applications can run their specific accelerated instructions on the same reconfigurable framework.

Nevertheless, the implementation of the proposed concept requires to extend the platform by modifying the processor itself and providing a new module called NMC Controller as shown in Fig. 3.

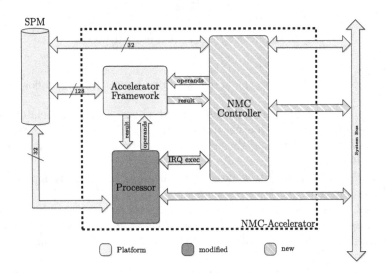

Fig. 3. Implementation overview

4.2 Processor

Due to its ability to run a broad range of tasks the internal processor is a key element to implement a very flexible NMA architecture along with the reconfigurable framework.

As a bus master, it can access not only the internal SPM but also other system components to load data if necessary. Therefore, clients do not have to provide all the data required to process the task if the missing values are accessible to the NMA internal processor.

To notify the processor about pending tasks in the software-assisted mode, it is directly connected to the NMC Controller. As our processor design allows customizable hardware traps, this feature is used to assert an interrupt each time the processor needs to start working on a region. Moreover, this approach allows the processor to execute unrelated tasks in parallel, which get interrupted automatically whenever the accelerator itself requires action. In our reference implementation, the operating system treats the reconfigurable processor like a normal processor, as it is able to execute generic workload in parallel.

4.3   NMC Controller

The main component of our implementation is the NMC Controller. It is placed between system bus and SPM to snoop bus transactions on the SPM. During execution, the NMC Controller can deny or delay write access to the SPM to prevent the NMC result from being affected by inconsistent values in memory. Moreover, in case of encryption algorithms it also allows to ensure that clients are not able to read the plaintext. When delaying a memory access, bus splits are used to avoid locking up the system bus. Figure 4 shows the architecture of the NMC Controller implementation.

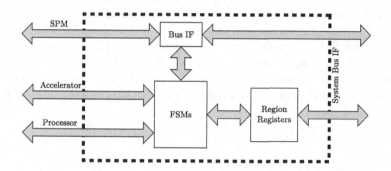

Fig. 4. Schematic of the NMC controller

When a write transaction to the SPM matches the processing condition of an enabled region, the corresponding action is triggered. Either an interrupt can be used in case of the software-assisted mode or the reconfigurable framework can be accessed directly using the COREFAB [3] interface. This interface allows to bypass the processor and directly execute a task in the accelerator framework. Input parameters required by the accelerator framework such as operands and the SI to run have to be configured as part of the region configuration prior to execution. Nevertheless, running SIs on the processor in parallel is still possible since the implementation of the extended framework comes with an arbiter to switch between local and NMC instructions.

5   Evaluation

We implemented a prototype of the NMA using the reconfigurable processor *i*-Core [2], based on the LEON3 core. This prototype is a dual-core system, where one core is the augmented near-memory processor and the second core is a standard LEON3 core acting as the remote user of the accelerator framework. The resulting hardware design has been tested both in simulation and on a Xilinx VC707 prototyping board with a Xilinx Virtex 7 FPGA. Cycle counts have been determined using a clock cycle counter in the debug unit. During all tests, there was no additional traffic on the system bus by other applications. Such traffic would reduce the performance of software implementations even further, with low impact on the NMA performance as it has its own memory interface.

5.1 Video Encoding Acceleration

As part of a H.264 video encoder implementation on our platform, the sum of absolute differences (SAD) algorithm has been implemented within the NMA architecture [8]. It is used to calculate the similarity of two 16×16 image sections.

To support our approach, SAD is used as a benchmark to compare software-based execution to the NMA: A remote processor configures a region and streams pixel data to that region. As soon as enough data is availabe for a SAD 16×16 operation, the NMC controller starts processing. In case of the accelerated implementation, the reconfigurable accelerator is triggered directly, not involving the processor at all. The software reference runs on the NMA processor, but does not use any accelerated instructions and is therefore limited to 32 bits bus width.

Table 1. Runtime comparison SAD 16×16

Interface	Software reference	Near-memory accelerator	
		4 Pixels/Iteration	8 Pixels/Iteration
32 bits	1.635 cycles	463 cycles	339 cycles
128 bits	N/A	223 cycles	126 cycles

Table 1 shows a runtime improvement of 72% when launching the NMA through the remote processor interface. It also quantifies the memory interface impact, taking only 48% resp. 37% cycles when using the high-bandwidth memory interface. Additionally, reconfiguration allows the SAD accelerator to be implemented twice, as enough resources are available in our sample design. Thus it can process eight pixels per iteration, almost doubling processing power.

5.2 AES Encryption

To demonstrate both the flexibility and performance of the software-assisted approach, an AES encryption benchmark is used. The implementation is based on the *MiBench* suite [7]. As the AES algorithm involves a diverse control flow as well as preliminary operations like key derivation, the software-assisted operation mode is used. The operations for a single encryption round are implemented in hardware. As a slightly different implementation is necessary in the last encryption round, we fall back to the original software implementation for that. This highlights a benefit of the processor-based approach: instead of having to implement the full AES algorithm in hardware, less demanding operations like preparation or finalization can still be handled in software. Although only parts of the algorithm are accelerated, we still see significant performance gains as shown in Fig. 5.

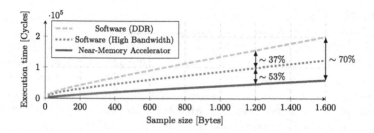

Fig. 5. AES performance comparison

It can be seen that the software performance increases by 37% when using the high bandwidth memory interface only. Using the LUT-based hardware acceleration, execution time improves by approx. 53% compared to the software implementation.

5.3 Resource Usage

The resource usage of our implementation can be divided in the processor core, the accelerator framework and the NMC Controller. To allow comparing our approach to other implementations we also provide numbers for a common LEON3 processor as well as a modified LEON3 core that can access a remote framework within its execution stage. Table 2 shows FF, LUT and BRAM resources for the individual components.

Table 2. FPGA resources by component

	FF	LUT	BRAM
LEON3	4,785	12,793	22
Reconf. processor	5,505	13,245	24
Framework	7,922	16,326	59
Instruction merging	1,032	9,661	0
Remote reconf. processor	5,471	13,741	24
NMC Controller (4 regions)	1,143	907	0

The reconfigurable framework holds the biggest share of resources. This is primarily caused by the reconfigurable containers, holding a fixed amount of FPGA resources required to fit different accelerators. The amount of resources for these regions represents a tradeoff between low resource usage and flexibility to fit larger accelerators for applications, whose requirements may not be known at design time.

6 Conclusion

Throughout this paper, we present an approach for a highly flexible, programmable and reconfigurable near-memory accelerator. The concept gains high flexibility through a general-purpose processor, allowing to port existing implementations with low effort. The attached reconfigurable accelerator can perform operations on the attached memory with high performance. It can be flexibly decided if the accelerator is used directly or if it is sufficient to accelerate only parts of the algorithm and execute remaining tasks in software.

A core feature of our NMA is transparent operation on memory by defining regions with associated operations. The near-memory controller can dynamically execute these operations whenever a block of data is fully written to memory and notify the client after operation has finished. Especially in PGAS architectures, configuring and using the accelerator is greatly simplified. For secure applications, the near-memory controller can lock access to data if required.

In future work, we will be looking into improving the control flow capabilities of the NMA to depend less on the general-purpose processor and reduce its resource usage.

Acknowledgement. This work was supported by the German Research Foundation (DFG) as part of the Transregional Collaborative Research Center Invasive Computing [SFB/TR 89].

References

1. Corda, S., Veenboer, B., Awan, A.J., Kumar, A., Jordans, R., Corporaal, H.: Near memory acceleration on high resolution radio astronomy imaging. In: 2020 9th Mediterranean Conference on Embedded Computing (MECO), pp. 1–6 (2020)
2. Damschen, M., Rapp, M., Bauer, L., Henkel, J.: i-Core: a runtime-reconfigurable processor platform for cyber-physical systems (2020)
3. Grudnitsky, A., Bauer, L., Henkel, J.: COREFAB: concurrent reconfigurable fabric utilization in heterogeneous multi-core systems. In: 2014 International Conference on Compilers, Architecture and Synthesis for Embedded Systems (CASES), pp. 1–10 (2014)
4. Gu, P., et al.: iPIM: programmable in-memory image processing accelerator using near-bank architecture. In: 2020 ACM/IEEE 47th Annual International Symposium on Computer Architecture (ISCA), pp. 804–817 (2020)
5. Harbaum, T., et al.: Auto-Si: an adaptive reconfigurable processor with run-time loop detection and acceleration. In: 2017 30th IEEE International System-on-Chip Conference (SOCC), pp. 153–158 (2017)

6. Koo, G., et al.: Summarizer: trading communication with computing near storage. In: 2017 50th Annual IEEE/ACM International Symposium on Microarchitecture (MICRO), pp. 219–231 (2017)
7. University of Michigan: MiBench Version 1.0 (2001). https://vhosts.eecs.umich.edu/mibench/
8. Wong, S., Vassiliadis, S., Cotofana, S.: A sum of absolute differences implementation in FPGA hardware. In: Proceedings 28th Euromicro Conference, pp. 183–188 (2002)

A Dataflow Architecture for Real-Time Full-Search Block Motion Estimation

Jesús Barba$^{(\boxtimes)}$![ORCID], Julián Caba ![ORCID], Soledad Escolar ![ORCID], Jose A. De La Torre ![ORCID], Fernando Rincón ![ORCID], and Juan C. López ![ORCID]

School of Computer Science, University of Castilla-La Mancha,
13071 Ciudad Real, Spain
jesus.barba@uclm.es

Abstract. Motion estimation is the cornerstone of main video compression standards, which are based on the reduction of the temporal redundancy between consecutive frames. Although the mechanism is simple, the best method, *Full Search*, uses a brute-force approach which is not suited for real-time applications. This work introduces a high performance architecture for performing on-the-fly full-search block matching estimation in FPGA devices, which has been modeled using C++ programming language and synthesized with Vivado HLS for a Xilinx ZC706 prototyping board. The architecture is based on a dataflow datapath and it is configurable, enabling a fast and easy exploration of the solution space. On-board results achieve a maximum performance of 743 fps, 247 fps and 110 fps for VGA, HD and FHD video resolutions, respectively, for a typical macroblock size of 16×16 pixels and a search area of ± 16 pixels.

Keywords: FPGA · High-level synthesis · Motion estimation · Full search · Block matching algorithm

1 Introduction

Motion Estimation (ME) explores temporal redundancy of a sequence, which is inherent in consecutive video frames, and it represents a basis for lossy video compression. Thus, ME techniques are present in standard video codecs, such as H.263, H.264, or HEVC, to exploit temporal redundancy in a sequence of frames. However, the relentless growth in digital video applications and their continuous resolution improvement make the ME phase a critical one; the total computing time varies between 60% and 80% depending on the Block Matching (BM) algorithm selected, which also determines the resulting accuracy reached. Thus, the

This research is partially funded by the Ministry of Economy and Competitiveness (MINECO) of the Spanish Government under project PLATINO (grant number TEC2017-86722-C4-R4), the Regional Government of Castilla-La Mancha under project SymbIoT (grant number SBPLY/17/180501/000334) and the EU's Horizon 2020 programme under project SHAPES (GA N° 857159).

© Springer Nature Switzerland AG 2021
S. Derrien et al. (Eds.): ARC 2021, LNCS 12700, pp. 232–241, 2021.
https://doi.org/10.1007/978-3-030-79025-7_16

Full-Search Block Matching (FSBM) algorithm gets the most accurate results since it performs all possible comparisons of macroblock, being a macroblock a group of $N \times N$ pixels.

The FSBM algorithm has the aim to get the best match for a block in the reference frame. Unfortunately, the computational costs of the FSBM algorithm is prohibitive on general purpose processors, because it is extremely demanding concerning the computing effort, rendering this technique unsuitable for real-time imaging applications. Contrarily, FPGA (*Field Programmable Gate Array*) architecture is well-suitable for this algorithm because of its parallel nature.

In this work, a high-performance architecture for Full-Search Block-Matching Estimation is introduced, with the following main contributions.

- A configurable hardware accelerator of the FSBM algorithm for different video resolution, i.e. VGA, HD and Full HD.
- Reduce the footprint of the proposed solution as low as possible to enable its deployment on embedded FPGA-based platforms with constraint resource (i.e. edge/fog computing nodes) or power (i.e. energy harvesting or battery powered) budgets.

2   Related Work

S. Ghosh et al. in [3] present an FPGA-based solution for the sum-of-absolute-differences (SAD) operator of the FSBM algorithm, in which the main optimization done is the reduced number of basic arithmetic operations performed. This optimization results in a the performance as well as reduces the silicon area. In the same line, H. Loukil et al. describe a VHDL implementation of the SAD operator in [5]. The optimizations of both works get good results for isolated macroblocks, but the scalability of these solutions do not work fine when a whole frame is processed. The arrangement pattern of the pixels would require extra bandwidth to access the memory in the required order.

J. Olivares et al. [7] apply the Online Arithmetic (OLA) that allows to speed up computation by early termination of the SAD calculation when the candidate is bigger than the current reference. The accelerator is optimized for area and is able to process 17.2 VGA frames per second on a Virtex-II with a 425 MHz clock for 16×16 macroblocks.

Furthermore, 1-D and 2-D Systolic array architectures for FSBM implementation have been regarded as an optimal solution due to the efficient use of resources, low power budget and their configurability properties in what concerns the macroblock dimension, the search area and parallelism level [9,11].

M. Mohammadzadeh et al. present in [6] an array processor written in VHDL and its optimization to achieve the minimum area occupation and maximum operating frequency. It includes control logic blocks to generate memory access addresses, which makes this work one of the few approaching the whole process at frame level, together with the proposal presented by Kasturi et al. in [8]. Implementation results are shown for a size of macroblock of 8×8 and different values for the search area. For the same configuration that the one set in this work ($N = 16$ and $p = 8$), the synthesis results show that the area occupied on a Vritex-II FPGA is about %11 of the chip and the maximum frame rate is 60 for CIF resolution and a 191 Mhz clock. It is not possible to project these results for other video formats.

Nuno et al. [10] validate several optimization strategies to obtain even more efficient systolic array architectures without sacrificing the quality of the result. Some of these techniques (i.e. reduced pixel precision) are of interest and its application to the solution proposed in this work is planned for future improve versions of the FSBM IP.

3   Full-Search Block Matching Implementation on FPGA

For the design of the FSBM architecture, a dataflow approach (see Fig. 1) has been followed, avoiding, as much as possible, the use of unnecessary intermediate memory storage. The simplicity of the HLS model and the optimization of the computations adds together to obtain and optimal outcome.

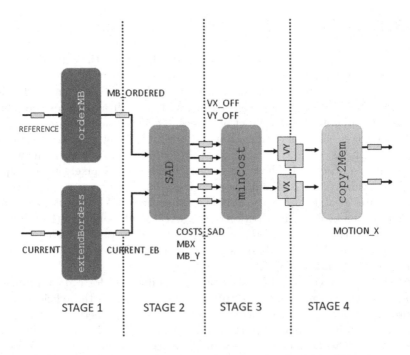

Fig. 1. Proposed dataflow architecture for the FSBM IP.

The C++ model defines four stages that operate concurrently (see Fig. 1).

Such model has also been fully parameterized by means of *#define* preprocessor directives, enabling easy adaptation by only changing the values for the video resolution and macroblock size.

All stages communicate by means of streams, implemented as FIFO channels, avoiding the need of large intermediate ping-pong buffers that would require of BRAM resources. The only exception to this rule are the two ping-pong buffer channels between *Stage 3* and *Stage 4* (VX and VY). These memories are used to store the values of the motion vectors computed so far in *Stage 3*.

In order to keep a sensible use of FPGA resources, such as BRAMs, the depth of the FIFO channels are set to the smallest possible value due to the balanced design of the stages. The width and depth of some of the channels depend on the width of the AXI-Stream interface to external memory and the resolution of the images.

Concerning the internal demand for resources by the individual modules, the focus is put in avoiding the need for unnecessary intermediate storage. The majority of such demand comes from the `orderMB` and `SAD` functions that implement two line buffers of size N and, for the latter, an additional buffer that holds one, three or five rows of macroblocks, depending on the search area configures (i.e. 8, 16 or 32 pixels).

3.1 Stage 1: Input Stream Accommodation

This step is responsible for the preparation of the video frames before the computation of the SAD values. In addition to the use of built-in Xilinx functions (i.e. *hls::AXIVideo2Mat*) so as to be compliant with the HLS utility video data types, two additional actions are carried out.

The general operation of the FSBM algorithm consists in finding the most likely position of a reference macroblock in the current frame within a delimited search area. Macroblocks placed at the borders of a frame are a special case since there are search positions that might not be valid because they are out of the frame area. This situation can be detected by checking the limits before proceeding to compute the cost function.

However, in order to ease the work of the HLS tool, the borders of the input reference frame are extended. This way, the implementation of the SAD function becomes a perfect loop, leading to an optimal pipeline architecture. This is the task of the `extendBorders` function which replicates the pixels placed at the borders of the current frame and fills out the empty search area.

Meanwhile, running in parallel to the adaptation of the current frame, the `orderMB` function re-arranges the pixels of the reference frame and feeds the second stage with an ordered flow of MBs. To this end, a line buffering approach is implemented which optimizes the number of BRAMs needed.

The user logic in `orderMB` packs the $16x16$ 8-bit pixels of the window in one 2048-bit word. This only happens when `row` and `col` loop indexes are multiple of the macroblock size (lower-right corner). Therefore, the packed word actually represents the content of a macroblock in the reference frame.

3.2   Stage 2: SAD Computation

In this stage, each macroblock of the reference frame is compared with all possible adjacent macroblocks within a delimited search area in the current frame. The correspondence of the reference macroblock in the current frame is established by selecting the current macroblock with the minimum cost (similarity) function. In this implementation, the *Sum of Absolute Differences* (SAD) is used [4].

The challenge is to perform all SAD computations as the pixels of the current (border-extended) frame are received. To this end, the implementation of the SAD function uses a similar line buffer structure than the one used in the orderMB function in Stage 1. However, it is introduced a new challenge derived from the need of synchronizing the stream of the current frame with extended borders and the ordered list of MBs of the reference frame.

Figure 2 sketches the synchronization mechanism and the macroblock consumption pattern. The picture represents a simplified version of the extended current and reference (light blue background) frames which are overlapped. In this example, each cell represents a 8×8 pixel sub-block and this representation assumes a macroblock size of 16×16 pixels and a search area of ± 8 pixels. The reference macroblocks are consumed only at the instants represented as black diamonds, filling the MB buffer which has a size equals to one row of macroblocks (steps a to d in Fig. 2).

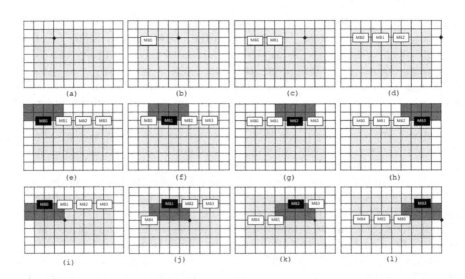

Fig. 2. Reference macroblock consumption pattern and SAD computing areas.

The SAD cost values for each reference macroblock are computed in two phases; upper half (steps e to h) and lower half (steps i to l). After the finalization of the second phase, the macroblock is replaced by a new one since it is not needed anymore. The dark blue cells represent, for the active reference macroblock (highlighted as a black box), the actual search area processed. This mechanism is also followed for values ±16 and ±32 pixels of the seach area. The only difference is that it must be stored three and five lines of reference macroblocks, respectively.

Furthermore, this stage also obtains the SAD cost by the costSAD function, which is responsible for the actual computation of the macroblock similarity metric. This function must accept a new window of pixels every clock cycle in order to keep the pace set by the dataflow path. Since the input stream has a width of 32-bits, at each iteration of the pipeline four new luminance components are accepted. This means that, at each iteration, four SAD cost values have to be computed; otherwise, three columns of pixels will be lost due to the shifting of the processing window.

Depending on the search area parameter, the number of instances of the costSAD function takes a value of 1, 9 or 25 in the architecture.

3.3   Stage 3: Selection of the Minimum SAD Cost

This stage receives the output of the previous SAD computation phase. For a reference macroblock, a new intermediate cost needs to be processed and checked to determine whether it is the minimum for that macroblock. If so, the current value of the motion vector is updated with the VX_OFFSET and VY_OFFSET components.

The minCost function initializes the MIN_COSTS matrix with the maximum possible value for SAD cost. Then, it starts the processing comparing the current minimum with the value took out off the input stream. In case that both SAD costs are equal, the one belonging to the current macroblock closest to the center of the search area is selected. A ROM is used to stored the pre-computed distance values in order to avoid higher latencies due to extra arithmetic operations.

As in the previous stages, only a well-known subset of the positions in VX and VY arrays are accessed for a macroblock in the current frame given a specific search area. Therefore, the bottleneck that would represent the minCost function when several instances of the costSAD functions are created, is solved by maintaining in registers only those positions that could be potentially affected by the arrival of a new minimum.

By the end of this phase, the VX and VY ping-pong buffer channels have the final values of the motion vectors for the pair of frames under processing. The copy2Mem function (Stage 4) only reads these memories and packs up to four components (depending on the specified width of the AXI-Stream interface) in a single memory word.

4   Experimental Results

A prototype of a video processing platform has been developed on a Xilinx ZC706 board, so the actual performance of the proposed architecture can be measured.

The FSBM core has been developed in C++ and then synthesized, packed and deployed using the Vivado 2019.2 toolchain provided by Xilinx. The high-level model is fully parameterized, allowing the possibility of varying the video resolution (VGA, High Definition, and Full HD), and the width of the AXI-Stream interfaces (16 or 32 bits) to access the memory where the frames are stored. Also, the FSBM core can instantiate three versions of the costSAD function, which perform 1, 2 or 4 (see Sect. 3.2) macroblock comparisons over the same window. The version of the core used in the prototype analyzed in this section has fixed the size of the macroblock to $N = 16$ and the search area parameter to ±16 and ±32.

Table 1. Nominal frame rate (ZC706 board, $\overline{T} = 8.69\,\text{ns} \pm 2.23\%$). Best configuration: 32-bit AXI-Stream interface and 4-pixel costSAD function.

	SEARCH AREA		
INPUT VIDEO	8	16	32
VGA	965	743	371
HD	322	247	124
FHD	143	110	55

Regarding the performance achieved by our design, Table 1 shows the nominal frames per second (fps) for the most performing configurations. That is, the use of a 32-bit AXI-Stream bus and the version of the costSAD function that process four new pixels in parallel. Synthesis results prompted a slight variation in the clock period for the proposed FSBM IP as the model parameters where modified. Thus, it is safe to say that the average period (8.69 ns ± 0.19 ns) is constant The nominal working frequency ($\simeq$115 Mhz) is enough to perform real-time processing of 60 Hz video stream for VGA and HD resolutions, with a combination of IP parameters that ensures the minimum occupancy of the FPGA. For Full HD resolutions, the core cannot meet the pixel time (i.e. 148.5 Mhz for 60 Mhz), so the designer might overcome this limitation by selecting a more aggressive combination of parameters to meet real-time requirements. This approach also applies to contexts where the performance is the principal driving force in the design.

The comparison with other works is not straightforward. Whilst our solution comprises the whole FSBM algorithm, most of the related proposals focus only on the implementation of the SAD operand. A comprehensive approach introduces additional challenges that are not taken into account such as the efficient management of the traffic to/from memory through reutilization of data.

Table 2 lists information on certain implementation results of other FPGA-based implementations of the FSBM algorithm. The use of RTL as the developing language is common in all them whereas in this proposal, HLS technology has

Table 2. Summary of other FPGA-based implementations of the FSBM algorithm and comparison with the proposed architecture.

Work	Platform	Clock (MHz)	MB size	Search area	Resolution	FPS
[7]	Xilinx Spartan3	366.8	16 × 16	±16	HD	13.62
[5]	Altera Stratix	103.8	16 × 16	±16	HD	5.15
[9]	Xilinx XCV3200E	76.1	16 × 16	±16	HD	20.98
[12]	Altera Flex20KE	197	16 × 16	±16	HD	4.91
[3]	Xilinx Virtex 4	221.2	16 × 16	±16	HD	55.33
[6]	Xilinx Virtex 2	191	16 × 16	±16	HD	2.09
[2]	Xilinx Virtex 5 LX330T	125	8× 8,16 × 6, 32 × 32,64 × 64	±64	FHD	26.9
	Virtex 6 LX240T					53.6
[1]	Xilinx Virtex 5	269.3	16 × 16	± 32	FHD	31
						30
Ours	**Xilinx ZCU706 (Kintex-7)**	**115**	**16 × 16**	**±16**	**HD**	**247**
					FHD	**110**
				±32	**HD**	**124**
					FHD	**55**

proved to be competitive in terms of performance. No development and testing times have been reported in any of these works, so it is not possible to establish a comparison framework in this regard, which is one the major pluses of HLS tools.

The approach presented in this article surpasses the performance levels reported by those works with the same configuration (i.e. macroblock size, search area and resolution of the video), despite running at a lower clock frequency. Also, the reader should notice that our approach also deals with the burden of moving efficiently the frames from/to the DDR memory.

Only D'huys et al. in [2] faced the implementation of a global solution, where it is also employed a macroblock reordering strategy to optimize the computation of the SAD costs. The comparison with this work is not direct since the solution is intended for a variable-size macroblock problem ranging from $N = 8$ to $N = 64$. Also, the search area is wider so the computational load increases significantly. Although current results look promising, it would be necessary revisiting the architecture to adapt it to this more challenging scenario.

Nevertheless, the comparison with [1] is more direct since the size of the block remains the same.

The impact on resource utilization, for different variations of the search area, is summarized in Table 3, where actual synthesis results (after place & poute) are shown. Firstly, the demand for resources remains stable despite the fact of dealing with higher resolutions of the video feed. This is specially true for LUTs and FFs. However, such demand slightly sees a moderate increment for BRAM resources. Secondly, the wider the search area the higher the increment

Table 3. Resource occupation after place & route (XC7Z045-FFG900-2 ZynQ-SoC). Best configuration: 32-bit AXI-Stream interface and 4-pixel `costSAD` function.

Search area	LUT	FF	18 Kbit BRAM
VGA			
8	30720 (14,05%)	22745 (5,20%)	48 (4,40%)
16	64304 (29,42%)	52145 (11,93%)	58 (5,32%)
32	131472 (60,14%)	110945 (25,38%)	68 (6,24%)
HD			
8	30680 (14,03%)	24176 (5,53%)	53 (4,86%)
16	64264 (29,40%)	53576 (12,25%)	71 (6,51%)
32	131432 (60,12%)	112376 (25,7%)	90 (8,26%)
FHD			
8	31548 (14,43%)	26880 (6,15%)	60 (5,50%)
16	65132 (29,8%)	56280 (12,87%)	89 (8,17%)
32	132300 (60,52%)	115080 (26,32%)	117 (10,73%)

in resource usage, specially in LUTs and BRAMs, due to the need to cache a greater number of macroblocks for concurrent `costSAD` computation.

5   Conclusions

In this work, a high performance implementation of the full search block matching motion estimation algorithm for real-time video processing has been presented. The proposed architecture is based on a dataflow and has been modeled using Vivado HLS. The model is parameterized, enabling the engineer to easily explore the solution space and select the combination of variables (video resolution, width of memory interface, number of parallel SAD computations) that best serve the design requirements.

Several optimizations and potential improvements are devised for future versions of the component. The reduction of the LUT resources has the highest priority since represents 60% of the total available. Also, alternative versions of the cost function will be explored, which might help to the rationalization of the FPGA resources (e.g. implementing the Mean of Absolute Differences would reduces the number of bits necessary to represent the cost), and variations on the technique to extend the borders of the current frame.

References

1. Asano, S., Shun, Z.Z., Maruyama, T.: An FPGA implementation of full-search variable block size motion estimation. In: 2010 International Conference on Field-Programmable Technology, pp. 399–402 (2010). https://doi.org/10.1109/FPT.2010.5681445

2. D'huys, T., Momcilovic, S., Pratas, F., Sousa, L.: Reconfigurable data flow engine for HEVC motion estimation. In: 2014 IEEE International Conference on Image Processing (ICIP), pp. 1223–1227 (2014). https://doi.org/10.1109/ICIP. 2014.7025244

3. Ghosh, S., Saha, A.: Speed-area optimized FPGA implementation for full search block matching. In: 2007 25th International Conference on Computer Design, pp. 13–18, October 2007. https://doi.org/10.1109/ICCD.2007.4601874

4. Manikandan, L.C., Nair, S., Anu H., Sanal Kumar, K.P., Selvakumar, R.K.: A study and analysis on block matching algorithms for motion estimation in video coding. Cluster Comput. 22(5), 11773–11780 (2017). https://doi.org/10.1007/s10586-017-1478-z

5. Loukil, H., Ghozzi, F., Samet, A., Ben Ayed, M.A., Masmoudi, N.: Hardware implementation of block matching algorithm with FPGA technology. In: Proceedings. The 16th International Conference on Microelectronics, ICM 2004, pp. 542–546, December 2004. https://doi.org/10.1109/ICM.2004.1434720

6. Mohammadzadeh, M., Eshghi, M., Azadfar, M.M.: Parameterizable implementation of full search block matching algorithm using FPGA for real-time applications. In: Proceedings of the Fifth IEEE International Caracas Conference on Devices, Circuits and Systems, 2004, vol. 1, pp. 200–203, November 2004. https://doi.org/10.1109/ICCDCS.2004.1393383

7. Olivares, J., Hormigo, J., Villalba, J., Benavides, I., Zapata, E.: Sad computation based on online arithmetic for motion estimation. Microprocess. Microsyst. 30(5), 250–258 (2006). https://doi.org/10.1016/j.micpro.2005.12.006, http://www.sciencedirect.com/science/article/pii/S0141933105000943

8. Rangan, K., Reddy, M., Reddy, V.: A FPGA-based architecture for block matching motion estimation algorithm. In: IEEE TENCON 2005, vol. 2007, pp. 1–5 (2005). https://doi.org/10.1109/TENCON.2005.301202

9. Roma, N., Sousa, L.: Efficient and configurable full-search block-matching processors. IEEE Trans. Circ. Syst. Video Technol. 12(12), 1160–1167, December 2002. https://doi.org/10.1109/TCSVT.2002.806818

10. Roma, N., Dias, T., Sousa, L.: Customisable core-based architectures for real-time motion estimation on FPGAs. In: Y.. K.. Cheung, P., Constantinides, G.A. (eds.) FPL 2003. LNCS, vol. 2778, pp. 745–754. Springer, Heidelberg (2003). https://doi.org/10.1007/978-3-540-45234-8_72

11. Ryszko, A., Wiatr, K.: An assessment of FPGA suitability for implementation of real-time motion estimation. In: Proceedings Euromicro Symposium on Digital Systems Design, pp. 364–367, September 2001. https://doi.org/10.1109/DSD.2001.952332

12. Wong, S., Vassiliadis, S., Cotofana, S.: A sum of absolute differences implementation in FPGA hardware. In: Proceedings 28th Euromicro Conference, pp. 183–188 (2002). https://doi.org/10.1109/EURMIC.2002.1046155

Providing Tamper-Secure SoC Updates Through Reconfigurable Hardware

Franz-Josef Streit[1]([✉])[iD], Stefan Wildermann[1][iD], Michael Pschyklenk[2], and Jürgen Teich[1][iD]

[1] Department of Computer Science 12, Friedrich-Alexander University Erlangen-Nürnberg (FAU), Erlangen, Germany
{franz-josef.streit,stefan.wildermann,juergen.teich}@fau.de
[2] Schaeffler Technologies AG and Co. KG, Herzogenaurach, Germany
pschymch@schaeffler.com

Abstract. Remote firmware updates have become the de facto standard to guarantee a secure deployment of often decentrally operated IoT devices. However, the transfer and the provision of updates are considered as highly security-critical. Immunity requirements, such as the authenticity of the update provider and the integrity and confidentiality of the content typically loaded from an external cloud server over an untrusted network are therefore mandatory. This is especially true for FPGA-based programmable System-on-Chip (PSoC) architectures, as they are ideal implementation candidates for products with a long lifetime due to their adaptivity of both software and hardware configurations. In this paper, we propose a methodology for securely updating PSoC architectures by exploiting the reconfigurable logic of the FPGA. In the proposed approach, the FPGA serves as a secure anchor point by performing the required authenticity and integrity checks before granting the system update to be installed. In particular, a hardware design called Trusted Update Unit (TUU) is defined that is loaded from memory for the duration of an update session to first verify the identity of an external update provider and then, based on this verification, to establish a secure channel for protected data transfers. The proposed approach is also able to secure the confidentiality of cryptographic keys even if the software of the PSoC is compromised by applying them only as device-intrinsic secrets. Finally, an implementation of the approach on a Xilinx Zynq PSoC is described and evaluated for the design objectives performance and resource costs.

Keywords: Security · FPGA · Secure update · Hardware/Software co-design

1 Introduction

The Internet of Things (IoT) paradigm depends on the ability to adapt the functionality of devices to permanently changing requirements and conditions. In this context, particular FPGA-based Programmable System-on-Chip (PSoC)

S. Derrien et al. (Eds.): ARC 2021, LNCS 12700, pp. 242–253, 2021.
https://doi.org/10.1007/978-3-030-79025-7_17

architectures are gaining more and more interest and visibility, as they provide the necessary flexibility in adapting both software and hardware [10]. Examples are platforms for the sensor and edge level in domains like the Industrial IoT (IIoT), autonomous driving, multi-camera surveillance, connected health and others [9,14,16]. However, the deployment of IoT devices everywhere requires to control and program them remotely to enable software as well as hardware changes on demand, which obviously is a challenge concerning security.

Particularly, when it comes to the reprogramming during an update or upgrade session, a) the source of the update (e.g., Cloud Server (CS)) must be uniquely identifiable to protect the configuration of the device against malicious network sources and b) the confidentiality of sensitive data such as secret keys and valuable Intellectual Property (IP) must be guaranteed over the entire product lifetime. Here, secure and trusted remote update mechanisms are needed that consider the following security aspects. First, a suitable protocol for secure authentication and key distribution between server and IoT device needs to be established. Unfortunately, in the past, software-only solutions such as Secure Shell (SSH), Secure Sockets Layer (SSL), and Transport Layer Security (TLS) have been proven to be highly vulnerable [3,13], while more robust attempts targeting FPGAs [5,6] often rely on parties sharing a secret key to reduce the required amount of hardware resources. Consequently, the whole root of trust depends on the confidentiality and integrity of the applied secret keys, which poses the entire system at an unacceptable risk.

To address these challenges, we advocate a hardware-centric authentication of remote updates and their content that extends beyond existing methods. As a solution, we propose an update protocol entirely relying on tamper-proof hardware primitives to enable the secure hardware/software reconfiguration of a PSoC from an external cloud server. The central component, realized in reconfigurable logic, is called Trusted Update Unit (TUU) and loaded through partial reconfiguration to guarantee among the integrity and authenticity of remote configurations a secure on-the-fly key generation.

In particular, the proposed hardware-based remote update protocol and implementation provides the following main features:

- Sophisticated PSoC device authentication and key exchange mechanism, using Physical Unclonable Function (PUF)-based Elliptic Curve (EC) cryptography.
- Cryptographic primitives entirely embedded in reconfigurable logic, enabling tamper-proof hardware security of remote system updates.
- Processor-free update validation to guarantee the confidentiality of keys even for the case the device's software-based processing system should get compromised.
- Low and only temporal (during the update process) resource overheads through partial reconfiguration of the FPGA during an update session.

In the following, we define the steps and flow of this secure update protocol and the concept and structure of the TUU in Sect. 3. Subsequently, we describe the implementation of this methodology on a Xilinx Zynq PSoC-platform containing an Artix-7-based FPGA and a dual-core ARM Cortex-A9 processor. Finally, we analyze performance as well as resource overheads of the proposed protection mechanisms in Sect. 4.

2   Related Work

In general, remote firmware updates for many IoT devices, including PSoCs, are mainly based on well-known software protocols such as TLS and its predecessor SSL [18]. In the past, however, these protocols have been heavily affected by numerous cryptographic breaks, often due to hidden flaws in the software implementation. Here, especially, buffer over-reads to access adjacent memory regions [13] and open side channels exposed by timing [3] and more recently by cache attacks [11] were used to leak secret passwords, cryptographic keys, login credentials, and other private data. To address these problems, we propose to rather embed the cryptographic primitives of the update protocol entirely in the programmable logic of the FPGA so to never reveal the keys to the processor or shared memory instances such as caches and RAM, which enables a tamper-proof isolation.

On the hardware side, previous research has been driven mainly by the industry's need to protect valuable IP against non-authorized use when updating FPGAs in the field. In this context, several protocols were presented, of which those of Simpson/Schaumont [12], Guajardo et al. [6], and Drimer/Kuhn [5] are particularly noteworthy. Unfortunately, all these approaches are based on the sharing of a secret key between a server instance and the FPGA. While such a symmetric key protocol provides obviously the necessary confidentiality protection while keeping hardware resource requirements low, it also represents a single point of failure, when the shared key gets compromised. In addition, the remote server's device management system requires to store unique symmetric keys of all connected devices, resulting in a cumbersome device management and, maybe worse, represents an attractive target for server attacks. As a remedy, out approach makes use of a public/private key exchange protocol, where the server knows only its own private key in addition to the public keys of the fielded devices.

While the general concept of such a public/private key protocol on FPGAs has already been presented in [7], newer approaches extend this to either secure the boot process of PSoCs, as in [17], or similar to our approach to enable secure PSoC updates [4]. However, in [4], Coughlin et al. rely on software of the Linux environment running on the PSoC processing system for the generation of the private/public key pairs, which breaks our restrictive trust assumptions. If an adversary tampers with the software running on the processing system, he or she might break the processor's memory protection barriers to compromise the confidentiality of secret keys. Our solution differs by leveraging a PUF circuit to generate a device intrinsic key that never leaves the internal programmable logic of the PSoC and thus allows to handle the entire update procedure within the FPGA. Moreover, special focus was given to keep the resource overhead to a minimum. Therefore, we make use of Elliptic Curve (EC) cryptography instead of RSA as in [4] to

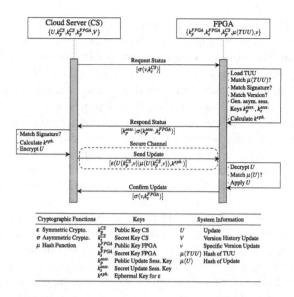

Fig. 1. Sequence diagram illustrating the communication between the update provider (Cloud Server (CS)) and the FPGA as part of a Programmable System-on-Chip (PSoC) within the proposed update protocol.

reduce logic resources for key generation by exploiting generally smaller key sizes. Finally, our partial reconfiguration flow as introduced in Sect. 3.2 is able to even further decrease the hardware footprint due to time-sharing parts of the logic as the cryptographic building blocks are only required during the update session.

3 Secure Update Process Using Reconfigurable Hardware

This section describes the remote update protocol for FPGA-based PSoCs from an external update server. The general approach is based on the idea of an isolated authentication of the server identity within the reconfigurable logic of the FPGA to guarantee a trustworthy system reconfiguration.

3.1 Update Protocol

The protocol as depicted in Fig. 1 is comprised of two communicating parties: a Cloud Server (CS) (which runs on trusted commodity) and the reconfigurable logic of the FPGA as part of the PSoC representing the client (which operates in an untrusted environment, and hence, may be exposed to malicious modifications). In the following, we propose the steps required to securely transfer the desired update. To establish a trusted communication channel between the server and the PSoC, the cloud server must first be in possession of certain system parameters and information about the current firmware version of the PSoC. Among the update denoted as U, the server requires its own public/secret key pair denoted as k_p^{CS}/k_s^{CS} together with the public key of the FPGA k_p^{FPGA} and a history of firmware versions V, while a specific update version is defined as $v \in V$. On the other side, the FPGA contains its own public/secret key pair denoted as k_p^{FPGA}/k_s^{FPGA}. In addition to that, the FPGA holds the public key of the corresponding cloud server k_p^{CS} and the currently running firmware version v.

Ahead of an update transfer, the server is required to send a *Request Status* to the FPGA. In this step, the server signs the version of the currently running PSoC firmware v with its secret key k_s^{CS} before sending the resulting signature, denoted as $\sigma(v, k_s^{CS})$, to the FPGA to authenticate itself as trustworthy. The reason for requesting the firmware version of the PSoC is to prevent replay attacks, e.g., by maliciously forwarding an old system configuration to downgrade the system to an older version. However, before any update request is processed, the FPGA decides whether it is currently possible to load a Trusted Update Unit (TUU) (cf. Fig. 2) by partially reconfiguring the FPGA. Furthermore, the integrity of the TUU is checked against a pre-calculated hash denoted as $\mu(TUU)$, which is hard-coded in a static FPGA area. As it will be discussed more detailed in Sect. 3.2, this allows both secure sharing of hardware resources and seamless updates without compromising system availability.

As soon as the TUU is loaded and its integrity is verified, the authenticity of the cloud server can be proven by making use of the senders public key k_p^{CS}, which is also hard-coded in the TUU's hardware design. In case that the CS cannot be identified by its signature, the update procedure is immediately paused to prevent possible Denial-of-Service (DoS) attacks. A successful authentication leads to the generation of an asymmetric update session key pair denoted as $k_s^{sess.}$ resp. $k_p^{sess.}$. Furthermore, the FPGA can now apply the secret session key $k_s^{sess.}$ and the public key of the cloud server k_p^{CS} to calculate an ephemeral key denoted as $k^{eph.}$ for an encrypted update channel. This ephemeral key is a symmetric key, which reduces considerable the de-/encryption overhead of any received/sent update compared to an entirely asymmetric approach.

After calculating the ephemeral key on the FPGA, the public update session key $k_p^{sess.}$ is send to the server in the *Respond Status* step. This message is not encrypted since the public update key doesn't have to be secret. Nevertheless, the FPGA signs the public session key $k_p^{sess.}$ with its private key k_s^{FPGA} to confirm authorship. Now, the cloud server can verify if the signed public update session key $k_p^{sess.}$ origins from the intended PSoC device. If the verification is successful, the remote server can securely agree on the ephemeral session key $k^{eph.}$ by making use of its private key k_s^{CS} and the sent public session key $k_p^{sess.}$ to calculate the symmetric ephemeral key for update encryption. These steps form the basis of the well-known Diffie-Hellman algorithm performed in our work by the TUU through an Elliptic Curve Diffie-Hellman Ephemeral (ECDHE) key exchange. As a result, the remote server can encrypt the PSoC update using this ephemeral key to protect the confidentiality when sending the data over an untrusted network. Moreover, through the generation of unique session keys for every update session, we achieve Perfect Forward Secrecy (PFS), since past communication cannot be decrypted. This holds even for the case the secret session key $k_s^{sess.}$ gets compromised, since such a key is always used for only one update. In case the secure key of the FPGA k_s^{FPGA} should get compromised, at least past update messages are protected this way. However, if this were to happen, it would be possible to forge the authorship of the FPGA, thus possibly compromising all future messages.

Once the secure channel is established, the cloud server can send the symmetrically encrypted update (denoted as ϵ with ephemeral key $k^{eph.}$) in the *Send Update* step. Beside the update itself, this message contains information indicating the new firmware version v to update the current version parameter and a new public key of the cloud server k_p^{CS} if required. Sending a new public key provides the option to revoke the private key of the server. This leads to the advantage that a legacy secure key of the cloud server k_s^{CS} can be refused, when being outdated or for the case when employees knowing the key would leave the company. In this context, however, it is important to point out that this revocation does not apply for the case that the server itself gets compromised. For instance, if an attacker has full access to the cloud server, he or she can compromise the cloud server's private key k_s^{CS} to apply its own key k_s^{CS*} and update the client with a malicious server public key k_p^{CS*} to get control over the client. In particular, if the attacker is able to push a malicious update U^* to the client before a legitimate server can revoke the malicious key k_s^{CS*}, the attacker gets full access as the server's public key is replaced on the client as part of the update that depends on the previous (now compromised) public key k_p^{CS*}. However, we consider the central cloud server to be secure, as these are typically embedded in a well-protected corporate network, unlike the client.

Concerning the integrity of the update, the server adds a secure hash value $\mu(U)$ to the message, which represents the content of the update in a compressed form. In this way, the FPGA can proof integrity and detect whether the update has been manipulated by calculating in the same way its own secure hash over the received update data. In a situation where an attacker should have tampered with the update data, the hash $\mu(U)$ calculated by the FPGA would consequently not match the sent one. In this case, the update procedure might be suspended for a certain amount of time and it would be possible to send an incident report to the cloud server.

After decrypting the received hardware/software update on the FPGA side, the update can now be applied by either loading it directly into system RAM or by persistently storing it on Non-Volatile Memory (NVM). While the first option only represents a temporal update that would get lost after system shutdown, the second option requires a secure boot cycle of the PSoC, such as the one in [15], to finally be activated. The last step is to send the *Confirm Update* message from the FPGA to the cloud server to confirm that the update was successfully applied and the firmware version has been updated.

3.2   Partial Reconfiguration and System Availability

This subsection describes the partial reconfiguration of the FPGA to time share the logic resources required for an update session and explains how the formulated security requirements are met. To enable seamless system updates, we separated the programmable logic of the FPGA into two areas, consisting of a static area (non run-time reconfigurable) and a dynamic area. Here, the dynamic area can be reconfigured at run-time, while the static area remains unchanged. In our design, the static area integrates a configuration controller, which has direct access to both, the system's RAM and NVM plus can write bitstreams directly to the FPGA's configuration memory via a dedicated interface called Internal Configuration Access Port (ICAP) in case of Xilinx devices.

However, in order not to impair system availability at any time, the controller decides if an update request can be safely served instantaneously as this would trigger a partial reconfiguration of the FPGA to load the TUU into the dynamic area. With this by default "delayed update" policy, the update procedure and thus reconfiguration can only start when no safety-critical applications are running. Indeed, this policy prevents the PSoC from DoS attacks where a potential Man-in-the-Middle (MITM) attacker controlling the communication channel could otherwise launch endless update requests. Once this has been checked, the TUU bitstream is passed in parallel to an SHA module, where the corresponding hash is compared with a pre-calculated signature hard-coded in the configuration controller, thus performing an integrity verification. Only upon success, the reset of the TUU is released and the update protocol is processed further. In consequence, we ensure that the FPGA side has full control over the protocol. In addition, only the FPGA can reprogram the PSoC by means of a secure update, by either writing the content to NVM, RAM, or directly into the FPGA's configuration memory. Thus, an adversary with access to the processor system's external memory could attack the availability through tampering with the storage of the TUU bitstream, but never compromise the confidentiality and integrity of secret keys.

3.3   Trusted Update Unit

This subsection shortly introduces the required building blocks to securely establish and process the proposed update protocol according to Fig. 1. During an update, the FPGA is in charge to handle all compute-intensive and security-critical operations, while the processing system of the PSoC is only responsible for forwarding the data of the send/received messages from the cloud server to the FPGA. Figure 2 illustrates a high-level description of the cryptographic modules of the TUU and their interaction with the individual steps of the update protocol introduced in Sect. 3.1.

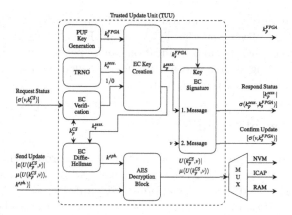

Fig. 2. Trusted Update Unit (TUU) building blocks enabling secure PSoC updates from an external cloud server.

For a proof of concept, we implemented the following cryptographic algorithms in dedicated hardware blocks: FPGA key provisioning within the TUU is done via a 163-bit PUF as an extension of the design proposed in [1], while session keys are obtained by a 32-bit ring oscillator based True Random Number Generator (TRNG) as proposed in [2]. We make use of a 163-bit Elliptic Curve Digital Signature Algorithm (ECDSA) module based on the Koblitz sect163k curve [8] for message signing and verification. To decrypt the received update data, a 128-bit AES decryption block is applied, while integrity is checked by a 256-bit SHA module (as part of the static area not shown in Fig. 2).

After loading the TUU, the PUF generates a response from which the secret device key k_s^{FPGA} is reproduced using a fuzzy extractor. Following a successful key generation, the *PUF key generation* module is ready to pass the secure key to an *EC Key Creation* module, where the corresponding public key k_p^{FPGA} is retrieved by elliptic curve point multiplication. When the signature $\sigma(v, k_s^{CS})$ of the cloud server in the *Request Status* step is verified by the *EC Verification* module (output = 1), the *EC Key Creation* is called to generate the public session key $k_p^{sess.}$ from the private session key $k_s^{sess.}$ generated by the TRNG.

For the creation of the signatures for the *Respond Status* and *Confirm Update* messages, the *EC Signature* module is in charge to sign the corresponding messages with the private FPGA key k_s^{FPGA}. To calculate the ephemeral symmetric key $k^{eph.}$, the secret session key $k_s^{sess.}$ and the public key of the cloud server k_p^{CS} are processed by a module implementing the *EC Diffie-Hellman* algorithm. If the cloud server sends the *Send Update* message, the *AES decryption block* applies the ephemeral key $k^{eph.}$ to decrypt the sent update data. Lastly, the configuration controller is in charge to write the received update data either temporally to RAM resp. ICAP or permanently to a boot partition of the NVM. After the update is applied, the current firmware version v is signed through the *EC Signature* module and just the signature is sent as *Confirm Update* status to the cloud server.

The software on the processor system only forwards the protocol commands between the cloud server and the TUU on the FPGA side. As a result, key generation, message signing, and verification can be performed without revealing keys to the processing system and remain in consequence protected even in the case of an infiltrated processing system.

4   Experimental Results

In this section, our proposed hardware-centric update protocol from Fig. 1 and TUU design according to Fig. 2 is evaluated on a Xilinx Zynq xc7z020clg484-1 PSoC placed on the ZedBoard evaluation board, while the Xilinx Vivado Design suite 2019.2 was utilized for synthesis. Since the resource overhead of the update unit should not surpass an actual user application, special focus was given onto area efficiency. The amount of required FPGA resources, separated into static and dynamic area is highlighted in Table 1. The static area represents the building blocks which are permanently not usable for user applications and accommodates the logic of the configuration controller including the ICAP interface and the SHA module for configuration and authentication of the TUU. The TUU, as part of the dynamic area, contains the PUF as well as the fuzzy extractor (which form the PUF key generation module), the TRNG for ephemeral key generation, and an EC module for the ECDSA as well as ECDHE key exchange in addition to the AES module for data decryption.

The numbers indicate that with 39% of Lookup Tables (LUTs) and only 15% of Flip-Flops (FFs), a user has more than 60% resp. 80% of the available LUTs and FFs for designing custom hardware applications that never interferes with the TUU. This means that more than half of the resources of the FPGA can always be used by the user for custom applications, while 37% of the FPGA's LUTs logic needs to be freed to load the TUU, when an update is pending.

As a second design objective, we evaluated the latency properties of the steps required to perform the update protocol, since a long update procedure might be not acceptable in some domains. Table 2 lists the measured latency and absolute time to verify the remote server request status at a target clock frequency of 150 MHz for a permanent PSoC boot image update of size 4 MB. Here, the time to reproduce the secret FPGA authentication key from a noisy PUF response amounts to 849 clock cycles. While, the time to generate the asymmetric session key pairs is more compute intensive and takes almost the same time as the calculation of the shared ephemeral key with the Diffie-Hellman algorithm. This is due to the fact that both operations are performed by a single elliptic curve point multiplication. The additional six clock cycles to generate the session keys are introduced by the TRNG, which produces 32 random bits per clock cycle and hence need six clock cycles to generate the required key length of 163-bit. Furthermore, the time required to verify a signature is higher than the one required to create a signature, while the small discrepancy in clock cycles of the sign *Respond Status* and sign *Confirm Update* is due to slightly different input values. Last but not least, the time required for decryption, linearly depends on the

Table 1. Resource requirements of the proposed TUU implementation and its cryptographic building blocks on a Xilinx Zynq 7z020 PSoC.

Module	Block	Num	LUTs	FFs	BRAMs
Static area	Conf. controller	abs	106	18	0
		(%)	0.2	0.1	0
	SHA-256	abs	1,217	1,358	0.5
		(%)	2.3	1.3	0.4
Dynamic area	PUF-163	abs	326	163	0
		(%)	0.6	0.2	0
	Fuzzy extractor	abs	927	1,896	0
		(%)	1.7	1.8	0
	TRNG-32	abs	192	544	0
		(%)	0.4	0.5	0
	AES-128	abs	1,515	1,054	4
		(%)	2.9	1.0	2.9
	EC (sect163k)	abs	16,454	11,472	9.5
		(%)	30.9	10.8	6.8
	Total	**abs.**	**20,737**	**16,505**	**14**
		(%)	**39.0**	**15.5**	**10.0**

update size and is only determined by the throughput of the AES module. Compared to the time for update verification and decryption, the time for loading the TUU bitstream by a partial reconfiguration is with measured 436 ns negligible. Overall, the resource and time overheads caused by the proposed TUU approach are tolerable for the sake of tamper-proof hardware security.

Table 2. Latencies and absolute times of the individual steps of the proposed update protocol in clock cycles and milliseconds for a target frequency of 150 MHz, when processing a PSoC update of size 4 MB.

Protocol step	Latency in cycles	Latency in [ms]
Secure fey generation	849	0.006
Verify request status	363,448	2.423
Gen. Asym. Sess. Key	138,098	0.921
Sign respond status	240,389	1.603
Diffie-Hellman algorithm	138,092	0.921
Decrypt update	3,792,826	25.285
Sign confirm update	232,751	1.552

5 Summary

In this paper, we presented a novel update approach for checking authenticity of a remote update provider and the integrity of transferred configuration data for programmable System-on-Chip (SoC) devices. In order to prevent any tampering of the update process, a fully hardware-centric solution is proposed in which a so-called Trusted Update Unit (TUU) is loaded first into the available reconfigurable region of the FPGA, which then initializes the communication interface of the PSoC with the server including authentication, integrity checking, and decryption of data. The protocol and its hardware implementation have been evaluated in terms of security, resource utilization, and performance. As a result, the lightweight TUU implementation can be used already in quite low cost, even IoT devices.

Acknowledgment. The work has been supported by the Schaeffler Hub for Advanced Research at Friedrich-Alexander University (SHARE at FAU).

References

1. Anderson, J.H.: A PUF design for secure FPGA-based embedded systems. In: ASPDAC. IEEE (2010)
2. Baudet, M., Lubicz, D., Micolod, J., Tassiaux, A.: On the security of oscillator-based random number generators. J. Cryptol. **24**(2), 398–425 (2010). https://doi.org/10.1007/s00145-010-9089-3
3. Canvel, B., Hiltgen, A., Vaudenay, S., Vuagnoux, M.: Password interception in a SSL/TLS channel. In: Boneh, D. (ed.) CRYPTO 2003. LNCS, vol. 2729, pp. 583–599. Springer, Heidelberg (2003). https://doi.org/10.1007/978-3-540-45146-4_34
4. Coughlin, A., Cusack, G., Wampler, J., Keller, E., Wustrow, E.: Breaking the trust dependence on third party processes for reconfigurable secure hardware. In: FPGA (2019)
5. Drimer, S., Kuhn, M.G.: A protocol for secure remote updates of FPGA configurations. In: Becker, J., Woods, R., Athanas, P., Morgan, F. (eds.) ARC 2009. LNCS, vol. 5453, pp. 50–61. Springer, Heidelberg (2009). https://doi.org/10.1007/978-3-642-00641-8_8
6. Guajardo, J., Kumar, S.S., Schrijen, G.-J., Tuyls, P.: FPGA intrinsic PUFs and their use for IP protection. In: Paillier, P., Verbauwhede, I. (eds.) CHES 2007. LNCS, vol. 4727, pp. 63–80. Springer, Heidelberg (2007). https://doi.org/10.1007/978-3-540-74735-2_5
7. Guajardo, J., Kumar, S.S., Schrijen, G.J., Tuyls, P.: Physical unclonable functions and public-key crypto for FPGA IP protection. In: FPL (2007)
8. Koblitz, N.: Elliptic curve cryptosystems. Math. Comput. **48**(177), 203–209 (1987)
9. Morris, K.: Xilinx Hits the Road with Daimler SoCs to Power Automotive AI Applications. https://www.eejournal.com/article/xilinx-hits-the-road-with-daimler. Accessed March 2021
10. Ray, S., Basak, A., Bhunia, S.: Patching the Internet of Things. IEEE Spectr. **54**(11), 30–35 (2017)
11. Ronen, E., Gillham, R., Genkin, D., Shamir, A., Wong, D., Yarom, Y.: The 9 lives of bleichenbacher's CAT: new cache attacks on TLS implementations. In: SP. IEEE (2019)

12. Simpson, E., Schaumont, P.: Offline hardware/software authentication for reconfigurable platforms. In: Goubin, L., Matsui, M. (eds.) CHES 2006. LNCS, vol. 4249, pp. 311–323. Springer, Heidelberg (2006). https://doi.org/10.1007/11894063_25
13. Somorovsky, J.: Systematic fuzzing and testing of TLS libraries. In: CCS (2016)
14. Streit, F., et al.: Data acquisition and control at the edge: a hardware/software-reconfigurable approach. Prod. Eng. **14**(3), 365–371 (2020). https://doi.org/10.1007/s11740-020-00964-x
15. Streit, F.J., Fritz, F., Becher, A., et al.: Secure boot from non-volatile memory for programmable SoC architectures. In: HOST. IEEE (2020)
16. Streit, F.J., Letras, M., Schid, M., Falk, J., Wildermann, S., Teich, J.: High-level synthesis for hardware/software co-design of distributed smart camera systems. In: ICDSC. ACM (2017)
17. Unterstein, F., Jacob, N., Hanley, N., Gu, C., Heyszl, J.: SCA secure and updatable crypto engines for FPGA SoC bitstream decryption. In: ASHES (2019)
18. Zandberg, K., Schleiser, K., Acosta, F., Tschofenig, H., Baccelli, E.: Secure firmware updates for constrained IoT devices using open standards: a reality check. IEEE Access **7**, 71907–71920 (2019)

Graviton: A Reconfigurable Memory-Compute Fabric for Data Intensive Applications

Ashutosh Dhar[1(✉)], Paul Reckamp[1], Jinjun Xiong[2], Wen-mei Hwu[1], and Deming Chen[1]

[1] University of Illinois at Urbana-Champaign, Urbana, USA
{adhar2,paulrr2,w-hwu,dchen}@illinois.edu
[2] IBM Research, Yorktown Heights, USA
jinjun@us.ibm.com

Abstract. The rigid organization and distribution of computational and memory resources often limits how well accelerators can cope with changing algorithms and increasing dataset sizes and limits how efficiently they use their computational and memory resources. In this work, we leverage a novel computing paradigm and propose a new memory-based reconfigurable fabric, Graviton. We demonstrate the ability to dynamically trade memory for compute and vice versa, and can tune the architecture of the underlying hardware to suit the memory and compute requirements of the application. On a die-to-die basis, Graviton provides up to 47X more on-chip memory capacity over an Alveo U250 SLR, with just an additional 1.7% area on a die-to-die basis than modern FPGAs, and is $28.7X$ faster, on average, on a range of compute and data intensive tasks.

Keywords: Reconfigurable architectures · Logic folding

1 Introduction

The slow down in CMOS device scaling has resulted in the adoption of accelerators across computing domains. Simultaneously, an explosion of algorithmic and data complexity has presented an increasing demand for computational performance, efficiency, and flexibility. In this age of big-compute and big-data, we observe two salient phenomena when considering the needs of accelerators: (1) rapidly changing computational problems require flexible and programmable accelerators, and (2) architects are adding more on-chip memory to accelerators as the cost of moving data to computational units is emerging as the key challenge to efficient and high performance computing.

Domain specific accelerators are often unable to provide the flexibility to adapt to fast evolving algorithms. Thus, we note that there is a need for reconfigurable architectures such as FPGAs. An FPGA is an array of configurable logic blocks (CLBs), each of which is comprised of look-up tables and flip-flops organized in an island layout with programmable routing structures – connection, switch boxes, and wires. While these routing structures are critical to the

© Springer Nature Switzerland AG 2021
S. Derrien et al. (Eds.): ARC 2021, LNCS 12700, pp. 254–264, 2021.
https://doi.org/10.1007/978-3-030-79025-7_18

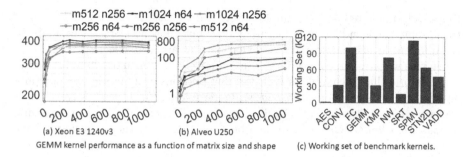

(a) Xeon E3 1240v3   (b) Alveo U250

GEMM kernel performance as a function of matrix size and shape   (c) Working set of benchmark kernels.

Fig. 1. (a, b) Average throughput (GOP/s) on dense matrix multiplication computation, as function of matrix dimensions. Input matrices A and B have shapes {MxK} and {KxN}, respectively, and the output matrix, C, has a shape of {MxN}. X-axis shows Kth dimension. (c) Minimum working set (KB) per accelerator unit across benchmarks.

FPGA's ability to realize large and arbitrary circuits, they are responsible for the bulk of the delay and can occupy significant area [3]. Similarly, the BRAM memory units include additional circuitry [9] to provide flexible memory organization, which limits their density and performance. Finally, the reconfiguration latency of FPGAs limits their ability to dynamically adapt to the varying characteristics of applications.

As the computational power of accelerators has increased, the amount of on-chip memory has increased proportionally, yet designers must perform hand-tuning via *data tiling* strategies to realize peak accelerator performance. Despite these efforts, the effective computational throughput and efficiency are determined by the shape and size of the *data tiles* that can be loaded into the accelerator, which are characteristic to the application and dataset. Accelerators feature a fixed distribution of on-chip memory and computational elements; often, a dedicated cache/scratchpad/FIFO is allocated to a computational element or a group of computational elements. This fixed *memory-to-compute ratio* and memory hierarchy leads to under utilization of on-chip compute and memory resources.

To illustrate the limitations of fixed memory-to-compute ratios, we consider two examples. First, we consider general purpose matrix multiplication (GEMM) evaluated on an Intel Xeon E3-1240 v3 CPU and a Xilinx Alveo U250 FPGA with their vendor-provided optimized kernels – Intel OneAPI (32 bit float) and Xilinx Vitis BLAS (16 bit integer) libraries. We present the observed throughput of each device in Fig. 1a and Fig. 1b as we sweep along one of the shared matrix dimensions. Here we see that each accelerator has a unique inflection point, determined by the underlying architecture of its compute units and memory organization, that saturates performance. Next, we consider a selection of benchmarks from the MachSuite [5] benchmark suite and a few handwritten kernels. The benchmarks' data parllelism allows several parallel and identical accelerator compute units to be instantiated. The smallest data tile that each compute unit can work independently on, called the *minimum working set*, is presented in Fig. 1c. The minimum working set varies significantly and limits the amount of parallelism that can be exploited. Both examples in Fig. 1 demonstrate that a fixed memory-to-compute ratio and memory hierarchy does not allow accelerators to adapt to the different levels of data reuse and sharing that are available.

In this work, we introduce Graviton – a novel dense-memory based reconfigurable fabric that is capable of transforming portions of its fabric into compute on-demand by leveraging *logic folding*. Logic folding [3,11] *folds* large circuits over time by partitioning a netlist into levels, such that each level is a stage in a *temporal pipeline*. Each level can then be implemented by the same shared logic resources by reconfiguring them at each time step, implementing large circuits in a smaller area with a longer latency.

Graviton creates a fabric comprised of thousands of dense SRAM-based memory arrays organized into computational-memory units called Mem-Compute (MC) tiles. The dense memory structures hold configuration bits for thousands of look-up tables (LUTs), that allow us to load new configurations every cycle and implement a stage in the *temporally pipelined* circuit. Accelerators in Graviton can be realized by *folding* and implementing them across one or more MCs, and large workloads can instantiate multiple accelerator units across the fabric. Alternatively, MC tiles may be used as regular memory buffers. The high density of the MC tiles and logic folding limits the spatial spread of circuits, and we do not require long routing paths via FPGA-like global routing structures. Thus, we operate our memory arrays at high clock speeds, compensating for logic folding overheads. Finally, we couple our MC tiles with a hierarchical on-chip network to enable high bandwidth communication between accelerators and memory buffers. Graviton is scalable, flexible, capable of fast reconfiguration, and features a large amount of on-chip memory. Crucially, Graviton can dynamically alter its memory-to-compute ratio. We present the following contributions:

- We introduce a novel reconfigurable fabric, Graviton, capable of dynamically altering its memory-to-compute ratio to suit application requirements.
- Our architecture provides high logic density compared to modern FPGAs, and is capable of high-speed dynamic reconfiguration.
- We compare our architecture on a die-to-die basis with a modern Xilinx FPGA. Compared to an Alveo U250 SLR, our architecture provides up to 47X more on-chip memory capacity, with just an additional 1.7% area. We also demonstrate an average of 28.7X performance advantage on computational and data-intensive workloads.

2   Graviton: A Novel Reconfigurable Fabric

Graviton, shown in Fig. 2a, is comprised of several *Super Tiles* (ST), which contain thousands of computational memory arrays coupled with a hierarchical on-chip network. Data intensive applications are accelerated by realizing hundreds of independent *accelerator unit and data tile* pairs in the STs, customized to suit the application and dataset characteristics. Graviton scales by connecting multiple STs on a shared bus that is used for off-chip memory access, IO, and accelerator to accelerator communication. Finally, we include several CPU cores to help manage the accelerator units and facilitate data orchestration.

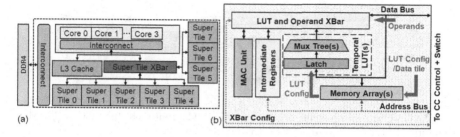

Fig. 2. (a) Graviton system architecture. (b) Memory-Compute (MC) tile.

Computational Clusters: Memory-Compute (MC) tiles are the smallest units in Graviton and are shown in Fig. 2b. We store the configuration bits of one or more LUTs in each row of the array and pair the output of the array with a multiplexer tree (mux-tree) and latch. For example, if the array provides 32 bits per access, then on each read we can implement a single 5-LUT or two 4-LUTs. We also include a crossbar (Xbar), similar to those in an FPGA's CLB, to help the resulting LUTs realize combinational circuits and state registers for the intermediate results of each level. Since the memory array(s) in the MC tile provides the configuration bits of one or more LUTs, we can reconfigure the LUT(s) by reading a new row and implementing a different level of the *folded* circuit or stage in the *temporal pipeline*. We call this *compute mode*. Alternatively, the MC tile can operate in *memory mode*, where the memory array can be used to store data tiles. To enable both modes of operation, the MC tile features a shared data bus which enables the memory arrays to drive the memory latches to form LUTs or be read/written by an external controller. The shared data bus also allows the MC tile to receive operands to feed directly into the LUT input or state registers. To facilitate this, MC tiles are driven by an external controller that arbitrates the bus and provides address logic for the memory arrays. To simplify the execution of the compute mode, we store the configuration bits of the LUTs in sequential addresses of the memory arrays, such that each row in an array holds the configuration for one timestep in the folded circuit. This simplifies the address generation unit and allows a single shared address bus for all memory arrays. Finally, to improve the computational performance, we add a dedicated integer multiply-accumulate (MAC) unit. The LUT input/output crossbars, the shared data bus, and the MAC units are arbitrated by a shared crossbar that we call the *operand crossbar*. Thus, the MC tile is capable of implementing either a memory buffer tile or a single independent folded accelerator unit.

A fabric made up of *thousands* of MC tiles, each with fully independent control and operation, is not feasible – each MC tile would require its own address generation unit, schedule controller, bus arbiter, etc. Instead, we rely on the regular nature of data intensive and computational applications, where we expect to see multiple instances of the same accelerator tile operating on independent data units, and group eight MC tiles into a *Compute Cluster* (CC). MC tiles in a compute cluster (CC) share common address generation, control,

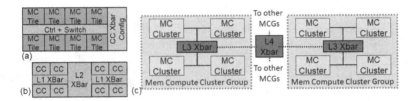

Fig. 3. Graviton component organization. (a) Compute cluster (CC), (b) Mem-Compute cluster (MCC), and (c) Super tile (ST).

and arbitration units. The CC controller is responsible for sequencing addresses to execute a logic folding schedule by driving the address and arbitration signals. The CC also provides an L0 crossbar, which acts as a fully connected switch and enables LUTs in MC tiles to drive each other. Thus, one or more MC tiles can be grouped to form accelerators with increased LUTs available per cycle, reducing the number of logic fold timesteps. The CC controller drives a shared address bus for all MC tiles, so all MC tiles operate in lock-step. Thus, the eight MC tiles in a CC will realize between one and eight identical accelerator units which operate in lock-step, but operate on independent data tiles, in *compute mode*. The data tiles may be stored in MCs within the same CC or external CCs. In *memory mode*, loads and stores from accelerators within the CC and external CCs are handled by the CC controller and arbitrated with the L0 Xbar. The eight MC tiles are fully addressable by the CC controller and may host data tiles belonging to accelerators in internal or external clusters. Finally, by storing configuration bits and data tiles in different locations within the array, it is possible to rapidly switch between compute and memory modes on-the-fly, using the same CC to implement an accelerator and the associated memory tile.

Scalable Cluster Design: Graviton deploys hundreds of independent accelerator units to collectively solve large computational problems, and accelerators communicate with each other by copying to-and-from shared memory buffers on chip. Each accelerator unit is logic folded and implemented within a constrained area – a compute cluster. Thus, accelerator circuits do not use long wire segments, and we do not require FPGA-styled complex global routing structures to enable large, spatially-spread circuits. This lack of FPGA-styled global routing provides several key advantages: (1) we can operate MC tiles at higher clock rates, which helps overcome the impact of logic folding and increases the internal memory bandwidth, and (2) Graviton easily scales up and provides significantly higher logic, memory, and compute density over traditional FPGAs.

To enable high-bandwidth communication between accelerators and the shared global address space across all MC tiles, we propose a light-weight hierarchical on-chip network within Super Tiles (ST). A full mesh network-on-chip (NoC) with packet switching would be expensive and would complicate mapping accelerators. Instead, we setup an H-tree network via crossbars that provides more predictable latency and high bandwidth access. We begin by creating a *Mem Compute Cluster* (MCC), comprised of eight compute clusters connected via a two-level crossbar so that the accelerators can share buffers at high speed. A transaction between compute clusters in an MCC experiences 2 cycles of latency across the L1 and L2 crossbars. The next level of the hierarchy is called an *MC Cluster Group* (MCG) and is made of four MC Clusters and with another 2 cycles of latency over the L3 crossbar. This network is illustrated in Fig. 3a, and 3b. Finally, sixteen MC Cluster Groups, organized in a 4 × 4 fashion, form the *Super Tile* unit, as shown in Fig. 3c, with the help of L4 crossbars. To keep the network simple, all crossbars in Graviton are blocking, and any over subscription of bandwidth results in increased latency. In this work, we use 128 bit wide transactions, and thus, each MCG has a total internal bandwidth of 4 × 8 × 128 bits (4 MCCs per MCG and 8 CCs per MCC). At an operating frequency of 3 GHz, this amounts to 1.5 TB/s per MCG, 24.5 TB/s per super tile, and a total of 196.6 TB/s for the full 8-ST fabric shown in Fig. 2.

Accelerator Control and Operation: All MC tiles in Graviton share a global memory address space, and the CPUs (Fig. 2a) drive configuration and control them via reserved addresses for control registers (managed by the MC tile's CC controller). By accessing the MC tile's control registers, the CPU can initialize, program, and control the accelerator. Each MC is provided with a *Run* and *Done* register to track the accelerator state and configuration offsets that point to the accelerator unit's configuration bits (stored in the MC's memory array). Additional control registers inform the CC controller to switch the MC tile from compute to memory mode. Memory arrays are typically large enough that we can store more than one accelerator's configuration bits in an MC tile and instantly switch between accelerators by changing the configuration offset. Moreover, MC tiles can be simultaneously used to store global data and implement accelerator units and scratchpad buffers. We map the control and operand address spaces of an entire super tile to a part of the shared global address space, visible to all accelerator units and CPUs. Naturally, CPU cores perform data orchestration and are responsible for loading and initializing data into memory buffers on the fabric. Accelerators can optionally run independently with their own address generation logic and *pushing* or *pulling* operands from memory buffers.

3   Evaluation

Accelerator Mapping: Accelerating applications with Graviton requires an accelerator circuit for each computational kernel, a logic folding schedule for each circuit, and the number of accelerator units to instantiate determined by the unique memory-to-compute ratios. Recall that each accelerator unit may be implemented in up to eight MC tiles in a compute cluster (CC), and all accelerator units in the CC will execute the same logic folding schedule, operating in lock-step. The schedule determines the number of times the circuit is folded, and which operations happen at each level. In this work we use the Machsuite [5] and hand tuned benchmarks we illustrated in Fig. 1c. Our benchmarks are written in C/C++ and synthesized via Xilinx Vivado HLS. Prior work on logic folding

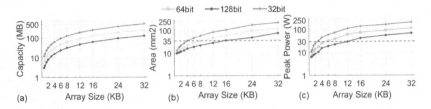

Fig. 4. Super tile architectural design space across different memory array technologies. Plots illustrate: (a) Total capacity (MB), (b) Area (mm^2), and (c) Peak Power (W) as a function of increasing memory array size, for arrays of different output width – 32, 64, and 128 bits. For clarity, 35 mm^2 and 30 W are marked on (b) and (c) in green. (Color figure online)

has extensively explored mapping and scheduling circuits [3,4,10], and in this work we use a flow similar to [3] to map the benchmarks to our fabric.

Area and Timing Modeling: We evaluated the area and performance of Graviton through models we developed targeting a 16 nm CMOS process and used data provided by Stillmaker et al. [6] to scale area, delay and energy to 16 nm when needed. Since Graviton does not have FPGA-styled global routing, we target a fabric clock frequency of 3 GHz. We used Cacti 7 [1] to model the SRAM arrays in a 22 nm process node and then scaled it to 16 nm [6]. Next, with the help of DSENT [7], we estimated the area of the mux-tree as 22 µm^2, the MC operand xbar as 297 µm^2, and the L0 CC xbar as 6094 µm^2. We then used COFFE [9] and estimated the CC switch latency as 109 ps and the MC tile operand crossbar latency as 47 ps. As shown in Fig. 2b, the memory latch and mux-tree form the LUT(s), and thus, the delay of the LUT is determined by the latency of the register and the mux tree, making it very fast. By using small, but dense, SRAM arrays, the latency of the arrays can be very small [3]. Thus, for our target frequency of 3 GHz, we can realize folded circuits that are spread across an entire compute cluster (CC) within a clock cycle, 330 ps. We then model the L1, L2, L3 and L4 crossbar areas in the super tiles and find them to be 4760 µm^2, 1710 µm^2, 4760 µm^2, and 4760 µm^2 respectively. Finally, we used RTL synthesis with a 45 nm CMOS library, scaled to 16 nm [6], to estimate the area of the MC tile's MAC unit as 243 µm^2, and used Cacti [1] to estimate the area of a 32 × 192 state register file to be 313 µm^2.

Architecture Design Space: We compare Graviton to two modern FPGAs: an Alveo U250 and an Ultra 96. Note that the Alveo U250 is comprised of four FPGA dies packaged together (each die is called a super logic region or SLR). We use area data provided by Wong et al. [8] for various FPGA resources (Logic blocks, BRAMs, routing, DSPs) scaled to 16nm [6], to estimate the die area of the FPGAs. We estimate that a single die of the Alveo U250 (1 SLR) occupies 286 mm^2, while an Ultra 96 FPGA occupies 25.89 mm^2. Since our fabric can be scaled by increasing or decreasing the number of *super tiles*, we compare a single super tile to an Ultra 96 (U96), and eight super tiles to an Alveo U250 die.

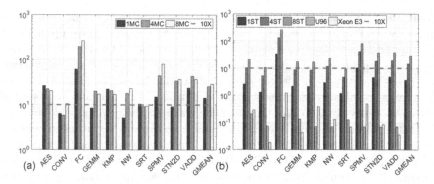

Fig. 5. Speedup shown over a single U250 die.(a) Impact of accelerator tile sizing on performance in fabric. (b) Scaling the fabric with increasing number of super tiles.

Dense SRAM memory arrays are the key building blocks of Graviton, and we begin by considering how to select and design SRAM arrays. Key factors such as the process node, process type, total array capacity, and array width determine the area and energy efficiency. To illustrate this trade-off, we performed a sweep of array size and width with Cacti 7 [1], for the architecture described in Sect. 2. Our exploration targets eight 4-LUTs per cycle per MC tile. We then estimate the peak power (Watts) that a single super tile can consume, and the total memory capacity (Megabytes) and area (mm^2) per super tile. Note that in practice we will not sustain the peak power, but it is still an important thermal design point. Figure 4 presents our analysis, and we include markers for 35 mm^2 and 30 W for clarity. As we can see, there is significantly lower energy associated with wider output widths, due to the shorter bitlines. During our analysis, we also considered 350 W to be the maximum peak power we can tolerate, as this is typically seen in high performance PCIe-attached accelerators. With the help of the peak power limit and the data in Fig. 4, we select SRAM arrays of 16KB and 128 bit words to implement the MC tiles. Thus, a single super tile has an area of 36.35 mm^2. This ST has a total capacity of 64 MB, and a total of 4096 MAC units (one per MC tile). Recall that due to the absence of FPGA-styled routing resources, Graviton has a significantly higher resource density. Thus, when we consider our complete 8 ST fabric, we see it has a total capacity of 512 MB, 32.7K MAC units, a peak power of 336 W, and an area of 291 mm^2. When compared to an Alveo U250 on a die-to-die (1 SLR) basis, Graviton is just 1.74% larger. However, compared to an Alveo U250 SLR's 10.8 MB of URAM/BRAM capacity and 3032 DSP units, we provide up to 47X more on-chip memory capacity, and 10.8X more computational units (DSPs/MACs). In practice, not all 512 MB and 32.7K MACs will be used. The effective usage is determined by: the size of the accelerator netlist, the number of folding steps, how many accelerator configurations are concurrently stored on-chip, and how much data tiling can be practically leveraged for the kernel.

Fabric Performance: We will now evaluate the performance of our fabric and demonstrate its ability to reconfigure itself to suit the memory-to-compute ratios of the applications. We use the gem5 [2] simulator to model Graviton as shown in Fig. 2, by using out-of-order ARM cores for the fabric CPU cores and implementing a cycle-level timing model for the reconfigurable fabric. We first perform an RTL simulation of each benchmark to generate traces of the memory accesses and the exact latency (cycles). We then run the trace on the gem5 model, accounting for: the folding schedule of each benchmark accelerator's synthesized circuit, the contention on the buses and crossbars when moving operands from memory buffers to clusters, cluster IO bandwidth, and loading of operands to the accelerator tiles [3]. For comparison, we consider an Ultra 96, Alveo U250 die, and Intel Xeon E3 E3-1240 v3 CPU. For the Alveo U250 and Ultra 96, we synthesize the benchmark circuits using Xilinx Vivado HLS at 100 MHz and use the reported simulation latency. We attempt to instantiate as many copies of the benchmark IPs as possible on the FPGA, to reflect the maximum data parallelism. If all copies do not fit, we batch the workloads and scale the latency accordingly. For the Xeon E3, we parallelize the benchmarks across all four available cores via OpenMP. On our Graviton fabric, we instantiate as many copies as possible, based on their respective memory-to-compute ratios, and allow the accelerators to have shared buffers spread across the MCG. We also scale the benchmark problem size and datasets to ensure that it saturates all devices. Finally, the cost of a PCIe transfer is a function of DMA and driver efficiency and is hard to simulate. Since our focus is only on fabric performance, we consider that the data has already been initialized on all devices. We present all data normalized to the performance of the Alveo U250 die (1 SLR), and show the relative speedup.

We begin by considering the impact of accelerator sizing. We consider accelerators mapped to 1, 4, and 8 MC tiles. Increasing the accelerator size can reduce the number of folding cycles, but decreases the number of concurrent accelerators. Moreover, the number of accelerator tiles is limited by their per-tile working set, as in Sect. 1 and Fig. 1b, and more accelerator units increases contention to memory buffers. We explore the impact of these factors in Fig. 5a, where we see that the best accelerator tile size varies significantly by application. However, Graviton is able to successfully adapt based on the memory-to-compute ratio of the application. Finally, we evaluate the scalability of our fabric in Fig. 5b by sweeping the number of super tiles. We consider 1, 4, and 8 STs, with accelerator units occupying a full CC (8 MC tiles). We compare the performance of one super tile to an Ultra 96 and all eight super tiles to an Alveo U250 die; our fabric demonstrates strong scaling with increased super tiles. With just a single super tile we significantly outperform the Ultra 96, by an average of 37.8X (Geometric mean). When compared to the Alveo U250, we demonstate an average speedup of 28.7X (Geometric mean) on a die-to-die basis (1 SLR). The key to Graviton's performance is: (1) its ability to adapt to the memory-to-compute ratio of the application, (2) its high density of memory and computational units, allowing it to keep large datasets on-chip, and (3) the lack of complex global routing structures, allowing it to operate at high clock frequencies.

4   Related Work

Prior attempts at leveraging logic folding [4,10] have focused on improving FPGA performance by using logic folding to help reduce wire lengths. These attempts did not approach the problem from a computation-first perspective, and focused on improving the performance of spatially distributed circuits. In contrast, we propose a novel fabric focused on accelerating compute based on the observation that applications have unique memory-to-compute ratios. Thus, our work provides a large amount of on-chip memory, capable of transforming itself into compute and back, while reconfiguring at very high speeds. Dhar et al. [3] attempted to leverage logic folding to realize a reconfigurable fabric in the last-level cache of a CPU. Their goal was to enable cheap near-memory computing. However, they were limited by the constraints of power and density in the cache, and do not demonstrate the level of flexibility that our fabric does.

5   Conclusion

In this work, we presented a novel reconfigurable fabric capable of dynamically transforming memory arrays into compute and back. This allows us to realize accelerators with finely tuned memory to compute ratios, while also providing high speed reconfiguration. Thus, we overcome limitations of traditional FPGAs by avoiding global routing structures, fixed memory and compute organizations, and slow reconfiguration speeds. Our architecture provides up to 47X more on-chip memory with just an additional 1.7% area on a die-to-die basis than modern FPGAs, and we demonstrated an average speedup of 28.7X over a variety of computational benchmarks.

Acknowledgement. This work was supported by the IBM-ILLINOIS Center for Cognitive Computing Systems Research (C3SR), Xilinx Center of Excellence, and Xilinx Adaptive Compute Clusters (XACC) at the University of Illinois Urbana-Champaign.

References

1. Balasubramonian, R., et al.: CACTI 7: new tools for interconnect exploration in innovative off-chip memories. ACM Trans. Archit. Code Optim. 14(2), 1–25 (2017)
2. Binkert, N., et al.: The Gem5 simulator. SIGARCH Comput. Archit. News 39(2), 1–7 (2011)
3. Dhar, A., et al.: FReaC cache: folded-logic reconfigurable computing in the last level cache. In: 2020 53rd Annual IEEE/ACM International Symposium on Microarchitecture (MICRO)
4. Lin, T.J., et al.: A fine-grain dynamically reconfigurable architecture aimed at reducing the FPGA-ASIC gaps. IEEE Trans. Very Large Scale Integr. (VLSI) Syst. 22(12), 2607–2620 (2014)
5. Reagen, B., et al.: MachSuite: benchmarks for accelerator design and customized architectures. In: 2014 IEEE International Symposium on Workload Characterization (2014)

6. Stillmaker, A., Baas, B.: Scaling equations for the accurate prediction of CMOS device performance from 180 nm to 7 nm. Integration **58**, 74–81 (2017)
7. Sun, C., et al.: DSENT - a tool connecting emerging photonics with electronics for opto-electronic networks-on-chip modeling. In: 2012 IEEE/ACM Sixth International Symposium on Networks-on-Chip (2012)
8. Wong, H., et al.: Comparing FPGA vs. custom CMOS and the impact on processor microarchitecture. In: Proceedings of the 19th ACM/SIGDA International Symposium on Field Programmable Gate Arrays (2011)
9. Yazdanshenas, S., Betz, V.: COFFE 2: automatic modelling and optimization of complex and heterogeneous FPGA architectures. ACM Trans. Reconfigurable Technol. Syst. **12**(1), 1–27 (2019)
10. Zhang, W., et al.: NanoMap: an integrated design optimization flow for a hybrid nanotube/CMOS dynamically reconfigurable architecture. In: 2007 44th ACM/IEEE Design Automation Conference (2007)
11. Zhang, W., et al.: NATURE: a hybrid nanotube/CMOS dynamically reconfigurable architecture. In: 2006 43rd ACM/IEEE Design Automation Conference (2006)

Dynamic Spatial Multiplexing on FPGAs with OpenCL

Pascal Jungblut[✉] and Dieter Kranzlmüller

Computer Science Department, MNM Team, Ludwig-Maximilians-Universität (LMU)
Munich, Oettingenstr. 67, 80538 Munich, Germany
{pascal.jungblut,dieter.kranzlmuller}@nm.ifi.lmu.de

Abstract. Recent advances in High-Level Synthesis (HLS) allow software developers to offload compute kernels to FPGAs without deep knowledge about low-level hardware description languages. However, this abstraction comes at the cost of control over the bitstream and thus complicates features like partial reconfiguration. We introduce a vendor-agnostic high-level approach for time and space multiplexing on OpenCL-programmed FPGAs. It dynamically adjusts the FPGA's configuration to provide load balancing between multiple kernels on the same device. Our method uses several configurations, each with a different amount of FPGA resources dedicated to the respective kernel. We introduce a model to decide which configuration is selected based on the projected runtime of the enqueued tasks. Our model and the implementation *Forecast* are demonstrated with an online scheduler on a current high-end FPGA. We find that Forecast makes automatic handling of configurations in HLS-applications possible.

1 Introduction

Since their introduction in the 1980s Field-Programmable Gate Arrays (FPGAs) have been used to process and accelerate computational workloads. They consist of logic blocks that can be set and combined through a configuration, the *bitstream*. The resulting logic circuit defines the functions an FPGA is able to perform.

Software developers program or rather configure an FPGA based on a high-level programming language like C, libraries based on these or even dedicated Domain Specific Languages (DSLs). In this case, a compiler generates Hardware Description Language (HDL) from the input program, which in turn is compiled to a configuration in the form of a bitstream. One of the more well known programming environments that have been adapted for reconfigurable computing is OpenCL [4]. It extends C with some keywords along with a well defined program- and memory model as well as a runtime.

© Springer Nature Switzerland AG 2021
S. Derrien et al. (Eds.): ARC 2021, LNCS 12700, pp. 265–274, 2021.
https://doi.org/10.1007/978-3-030-79025-7_19

1.1   OpenCL

The free OpenCL standard defines a programming model targeted at heterogeneous architectures. It consists of two parts: an API to control the execution of parallel computations and a dedicated, C-based language to define *kernels* in a well-defined computation and memory environment. The programming model is divided into the *host* part, which controls the execution, defines tasks and memory movement, and a *device* part. The host offloads kernel computation to devices. The kernels are defined in the OpenCL programming language which is similar to ANSI C.

1.2   Partial Reconfiguration

An FPGA that is intended to be used as a computing accelerator has to support the dynamic software environment. Two features supported by most high-performance FPGA-accelerators are: **Dynamic reconfiguration** where the FPGA can be reconfigured without interruption and **Partial reconfiguration**, i.e., it supports changing only parts of its configuration while the rest of the chip operates.

With (dynamic) partial reconfiguration (PR) it is possible to reconfigure only a part of the resources of the FPGA while the rest of the circuits operate. To support PR, the configuration has to be prepared: *reconfigurable regions* have to be designed that can be filled with configuration modules. While PR makes fine grained, dynamic reconfiguration possible, it has some drawbacks. The configuration is limited by the region's interface and the constrained area may have a negative impact on the performance. Additionally, the configuration has to be compiled for each slot and the process causes an overhead for developers.

In practice PR *is* used in the OpenCL environment. The bitstreams generated by the compiler are dynamically loaded at runtime via PR. However, it is not possible to explicitly replace one kernel function with another one. Instead, all kernels inside an OpenCL-file are considered one reconfigurable module. This makes it possible to combine kernels into one module, but also prevents developers from using true PR at a kernel-level granularity.

1.3   Motivation

The lack of kernel-level partial reconfiguration and the practical limitations of the OpenCL environment are the primary motivation for this work. In a software environment the amount and type of workloads can be dynamic and the reconfigurability of FPGAs is potentially a good mechanism to react to these changes.

In this paper we present a novel and simple approach to handle dynamic workloads with multiple configurations. This works for OpenCL but it can also be applied to other, similar High-Level Synthesis (HLS) programming environments.

Without partial reconfiguration, we consider a different approach to dynamically adjust the FPGA's configuration to the current workload. Naively, we could pursue the two extremes:

1. Put each kernel function into its own configuration file, maximizing the available FPGA-resources for each kernel at the cost of configuration overhead.
2. Bundle as many kernels as possible into one configuration which may affect the routing negatively.

With our approach we aim to find the balance between both ends of the scale and we take a deliberately high-level point of view to be vendor-agnostic.

2   Approach

For that goal we extend the OpenCL runtime with two components:

1. a reconfiguration-aware task scheduler
2. a model to predict the cost of task execution and reconfiguration

The runtime applies the model to predict the cost of executing the currently enqueued tasks for each configuration. Switching to another configuration results in overhead and therefore potentially in additional cost. A loss function could consider the total task runtime, throughput, latency or the total consumed energy.

Given kernels K, we create multiple configurations C from the kernels by compiling them from a single OpenCL-file per configuration. In a configuration $C_i \in C$ each kernel $k_j \in K$ has resources $0 \leq R_i^r(k_j) \leq 1$ of resource type r allocated. The function R describes the fraction of resources of the targeted hardware that are reserved for a kernel. For a given configuration C_i to be valid $\sum_{k \in K} R_i^r(k) \leq 1$ must hold. To balance the resource usage it is possible to influence $R_i^r(k_j)$ deliberately.

2.1   Manipulating Utilization

There are several ways to purposely influence R_i^r. We identified three categories of manipulation mechanisms: **explicit** changes to the kernel code, **semi-explicit** annotations that influence the code generation and **implicit** factors that affect allocation (e.g., compiler version).

2.2   Configurations

Since the compile times for FPGAs are orders of magnitudes longer than for traditional software, it is important to extract sensible information about the resources $R_i^r(k_j)$ early in the compilation process. It is possible to get estimates for the consumed resources for a given kernel before the costly place-and-route step is executed. These can be extracted from the compiler-generated reports and allow both a prediction of $R_i^r(k_j)$.

2.3 Tasks

In OpenCL there are three types of commands that can be enqueued into command queues: computation, data movement and synchronization,

Data movement commands write data from the host to an OpenCL device or vice-versa. Synchronization points in a command-level are either explicitly introduced by enqueuing computation commands or by submitting barriers. In this work, we mainly focus on the computation commands, which we will call tasks. Note that the OpenCL standard uses "task" for single work-item kernels, i.e., kernels that have extent 1 in all dimensions, but we will include all compute *kernel instances*. A kernel instance consists of a kernel function, its arguments and the NDRange index space.

3 Model

To find the best point in time to switch to a different configuration, we employ a model that calculates the cost for all currently enqueued tasks. Depending on the cost function, the reconfiguration implies some overhead that has to be accounted for. For example if the objective is to minimize the overall runtime of all tasks and each reconfiguration takes one second, a reconfiguration has to reduce the runtime of the remaining tasks by more than one second.

Given the cost-function $l_n(q_i)$ for queue $q_i \in Q$ under the configuration C_n, we define the model to predict the cost of executing all tasks T in all active queues Q:

$$L_n = O_{r_n} + \Theta(l_n(q_1), l_n(q_2), \ldots, l_n(q_j))$$

We compute the cost for each queue q_n and use a function $\Theta : \mathbb{R}^j \to \mathbb{R}$ to reduce their cost to a single value, for example a sum or the maximum. The overhead of reconfiguring is denoted as O_{r_n}. Clearly, the cost is 0 if the target configuration is already loaded.

$$O_{r_n} = \begin{cases} 0 & \text{if n is the current configuration} \\ o_{r_n} \in \mathbb{R} & \text{otherwise} \end{cases}$$

The optimization in this work is the minimization of total runtime. The cost functions of the queues have to be designed accordingly. Here, we use a simple α-β-model to predict a task's runtime: $R = \alpha + \beta n$

The two parameters must be determined empirically: α is the constant overhead for each kernel call. β denotes the maximum throughput in FLOPS that a kernel function achieves and n is the number of floating point operations a task requires. The runtime of all tasks is summed up to reflect the cost of a queue: $l_n(q_i) = \sum_{t \in q_i} R(t)$.

4   Implementation: Forecast

Forecast is our implementation[1] of the approach we present in this paper. In it we provide a reconfiguration-aware scheduler on top of OpenCL and a model that provides information for the scheduler using its current state. Forecast is built as a C++-library on top of OpenCL.

A major challenge is the workflow of OpenCL. The `cl::kernel` that is offloaded to a device is built using a `cl::program`, i.e., the configuration. Typically a kernel object is created and directly enqueued. In our scenario this creates the problem that Forecast is unable to switch the configuration of an already created kernel, because it was already built from a `cl::program`. Additionally, it is not possible to *unqueue* a previously enqueued kernel. Therefore, we expand Forecast to lazily create the kernel objects when they are enqueued into the OpenCL-queue.

4.1   Interface

We introduce a new scheduler that accepts *tasks* as an input and uses the model from Sect. 3 to select the best configuration for the current work load. The tasks are enqueued as C++11-lambdas, because `cl::kernel` objects can only be created after a configuration is selected. A typical lambda, like the example in Listing 1.1, takes a `cl::program&` as an input and creates the `cl::kernel`. By the time the scheduler calls the lambda, the correct configuration and hence the corresponding `cl::program` is known and passed to the lambda.

Listing 1.1. Enqueuing a task lambda with Forecast (simplified).

```
auto create_kernel = [&args](const cl::Program &prg) {
  cl::Kernel kernel(prg, "my_kernel");
  kernel.setArg(0, args[0]);
  return kernel;
};
auto dimensions = forecast::TaskDims{glob_range, loc_range};
forecast_scheduler.enqueue(create_kernel, task_dimensions);
```

From the user's perspective this wrapper around kernel-calls is the only difference to the standard OpenCL-interface. All events and dependencies work as described by the OpenCL-standard. There is also semantic change: each kernel has its own implicit in-order queue. However, even with native OpenCL, if the goal was to offload kernels to the FPGA accelerator truly in parallel, one has to use a dedicated queue per kernel. Synchronization between multiple queues is supported by the standard.

4.2   Scheduler and Model

The scheduler holds one in-order queue for each kernel function. This is a good compromise between reasonable semantics and true parallelism. Forecast starts

---

[1] https://github.com/pascalj/forecast.

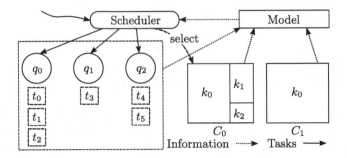

Fig. 1. Architecture of the Forecast scheduler with two configurations C_a, three queues q_b and five tasks t_c. The area of the kernels k_d represent the allocated resources.

a thread for each queue (kernel function) that waits for incoming tasks and manages the submission to its dedicated OpenCL-queue. The queue threads spend most of the time waiting either for incoming work or for the current task to finish and require little resources using C++11 condition variables.

Before the Forecast-scheduler submits any work to the underlying OpenCL-queue, it requests the estimated cost $L_1, \ldots, L_n$ for all n configurations. To estimate the runtime, the model has access to the static information as well as the trip count t of each pending task. We can extract the trip count either from the specified NDRange, i.e., the problem size, or by reading out a specified kernel argument. If the model finds that, despite the reconfiguration overhead t_{r_n}, another configuration has less cost, the respective cl_program is selected. This cl_program is then passed as a parameter to the user-provided lambdas for task creation.

Figure 1 shows the overall architecture of Forecast with some example workload and two loaded configurations C_0 and C_1. The scheduler holds three queues, each with some tasks ($t_{0...5}$) enqueued. At any point in time the scheduler selects the current configuration. The model provides the best candidate for the current configuration based on the enqueued tasks and L_n.

5   Experiments

We tested Forecast on a dual-socket system with two Intel Xeon E5-2630L each with 6 cores at 2.4 GHz and 64 GB of DDR3 running CentOS 7.7. The FPGA accelerator card is an Intel FPGA PAC D5005 which contains an Intel Stratix 10 SX. All host programs were compiled using GCC 8.3.0 with -O3 enabled. The Intel FPGA SDK for OpenCL Version 19.2.0 was used to compile the OpenCL code to the bitstream. Conversely, the 19.2.0 Version of the Intel RTE for OpenCL Pro Edition is used as the runtime. The D5005 card is connected via 16 PCIe 3 lanes.

5.1   Reconfiguration Overhead

The model needs several input parameters as described in Sect. 3. One is the reconfiguration overhead. We are interested in the time characteristics of this overhead and measured the reconfiguration duration as o_{r_n} on the Intel platform. The OpenCL-runtime switches the configurations based on the cl_kernel to be executed next. We queued kernels from two cl_program and measured the time overhead of a call to an empty kernel. This overhead is large with around 2.2 s ($\sigma = 12$ ms), especially compared to the overhead of copying a configuration. An experiment on the Xilinx platform yielded similar results. This overhead can be traced back to an *ioctl* call to the driver.

5.2   Determining Parameters

The runtime prediction also relies on the parameters α and β. While α represents the constant overhead per task invocation, β reflects the throughput, here in terms of FLOPS. These parameters may be determined online or offline. While the online approach may be considered for convenience, it does impose an overhead during the execution of the program. The offline evaluation requires the execution of a set of tasks beforehand, but the scheduler can select the best projected configuration from the start.

Determining α *offline* can be straightforwardly achieved by enqueuing an empty kernel function, result in $\alpha = 88.2\,\mu s$ with a standard deviation of $\sigma = 0.67\,\mu s$.

The throughput and therefore the β-parameter must be determined per-kernel k and per configuration C_n, because it depends on the reserved resources $R_i^r(k)$. With the total number of floating point operations O and the runtime t known, we can approximate $\beta = \frac{t-\alpha}{O}$.

It is also possible to approximate α and β *online* during runtime. However, the model and scheduler lack information to select the most efficient configuration from the start. An implementation must therefore force all C_n to execute.

To illustrate the effects of the resources allocated per kernel, we implemented several configurations, varying $R_i^r(k_j)$ for each kernel. We chose three kernels, two Dense Matrix-Matrix Multiplication (GEMM) functions (single- and double-precision) and one 1-dimensional Fast Fourier Transform (FFT). All kernels are based on an implementation from Intel.

5.3   Influence of Resources

Figure 2 shows the FLOPS for different configurations evaluated for a range of matrix sizes. For smaller matrices the overhead of the kernel-invocation is clearly visible, resulting in lower performance. Once the input size is large enough, the overhead becomes negligible. The plot also contains the predictions of the hybrid Forecast-model for the performance and thus its predicted runtime for the scheduler. It shows the effect of resource utilization on kernels. We want to emphasize two patterns in these plots. First is the influence of the resource consumption of other kernels within the same configuration. Compare the performance of the *float* kernel in the *SIMD 1* configuration to the one in *SIMD 4*. Although both contain the exact same code, the resources consumed by the *double* kernel in the same configuration causes the performance to degrade from 38 GFLOPS to 25 GFLOPS. Second is the near-linear performance gains for SIMD-enabled kernels.

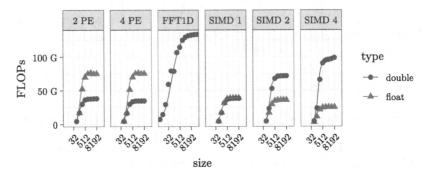

Fig. 2. Performance and model predictions for different configurations and kernels. Points represent measurements while the line represent the predictions of the offline-model.

5.4   Scheduler Performance

We evaluate the influence of the scheduler with the configurations from the previous section. All of the configurations contain two kernels: a single precision and a double precision GEMM code. We then generate tasks randomly using a binomial distribution. With probability p a single precision task is generated, else the double precision version is enqueued.

Figure 3 shows the performance achieved by each configuration without any involvement of Forecast as colored lines. The box plots show the execution of 10 runs with the same p using Forecast and the offline model. Here, two things are notable. On the one hand, it shows that the achieved FLOPs by Forecast are relatively noisy. This is a result from O_{r_n} in combination with the randomly generated tasks which also have uniformly randomly chosen matrix sizes between 64×64 and 4096×4096. In some cases, the incoming tasks change the optimal configuration multiple times over one run, introducing noise due to the reconfiguration overhead. On the other hand, it is apparent that Forecast achieves comparable performance to the best configuration, i.e., it selects the optimal configuration(s) during runtime.

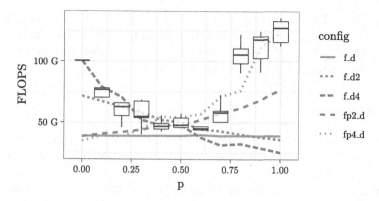

Fig. 3. Achieved FLOPs of the Forecast scheduler (box plots) and bare OpenCL with each configuration (colored lines).

6 Related Work

To the best of our knowledge, no approach thus far deliberately ignored the details of Partial Reconfiguration (PR) as we do in this paper. However, there are similar approaches that do use PR for spatial multiplexing and support OpenCL or similar HLS-techniques.

Intel provides multiple HLS-programming environments for its hardware, most notably an OpenCL-implementation [2]. The runtime changes the configuration based on the enqueued kernel invocation. In contrast, Xilinx' Vitis with its Xilinx Runtime (XRT) also supports OpenCL and initiates the configuration based on a created `cl_program` object [7]. This is slightly more flexible, because a programmer decides when to instantiate such an object, without relying on the OpenCL queue.

PCIeHLS by Vesper et al. supports more than one dynamically reconfigurable region, in contrast to both Vitis and Intel's OpenCL SDK [6]. While we focus on one reconfigurable region (i.e. configuration), PCIeHLS supports multiple regions that can be configured per kernel. Additionally, the overhead compared to a full reconfiguration is minimized. One drawback is that each kernel function must occupy a multiple of a reconfigurable region, possibly negatively affecting routing. As a research project, PCIeHLS's support for data types and hardware is not as wide as for the industry standards. Similar is the work on *Zucl* by Pham et al. in which the same idea is used to enable the scheduling of OpenCL-kernels on ZYNQ UltraScale+ devices [3]. Both use a bitstream manipulation tool to avoid recompilations.

Vaishnav et al. introduced reconfiguration-aware scheduling strategies [5] and evaluated these with their previous work. The scheduling uses preemption on an OpenCL work-group basis to resume tasks later and balance the resources between tasks. The approach also requires that each kernel occupies an integer-multiple of a reconfigurable region. Forecast does not support preemption but uses a model to balance the resources accordingly.

OmpSs@FPGA [1] is an approach with OpenMP-support for FPGAs that also handles dynamic scheduling. However, it relies on tools specific for Xilinx and its scheduler does not consider reconfiguration overhead. Instead, the focus lies on work sharing between CPU and FPGA.

7   Conclusion

In this paper we present our approach for seamless dynamic multiplexing on FPGAs. It uses a simple α-β-model to select the best configuration for the enqueued tasks. Methods to determine the necessary parameters are described and evaluated. Our implementation *Forecast*, consisting of a reconfiguration-aware scheduler that uses the model, is compared against a vanilla OpenCL-approach on a current high-end FPGA. We find that Forecast performs similarly to the best configurations but additionally adjusts flexibly at runtime to changes in the load.

In the future we want to apply Forecast to applications with multiple kernels and evaluate potential benefits. Also we plan to look into other cost functions. Specifically the reduction of the total energy consumption is of interest.

References

1. Bosch, J., et al.: Application acceleration on FPGAs with OmpSs@FPGA. In: 2018 International Conference on Field-Programmable Technology (FPT), pp. 70–77. IEEE (2018)
2. F Intel: SDK for OpenCL. In: Programming Guide. UG-OCL002 31 (2016)
3. Pham, K.D., et al.: ZUCL: a ZYNQ Ultrascale+ framework for OpenCL HLS applications. In: FSP Workshop 2018; Fifth International Workshop on FPGAs for Software Programmers, pp. 1–9. VDE (2018)
4. Stone, J.E., Gohara, D., Shi, G.: OpenCL: a parallel programming standard for heterogeneous computing systems. Comput. Sci. Eng. **12**(3), 66–73 (2010)
5. Vaishnav, A., et al.: Resource elastic virtualization for FPGAs using OpenCL. In: 2018 28th International Conference on Field Programmable Logic and Applications (FPL), pp. 111–1117. IEEE, Dublin (August 2018)
6. Vesper, M., Koch, D., Phama, K.: PCIeHLS: an OpenCL HLS framework. In: FSP 2017; Fourth International Workshop on FPGAs for Software Programmers, pp. 1–6. VDE (2017)
7. Wirbel, L.: Xilinx SDAccel: a unified development environment for tomorrow's data center. The Linley Group Inc. (2014)

Accelerating Convolutional Neural Networks in FPGA-based SoCs using a Soft-Core GPU

Hector Gerardo Munoz Hernandez$^{(\boxtimes)}$ (ID), Mitko Veleski (ID),
Marcelo Brandalero (ID), and Michael Hübner (ID)

Computer Engineering Group, Brandenburg University of Technology
Cottbus - Senftenberg, Cottbus, Germany
{hector.munozhernandez,mitko.veleski,marcelo.brandalero,
michael.huebner}@b-tu.de,
https://www.b-tu.de/fg-technische-informatik

Abstract. Field-Programmable Gate Arrays (FPGAs) have increased in complexity over the last few years. Now available in the form of Systems-on-Chip (SoCs) such as Xilinx Zynq or Intel Stratix, users are offered significant flexibility in deciding the best approach to execute their Deep Learning (DL) model: a) in a fixed, hardwired general-purpose processor, or b) using the programmable logic to implement application-specific processing cores. While the latter choice offers the best performance and energy efficiency, the programmable logic's limited size requires advanced strategies for mapping large models onto hardware. In this work, we investigate using a soft-core Graphics Processing Unit (GPU), implemented in the FPGA, to execute different Convolutional Neural Networks (CNNs). We evaluate the performance, area, and energy tradeoffs of running each layer in a) an ARM Cortex-A9 with Neon extensions and in b) the soft-core GPU, and find that the GPU overlay can provide a mean acceleration of 5.9× and 1.8× in convolution and max-pooling layers respectively compared to the ARM core. Finally, we show the potential of the collaborative execution of CNNs using these two platforms together, with an average speedup of 2× and 4.8× compared to using only the ARM core or the soft GPU, respectively.

Keywords: FPGA · Soft core · GPU · System-on-chip · Convolutional Neural Networks

1 Introduction

Convolutional Neural Networks (CNNs) have attracted significant attention in the past few years for their high accuracy in Machine Learning (ML) tasks, such a classification, autonomous driving, and drone navigation [16]. However, running ML applications on low-power embedded devices with limited compute capabilities has proven not to be trivial and has motivated several work [4]. Due to their high computational density, GPUs and FPGAs are the usual platforms

© Springer Nature Switzerland AG 2021
S. Derrien et al. (Eds.): ARC 2021, LNCS 12700, pp. 275–284, 2021.
https://doi.org/10.1007/978-3-030-79025-7_20

of choice [13]. While GPUs are known for offering high performance for parallel computation, FPGAs are known for their increased energy efficiency but requires hardware knowledge and more development time than its counterpart. Even with tools such as High-Level Synthesis (HLS), where higher-level programming languages like C or C++ can be used, the designer of the application that will run in the FPGA still has to bear in mind the hardware structure of the target to write an efficient code.

Besides FPGAs and GPUs, a third option for CNN implementations is using an *overlay*, a software-programmable processor implemented in the FPGA. The FGPU [1] is such an overlay architecture that implements a GPU-like architecture, saving space compared to the FPGAs since the hardware must be programmed only once and can then be reused for several applications. Previous works have investigated the benefits of executing Deep Learning (DL) models in the FGPU [11]; however, the potential of collaborative execution of all SoC resources such as the dedicated General-Purpose Processing (GPP) core and an overlay architecture using the FPGA has not yet been investigated.

In this work, we use FPGA-based SoCs with a dedicated Processing System (PS) and Programmable Logic (PL) as a first step towards the approach mentioned above. We do this by first introducing a new methodology to map trained CNNs from Tensorflow/Keras [14] into different execution platforms: a dedicated embedded GPP (ARM Cortex-A9) and the FGPU overlay. Our methodology is based on a library of OpenCL kernels that modularly implement all layers typically used in CNNs coupled with semi-automatic tools that customize these implementations for the different hardware platforms. Using this library, we compare the execution in the ARM core with the FPGU and show the conditions (types of layer and sizes) under which FGPU performs better in terms of performance than the dedicated ARM processor. In summary, our contributions are as follows:

- We propose a new approach to run complex DL/CNN models in FPGA-based SoCs by considering two possible execution platforms that can run pieces of a CNN: a hardwired General-Purpose Processor and the FGPU (these platforms are described in Sect. 3);
- We propose our flow for mapping complex CNNs onto these different hardware platforms using a unified approach based on a library of OpenCL kernels (Sect. 4);
- We investigate the performance, area, and energy tradeoffs from executing in three CNNs (MNIST_basic, LeNet [10], and AlexNet [9]) in these different execution platforms using a Xilinx ZC706 board with a Zynq-7000 SoC, and show that the FGPU excels at executing convolutional and max-pooling layers, achieving average speedups of 5.9× and 1.8× over the ARM core with the NEON optimization compiler option, which uses the Single Instruction, Multiple Data (SIMD) extension (Sect. 4).

2   Related Work

FPGAs have also been thoroughly used to accelerate the inference of DNN in recent years [2,6,15,17]. Two strategies are widely used: mapping these CNNs onto dedicated IP blocks using HLS or using a (single) accelerator overlay on which the CNN layers are mapped to and executed. We compare these two strategies and then present our contributions.

SqueezeJet-3 [12] enables mapping CNNs onto a single accelerator architecture implemented in FPGA, but the mapping process must be performed manually using HLS templates. Systolic-CNN [5] is a framework that allows mapping CNNs described in OpenCL onto a systolic array implemented in FPGA, achieving a peak computational throughput of 80–170 GFLOPS/s.

In this work, we focus on using a GPU-like overlay, FGPU [1]. To the best of the authors' knowledge, Ma et al. [11] is the most recent work that used the FGPU to develop DNN applications. It achieves approximately 5 to 35% fewer cycles than the baseline version and is only 4–7× slower than an Nvidia Volta V100 GPU [11]. However, it achieves a faster and more specialized execution of DNNs by modifying the original RTL codes on the VHDL sources and targets only Recurrent Neural Networks (RNNs). The source code for the project is not yet available for recreating the experiments.

We address the efficient execution of CNNs on FPGA-based SoCs such as the Zynq-7000 series from Xilinx, which features two ARM Cortex-A9 processors coupled to an FPGA block while also considering the possibility of execution in a GPU soft-core. Unlike past works that focused on generating efficient CNN implementations using HLS or implementing specialized accelerators, we address the execution of CNNs also on the FGPU. Compared to work that evaluated the FGPU, ours is the first to consider the execution of CNNs. Finally, we present the foundations of a framework that maps a trained network from a common high-level language like Python using the Tensorflow/Keras [14] to the required platform. Our approach will be made publicly available once we have an automated version since we follow open science strategies.

3   Target Platforms

Our approach targets FPGA-based SoCs like Intel Stratix or Xilinx Zynq. These platforms feature general-purpose processors combined with an FPGA reconfigurable unit where other IPs can be implemented. This section presents the two platforms for evaluating the proposed approach: The hard-core ARM Cortex-A9 General-purpose processor (Sect. 3.1) and the soft-core FGPU Overlay implemented in the FPGA (Sect. 3.2). As stated in Sect. 1, we focus on the ZC706 evaluation board from Xilinx, but the discussion that follows can be generalized to other platforms as well. The ZC706 Processing System (PS) contains two ARM Cortex-A9 processor cores, internal memories, external memory interfaces, and standard peripherals interconnected through the AMBA bus. The Programmable Logic block (PL) is composed of 218,600 Look-Up Tables (LUTs),

437,200 Flip-Flops (FFs), 545 Block RAMS (BRAMs), and 900 Digital Signal Processing (DSP) slices [18].

3.1 ARM Cortex-A9

The ARM Cortex-A9 [8] is a 32-bit superscalar processor implementing the ARMv7-A architecture. Each of the two cores in the system contains 32 KB private L1 instruction/data caches, and 512 KB shared L2 cache. An external memory interface provides access to 1 GB DDR3 SDRAM. The 8-stage pipeline supports multi-issue, out-of-order speculative instruction execution. Furthermore, the advanced combined 64- and 128-bit SIMD instruction set extension (Neon) enables standardized acceleration for media and signal processing applications and supports the execution of up to 16 operations per instruction. Finally, floating-point operations are provided by a high-performance VFPv3 FPU.

3.2 FGPU

The FGPU is an open-source 32-bit multi-core GPU-like processor based on the Single Instruction Multiple Thread (SIMT) execution model. The FGPU implements a custom 32-bit Instruction Set Architecture (ISA) composed of 49 MIPS-like instructions inspired by the OpenCL execution model. The translation from a high-level OpenCL code is performed by deploying the dedicated LLVM-based compiler. Another significant feature is that FGPU supports floating-point operations. Up to 8 Compute Units (CUs) can be accommodated, each consisting of 8 processing elements (PEs). A single CU can run up to 512 work items (threads). Each work item owns a private memory of 32 registers that can be extended using scratchpad memories. Additionally, an off-chip memory limited to 4 GB can be accessed by any working item. The FGPU includes a direct-mapped, multi-ported, and write-back cache system that can simultaneously serve multiple read/write requests. Finally, the FGPU is interfaced and controlled over an AXI4-lite bus. A detailed description of FGPU is presented in past works [1,3].

4 Evaluation Methodology

We evaluated our approach for its performance, energy consumption, and resource utilization on the FPGA by executing three CNNs architectures (basic MNIST, LeNet [10], AlexNet [9]) containing three different types of layers (convolution, maxpooling, fully-connected) in an FPGA-based SoC. Table 1 presents these network architectures in detail. Note that in this work, the last layer is referred to as a fully connected layer, although they might be referred to as Gaussian, output, or classification layer in other publications. Finally, it should be mentioned that all data is handled as 32-bit wide floating-point values.

Figure 1 gives an overview of how each CNN was mapped to the selected hardware architectures. The complete flow starts from a Tensorflow/Keras trained model (1), from which the topology and weights are extracted. Our framework

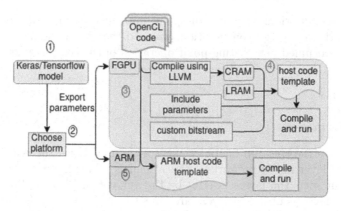

Fig. 1. Overview of our design flow for mapping trained CNNs onto different platforms.

uses this information to map these kernels onto a library of OpenCL functions that implement each type of layer. The user can then choose to implement the network in one of the two available platforms: FGPU or ARM core (2) by making minor adjustments to the OpenCL kernels. For the FGPU (3), the OpenCL kernels are compiled using the LLVM compiler that is shipped with the FGPU (4) and, for the ARM core, the OpenCL kernel is embedded into an ARM host template and compiled in the Vivado tools using the standard ARM compiler. The ARM core binaries were compiled with Neon extensions, which enable advanced SIMD execution, making this the best optimized for performance compilation option offered from the Vivado tool.

Both target architectures (ARM and the FGPU) were operated using the maximum frequency they could be implemented with: the ARM core runs at 666 MHz and the FGPU at a 250 MHz frequency. The ARM core is used to control the execution of both platforms. In order to run the CNNs in ARM, we use only one core and the application was written in C++ in Vivado SDK. As a means to measure the execution time of the networks, a timer was triggered before and stopped after executing every layer. The results were then summed up to get the overall execution time of the network. As the FGPU has customizable parameters that configure the hardware parameters of the soft GPU, we investigated three different configurations with 1, 2, and 4 compute units (CUs).

Table 1. Topology of networks

Network	MNIST_basic	LeNet	Alexnet
# Convolutional layers	1	2	5
# Maxpooling layers	1	2	3
# Fully-Connected layers	2	3	4
KFLOPs	1433.4	822.1	92766.8
Parameters (Kbytes)	1581.2	4267.2	100343.6

All of the configurations have floating-point implemented in hardware. Finally, to benchmark the energy consumption, we used the Vivado analysis tools and the energy consumed per floating-point operation of the complete network.

5   Results

5.1   Performance

Figure 2 shows the speedup factor (y-axis) of the FGPU vs. the ARM core for each type of layer in the networks (vertical panels). This figure mixes all three networks but sorts the layers (x-size) by the amount of Floating-Point Operations that they execute. The layers are coded in a *CNN_layer* fashion, where CNN corresponds to MNIST, LeNet, or AlexNet, followed by the specific layer (convolution, maxpool, and FC).

The FGPU is faster in the convolutional and maxpooling layers than the ARM core when using a 2CUs and a 4CUs configuration peaking at a 15.1x speedup in the MNIST_basic first convolutional layer. However, when using a 1CU configuration, the FGPU was slower only in one convolutional and all the maxpooling layers. On the other hand, the ARM core was faster than the FGPU in the FC layers, regardless of the configuration. The reason behind the FGPU's great performance in executing convolutional layers is due to the compute-intensive nature of this type of layer since a single kernel is reused multiple times, as discussed in [7].

5.2   Energy

To understand the energy-efficiency of each network-platform combination, we plot the total of all the layer's energy consumed for each different network in Fig. 3. The ARM core consumes less energy per operation when compared to every FGPU configuration, which translates into a trade-off considering that the FGPU outperforms the ARM core in convolutional and maxpooling layers when using a 4CUs configuration.

5.3   Resoure Utilization

Table 2 shows the resource utilization for the three different configurations of the FGPU quantified in percentage with respect to the available resources on the ZC706 board. As a quick reminder, creating dedicated IPs from HLS, for example, will have different resource utilization depending on how many layers the network has. In contrast, the FGPU has a fixed resource utilization that depends only on the GPU configuration.

5.4   Hybrid Between the FGPU and the ARM Core

As the FGPU in the ZC706 uses the ARM core to trigger the execution of the independent layers, a question arises: What happens if, for a specific network,

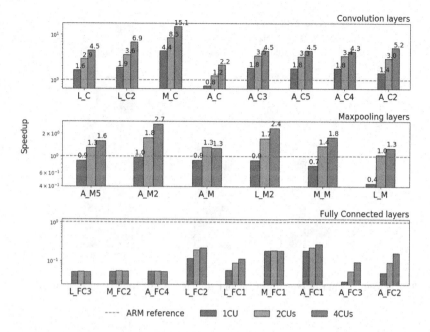

Fig. 2. Speedup normalized to the ARM core using 4CUs in the FGPU

Table 2. Resource utilization relative to the ZC706 board

Platform	Network or config.	LUT	FF	DSP	BRAM
FGPU	1CU	18.8%	12.9%	7.1%	10.2%
	2CU	30.8%	23.3%	14.2%	17.7%
	4CU	54.6%	44.1%	28.4%	33.5%

the FGPU only executes the layers in which it has better performance than its counterparts, namely the convolutional and maxpooling layers, but leaves the execution of the FC layers to the ARM core? In Table 3 we present how much benefit this setup could bring in terms of performance (ms) and energy consumed per operation (uJ/FLOP) for all FGPU configurations with respect to the old approach of FGPU or ARM only execution. The values presented stand for how better these metrics would be, which means that anything greater than 1 in this table is better than the original setup where each hardware platform was responsible for executing all layers.

Table 3 shows that the hybrid mode between the FGPU and the ARM core significantly improves the networks' execution in terms of both performance and energy needed per operation when comparing it to an FGPU only execution. We report an average speedup of 4.82× and an average of 12.35× less energy per operation used. When comparing the hybrid model with an ARM only, there is also an improvement in the performance among every network. Still, this

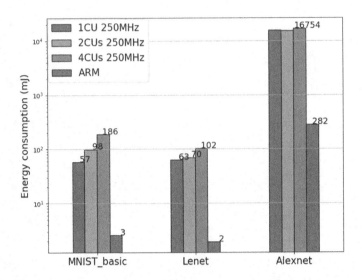

Fig. 3. Average of energy consumption per floating point operation for complete networks

model has an increase in energy consumed per operation when compared with its ARM-only counterpart. This can be seen as a trade-off, where the designer could choose to use a model that fulfills the application requirements in terms of performance or energy consumption.

In terms of energy consumption per operation, we present the new values in Table 4, where we considered the energy consumed while executing the complete network in a specific platform.

Table 3. Theoretical improvement in performance and energy for an FGPU and ARM core hybrid with respect of both independent approaches

Network	Theoretical improvement	Speedup vs. FGPU			Speedup vs. ARM		
		1CU	2CUs	4CUs	1CU	2CUs	4CUs
M_Basic	Speedup	4.14	4.58	5.00	1.81	2.11	2.28
	uJ/FLop	11.05	19.71	33.94	0.50	0.52	0.47
LeNet	Speedup	5.00	4.86	5.02	1.51	2.37	3.18
	uJ/FLop	6.48	7.74	10.39	0.20	0.22	0.20
AlexNet	Speedup	6.10	4.92	3.79	1.07	1.59	2.12
	uJ/FLop	7.64	7.34	6.90	0.14	0.13	0.12
Average	Speedup	4.82			2.01		
	uJ/FLop	12.35			0.28		

Table 4. Hybrid's overall energy consumption per operation ($nJ/FLOP$)

Network	1CU	2CUs	4CUs
M_Basic	3.60	3.46	3.83
LeNet	11.76	11.00	11.92
AlexNet	22.00	22.56	26.16

6   Conclusions

This work presented an evaluation of the performance and energy consumption of executing CNNs in modern FPGA-based SoCs, considering two different target platforms: an ARM Cortex-A9 core (with Neon extensions) and an FGPU overlay implemented in the FPGA fabric. Different configurations of the FGPU were employed, changing the number of CUs to show results and scaling in terms of performance, energy consumption per operation, and resource utilization. We find that the FGPU is faster than the ARM core for convolutional and maxpooling layers. The ARM core was faster than the FGPU in the FC layers. Moreover, the FGPU has a fixed resource utilization for a particular soft GPU configuration (18% of the LUT available in the ZC706 board for a 1CU configuration), which will also be advantageous when using the FGPU for bigger networks.

We finally showed the results for a hybrid execution of the networks, consisting of the FGPU executing the convolutional and maxpooling layers and the ARM core executing the FC layers. This experiment obtained an average 4.8x speedup in performance and 12.35x less energy consumption per operation compared to an FGPU only version. On the other hand, when comparing it to an ARM-only execution, there is an average speedup of 2x, with a 3.6x of increased energy consumed per operation.

We also show the toolflow, which was developed to map a network to the specific hardware, starting from a TensorFlow/Keras trained model. This method is, at the moment, not completely automated. We are working on automating the flow to enable fast prototyping and automated design space exploration.

References

1. Al Kadi, M., Janssen, B., Huebner, M.: FGPU: an SIMT-architecture for FPGAs. In: ACM/SIGDA 2016, FPGA 2016, pp. 254–263. Association for Computing Machinery (2016). https://doi.org/10.1145/2847263.2847273
2. Bacis, M., Natale, G., Del Sozzo, E., Santambrogio, M.D.: A pipelined and scalable dataflow implementation of convolutional neural networks on FPGA. In: IEEE IPDPSW, pp. 90–97 (2017)
3. Brandalero, M., Munoz Hernandez, H.G., Veleski, M., Kadi, M.A., Rech, P., Huebner, M., et al.: (Special topic submission) Enabling domain-specific architectures with an open-source soft-core GPGPU. In: IEEE IPDPSW, pp. 36–43 (2020)

4. Dean, J., Patterson, D., Young, C.: A new golden age in computer architecture: empowering the machine-learning revolution. IEEE Micro **38**, 21–29 (2018). https://doi.org/10.1109/MM.2018.112130030

5. Dua, A., Li, Y., Ren, F.: Systolic-CNN: an OpenCL-defined scalable run-time-flexible FPGA accelerator architecture for accelerating convolutional neural network inference in cloud/edge computing. In: IEEE FCCM, p. 231 (2020)

6. Guan, Y., et al.: FP-DNN: an automated framework for mapping deep neural networks onto FPGAs with RTL-HLS hybrid templates. In: IEEE FCCM, pp. 152–159 (2017)

7. Hanif, M.A., Putra, R.V.W., Tanvir, M., Hafiz, R., Rehman, S., Shafique, M.: MPNA: a massively-parallel neural array accelerator with dataflow optimization for convolutional neural networks. arXiv: 1810.12910 (2018)

8. ARM Holdings: Arm Cortex-A9 Processor. 2

9. Krizhevsky, A., Sutskever, I., Hinton, G.E.: ImageNet classification with deep convolutional neural networks. Commun. ACM **60**(6), 84–90 (2017). https://doi.org/10.1145/3065386

10. Lecun, Y., Bottou, L., Bengio, Y., Haffner, P.: Gradient-based learning applied to document recognition. Proc. IEEE **86**(11), 2278–2324 (1998). https://doi.org/10.1109/5.726791

11. Ma, R., et al.: Specializing FGPU for persistent deep learning. In: FPL, pp. 326–333 (2019)

12. Mousouliotis, P., Papaefstathiou, I., Petrou, L.: SqueezeJet-3: an accelerator utilizing FPGA MPSoCs for edge CNN applications. In: IEEE FCCM, p. 236 (2020)

13. Nurvitadhi, E., et al.: Can FPGAs beat GPUs in accelerating next-generation deep neural networks?. In: ACM/SIGDA 2017, FPGA 2017, pp. 5–14. ACM (2017). https://doi.org/10.1145/3020078.3021740

14. Tensorflow Keras. https://www.tensorflow.org/guide/keras. Accessed 24 Oct 2020

15. Umuroglu, Y., et al.: FINN: a framework for fast, scalable binarized neural network inference. In: ACM/SIGDA 2017, FPGA 2017, pp. 65–74. Association for Computing Machinery (2017). https://doi.org/10.1145/3020078.3021744

16. Venieris, S.I., Kouris, A., Bouganis, C.-S.: Toolflows for mapping convolutional neural networks on FPGAs: a survey and future directions **51**(3) (2018). https://doi.org/10.1145/3186332

17. Wang, D., Xu, K., Jia, Q., Ghiasi, S.: ABM-SpConv: a novel approach to FPGA-based acceleration of convolutional neural network inference. In: Proceedings of the 56th Annual Design Automation Conference 2019, DAC 2019. Association for Computing Machinery (2019). https://doi.org/10.1145/3316781.3317753

18. ZC706 Evaluation Board for the Zynq-7000 xc7z045 SoC Users Guide. https://www.xilinx.com/support/documentation/boards_and_kits/zc706/ug954-zc706-eval-board-xc7z045-ap-soc.pdf. Accessed 15 Dec 2020

Evaluating the Design Space for Offloading 3D FFT Calculations to an FPGA for High-Performance Computing

Arjun Ramaswami$^{(\boxtimes)}$, Tobias Kenter, Thomas D. Kühne, and Christian Plessl

Paderborn University, Warburger Str. 100, 33098 Paderborn, Germany
`arjun.ramaswami@uni-paderborn.de`

Abstract. The 3D Fast Fourier Transformation (3D FFT) is a critical routine in a number of applications of today's HPC workloads. Optimising it for computational performance with the use of FPGAs has been a focus of several studies. However, a systematic study has been missing on the viability of different scenarios how FPGA-accelerated 3D FFT implementations can be integrated into real world applications originally implemented on high-end CPUs. In this paper, we address this with two scenarios for offloading 3D FFT computations to an FPGA and investigate their feasibility in comparison to highly optimised FFTW based executions on CPU in terms of computation time and power consumption. In the first scenario, performance of individual 3D FFT offloading to FPGA is found to be limited by latency and unidirectional bandwidth of PCIe data transfers. This bottleneck is overcome in the second scenario by overlapping in a batched mode data transfers and computations in the FPGA to find performance competitive to CPU. In both these scenarios, projections to next generation PCIe connections show additional potential for the FPGA with up to 2x speedup over CPU executions. Furthermore, measurements indicate 3.7x to 4.1x lower average power consumption on the FPGA.

Keywords: 3D FFT · FPGA · HPC · OpenCL

1 Introduction

Field Programmable Gate Arrays (FPGAs) are increasingly used in High Performance Computing (HPC) workloads to offload intensive computations. In real world workloads, one can either offload individual functions that lie on the critical path of an application such as Fast Fourier Transformation (FFT) or matrix multiplication, or a series of functions that could form a critical part of the entire application such as linear algebra solvers or convolutions using FFTs.

The Three-Dimensional Fast Fourier Transformation (3D FFT) is one of the widely used algorithms in HPC workloads such as in long range force calculation in Molecular Dynamics (MD) simulations [1]. Offloading this computation to

© Springer Nature Switzerland AG 2021
S. Derrien et al. (Eds.): ARC 2021, LNCS 12700, pp. 285–294, 2021.
https://doi.org/10.1007/978-3-030-79025-7_21

FPGA has been a focus of several studies. Works by [4,8] optimise 3D FFT computation given that the required input is already available on the FPGA and compare its kernel execution performance to CPUs or GPUs. Pascoe et al. [6] offloads the entire long range force computation in MD simulations to FPGA. Initial impressions on offloading individual 3D FFT computations to FPGA from the CP2K software package are discussed in [7]. However, in the studies so far, there is a lack of a systematic study on the different scenarios for offloading 3D FFT computations from real world applications and their viability given the current FPGA technologies. We have identified three scenarios:

1. Scenario A: Offloading individual 3D FFT computations
2. Scenario B: Batching multiple 3D FFT computations
3. Scenario C: 3D FFT in an application – not investigated further in this work.

Scenarios A and B are the common cases when replacing existing 3D FFT function calls in applications with an FPGA library for FFT, similar to the interfaces in FFTW [2] for CPU or cuFFT [5] for GPU. Performance of both these scenarios should not only include the time to compute 3D FFT but also the data transfer time between the host CPU and the FPGA. The difference between them being the input data in the latter scenario allows multiple 3D FFT computations to be scheduled simultaneously. Thereby, benefitting from the data transfer and 3D FFT execution overlap. Scenario C though, refers to offloading a specific application entirely to FPGA, where 3D FFT is a sub-function as described in some of the related works mentioned above. This requires domain knowledge and performance optimization for every desired application. In this paper, we investigate Scenarios A and B in detail and compare their performance to highly optimized FFTW executions. Our results demonstrate that despite competitive performance of the raw FFT kernels on FPGA in Scenario A, only with the integration of batching in Scenario B are actual speedups achieved with the current PCIe Gen3 FPGA boards. However, given that the CPU reference uses up to 40 cores of a two-socket HPC system, the FPGA delivers this performance at much lower power consumption. The contributions of this paper include:

– An OpenCL-based FPGA implementation and host wrapper for 3D FFT that is flexibly used for the discussed scenarios.
– FPGA measurements and performance models that demonstrate the impact of data transfers on the viability of each scenario and allow to make projections for PCIe Gen4 accelerator boards.
– A comparison to highly optimised CPU references that demonstrate the performance but also the high power consumption of the CPU in comparison to the FPGA accelerator.

The remainder of this paper is organised as follows: Sect. 2 introduces the target infrastructure. Section 3 describes an optimised design and models performance for computing 3D FFT on the targetted FPGAs. Section 4 explains the experimental setup used to measure FPGA and CPU executions. Section 5 and 6 discuss the scenarios A and B respectively. Section 7 compares the power consumed by CPU and FPGAs. Section 8 concludes with a discussion on future work.

2   Target Platform

In this work, two different FPGA boards are used, `Nallatech 520N` and `Intel PAC D5005`. The `Nallatech 520N` board houses a Stratix 10 GX2800 FPGA that accesses four 8 GB banks of DDR4 memory and is connected to the host node using a PCIe Gen3 x8 bus. The `PAC D5005` board houses the SX2800 variant of Stratix 10 accessing the same DDR memory configuration, but is connected to the host via PCIe Gen3 x16 bus. Both FPGAs contain 28.625 MB of on-chip block memory (BRAM) arranged in 11721 blocks. The off-chip DDR/global memory can be accessed in a burst interleaved manner whereby buffers are burst-width interleaved across all the banks. Buffers can also be manually partitioned to individual banks. The theoretical peak bandwidth from each bank is 19.2 GBs^{-1}. Each bank is connected to the FPGA using a memory controller, which has a 512 bit wide interface, running at a maximum frequency of 300 MHz to match the throughput of the global memory bank.

The Open Computing Language (OpenCL) framework provide a high-level entry to program the FPGA boards to offload 3D FFT computations. The Intel FPGA SDK for OpenCL v20.4 is used for compilation and synthesis of the OpenCL kernels for both the FPGAs. For the `520N` board, the latest Board Support Package (BSP) based on Quartus 19.4 is providing the PCIe interface and DDR memory controller, whereas for the `PAC D5005` board, a BSP shipped with the oneAPI beta 10 is used, targetting Quartus 19.2. This latter BSP offers additionally a feature denoted as Unified Shared Memory (USM) by Intel that also supports the OpenCL Shared Virtual Memory (SVM) extensions. SVM allows the FPGA to access specifically allocated sections of host node's memory transparently through PCIe. The HPC server used to execute the OpenCL host code in the offloading scenarios and as CPU reference has a two socket Intel Xeon Gold 6148 CPU, featuring 20 cores per socket. The host code is compiled using GCC 9.3 and built using CMake 3.16.4.

3   Design and Model

3D FFT is an algorithm to compute the 3D Discrete Fourier Transformation (DFT) efficiently. The 3D FFT of N^3 points can be decomposed into N^2 1D FFTs in x-dimension, followed by the same in y and z-dimensions for a total of $3N^2$ N-point 1D FFTs. In order to facilitate efficient accesses to column-wise data required for the second FFT, a 2D Transpose is performed on every N^2 plane of points. Similarly, accessing points at strides of N^2 for the final FFT can be accomplished by retrieving xz planes and computing 2D Transposes on them, which is called here the 3D Transpose. Thus, the first $2N^2$ transformations need to be completed on the N^3 points before the final N^2 FFTs can be computed. In this section, a design of the 3D FFT for an FPGA is explored in terms of its individual components and a model of its performance is formulated.

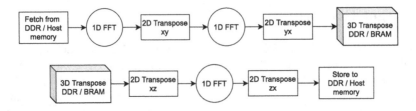

Fig. 1. Illustration of a 3D FFT design for FPGA

3.1 3D FFT Design

Figure 1 shows a general design for 3D FFT on an FPGA. Each step of this design is realized using distinct kernels: a kernel to fetch input data, three 1D FFT kernels, four 2D Transpose kernels, a 3D Transpose kernel and a kernel to store the results. The two phases shown share the same 3D Transpose kernel. In the following paragraphs, the design of these individual kernels are discussed.

Fetch and Store Kernels: These kernels retrieve or store N^3 complex single precision points either from the DDR memory of the device or the host node's memory in case of SVM-enabled boards. This is executed at a rate of 8 complex points per cycle, matching the 512 bit data width of the memory controller.

1D FFT Kernel: This is based on the reference OpenCL FPGA design provided with the Intel OpenCL FPGA SDK v20.2. This design uses a radix-2^2 FFT architecture [3] for an N-point transformation. It is implemented as a fully unrolled loop pipeline with an initiation interval of 1 and an 8 point throughput in bit reversed order. There is an initial buffering delay of $\frac{N}{8} - 1$ cycles, and an additional latency of $\frac{N}{8}$ cycles before and after the computation for bitreversal.

2D Transpose Kernel: This kernel is implemented by buffering N^2 points in the BRAM of the FPGA with the same 8 point throughput as the FFT kernel, therefore having an initial latency of $\frac{N^2}{8}$ cycles to buffer. The diagonal data mapping scheme [9] and double buffering are used to avoid replications and private memories respectively, restricting BRAM usage to only $2 \cdot N^2$ points.

3D Transpose Kernel: This step is required to access data at a stride of N^2 points to compute the final FFT computation. Firstly, N^3 points are buffered either in the BRAM or the DDR memory of the FPGA as shown in the first phase in the illustration. Then, N point rows are read at a stride of N^2 points, obtaining a plane of data along the xz-dimensions. This is transposed to produce the required input in the z-dimension. This kernel incurs a latency of $2 \cdot \frac{N^3}{8}$ cycles, half of which to fill the buffer and the other to read the transposed data, considering the same throughput as the previous kernels.

3.2 3D FFT Model

The performance of a complete 3D FFT execution can be modelled based on latency of its constituent kernels to fill their pipelines or buffers along with the time spent in steady state with compute and streaming pipelines fully occupied. The latency in buffering data is calculated from the measure that every kernel, as discussed previously, consumes and produces 8 complex points per cycle. The latency for arithmetic operations and memory operations within each loop can be obtained from the High Level Design reports generated by the Intel FPGA SDK for OpenCL. This model of latency is expressed using Eq. 1, where N is the number of points in a dimension and L_{Loop} is the loop latency.

$$
\begin{aligned}
L_{3DFFT} &= L_{3DTranspose} + 4 \cdot L_{2DTranspose} + 3 \cdot L_{1DFFT} + L_{Loop} \\
&= 2 \cdot \frac{N^3}{8} + 4 \cdot \frac{N^2}{8} + 3 \cdot \left(\left(\frac{N}{8} - 1 \right) + 2 \cdot \frac{N}{8} \right) + L_{Loop}
\end{aligned} \tag{1}
$$

In the following sections, this model of latency is used to compare the performance obtained from different implementations of 3D FFT in FPGA.

4 Experimental Setup

This section describes the setup used for the CPU and FPGA measurements. The CPU measurements are obtained using the single precision floating point variant of FFTW v3.3.8. The best runtime from all four planning heuristics of distinct MPI and OpenMP multithreaded FFTW executions is used, wherein the execution units are pinned to and scaled from 1 to 40 cores. Runtime is measured by recording the wall clock time of the `fftwf_execute` function call over an average of hundred iterations for each 3D FFT configuration. For the FPGA measurements, the kernels are invoked in the reverse order of their execution and the difference between the first and last kernel's starting and ending time respectively is used as the time for kernel execution. This is done to avoid the latency of the invocation of the first kernel execution command in the measurement of the kernel execution time. Similarly, the OpenCL function calls for transferring data to and from global memory are measured using the profiling information available from the commands. For the SVM enabled FPGA board, the kernel execution time also includes the time taken to transfer data. The time reported in the following experiments is an average of a hundred iterations.

5 Scenario A: Offloading Individual 3D FFT

Offloading individual 3D FFT computations involves transferring data to FPGA, performing the transformation and receiving the results back to the host before the subsequent computation.

Implementation Variants and Model: The 3D Transpose kernel can buffer data either in the BRAM or the DDR memory of the FPGA. The 3D FFT performance of these two variants are compared in Table 1 for powers-of-2 input sizes implemented on the **Nallatech 520N** board. The column labelled *520N BRAM* is the variant that buffers in the BRAM, similarly the column *520N DDR* buffers

Table 1. Runtimes of 3D FFT executions on the `Nallatech 520N` board, where the 3D Transpose is either implemented in the BRAM or the DDR memory of the FPGA.

# pts	520N BRAM			520N DDR	
	Model	No-interleaving	Burst-interleaving	Model	No-interleaving
32^3	0.036	0.042	0.037	0.038	0.105
64^3	0.232	0.290	0.184	0.234	0.348
128^3	1.783	2.737	2.157	1.785	2.776
256^3	–	–	–	14.100	18.676
512^3	–	–	–	112.296	141.354

in the global memory. The largest configuration that can be synthesized for the *520N BRAM* design is 128^3. This uses 61% of the BRAM owing to the 16MB (57%) that is required to store N^3 complex floating points in BRAM. For the *520N DDR* design, the maximum number of points that fits is 512^3.

The *520N DDR* variant is implemented using non-interleaved global memory accesses, whereas the *520N BRAM* variant uses both burst-interleaved and non-interleaved global memory accesses. This is because the latter either exclusively uses the read or the write channels of the global memory at any point in its execution, therefore it can benefit from the additional bandwidth from the other banks of the global memory. This is also observed in the comparison as the interleaving implementation of the *520N BRAM* variant is faster than the no-interleaving one. Hence, for configurations upto 128^3 points of 3D FFT, the burst-interleaved *520N BRAM* design shows better performance. The *520N DDR* variant enables scaling to larger configurations of 3D FFT.

In comparison to the measured performance, a model runtime is calculated from Eq. 1 and added to Table 1 using 300 MHz as kernel frequency matching the maximum memory controller frequency. The model difference in runtimes of the *520N BRAM* and *520N DDR* models lie in the loop latency values. The latter has an increased latency due to global memory accesses. Differences between model and measured execution times can also be attributed to the memory interface. In practice the memory doesn't reach the 100% efficiency of the model, but with burst-interleaving the interface can sometimes supply a kernel running at >300 MHz with higher bandwidth than modelled.

Comparison to FFTW: In order to determine the feasibility of this scenario, a comparison with highly optimised FFTW 3D FFT execution on the CPU is made. The measurement details are explained in Sect. 4. Table 2 shows the comparison between FFTW and the different FPGA implementation variants. The *520N BRAM* and the *520N DDR* columns denote their respective variants implemented on the `Nallatech 520N` board. Their total runtimes are calculated from the sum of their kernel runtimes and data transfer times between the host and the global memory as denoted by the *PCIe Gen3 x8 Host to Dev* and *Dev to Host* columns. The burst-interleaving variant is considered here in the *520N BRAM* column due to its better performance. The *PAC SVM Gen3 x16* column

Table 2. Runtimes of 3D FFT executions in milliseconds of FFTW and FPGA implementations. The *SVM* column denotes the *DDR* variant that uses SVM enabled PCIe transfers available on the **PAC D5005** board.

# pts	CPU	FPGA						
	FFTW	PCIe Gen3 x8		520N BRAM		520N DDR		PAC SVM
	≤40 Cores	Host to Dev	Dev to Host	Kernel	Total	Kernel	Total	Gen3 x16
32^3	0.029	0.105	0.099	0.037	0.241	0.105	0.309	0.220
64^3	0.141	0.446	0.425	0.184	1.055	0.348	1.219	0.484
128^3	0.711	2.770	2.718	2.157	7.645	2.776	8.264	2.863
256^3	6.940	21.378	21.052	–	–	18.676	61.106	21.272
512^3	109.63	170.28	167.766	–	–	141.354	479.40	168.836

Table 3. Measured runtimes of FFTW and PCIe latencies from targetted FPGA boards vs estimated latencies from higher bandwidth PCIe connections in milliseconds. PCIe Gen4 x16 latency estimations are used to further estimate FPGA runtimes.

# pts	Measured runtime	Measured latencies		Idealized latencies		Estimated runtime with PCIe Gen4 x16		
	CPU FFTW	PCIe	PCIe	PCIe	PCIe	FPGA	FPGA	FPGA
	≤40 cores	Gen3 x8	Gen3 x16	Gen3 x16	Gen4 x16	BRAM	DDR	SVM
32^3	0.029	0.204	0.054	0.030	0.014	0.051	0.119	0.102
64^3	0.141	0.871	0.341	0.244	0.120	0.304	0.468	0.238
128^3	0.711	5.488	2.645	1.940	0.976	3.133	3.752	1.440
256^3	6.940	42.430	21.070	15.620	7.800	–	26.476	10.622
512^3	109.63	338.04	168.476	125.0	62.50	–	203.854	84.418

denotes the *DDR* implementation variant that uses SVM enabled PCIe transfers available on the **PAC D5005** board.

Even though the two smaller 3D FFT sizes of *520N BRAM* kernel and the 512^3 *520N DDR* kernel alone are roughly comparable to the 40-core CPU reference, the overhead of PCIe data transfers makes the total execution time of individual offloading scenario much slower than on the CPU. The **PAC D5005** platform not only improves upon this with the higher bandwidth of the Gen3 x16 PCIe interface, but also with its SVM feature, overlapping transfers and computations such that the entire 3D FFT completes in roughly the time of a single data transfer from or to the **520N**, however this is still slower than the optimised FFTW reference. Even though the latency in data transfers cannot be directly improved, the kernel runtime might be further optimised by creating multiple lanes to better utilise the bandwidth available from the rest of the global memory banks by computing several individual FFTs in parallel.

Impact of Higher Bandwidth PCIe Connections: The potential in using higher bandwidth PCIe connections to overcome the communication bottleneck in offloading individual 3D FFTs is discussed here. In Table 3, the latencies of cur-

Table 4. Individual and batched 3D FFT runtimes using SVM and non-SVM based data transfers in milliseconds. *Indiv.* denotes individual 3D FFT computations discussed under Scenario A. FPGA SVM Gen4 x16 column is an estimation of the runtime using higher PCIe bandwidth bus.

# points	Measured						Estimated	
	CPU		FPGA 520N		FPGA PAC		FPGA PAC	
	FFTW		DDR		SVM Gen3 x16		SVM Gen4 x16	
	Serial	Batch	Indiv.	Batch	Indiv.	Batch	Indiv.	Batch
32^3	0.029	0.007	0.309	0.350	0.220	0.310	0.102	0.143
64^3	0.141	0.058	1.219	0.940	0.484	0.520	0.238	0.255
128^3	0.711	0.790	8.264	5.530	2.863	1.960	1.440	0.985
256^3	6.940	8.170	61.106	42.310	21.272	12.570	10.622	6.276
512^3	109.63	103.20	479.40	336.46	168.836	**98.50**	84.418	49.250

rent PCIe connections of the targetted FPGA boards (column *Measured Latencies*) are compared to the idealized latencies of *PCIe Gen3 x16* and *PCIe Gen4 x16* connections from theoretical bandwidths of 16 GB/s and 32 GB/s respectively (column *Estimated Latencies*). The measured *PCIe Gen3 x8* latency from the `Nallatech 520N` board is the sum of transfer latencies to and from the global memory and the host. Similarly the measured SVM based *PCIe Gen3 x16* latency from the `PAC D5005` board is measured explicitly using a memory-to-memory copy kernel via FPGA kernel logic. All the estimated latency measurements are doubled to account for bi-directional latencies. Furthermore, the idealized *PCIe Gen4 x16* column is used to calculate the estimated runtimes of individual 3D FFTs computations for different envisioned implementation variants (column *Estimated Runtime using PCIe Gen4 x16*). While the estimated *FPGA DDR* variant would still not catch up, the estimated *FPGA SVM* variant could achieve a speedup of 1.29x over the *CPU FFTW* execution simply by improving the PCIe bandwidth. Considering further optimisation potential, the two phases for filling and using the 3D transpose buffer are still disjoint in this scenario, as well as PCIe transfers and computations unless SVM is used.

6   Scenario B: Batching 3D FFT

In this scenario, multiple 3D FFT executions are scheduled by overlapping computation of one with the data transfer of the next. The `Nallatech 520N` variants have 3 stages that can be overlapped due to distinct data transfer and computation phases. The SVM based `PAC D5005` board has a 2 stage overlap because data can be directly transferred between the host and the FPGA kernels.

Table 4 summarizes measurements on the `Nallatech 520N` board under the *FPGA 520N DDR* column. Here, the maximum speedup obtained is only 1.5 because full duplex PCIe transfers between the host and the global memory is

Table 5. Power consumption in Watt (W) between CPU and FPGAs for individual 3D FFT executions

3D FFT	CPU 2x Xeon	FPGA 520N	FPGA PAC
Average	288.38	77.04	69.22
Peak	315.64	83.32	81.07

not supported, thereby only overlapping either one of the data transfers with the FPGA kernel execution. Similarly, the FPGA SVM column summarizes the measurements on the PAC D5005 board. The max speedup obtained here on batching is 1.7 for the 512^3 point configuration.

When comparing *CPU FFTW* with *FPGA PAC SVM Gen3 x16*, specifically larger configurations such as 512^3 points, we now see FPGA measurements that outperform FFTW reference, which was for this input running close the CPU peak performance already without batching. On the other hand, the CPU profits more than the FPGA implementation from batching for small FFTs, where an individual call didn't scale well to 40 cores. Projecting to a higher bandwidth PCIe connection, shown in the column *FPGA PAC SVM Gen4 x16*, a speedup of 2.09x the FFTW measurements is estimated on batching. These estimations are based on the corresponding speedups obtained on measured individual and batched values.

7   Power Consumption

While the previous discussions focused purely on performance, an important advantage of FPGA accelerators can be power consumption, in particular when compared to a two-socket high-end CPU reference. Table 5 shows the average and peak power consumption of the FPGA boards - Nallatech 520N and PAC D5005, compared to the 2 Intel Xeon Gold 6148 CPU node for 3D FFT executions. The power consumed by the CPU is the aggregate CPU and DRAM power measured at 10 s interval using Likwid for the duration of the computation. The power consumed by the FPGAs are measured using two different commandline tools provided by the respective board vendors and is measured for the total time of execution that also includes data transfers. The average and peak power consumptions shown are calculated for a workload of 500 iterations of the 512^3 configuration in order to provide sufficient points of measurement.

The measurements show that both FPGA platforms reach their respective performance points at a much lower power consumption than the CPU platform in average and peak power. The average values are between 3.74x lower for the 3D FFT on *520N* and 4.16x on *PAC*.

8   Conclusion

In this article, we analyzed scenarios for offloading 3D FFT calculations to FPGA boards. Our results underline the critical impact of data transfers via PCIe on the overall viability of this approach. It turns out that the SVM execution model provides a tangible benefit for FPGA platforms, which may be further improved by the upcoming PCIe Gen4 standard. The usage mode is also crucial. While for offloading individual calls to the FPGA board only best-case projections for PCIe Gen4 platforms may provide speedups, batching multiple 3D FFTs already demonstrates competitive performance over a modern dual-socket CPU system. At the same time both FPGA platforms exhibit a much lower power consumption of utmost 84 W compared to up to 316 W of the CPU reference. Using the FFT pipeline inside an integrated application on FPGA is likely to provide further benefits, as data transfers between host and accelerator become less critical. Future work can also investigate the viability of different usage scenarios in a distributed setup following an optimized multi-FPGA 3D FFT implementation.

Acknowledgments. The authors kindly acknowledge funding by the German Research Foundation (DFG) under grant "PerficienCC" (PL 595/2-1), funding from Paderborn University's research award for "GreenIT", and funding by computing time provided by the Paderborn Center for Parallel Computing (PC^2).

References

1. Essmann, U., Perera, L., Berkowitz, M.L., Darden, T., Lee, H., Pedersen, L.G.: A smooth particle mesh Ewald method. J. Chem. Phys. **103**(19), 8577–8593 (1995)
2. Frigo, M., Johnson, S.G.: The design and implementation of FFTW3. Proc. IEEE **93**(2), 216–231 (2005)
3. Garrido, M., Grajal, J., Sanchez, M., Gustafsson, O.: Pipelined radix-2^k feedforward FFT architectures. IEEE Trans. Very Large Scale Integr. (VLSI) Syst. **21**(1), 23–32 (2011)
4. Humphries, B., Hansen Zhang, J.S., Landaverde, R., Herbordt, M.C.: 3D FFTs on a single FPGA. In: Proceedings of International Symposium on Field-Programmable Custom Computing Machines (FCCM), vol. 2014, p. 68 (2014)
5. Nvidia, C.: CUFFT library (2010)
6. Pascoe, C., Stewart, L., Sherman, B.W., Sachdeva, V., Herbordt, M.W.: Execution of complete molecular dynamics simulations on multiple FPGAs. In: 2020 IEEE High Performance Extreme Computing Conference (HPEC), pp. 1–2. IEEE (2020)
7. Ramaswami, A., Kenter, T., Kühne, T.D., Plessl, C.: Efficient ab-initio molecular dynamic simulations by offloading fast Fourier transformations to FPGAs. In: 2020 30th International Conference on Field-Programmable Logic and Applications (FPL), pp. 353–354. IEEE (2020)
8. Sanaullah, A., Herbordt, M.C.: FPGA HPC using OpenCL: case study in 3D FFT. In: Proceedings of the 9th International Symposium on Highly-Efficient Accelerators and Reconfigurable Technologies, p. 7. ACM (2018)
9. Shang, Q., Fan, Y., Shen, W., Shen, S., Zeng, X.: Single-port SRAM-based transpose memory with diagonal data mapping for large size 2-d DCT/IDCT. IEEE Trans. Very Large Scale Integr. (VLSI) Syst. **22**(11), 2423–2427 (2014)

FPGA Implementation of Custom Floating-Point Logarithm and Division

Nelson Campos[1]([✉]) [iD], Slava Chesnokov[2], Eran Edirisinghe[1] [iD], and Alexis Lluis[3]

[1] Loughborough University, Loughborough, UK
{N.C.S.Campos,E.A.Edirisinghe}@lboro.ac.uk
[2] Imaging CV Ltd., London, UK
slava@chesnokov.org
[3] ARM Holdings PLC, Manchester, UK
alexis.lluis@arm.com

Abstract. The mathematical operations logarithm and division are widely used in many algorithms, including those used in digital image and signal processing algorithms and are performed by approximated computing through piece-wise polynomial functions. In this paper we present dedicated FPGA architectures for implementing the logarithm and division operations in floating-point arithmetic. The proposed hardware modules are customizable, with the mantissa and exponent fields of the floating-point representation defined as parameters that can be customized by the hardware designer. The design flow of the arithmetic blocks allows the generation of a set of architectures of custom-precision floating-point, which can result in compact hardware, when the numerical computations require less numerical range or precision. The paper also describes bit-width optimization using precision analysis and differential evolution (a genetic algorithm based method) is applied to reduce the power consumption and the resource usage in the FPGA minimizing the number of flip-flops, lookup tables and DSP blocks according to a desired accuracy chosen in the design, leading to significant resource savings compared to existing IP cores.

Keywords: Floating-point · FPGA · VLSI · Divider · Logarithm · Polynomial approximation · Differential evolution

1 Introduction

Most of the modern embedded systems are powered by 32-bit CPUs capable of performing operations in both integer and single-precision floating-point operations [2]. Although the development of algorithms using fixed-point representation is less expensive in terms of computational power, the dynamic range and precision of the floating-point are typically the criteria used by designers

Supported by CDT-EI at Loughborough University and ARM Holdings PLC.

when choosing between the two formats. Furthermore, the development of most of the algorithms are generally easier when using floating-point representation, as fixed-point format often requires additional numeric manipulations to reduce the quantization noise [10]. However, fixed-point processors are still used more extensively than the floating-point processors due to their reduced cost, size and power consumption.

Dedicated hardware architectures prototyped in FPGAs are usually implemented over their software-based models due to their advantages in flexibility and speed. However, the development of such architectures is generally a complex task which involves a tradeoff of resource usage of memory, circuit area and number of Digital Signal Processing (DSP) blocks. For instance, digit-recurrence methods to perform division operations require extensive use of hardware resources (lookup tables and flip-flops) and have high latency, whilst polynomial approximation techniques use excessive memory and DSP blocks [4].

One of the main objectives in the FPGA design flow is to produce an efficient design in terms of small circuit area and low latency, throughput and power consumption. A common optimization technique is to find the minimum number of bits that represents a signal within each design. This technique is often expensive in search space and an analytic range analysis is required to determine the bit-width of each signal [5].

In this paper we present dedicated FPGA architectures for implementing the logarithm and division operations in floating-point arithmetic. A numeric analysis is provided to find the optimum bit-width of each coefficient of the polynomial approximations used to compute the transcendental functions such as division and logarithm, but it is shown that the method can be expanded to implement any other function that can be approximated to a polynomial. These coefficients are also dependent on the width of the mantissa, once the modules are customizable, being compatible with the 32-bit IEEE-754 [1] standard format and also being expandable to fit for other numerical representations, such as the 16-bit half-precision floating-point, more suitable for embedded image processing applications.

To summarize, the main contributions of this paper are:

- propose floating-point hardware architectures for mathematical division and logarithm modules;
- parameterizable modules with the mantissa and exponent widths as inputs defined by the user;
- apply techniques of precision analysis and bit-width optimization using differential evolution in polynomial approximations to reduce the resource usage of the division and logarithm hardware modules.

The rest of this paper is organized as follows: Sect. 2 reviews previous published papers to provide a contextual support to this current work. Section 3 presents an overview of the proposed architectures of the floating-point hardware modules for division and logarithm. Section 4 discusses the results of precision analysis, synthesis and optimization of the proposed architecture and Sect. 5 gives conclusions and recommendations for future work.

2 Previous Work

Floating-point arithmetic have been widely implemented in FPGAs to speed up applications which require extended dynamic range and higher precision. Hardware architectures for the single precision natural logarithm and exponential, targeting FPGA architectures such as the Arria 10 and Stratix 10 FPGAs were presented in [4]. For both functions, the proposed implementations made efficient use of the available resources including: DSP blocks in fixed-point arithmetic mode, memory blocks, etc. Overall, the proposed cores offered high-performance, while generally reducing logic consumption, at the expense of DSP and M20K blocks. The work also presented a comparison of resource usage of the proposed modules with that at both industry and open-source competitors. Their analysis were only shown for single-precision. We extend the analysis of our results to both single and half-precision.

There is a number of commercial floating-point arithmetic hardware cores available in the market, which provide a high level of user specification. Xilinx LogiCORE [11] is a floating-point library, which enables the specification of floating-point functions such as adders and multipliers, logarithms and exponentiation. The exponent and mantissa fields can be customized by the user (with bit-width between 4 and 16 bits for the exponent and 4 to 64 bits for the mantissa). Another popular state-of-the-art in both industry and academia is FloPoCo (Floating-Point Cores) [3], which is an open-source C++ framework for generating custom data-path arithmetic cores in VHDL.

Section 4 compares the synthesis results of our proposed architectures with the synthesis of FloPoCo and LogiCORE for the mathematical operations of division and logarithm. Our experiments were performed in the Artix 7 FPGA using the software tool Vivado.

As mentioned previously, the implementation of transcendental functions are often performed through the use of polynomial approximations and one of the main bottlenecks in the design is to find the optimum bit-with to minimize resource usage in FPGAs. In [5] and [7] methodology for bit-width optimization were presented in the context of polynomial approximations. The methodology was based on Affine Arithmetic and Adaptive Simulated Annealing (ASA) aiming to reduce the fractional bits of the coefficients of the polynomial represented in fixed-point format. Although these works are relevant to us, their proposed techniques deal with fixed-point functions. In this paper we present a methodology to minimize the bit-widths of the coefficients of polynomials according to the accuracy desired, i.e. enabling variable range and precision. Further the optimisation technique used by the proposed approach uses Differential Evolution in order to reduce the resource usage of FPGAs when implementing floating-point cores of logarithms, division and exponentiation.

3 Proposed Architecture

In this section we describe the proposed floating-point architectures for mathematical operations of division and logarithm. The implementations are based on polynomial approximation functions that use read-only memory (ROM) to store the coefficients of the polynomials. We also present the novel method used for bit-width optimization, Differential Evolution, that is proposed to be used to minimize the FPGA resource usage within the hardware modules.

3.1 Division

Consider two numbers x and y represented in floating-point format. The number $z = \frac{x}{y}$ can be expressed according to the Eq. 1:

$$\frac{x}{y} = (-1)^{(s_x - s_y)} \times \frac{1.m_x}{1.m_y} \times 2^{(e_x - e_y) - bias} \tag{1}$$

The proposed architecture for the division is depicted in Fig. 1. As can be seen in Eq. 1, the determination of the sign of z s_z can be directly obtained with a xor of the two input signs s_x and s_y and the exponent is computed with just one subtraction.

The output mantissa $m_z = \frac{m_x}{m_y}$ can be expressed as a product $m_x \times m_y'$, where $m_y' = \frac{1}{m_y}$ and m_y' can be approximated by a degree-2 piecewise polynomial approximation with 4 segments [6]. Once $1.0 \leq 1.m < 2.0$, the reciprocal of $1.m$ can be approximated to $\frac{1}{m+1} = (c_0 \times m + c_1) \times m + c_2$, where the coefficients c_0, c_1 and c_2 are obtained through polynomial approximation and they are defined in the Table 1b. Each coefficient is stored in a ROM memory that is indexed according to the range of the mantissa. To ensure normalised floating-point numbers, if the reciprocal of the mantissa is a number smaller than one, then the resulted mantissa is right-shifted by one bit, whereas the exponent is increased by one. The datapath uses multiplexers to check this normalisation.

3.2 Binary Logarithm

The computation of the binary logarithm $y = log_2(x)$ is given by the Eq. 2.

$$log_2(x) = \begin{cases} log_2(1.m_x) + (e_x - bias), & s_x = 0, \\ NaN, & s_x = 1 \end{cases} \tag{2}$$

As the logarithm is defined only for positive numbers in the real domain, when the x is negative the result y should be not a number (NaN). One multiplexer is used to check the sign of the number comparing the exponent with the floating-point bias. When x is positive, the computation is the sum of the exponent e_x + $log_2(1.m_x)$. The architecture of the logarithm is illustrated in Fig. 1. A similar module for piecewise polynomial approximation is used in order to compute $log_2(1 + m_x)$, where the coefficients can be seen in Table 1 and the result of $log_2(1 + m_x)$ is added to the exponent normalised[1] e_x and then converted from fixed-point to floating-point.

---

[1] The exponent e_x is left-shifted by M bits, where M is the mantissa width.

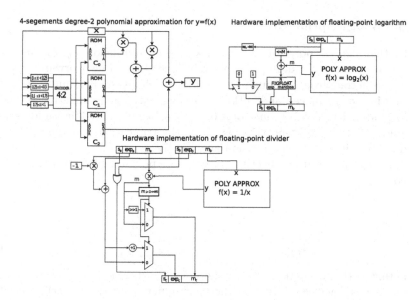

Fig. 1. Floating-point divider and logarithm FPGA architectures

Table 1. Coefficients of the polynomial approximation for $log_2(1+m)$ and $\frac{1}{m+1}$, where $m \in [0,1)$

(a) Logarithm approximation

Range	c_0	c_1	c_2
$1.0 \leq 1.m < 1.25$	-0.573	1.4288	0.0003
$1.25 \leq 1.m < 1.5$	-0.3829	1.3381	0.0115
$1.5 \leq 1.m < 1.75$	-0.2739	1.2312	0.0379
$1.75 \leq 1.m < 2.0$	-0.2056	1.1299	0.0756

(b) Reciprocal approximation

Range	c_0	c_1	c_2
$1.0 \leq 1.m < 1.25$	0.7099	-0.9736	0.9995
$1.25 \leq 1.m < 1.5$	0.3874	-0.8222	0.9811
$1.5 \leq 1.m < 1.75$	0.2342	-0.6729	0.9444
$1.75 \leq 1.m < 2.0$	0.1523	-0.5517	0.8995

In order to illustrate the conversion from fixed to floating-point consider the following example. If $x = 6.75$, in floating-point format x is 1.6875×2^2 and $y = log_2(6.75) = 2 + log_2(1.6875) = 2.7549 = 1.37745 \times 2^1$. The value y can represented as a signed fixed-point number in the format $Q5.10$ as $y = 0000010.1100000101_2$. Since y can also be expressed as $y = 1.m \times 2^{exp}$, to convert this number to a half-precision floating-point, where the exponent and mantissa widths are 5 and 10 respectively, the exponent is found as the position of the Most Significant Bit (MSB) and the mantissa is composed by the 10 least significant bits (LSB) of y, where the MSB of the mantissa is at the position 0 and the LSB of y is discarded in the conversion[2].

---

[2] The MSB position of the fixed-point number is found using a combinational priority encoder.

3.3 Bit-Width Optimization

Consider the degree-1 polynomial $y = c_0 \times m + c_1$ and denote ϵ_y, ϵ_{c_0} and ϵ_{c_1} the errors at signals y, c_0 and c_1, respectively. The most straightforward way to quantize y is accomplished through truncation, which gives a maximum error of 1 *ulp* (unit in the last place), and faithful rounding, with maximum error of $(1/2)$ *ulp*. As rounding (which gives one additional bit of accuracy) requires additional hardware in contrast to truncation, we chose the truncation as a quantization method for the signals in the precision analysis [7].

Adding the quantization effect to the degree-1 polynomial, Eqs. 3 and 4 are obtained.

$$y + \epsilon_y = (c_0 + \epsilon_{c_0}) \times (m + \epsilon_m) + c_1 + \epsilon_{c_1} \tag{3}$$

$$\epsilon_y = m \times \epsilon_{c_0} + c_0 \times \epsilon_m + \epsilon_m \times \epsilon_{c_0} + \epsilon_{c_1} \tag{4}$$

Denoting ϵ_x the truncation error of the signal x, where $\epsilon_x = 2^{-FB_x}$ and FB_x is the number of fractional bits of x, the maximum output error $max(\epsilon_y)$ needs to be less than 1 *ulp*:

$$max(\epsilon_y) \leq 2^{-FB_y} \tag{5}$$

Since $max(m) = 1$, the maximum accuracy of y for a given mantissa with M-bits width is given as $max(acc_y) = \alpha \times 2^{-FB_{c_0}} + \beta + 2^{-FB_{c_1}}$, where $\alpha = 1 + 2^{-M}$ and $\beta = |c_0| \times 2^{-M}$.

As a design decision, suppose that y is accurate to 16 bits. Combining Eqs. 4 and 5 gives the Eq. 6:

$$\alpha \times 2^{-FB_{c_0}} + \beta + 2^{-FB_{c_1}} < 2^{-16} \tag{6}$$

A straightforward solution to the expression 6 is to use Uniform Fractional Bit-widths (UFB), which results in a sub-optimal solution. Rather than using UFB, i.e., assigning the same number of bits for each signals, using Multiple Fractional Bit-width (MFB) leads to the optimal solution [7]. Lee *et al.* [7] propose to use Simulation Annealing (ASA) to optimize the bit-widths of c_0 and c_1 and the with the estimated bit-widths FB_{c_0} and FB_{c_1} compute the FB_{c_2}. In this work we apply differential evolution using *mystic* [8], a python library for non-linear and constrained global optimization, to minimize the area of the expression $y = c_0 \times m + c_1$, which is composed of one addition $(x_0 + x_1)$ and one multiplication $(x_0 \times x_1)$ modeled as a cost function $area_y(x_0, x_1) = max(\lceil FB_{x_0} \rceil, \lceil FB_{x_1} \rceil) + \lceil FB_{x_0} \rceil \times \lceil FB_{x_1} \rceil$ constrained to Eq. 6. After finding FB_{c_0} and FB_{c_1}, the determined values using *mystic* are substituted in the expression 7 to compute FB_{c_2}.

$$max(\epsilon_z) = \alpha \times \epsilon_y + max(|y|) \times \epsilon_m + \epsilon_{c_2} \tag{7}$$

4 Results and Discussion

The bit-widths for each coefficients of the polynomial approximations c_0, c_1 and c_2 were obtained using differential evolution[3] and the results are shown in Table 2a. For both division and logarithm mathematical operations, the maximum accuracy is 10^{-7} when the mantissa is of precision 10-bit, which resulted in a reduction of 1-bit in c_1 and c_2 (when the coefficients has uniform fractional bit-width) in the division operation. When the desired accuracy is 2^{-16}, which guarantees the correctness up to the fourth decimal digit, the signals c_0, c_1 and c_2 decreased the bit-width from 23 bits to 19, 17 and 18 bits, respectively.

Table 2. Multiple Fractional Bit-width (MFB) coefficients found using differential evolution

(a) Divider

m	c_0	c_1	c_2	a_{cc}
10	10	9	9	10^{-7}
13	12	12	12	10^{-10}
16	15	16	15	10^{-13}
19	19	18	18	10^{-16}
23	17	18	19	10^{-16}

(b) Logarithm

m	c_0	c_1	c_2	a_{cc}
10	10	10	8	10^{-7}
13	13	13	11	10^{-10}
16	16	16	14	10^{-13}
19	19	19	17	10^{-16}
23	19	17	18	10^{-16}

The accuracy of the floating-point division and logarithm will be directly dependent on the accuracy of the polynomial approximations of $log_2(m+1)$ and $\frac{1}{(m+1)}$ over the interval $[0, 1)$. Better accuracy is achieved with higher degrees of the polynomial approximations, as well as with a large number of intervals with smaller segments[4]. The approximation of $log_2(m+1)$ and $\frac{1}{(m+1)}$ over $[0, 1)$ using degree-2 piecewise polynomial approximations is accurate to 12 bits with 1 *ulp* and 2 *ulp*, respectively[4].

The number of lookup tables , flip-flops, DSP blocks and Block RAM (BRAM) are of particular interest for this experiment. The LUT and flip-flops are the basic building blocks of an FPGA and are generally used for the implementation of combinational and sequential logic, respectively. The BRAM is an embedded memory on-chip which provides a relatively large amount of data and is often used when inferring memory. DSP blocks are arithmetic logic units embedded into the fabric of the FPGA and are usually inferred to perform multiplication operations.

---

[3] Using the parameters maximum iterations to run without improvement **gtol = 2000** and population size **npop = 500**.

[4] According to [9] the Flopoco operator for division is correctly rounded and has accuracy of 0.5 ulp, whereas the LogiCORE documentation states that the division and logarithm has accuracy of 1 ulp.

Table 3. Resource usage and latency for division and logarithm on Artix 7 FPGA

Precision	Function	Architecture	LUTs	FFs	DSPs	BRAM	Latency
Half-precision	Div	Proposed UFB	43	0	3	0.0	6 cycles
		Proposed MFB	41	0	3	0.0	6 cycles
		LogiCORE Div	253	431	0	0.0	Variable
		FloPoCo Div	498	212	0	0.0	10 cycles
	Log	Proposed UFB	211	49	2	0.0	7 cycles
		Proposed MFB	210	49	2	0.0	7 cycles
		LogiCORE Log	274	469	2	0.0	Variable
		FloPoCo Log	411	377	1	0.5	17 cycles
Single-precision	Div	Proposed UFB	137	0	7	0.0	6 cycles
		Proposed MFB	127	0	6	0.0	6 cycles
		LogiCORE Div	809	1487	0	0.0	Variable
		FloPoCo Div	1617	624	0	0.0	17 cycles
	Log	Proposed UFB	534	65	5	0.0	7 cycles
		Proposed MFB	555	65	4	0.0	7 cycles
		LogiCORE Log	721	1191	4	0.0	Variable
		FloPoCo Log	681	842	3	2.0	23 cycles

Table 3 shows the FPGA resource usage for piecewise polynomial approximations for both $\frac{1}{m+1}$ and $log_2(1+m)$. The maximum latency of the Floating-Point for LogiCORE operators can be found on the Vivado IDE [11]. The throughput of the operations is one operation per clock cycles, which gives a performance of 100 million floating-point operations per second for a clock frequency of 100 MHz. The modules were synthesized in the Artix 7 FPGA from Xilinx using the Vivado 2018.3. The polynomial approximation for division, when the mantissa width is 23 bits and the desired accuracy is 2^{-16}, the bit-width optimization showed a reduction of 10.3093% and 20% in the number of LUTs and DSP blocks, respectively. Similarly, for the same mantissa bit-width and accuracy, in the logarithm approximation the LUTs increased by 41.5584% and the DSP blocks reduced 20%. The trends observed for both logarithm and division approximations showed a smaller reduction in terms of LUTs and DSP blocks when the mantissa is 10 bits wide. The designs of the floating-point division and logarithm have a latency of 6 and 7 clock cycles, respectively, and throughput of one operation per clock cycle and RTL was written in SystemVerilog.

The logarithm and divider in floating-point half-precision (mantissa $M = 10$-bit and exponent $E = 5$-bit) and in single-precision ($M = 23$-bit and $E = 8$-bit) modules were also synthesized in Vivado. The synthesizer converts hardware description language into a gate-level netlist. The implementation stage is a step followed by the synthesis in the Vivado design flow. In this stage the netlist is placed and routed in the FPGA device. The target used is the Artix 7 FPGA at a clock frequency of 100 MHz and the designs are described in SystemVerilog.

We have compared the proposed cores (both architectures with uniform fractional bit-width and multiple fractional bit-width obtained with the optimization using *mystic*[5]) with the available cores from the open-source framework FloPoCo[6] [3] and with the Xilinx LogiCORE floating-point cores for division and logarithm [11]. For the logarithm, our proposed core is a base 2 logarithm as opposed to the natural logarithm from FloPoCo and LogiCORE. However, our comparison is still fair, once the base conversion of logarithms can be performed with just one multiplication by constant[7]. Table 3 explores the FPGA resource usage for the logarithm and division cores. The optimization showed a reduction in the resource usage as compared to the same architectures without the bit-width optimization. To measure this reduction, we first synthesize the hardware modules (floating-point logarithm and divider cores) in Vivado using uniform bit-width for all the coefficients c_0, c_1 and c_2 in the polynomial approximation cores. Thereafter, for a given precision (single or half-precision) we use our optimization framework using *mystic* in two stages. Firstly, we find the minimum number of bits of c_0 and c_1 using Eq. 6. At this stage, we also estimate the error ϵ_y, defined in Eqs. 3, 4 and 5. During the second stage, we use the error ϵ_y found previously in Eq. 7 to compute c_2. Finally, with the new values of c_0, c_1 and c_2, we synthesize again the modules in Vivado and compare the synthesis results using both uniform and multiple fractional bit-widths.

Overall, the proposed cores showed less resource usage than FloPoCo and LogiCORE. It is important to note that unlike FloPoCo, our modules do not round the operations to the final result. In addition to that, the polynomial approximations are of order 2 with only 4-piecewise segments. Furthermore, for simplicity the proposed cores in this work does not have the exceptional cases to deal with subnormal numbers or infinity and not-a-numbers. These limitations were not an issue, as the accuracy and precision are sufficient for our applications in image processing and hardware compactness had higher priority during the design decisions. As can be observed from Table 3, as opposed to FloPoCo, the proposed division cores consume fewer resources because it uses the embedded DSP blocks to perform the polynomial approximations, whilst FloPoCo implementation makes more use of LUTs and flip-flops. Furthermore, the FloPoCo logarithm also inferred block RAM memory.

---

[5] We chose this framework because of its simplicity to solve highly-constrained non-convex problems using Python.

[6] The Flopoco Div and Log (VHDL divider and logarithm modules) are obtained from the framework with the command **flopoco FPDiv we = 8 wf = 23** and **flopoco FPLog we = 8 wf = 23** for single-precision. For half-precision, the parameters are **we = 5** and **wf = 10**.

[7] If the logarithm base is known during synthesis time, than the coefficients of the polynomial approximation will be different than that for the approximation for $log_2(x)$. Otherwise, a change of base during runtime will require one floating-point multiplier, which increases the latency by one clock cycle and consumes one additional DSP block.

We also compared the proposed cores with the IP-Cores from Xilinx Logi-CORE, which resource usage was roughly half of the LUTs and double of the flip-flops consumed by FloPoCo for the divider module. For the logarithm, FloPoCo consumed less resources (LUTs, flip-flops and DSP blocks) than LogiCORE because FloPoCo also uses BRAMs in contrast to our proposed modules and LogiCORE.

5   Conclusion

In this paper we have presented dedicated FPGA architectures for logarithm and division mathematical operations in floating-point arithmetic. For both modules, the mantissa and exponent are flexible parameters that can be defined by the user. The bit-width optimization of both methods is dependent of the desired accuracy defined in the design stage and is accomplished using differential evolution with the Python library *mystic*. For both modules, the bit-width optimization showed a reduction of LUTs, flip-flops and DSP blocks, leading to significant resource savings compared to existing IP cores.

References

1. Committee, I., et al.: 754–2008 IEEE standard for floating-point arithmetic. In: IEEE Computer Society Std, vol. 2008 (2008)
2. Dang, D., Pack, D.J., Barrett, S.F.: Embedded systems design with the Texas instruments MSP432 32-bit processor. Synth. Lect. Digit. Circ. Syst. **11**(3), 1–574 (2016)
3. De Dinechin, F., Pasca, B.: Designing custom arithmetic data paths with FloPoCo. IEEE Des. Test Comput. **28**(4), 18–27 (2011)
4. Langhammer, M., Pasca, B.: Single precision logarithm and exponential architectures for hard floating-point enabled FPGAs. IEEE Trans. Comput. **66**(12), 2031–2043 (2017)
5. Lee, D.U., Gaffar, A.A., Cheung, R.C., Mencer, O., Luk, W., Constantinides, G.A.: Accuracy-guaranteed bit-width optimization. IEEE Trans. Comput. Aided Des. Integr. Circ. Syst. **25**(10), 1990–2000 (2006)
6. Lee, D.U., Cheung, R., Luk, W., Villasenor, J.: Hardware implementation trade-offs of polynomial approximations and interpolations. IEEE Trans. Comput. **57**(5), 686–701 (2008)
7. Lee, D.U., Villasenor, J.D.: A bit-width optimization methodology for polynomial-based function evaluation. IEEE Trans. Comput. **56**(4), 567–571 (2007)
8. McKerns, M., Strand, L., Sullivan, T., Fang, A., Aivazis, M.: Proceedings of the 10th Python in Science Conference (2011)
9. Pasca, B.: Correctly rounded floating-point division for DSP-enabled FPGAs. In: 22nd International Conference on Field Programmable Logic and Applications (FPL), pp. 249–254. IEEE (2012)
10. Renczes, B., Kollár, I.: Roundoff errors in the evaluation of the cost function in sine wave based ADC testing. In: 20th IMEKO TC4 International Symposium and 18th International Workshop on ADC Modelling and Testing, pp. 15–17 (2014)
11. Xilinx: LogiCORE IP Floating-Point Operator v7.0. https://www.xilinx.com/support/documentation/ip_documentation/floating_point/v7_0/pg060-floating-point.pdf

On the Suitability of Read only Memory for FPGA-Based CAM Emulation Using Partial Reconfiguration

Muhammad Irfan[1(✉)] ⓘ, Kizheppatt Vipin[2] ⓘ, and Ray C. C. Cheung[1] ⓘ

[1] City University of Hong Kong, Kowloon Tong, Hong Kong
m.irfan@my.cityu.edu.hk
[2] Birla Institute of Technology and Science (BITS) Pilani, KK Birla Goa Campus,
Pilani, India

Abstract. Content-addressable memory (CAM) is a high-speed searching memory that provides the address of the input search key in one clock cycle. Traditional implementations of large CAMs on FPGAs with updatable memory elements are resource intensive requiring bigger and more expensive chips. Additional circuitry required for updating the CAM content is a major contributor to this which also impacts the overall clock performance of the circuit thus hampering the system throughput. To reduce the resource requirement, we investigate CAM implementation using read only memories (ROMs) and using partial reconfiguration (PR) to update their contents. Using a high-speed reconfiguration controller and bitstream compression, the reconfiguration overhead due to PR is offsetted. The results show 10% and 200% improvement in hardware resources and speed, respectively, compared to the state-of-the-art available FPGA-based TCAMs.

Keywords: Field-programmable gate arrays · Content-addressable memory · Partial reconfiguration · Memory

1 Introduction

A content-addressable memory (CAM) performs the search operation using input data unlike traditional memory which uses an address[4]. Typically it searches the entire memory in one clock cycle. CAM is classified into two types based on the storing bits; binary CAM (Bi-CAM) can store '1's and '0's, while ternary CAM (TCAM) can also store a don't care bit ('X'). Due to its high-speed searching capability, CAMs are suited for a wide range of applications, including pattern recognition, packet classification [9], data compression [5], and cache tags.

CAMs are widely used in ASIC implementations and are becoming popular on re-configurable architectures such as FPGAs due to their hardware-like performance and software-like flexibility. CAM is one of the missing dots in FPGAs for packet classifications and processing. It makes sense not to include them as

© Springer Nature Switzerland AG 2021
S. Derrien et al. (Eds.): ARC 2021, LNCS 12700, pp. 305–314, 2021.
https://doi.org/10.1007/978-3-030-79025-7_23

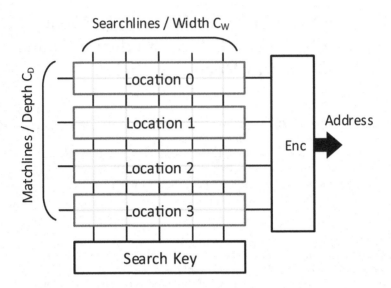

Fig. 1. A 4 × 5 CAM architecture, where C_D is 4 and C_W is 5.

hard macros because of the different configurations required to support a variety of applications. Therefore, soft IP cores are developed by vendors as well as researchers to utilize the underlying hardware as CAM in modern data-intensive applications.

Since the content of a CAM are dynamic in most applications, the traditional way of CAM implementation on FPGAs is to emulate it using random access memory (RAM). These RAMs can be implemented using discrete memory elements such as flip-flops or specialized memory primitives such as block RAMs (BRAMs). In either case, using the *write* interface of the memory, the content of the CAM can be updated. The drawback is, flip-flop (FF) based implementation of large CAMs are resource intensive and have high routing complexity. A binary CAM requires one memory element (FF) while a ternary CAM requires two memory elements; to store a single bit of data The interface for updating the CAM further increases the resource requirement. At the same time, BRAM-based implementations are highly inefficient in implementing smaller CAMs and their numbers are quite limited restricting the implementation of large CAMs. Researchers have proposed directly instantiating other FPGA primitives such as LUTs and LUTRAMs to reduce the resource requirement. But forcing the implementation tool to use specific primitives may make the resultant circuit less optimal. Again the number of specific primitives such as LUTRAMs are quite limited compared to LUTs and flip-flops. Direct instantiation of low-level FPGA primitives also makes the system-level design quite cumbersome.

In this work we propose using generic ROMs for emulating CAMs on FPGAs. Using ROMs, the requirement for update circuitry can be completely avoided, thus reducing the resource requirement. Partial reconfiguration (PR) technique

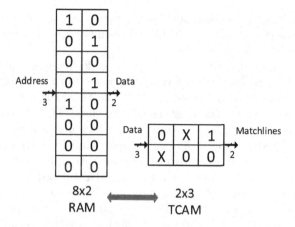

Fig. 2. Emulation of TCAM Using RAM.

available in modern FPGAs is then used for updating the CAM contents. By allowing the EDA tool to choose the appropriate primitives for implementation, the resultant circuit can achieve better clock performance. A high-speed reconfiguration controller and bitstream compression are utilized to reduce reconfiguration time overhead.

The rest of the paper is organized as follows: Sect. 2 discusses the related work, Sect. 3 presents the proposed CAM architecture, Sect. 4 discusses implementation on FPGAs and compares with state-of-the-art, and Sect. 5 concludes the work and gives some future directions.

2 Background and Related Works

Figure 1 shows an ASIC-like CAM design of size $C_D \times C_W$, where C_D (Depth of the CAM) is 4 and C_W (Width of the CAM) is 5; making the size of CAM as 4×5. A common method to emulate the CAM functionality using RAM is to treat the address lines of the RAM as search lines of the CAM, while the data out is treated as matchlines. The matchlines consists of information about the presence or absence of the input search key. Figure 2 shows the emulation of a RAM into a TCAM. The required depth and width of the RAM to emulate a 2×3 TCAM are 2^3 and 2 respectively.

Earlier, SRAM-based TCAM architecture was impractical on FPGAs due to the exponential increase in SRAM requirement with increase in TCAM width [8]. A 512 × 36 TCAM requires 64 GB RAM cells to emulate it using FPGA. Through to the partitioning of TCAM table, a large size (512 × 36) TCAM was implemented using 1080 kB SRAM in HP-TCAM [11]. Here the address formation and the data validation are done in separate blocks of SRAM. This makes the design inflexible and dependent on the arrangement of TCAM entries in a specific (ascending/descending) order. REST was proposed to reduce the hardware utilization by accessing multiple locations in multiple clock cycles [1]. However the reduction in hardware utilization comes with an increase in latency affecting the overall system performance.

UE-TCAM comes up with a flexible and order-independent architecture where the data information and data validation is done in a single block of SRAM rather than different SRAM blocks. A 512 × 36 TCAM is implemented using 32 BRAMs of size 36 KB. The existing BRAM-based TCAM design activates all of the BRAMs for a single search operation which makes it power inefficient. Our proposed TCAM automatically infers memory in FPGAs to store the initial data which can be updated using partial reconfiguration. It results in significant hardware resource reduction compared to other RAM-based TCAMs.

Distributed RAM-based TCAMs support higher density and are implemented using high performance logical blocks. D-TCAM take full advantage of the LUT-FF pair nature in modern FPGAs and tremendously improved the throughput without extra hardware resources. It utilizes the redundant FFs as pipeline registers.

FF-based TCAMs reduce the cost in terms of transistor count but due to the specialized nature of FPGA blocks, it does not efficiently use the hardware and the overall hardware utilization is high. Moreover, routing complexity is high compared to BRAM and distributed RAM-based CAM because of its fine grained structure implementing TCAM bit by bit. BRAM and distributed RAM design implementations are chunk by chunk rather than bit by bit.

FPGA has two types of LUTs; one in slices SLICEM and other in slices SLICEL. LUTs of SLICEM can be used for both logic implementation as well as memory while LUTs of SLICEL can only be used for logic implementation. PR-TCAM [7] uses LUTs of the SLICEL to emulate an FPGA-based TCAM. One problem in LUTs of SLICEL is the run-time updating of the content which is addressed by PR-TCAM using partial reconfiguration. The drawback of this implementation is the designer has to directly instantiate LUTs in their design with the corresponding TCAM initialization data. Mapping to TCAM data to LUTs is not straight forward and this makes system-level design cumbersome. Direct instantiation of FPGA primitives also restricts the implementation tools from fully exploiting the available resources for efficient implementation.

3   Architecture and Design

In this section we discuss the implications of using ROM based CAM emulation. Initially we investigate potential resource savings with ROM and later discuss the issue of updating the CAM contents.

3.1   ROM-Based CAM Emulation

Both ROM and RAM memory blocks can be used in design by explicitly instantiating Vendor supported IP cores or by inferring memories through specific coding styles [2]. Since the target implementation style (whether BRAM or distributed RAM) can be controlled using appropriate attributes, inferring through HDL is

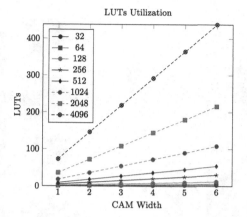

Fig. 3. Lookup Tables (LUTs) Utilization for varying sizes of proposed CAM.

more efficient. For large CAMs, *emph*implementation style=BRAM can be used for BRAM-based CAM implementation. Table 1 shows the resource utilization for RAM and ROM implementation on Xilinx 7-series FPGAs for a width of 6 and varying depth.

Table 1. Resource utilisation for RAM and ROM for memory width of 6 and varying depth.

Depth	RAM			ROM		
	LUTs	LUT RAMs	FFs	LUTs	LUT RAMs	FFs
512	53	48	6	54	0	6
1024	106	96	6	108	0	6
2048	212	192	6	216	0	6
4096	424	384	6	438	0	6
8192	854	768	6	870	0	6

It could be seen that for non-BRAM based implementations, ROMs do not consume any LUT RAMs. They are implemented purely using LUTs, which are the most abundant resource in FPGAs. It should be noted that for RAM implementation, the number of LUTs reported includes both LUTs as well as LUT RAMs. Due to the special architecture of LUT RAMs, they can efficiently implement RAM with out additional resources for the write interface. But such primitives are available only in Xilinx FPGAs and their availability will be half of that of ordinary LUTs. Figure 3 shows the resource utilization of CAM when implemented using LUT-based ROM. The resource utilization increases linearly

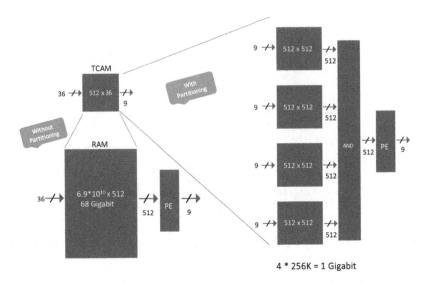

Fig. 4. Resource reduction by partitioning the TCAM memory.

with the increase in depth. This linear relation helps us to predict the size of the re-configurable region later when the design is implemented to support partial reconfiguration. It is possible that the implementation tool will optimize the LUTs if the contents of the ROM are not initialized. We used a script to generate an memory initialization file, which initializes all the ROM locations with random data. This makes sure that all the required LUTs are preserved during the implementation of the design.

3.2 Partitioning of CAM

A TCAM of size $C_D \times C_W$ requires RAM of size 2^{C_W}. This makes it very difficult to emulate a reasonable size of TCAM using RAM/ROM on the limited resources of FPGA. Thus partitioning of the TCAM is introduced.

The width of CAM is partitioned to store the information in multiple blocks of RAM instead of one block. During the search operation, the information from all of the RAM blocks is accumulated (ANDed) together to get the output matchlines. Multiple RAM blocks are combined in series and parallel to form larger TCAMs using partitioning and they are able to be implemented on FPGAs.

Concept of partitioning is not new. Researcher have used it on different memory elements available on FPGAs, i.e., FFs, LUTRAM, and BRAMs. We also inherit the idea of partitioning to emulate CAM on FPGA using multiple ROM blocks in FPGA.

Figure 5 shows the overview of the RAM- and ROM-based TCAM architecture where the content of RAM/ROM is ANDed together to generate the matchlines which are converted to an address by the priority encoder. In most of the designs,

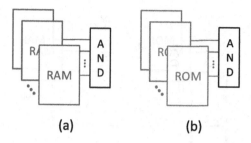

(a)   **(b)**

Fig. 5. Emulated RAM-based CAM and ROM-based CAM. (a) Multiple RAM blocks are connected to construct a larger CAM. (a) Multiple ROM blocks are connected to construct a larger CAM.

priority encoder is not part of the whole architecture because in networking applications, the output is in the form of matchlines is also very useful. Several priority encoder designs are available to opt in the TCAM architecture, such as the 2D encoder design [6].

3.3   Partial Reconfiguration

BRAM and LUTRAM can be updated at runtime by simply providing the data and corresponding address where the new data needs to be written. The read/write port is used during the search and update operation with the enable/disable signal. This helps in run-time modification of CAM contents. This method cannot be used for ROM-based CAM implementation. In order to update the contents of the ROM at run-time, we can exploit the partial reconfiguration (PR) feature available in modern FPGAs.

Partial reconfiguration (PR) enables FPGA to dynamically update part of the logic design keeping the remaining to operate normally [10,12]. It is a powerful feature when we need to update only a portion of the underlying design. The minimum reconfiguration area in FPGA is one frame which is updated using partial bitstream file as shown in Fig. 6. Multiple frames can be selected to update the different locations of FPGA with different partial bitstream files. CAM is continuously updated with new content where the old data is simply replaced by new data. RAM-based CAMs require large number of clock cycles to update a single entry that are stored in multiple distributed RAMs or Block RAMs (BRAM). However, PR can be utilized to update the content of FPGA-based CAM dynamically using ROMs.

Partial reconfiguration allows us to update the content of the ROM by updating the bitstream file of the FPGA. We exploit this feature of the FPGA to save the hardware resources and design the TCAM on ROM blocks instead of BRAM and LUTRAM blocks. The update time is more than that of the RAM and LUTRAM but we get the reduced hardware resources and high speed at the cost of update operation. Search operation are in large number than update operation, so the overall performance is improved by improving the search operation and compromising on the update operation.

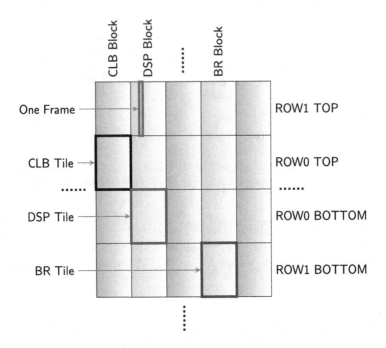

Fig. 6. FPGA Architecture

Table 2. Comparison with other TCAM architectures.

Design	512×40				512×80			
	BRAMs	LUTs	FFs	Speed	BRAMs	LUTs	FFs	Speed
LUTRAM-based	0	4096	4096	32	0	8192	8192	27
BRAM-based	58	512	512	374	116	1024	512	194
LUT-based	0	3574	N/A	82	0	6108	N/A	76
Proposed	0	3072	4136	252	0	5632	8272	237

4   Results and Discussion

To evaluate the feasibility and performance, the proposed design is implemented on Xilinx Artix 7 FPGA devices using Xilinx Vivado 2018.3. The hardware utilization is realised in terms of LUTs and FFs.

Based on the types of memory used for FPGA-based CAMs, we cannot compare our design with BRAMs as they are completely different in terms of area utilization and overall performance of the design. However, we can compare with distributed RAM-based CAMs which used LUTRAM to emulate TCAM. Similarly, as discussed in Sect. 2, PR-TCAM uses LUTs of the SLICEL and updates it using partial reconfiguration. We compare our design with LUTRAM-based

TCAM (i.e., D-TCAM [3]) and PR-TCAM [7], where our design shows better hardware utilization and enhanced performance on the target FPGA.

Table 2 shows the comparison of our proposed design with the conventional LUTRAM-based TCAM and LUT-based TCAM [7]. Our design has upto 10% better hardware utilization and upto 200% better performance (speed) than state-of-the-art available FPGA-based TCAM architectures.

The decrease in LUTs for 512 × 40 TCAM is from 3574 to 3072 and for 512 × 80 TCAM is from 6108 to 5632, which are 14% and 10%, respectively. Similarly, the increase in speed for 512 × 40 TCAM is from 82 MHz to 252 MHz and for 512 × 80 TCAM is from 76 MHz to 237 MHz, which are 207% and 222%, respectively.

5   Conclusion and Future Work

We propose a novel ROM-based TCAM architecture which reduces the hardware utilization and enhances the performance compared to the state-of-the art available FPGA-based TCAMs. The problem of updating the ROM with new content is addressed using partial reconfiguration by keeping the fact that update operations are far less than the search operations per second. Thus, improving the search operation improves the overall performance of the whole system. Our future work involves the exploration of how efficiently we can update the TCAM and further reduce the hardware utilization.

References

1. Ahmed, A., Park, K., Baeg, S.: Resource-efficient SRAM-based ternary content addressable memory. IEEE Trans. Very Large Scale Integr. (VLSI) Syst. **25**(4), 1583–1587 (2017)
2. Garrault, P., Philofsky, B.: HDL coding practices to accelerate design performance. Technical Report. Xilinx Inc. (2006)
3. Irfan, M., Ullah, Z., Cheung, R.C.: D-TCAM: a high-performance distributed ram based TCAM architecture on FPGAs. IEEE Access **7**, 96060–96069 (2019)
4. Karam, R., Puri, R., Ghosh, S., Bhunia, S.: Emerging trends in design and applications of memory-based computing and content-addressable memories. Proc. IEEE **103**(8), 1311–1330 (2015)
5. Kornijcuk, V., et al.: Reconfigurable spike routing architectures for on-chip local learning in neuromorphic systems. Adv. Mater. Technol. **4**(1), 1800345 (2019)
6. Nguyen, X.T., Nguyen, H.T., Pham, C.K.: A scalable high-performance priority encoder using 1D-array to 2D-array conversion. IEEE Trans. Circ. Syst. II Express Briefs **64**(9), 1102–1106 (2017)
7. Reviriego, P., Ullah, A., Pontarelli, S.: PR-TCAM: efficient TCAM emulation on Xilinx FPGAs using partial reconfiguration. IEEE Trans. Very Large Scale Integr. (VLSI) Syst. **27**(8), 1952–1956 (2019)
8. Somasundaram, M.: Circuits to generate a sequential index for an input number in a pre-defined list of numbers. US Patent 7,155,563, 26 Dec 2006

9. Srinivasavarma, V.S., Vidhyut, S.: A TCAM-based caching architecture framework for packet classification. ACM Trans. Embed. Comput. Syst. (TECS) **20**(1), 1–19 (2020)

10. Tang, Q., Wang, Z., Guo, B., Zhu, L.H., Wei, J.B.: Partitioning and scheduling with module merging on dynamic partial reconfigurable FPGAs. ACM Trans. Reconfig. Technol. Syst. (TRETS) **13**(3), 1–24 (2020)

11. Ullah, Z., Ilgon, K., Baeg, S.: Hybrid partitioned SRAM-based ternary content addressable memory. IEEE Trans. Circ. Syst. I Regul. Pap. **59**(12), 2969–2979 (2012)

12. Vipin, K., Fahmy, S.A.: FPGA dynamic and partial reconfiguration: a survey of architectures, methods, and applications. ACM Comput. Surv. (CSUR) **51**(4), 1–39 (2018)

Domain-Specific Modeling and Optimization for Graph Processing on FPGAs

Mohamed W. Hassan$^{(\boxtimes)}$, Peter M. Athanas, and Yasser Y. Hanafy

ECE department, Virginia Tech, Blacksburg, USA
{mwasfy,athanas,yhanafy}@vt.edu

Abstract. The use of High Level Synthesis (HLS) tools is on the rise; however, performance modelling research has been mainly focused on regular applications with uniform memory access patterns. These performance models fail to accurately capture the performance of graph applications with irregular memory access patterns. This paper presents a domain-specific performance model targeting graph applications synthesized using HLS tools for FPGAs. The performance model utilizes information from the hardware specification, the application's kernel, and the graph input. While the compilation process of HLS tools takes hours, the information required by the performance model can be extracted from the intermediate compilation report, which compiles in seconds. The goal of this work is to provide FPGA users with a performance modelling framework for graph applications, to estimate performance and explore the optimization space. We tested the framework on Intel's new Devcloud platform and achieved speedup up to 3.4× by applying our framework's recommended optimization strategy compared to the single pipeline implementation. The framework recommended the best optimization strategy in 90% of the test cases.

Keywords: Graph processing · Performance modelling · Domain-specific optimization · FPGA · Graph data-sets

1 Introduction

High-Level Synthesis (HLS) tools significantly improved the ease of use of FPGAs and allowed them to be accessible to the masses. Since then, the potential of FPGAs has been maximized making them important in high-performance computing. Previous research explored optimizing and modeling the performance of HLS designs [5,10–12,14,15]; however, much of the previous work targeted regular applications with uniform memory access patterns that are easily predictable. However, these performance models fail to accurately capture the expected performance of irregular applications. This study explores performance modelling of graph applications, which are characterized by irregular memory access patterns. In many instances, the processing requirements of a given graph computation are heavily data-dependent with a major impact on the computational solution and in

© Springer Nature Switzerland AG 2021
S. Derrien et al. (Eds.): ARC 2021, LNCS 12700, pp. 315–326, 2021.
https://doi.org/10.1007/978-3-030-79025-7_24

turn the resulting performance [6]. In this paper, we propose a domain-specific performance model for graph applications. However, Not only performance is of concern, but exploring the optimization space is also a major concern. For an FPGA developer to test the efficacy of myriad optimizations, one has to spend days synthesizing them. Many FPGA developers wish for an answer to some optimization questions without the need to fully synthesize many design optimizations. The framework is built using information from three sources; the hardware intermediate compilation report, the application's kernel, and the graph input size. The intermediate compilation report can be generated in seconds; hence, we acquire the information needed without resorting to the lengthy compilation process of full hardware generation. Moreover, the model derives useful information about the graph input characteristics using information readily available upon reading the graph. Therefore, no time-intensive pre-processing of the graph input is required to extract the graph characteristics. Finally, we extract application properties directly form the source kernel. The framework explores the optimization space and guides the user on how to optimize the hardware design for a specific graph input. Using our approach, we were able to achieve up to 3.4× speedup compared to the baseline implementation of Pannotia benchmark [2], with an average of 2.1×. Exploring the optimization space, the framework was able to identify the best optimization strategy in over 90% of the test cases. The contributions of this work are:

- We devise an automated domain-specific framework for performance modelling and optimization space exploration of graph applications, and
- We augment graph input characteristics into the framework to exploit knowledge of the input properties in the decision-making process.

2   Background

2.1   Graph Applications

Three graph applications are used to test the efficacy of the proposed framework, PageRank (PR), Single Source Shortest Path (SSSP), and Maximal Independent Set Algorithm (MIS). PR is an algorithm used by Google search engine to rank web pages [8]. SSSP is the problem of finding the shortest path tree from one source node to the rest of the graph nodes [3]. MIS finds a maximal subset of nodes in a graph such that no nodes outside that set may join it (per the independent set theory) [1].

2.2   Hardware Parallelism Extensions

Parallel extension optimizations in the scope of HLS can be categorized into three main groups; SIMD vectorization, Compute Unit replication (CU), and Loop Unrolling (LU). Firstly, SIMD optimization is not allowed by the compiler due to cross iteration dependency. However, we use multiple compute units to explore the data parallelism space. On the other hand, loop unrolling synthesizes multiple copies of the loop while decreasing the iteration count by the same factor. This deepens the pipeline, so we categorized it as a pipeline parallelism extension.

3   The Performance Model Framework

This section discusses the construction of the performance model, starting by introducing some terminology, then elaborating on the details of the performance model. The source code for the performance model and the implemented applications are open-sourced and available at (https://github.com/mwasfy/gale).

3.1   Information Collection and Terminology

Our approach is simple and easy to use, with an easily obtainable set of information, one can predict the performance of a graph application. Not only that, but the optimization space is automatically explored without any additional information. As shown in Fig. 1, a user starts by generating the intermediate compilation report of the original application using the HLS tool, which takes seconds to compile. The second step is to collect information from the source code and the data-set, as seen in Table 1. Finally our analytical model is executed to retrieve performance predictions and optimization recommendations. This is all done without the need for any long compilation process, or any dynamic profiling, or pre-processing of the graph data-set to extract information.

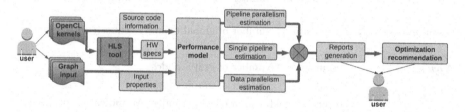

Fig. 1. Overview of the performance model framework. Information flowing from the user, through the framework, then back to the user.

Performance Model Terminology. As shown in Table 1, the parameters are divide into three groups; hardware specifications, application characteristics, and input properties. Table 1 explains the meaning of each parameter and its source, however, additional derived parameters are explained in detail in Subsect. 3.2.

Model Parameters' Impact on Performance Estimation. We will start by discussing key parameters obtained from the input graph. Pre-processing a graph input is time-intensive and defeats the purpose of fast exploration of the optimization search space. Hence, we only depend on information readily available by reading the graph, the number of nodes ($Nodes$), and the number of edges ($Edges$). However, the ratio of edges to nodes ($Chunk\_size = Edges/Nodes$), directly translates to the average degree of the graph, which we use to infer the average number of memory requests in the inner loop of the graph application. As for the application parameters, we observed that most graph applications

Table 1. Performance model parameters, source, and description

Parameter	Source	Description
N	Compiler	Number of pipeline stages
F_{pipe}	Compiler	Pipeline frequency
F_{mem}	Compiler	Memory frequency
II	Compiler	Initiation Interval: Number of stall cycles between iterations
Mem_cycles_{outer}	Compiler	Number of clock cycles to access the global memory in the outer loop
Mem_cycles_{inner}	Compiler	Number of clock cycles to access the global memory in the inner loop
$BURST\_SIZE$	Compiler	Number of maximum memory access transactions per cycle
CU	Compiler	Data parallelism degree: The number of Compute Units
LU	Compiler	Pipeline parallelism degree: Loop unrolling factor
$Mem\_accesses_{outer}$	Application	Number of global memory requests in the outer loop
$Mem\_accesses_{inner}$	Application	Number of global memory requests in the inner loop
$Nodes$	Input	Number of graph nodes
$Edges$	Input	Number of graph edges
$Chunk\_size$	Input	Ratio of edges to nodes. An indication of the average number of neighbours for each node

have a double nested loop structure. The outer loop retrieves pointers to the nodes of interest, while the inner loop retrieves the nodes actual state. Hence, the performance model features $Mem\_accesses_{outer}$ & $Mem\_accesses_{inner}$.

3.2   Performance Model Construction

To better understand the performance model, we broke down the model's structure to first introduce the single pipeline model, then we extend the approach for pipeline and data parallelism. Execution time estimation is the sum of the pipeline and memory access latency ($est\_pipe\_time + est\_mem\_time$).

Pipeline Latency. The performance model starts by quantifying an estimate of the pipeline's computational time est_pipe_time. Equation 1 depicts how to quantify the number of computational clock cycles.

$$est\_pipe\_time = \frac{N + (Nodes \times (II + 1))}{F_{pipe}} \tag{1}$$

Memory Access Latency. First, the memory access model calculates the total number of memory requests that will be generated in the outer loop, which makes use of the $BURST\_SIZE$ parameter to accurately model its latency. The number of clock cycles required to fetch this amount of data from global memory is quantified in Eq. 2.

$$Loop\_latency_{outer} = \frac{Nodes \times Mem\_accesses_{outer}}{BURST\_SIZE} \times Mem\_cycles_{outer} \tag{2}$$

On the other hand, inner loop modelling uses $Chunk\_size$ to quantify how it utilizes the burst coalescing feature of the global memory access as depicted in Eq. 3. With the number of inner loop iteration $Iters_{inner} = Nodes$, the total memory access requests generated by the inner loop are estimated as shown in Eqs. 4, 5. Finally, Eq. 6 estimates the total memory access latency.

$$Loop\_reqs_{inner} = \lceil \frac{Chunk\_size}{BURST\_SIZE} \rceil \tag{3}$$

$$Loop\_accesses_{inner} = Loop\_reqs_{inner} \times Iters_{inner} \times Mem\_accesses_{inner} \tag{4}$$

$$Loop\_latency_{inner} = Loop\_accesses_{inner} \times Mem\_cycles_{inner} \tag{5}$$

$$est\_mem\_time = \frac{Loop\_latency_{inner} + Loop\_accesses_{outer}}{F_{mem}} \tag{6}$$

3.3 Parallelism Extension

Loop Unrolling Extension - Pipeline Parallelism. The offline compiler synthesizes loop unrolling by adding by more pipeline stages and coalescing the load operations so that the compute unit can maximize its bandwidth efficiency. The loop's trip count is reduced to $Iters_{inner\_LU} = Nodes/LU$, while the projected memory bandwidth efficiency is depicted in Eq. 7.

$$Loop\_reqs_{inner\_LU} = \lceil \frac{Chunk\_size \times LU}{BURST\_SIZE} \rceil \tag{7}$$

The model accounts for the extra memory pressure exerted on the global memory interface. Through studying the execution schedule, we observed that the memory access units are overloaded by a factor of $(LU - 2)$. Hence, we calculate a metric to quantify the memory overhead pressure factor as shown in Eq. 8. It can be observed that as long as $Loop\_reqs_{inner\_LU} > 1$, loop unrolling will show great performance gains. However, values < 1 show degradation in performance, due to the extra un-amortized memory pressure. Equation 9 demonstrates how to calculate the total number of accesses estimated for the unrolled loop.

$$Mem\_ovh\_factor = \frac{1}{Loop\_reqs_{inner\_LU}} \times (LU - 2) \tag{8}$$

$$Loop\_accesses_{inner\_LU} = Iters_{inner\_LU}(Loop\_accesses_{inner} + Mem\_ovh\_factor) \tag{9}$$

Multiple Parallel PEs Extension - Data Parallelism. The major difference between loop unrolling and compute unit replications is in the synthesized load/store units. Unlike loop unrolling, each compute unit has its own memory access interface. While this diminishes the memory bandwidth available to each compute unit, graphs with low $Chunk\_size$ show significant performance gains compared to the Single Work Item (SWI) implementation. The memory overhead coefficient is now calculated as in Eq. 10. Hence, to calculate the total $Loop\_latency_{inner\_CU}$, we quantify the size of memory accesses as shown in Eq. 11, where $Iters_{inner\_CU} = Nodes/CU$.

$$Mem\_ovh\_factor = \frac{Loop\_reqs_{inner}}{CU} + (\frac{Chunk\_size}{BURST\_SIZE} \times CU) \tag{10}$$

$$Loop\_accesses_{inner\_CU} = Iters_{inner\_CU}(Loop\_accesses_{inner} + Mem\_ovh\_factor) \tag{11}$$

4   Evaluation and Analysis of the Framework

The computational platform used is the new Intel Devcloud [7]. The computational node includes an Intel Arria 10 GX FPGA and an Intel Xeon Gold 6128 CPU. The FPGA designs run at an average frequency of 240 MHz, while the CPU includes 24 cores running at 3.40 GHz. We implement six designs for each of the three tested applications (PR, SSSP, and MIS). One design for the SWI, three designs for pipeline parallelism (2, 4, and 8 loop unrolling factors), and two designs for data parallelism (2, and 4 CUs). The network data repository [9] is used as the source of real-world graphs dataset. To ensure the generality of different types of graphs, we use a set of graphs with sizes up to 100M edges adopting a wide range of properties including road networks, web-graphs, social networks, and more. All designs were tested across the input data-set to measure the execution time for accuracy calculation purposes. Hence, we have a total of 18 designs executed over 20 graphs for a total of 360 test cases.

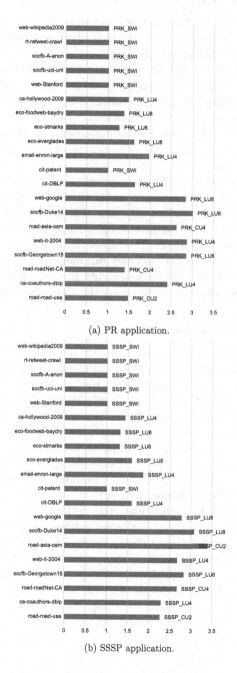

(a) PR application.

(b) SSSP application.

Fig. 2. Speedup of the recommended optimization strategy compared to SWI.

4.1 Optimizations and Performance Analysis

To quantify the accuracy of the framework's recommendation, we measured the execution time of all test cases, **90%** of which, the framework recommended the best optimization maximizing performance.

As depicted in Fig. 2, we achieve up to 3.4× speedup with an average speedup of 2.1×. It should be noted that a speedup of 1× is not a bad result, in fact, it is counted as an advantage of our framework. A speedup of 1× means that the framework recommended the SWI implementation. After exhaustively measuring the real execution, it showed that expanding pipeline or data parallelism slows down the performance in these cases. Hence, the single pipeline turned out to be the best choice indeed.

While SSSP application's recommendations were correct for all test cases, PR application had two errors mispredicting the fastest optimization strategy, `road-road-usa` and `road-roadNet-CA`. This will be detailed later in Sect. 4.3. MIS application is not included in the figure because the framework always recommended SWI which showed a speedup of 1×. The MIS application includes three memory access in the outer loop and four memory access in the inner loop, which is almost 3× the memory requirements for both PR and SSSP. Hence, parallelism extension only adds pressure on the global memory interface.

4.2 Performance Model Accuracy

It should be noted that analytical performance models for FPGA designs, that use compile-time information only, rarely achieve accurate performance estimation for graph applications. We reproduced the performance model proposed in [15], which showed up to two orders of magnitude deviation from actual performance when tested on graph applications. We elaborate on this later in Sect. 5. Our performance model shows accuracy within 2× of the measured performance, which can be considered acceptable considering the data-driven execution profile of graph applications. As shown in Fig. 3, only 5% of the tested cases were out of bounds of the 2× performance prediction threshold. Moreover, 25% of the test cases achieved over 80% prediction accuracy.

For the PR and SSSP applications, the performance model sustains over 85% prediction accuracy for data parallelism extensions. However, pipeline parallelism prediction accuracy drops to 50%. We analyzed the execution profile and identified the root causes. The analysis showed that typically graphs with a high or low average degree are well predicted achieving over 85% prediction accuracy. However, it was observed that graphs with an average degree in the spectrum $4 < Chunk\_size < BURST\_SIZE$, show unpredictable memory access patterns that are not well captured by the model. This misprediction is compounded by the pipeline parallelism extension.

4.3 Discussion

Analyzing the PR application results showed that our framework diverges from optimal recommendations as shown in Fig. 4. The performance model estimated

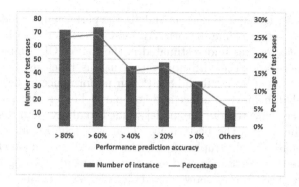

Fig. 3. Performance prediction accuracy in percentiles.

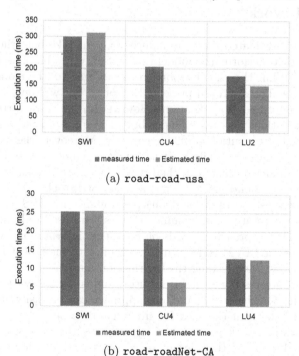

Fig. 4. Measured and estimated time for three PR configurations, the baseline (SWI), framework's recommendation (CU), optimal configuration (LU).

that road network graphs showed the best performance by applying data parallelism extensions. This was true for all road network graphs for both PR and SSSP applications, except road-road-usa and road-roadNet-CA in the case of PR application. Figure 4 shows the measured execution time compared to the estimated execution time for three configurations, the baseline (SWI), the performance model recommended strategy (CU), and the optimal optimization strategy (LU). As depicted in Figs. 4a and 4b, the performance model accurately estimated the execution time in both SWI and LU implementations. However, the Mem_ovh_factor was underestimated in the case of CU4 implementation.

On the other hand, the MIS application has as much as 3× the memory access requirements of both PR and SSSP. Our performance model depicts pressure on the global memory interface and how parallel extensions may compound that problem. For that reason, the model seemed to always find the SWI implementation to be always the best choice. That was true for all graphs except those exceptionally small graphs that make efficient use of on-chip memory, `eco-everglades`, `eco-stmarks`, and `eco-foodweb-baydry`. Using CU4 configuration for these three graphs shows an average of 1.4× speedup.

5 Related Work

Zohouri et al. [15] evaluated the performance of OpenCL kernels where they proposed an analytical performance model that captures the baseline performance of HLS designs. While they don't report on the accuracy of the model, we reproduced the results. The approach presented is sound but will only be feasible in the case of compute-bound applications. However, in the case of irregular memory access applications such as memory-bound graph applications, the model failed to depict the execution profile accurately. Moreover, the exploration of optimization techniques was wildly off par. This is mainly due to the simplistic memory access model presented in their work. On the other hand, our work is focused on memory-bound, irregular memory access kernels.

One of the earliest works on modeling performance for HLS design was presented in [12] where static and dynamic analyses were used to build the performance model. This approach depends on collecting information by performing static analysis of the LLVM code, dynamic profiling of the OpenCL application execution on GPUs, then feeding the information into the model. This amount of information is not readily available for users and is not easily reproducible for new applications. On the other hand, our approach can be easily applied to any graph application without the need for any dynamic profiling.

Other interesting work proposed in [4], explores the idea of extending the roofline model [13] to the HLS design space. This work considers the resource utilization on the FPGA to maximize area usage by replicating the Processing Entities (PEs), and in turn, maximize performance. However, in addition to the limited bandwidth of global memory on FPGAs, complications may arise due to the irregular memory access patterns of graph applications, as shown in Sect. 4. Moreover, this work only recognizes the peak performance attainable on the FPGA design, which is not realistic considering the irregularity of the graph applications domain.

Another effective design space exploration work was proposed in [14], where they recursively quantify the loop latency through an analysis on the LLVM-IR. However, a major drawback that would make this work not well suited for graph applications, is that their analysis depends on having static loop bounds.

This work is efficient in the case of regular memory access applications, where the loop bounds can be fixed and global memory can be accessed through fixed stride accesses, which unfortunately is not the case for graph applications.

6 Conclusion

Graph applications have a challenging execution profile that is hard to optimize and harder to model. The data-driven execution profile makes it hard to capture performance estimations using compile time analytical models. However, in this work, we presented a domain-specific performance modelling framework that projects the performance of graph inputs on HLS-based FPGA designs. Furthermore, the framework explores the optimization space without the need for a lengthy hardware synthesis process for each optimization strategy. The framework recommended the best optimization strategy in 90% of the test cases. We show up to 3.4× speedup with an average of 2.1× compared to the single pipeline implementation by using optimization strategies suggested by our framework.

References

1. Alon, N., Babai, L., Itai, A.: A fast and simple randomized parallel algorithm for the maximal independent set problem. J. Algorithms **7**(4), 567–583 (1986)
2. Che, S., Beckmann, B.M., Reinhardt, S.K., Skadron, K.: Pannotia: understanding irregular GPGPU graph applications. In: 2013 IEEE International Symposium on Workload Characterization (IISWC) (2013)
3. Cormen, T.H., Leiserson, C.E., Rivest, R.L., Stein, C.: Section 22.4: topological sort. In: Introduction to Algorithms, 2nd edn., pp. 549–552. MIT Press and McGraw-Hill (2001)
4. Da Silva, B., Braeken, A., D'Hollander, E.H., Touhafi, A.: Performance modeling for FPGAs: extending the roofline model with high-level synthesis tools. Int. J. Reconfigurable Comput. **2013** (2013)
5. Hassan, M.W., Helal, A.E., Athanas, P.M., Feng, W.C., Hanafy, Y.Y.: Exploring FPGA-specific optimizations for irregular openCL applications. In: 2018 International Conference on ReConFigurable Computing and FPGAs (ReConFig) (2018)
6. Hasssan, M.W., Athanas, P.M.: Graph analytics on hybrid system (GAHS) case study: Pagerank. In: 2021 IEEE International Parallel and Distributed Processing Symposium Workshops (IPDPSW) (2021)
7. Intel: Intel devcloud for oneAPI projects (2019). https://software.intel.com/en-us/devcloud/oneapi
8. Page, L., Brin, S., Motwani, R., Winograd, T.: The PageRank citation ranking: bringing order to the web. Technical report, Stanford InfoLab (1999)
9. Rossi, R.A., Ahmed, N.K.: The network data repository with interactive graph analytics and visualization. In: Proceedings of the Twenty-Ninth AAAI Conference on Artificial Intelligence (2015). http://networkrepository.com
10. Umuroglu, Y., Morrison, D., Jahre, M.: Hybrid breadth-first search on a single-chip FPGA-CPU heterogeneous platform. In: 2015 25th International Conference on Field Programmable Logic and Applications (FPL), pp. 1–8, September 2015. https://doi.org/10.1109/FPL.2015.7293939

11. Wang, Y.: Accelerating Graph Processing on a Shared-Memory FPGA System. Ph.D. thesis, Carnegie Mellon University, Pittsburgh, USA (2018)
12. Wang, Z., He, B., Zhang, W., Jiang, S.: A performance analysis framework for optimizing openCL applications on FPGAs. In: IEEE International Symposium on High Performance Computer Architecture (HPCA), pp. 114–125, March 2016
13. Williams, S., Waterman, A., Patterson, D.: Roofline: an insightful visual performance model for multicore architectures. Commun. ACM **52**(4), 65–76 (2009)
14. Zhao, J., Feng, L., Sinha, S., Zhang, W., Liang, Y., He, B.: Performance modeling and directives optimization for high-level synthesis on FPGA. IEEE Trans. Comput. Aided Des. Integr. Circ. Syst. **39**(7) (2019)
15. Zohouri, H.R., Maruyama, N., Smith, A., Matsuda, M., Matsuoka, S.: Evaluating and optimizing openCL kernels for high performance computing with FPGAs. In: Proceedings of the International Conference for High Performance Computing, Networking, Storage and Analysis, pp. 35:1–35:12 (2016)

Covid4HPC: A Fast and Accurate Solution for Covid Detection in the Cloud Using X-Rays

Dimitrios Danopoulos[1]([⊠])[iD], Christoforos Kachris[1,2][iD], and Dimitrios Soudris[1][iD]

[1] Department of Electrical and Computer Engineering, NTUA, Athens, Greece
{dimdano,kachris,dsoudris}@microlab.ntua.gr
[2] Democritus University of Thrace, Komotini, Greece

Abstract. Covid-19 pandemic has devastated social life and damaged the economy of the global population with a constantly increasing number of cases and fatalities each day. A popular and cheap screening method is through chest X-Rays, however it is impossible for every patient with respiratory illness to be tested fast and get quarantined in time. Thus, an automatic approach is needed which is motivated by the efforts of the research community. Specifically, we introduce a Deep Neural Network topology that can classify chest X-Ray images from patients in 3 classes; Covid-19, Viral Pneumonia and Normal. Detecting COVID-19 infections on X-Rays with high accuracy is crucial and can aid doctors in their medical diagnosis. However, there is still enormous data to process which takes up time and computer energy. In this scheme, we take a step further and deploy this Neural Network (NN) on a Xilinx Cloud FPGA platform which as devices are proven to be fast and power efficient. The aim is to have a medical solution on the Cloud for hospitals in order to facilitate the medical diagnosis with accuracy, speed and power efficiency. To the best of our knowledge, this application has not yet been considered for FPGAs while the accuracy and speed achieved surpasses any previous known implementation of NNs for X-Ray Covid detection. Specifically, it can classify X-Ray images at a rate of 3600 FPS with 96.2% accuracy and a speed-up of 3.1× vs GPU, 17.6× vs CPU in performance and 4.6× vs GPU, 13.1× vs CPU in power efficiency.

Keywords: Deep learning · Neural networks · Covid-19 · Medical diagnosis · X-rays · FPGA · Xilinx

1 Introduction

The sudden spike in the number of patients with COVID-19, a new respiratory virus, has put unprecedented load over healthcare systems across the world. The

---

Covid4HPC has been open-sourced and is available online in the following Github repository: https://github.com/dimdano/Covid4HPC.

© Springer Nature Switzerland AG 2021
S. Derrien et al. (Eds.): ARC 2021, LNCS 12700, pp. 327–336, 2021.
https://doi.org/10.1007/978-3-030-79025-7_25

COVID-19 pandemic continues to have a devastating effect on the health and economy of the global population.

A critical step towards the fight against Covid is the effective screening of infected patients so that those infected can receive immediate treatment and get quarantined in time, especially those at high risk. The detection of the disease is commonly performed through chest X-Ray radiograph (CXR) examination by highly-trained specialists. It's a popular and widespread method which usually manifests as an area of increased opacity on CXR. However, it is a very time-consuming, and complicated manual process that can put additional stress on healthcare systems. Also, X-Ray images of pneumonia in the case of Covid-19 are often not very clear and can be misclassified to other diseases or other benign abnormalities which can lead to wrong medication or late quarantine [9,13].

In this scheme, an automated method is needed to categorize chest X-rays and determine the type of disease. Inspired by the open source efforts of the research community and the urgent need to develop solutions to aid in the fight against the COVID-19 pandemic we will introduce a Deep Learning application for automatic Covid-19 detection through chest X-Rays. The aim of this project is to port our tool in the Cloud so that doctors and clinics from all around the world can have access to a Cloud Medical AI Assistance remotely. Cloud Computing will enable the on-demand availability of computer system resources that will perform Medical Diagnosis using our tool. However, CNN models have high demands in compute power as they are often computationally intensive [7]. Thus, modern companies that operate the data centers will require a demanding workload and computer power due to these algorithms, especially in the pandemic era with terabytes of patient data to be processed everyday.

In this project we take a step further to this modern challenge and provide a solution which, to the best of our knowledge, has not been considered yet. This computational complexity motivated our efforts to enhance these AI task using hardware-specific optimizations by leveraging a hardware architecture known as Field-programmable gate array (FPGA). FPGA-based acceleration has shown great potential [5,6] as they offload specific tasks from the CPU improving the global performance of the system and reducing its dynamic power consumption. These implementations have seen great advancement on Deep Learning as is it shown that they have been extremely effective on CNN tasks due to their massive parallelism and reconfigurability on the bit level. Thus, by deploying our CNN model to FPGA platforms we accelerated the Image Recognition process with great speed and power efficiency as well, which is essential in datacenter workloads.

In this project, we will describe several highly accurate Deep Learning models using custom and novel Convolutional Neural Network topologies that can detect Covid-19 disease in chest X-Ray images which are also deployed in a Xilinx Cloud FPGA platform. In summary, the main contributions of the paper are as follows:

- We describe three efficient CNN model architectures in terms of memory and size which can classify chest X-Rays in 3 classes (Covid, Viral Pneumonia, Normal). Trained on Tensorflow Deep Learning framework we achieved a maximum of ~97% accuracy which surpasses the performance of previous CNNs for chest X-Ray Covid detection.

- We introduce FPGA-specific optimizations on the model topologies and use 8-bit quantization for the arithmetic precision. We select the most efficient model and accelerate it on a Xilinx Alveo U50 FPGA using an heterogeneous architecture that is also scalable and can be seamlessly ported in datacenters for cloud workoads.
- We ran the FPGA application in a containerized environment and measure the results in terms of accuracy, speed and power efficieny. We outperformed other high performance devices (Xeon CPU, V100 GPU) in performance and performance/watt. Also, we make an evaluation on the model classification ability using heatmaps on top of X-Rays and show other useful classification metrics.

2   Related Work

X-Ray detection algorithms have been explored by many researchers especially in the past, usually for lung diseases such as Viral Pneumonia. In the last year (2020), due to the Covid-19 pandemic there is a continuous growing interest from the research community on developing AI models for the detection of Covid-19 disease. There is an urgent need to aid clinicians in their medical diagnosis using automated tools through Deep Learning. However, as the computational complexity of AI models is large and the laboratory data from new patients grows exponentially a new robust platform is needed to handle all these requests with high speed and efficiency. The following related work involves similar design methods for relatively similar problems or present a related problem that covers our problem domain.

Several studies have investigated the use of Neural Networks towards Covid detection through chest X-Rays. Mangal et al. [11] presented CovidAID, a deep neural network based model to triage patients for appropriate testing. On the publicly available covid-chestxray dataset their model gave 90.5% accuracy for the COVID-19 infection. On the same scheme, Wang et al. introduced CovidNet [16], a deep convolutional neural network design tailored for the detection of COVID-19 cases from CXR images. They showed a classification report with 93.3% achieved accuracy. Although, these projects were some of the early work towards the fight against Covid and were very useful for the community, they lack the performance of our CNN model which achieves an accuracy of 96.2%.

Also, various deep learning based approaches have been developed to identify Covid-19 [3,12,17] but lack the accuracy or precision of our model. Others, such as Jain et al. [10] who presented an Xception model topology for the same problem domain, they achieved slightly higher accuracy as our model (97,9%) but they do not include a method to accelerate or run more efficiently the inference procedure. Last, there is numerous work that focus on two-class classification between Covid and non-Covid images [8,14] in contrast with ours which employs a third classification category called Viral Pneumonia. This is essential for the treatment strategy since Viral Pneumonia patients require different treatment plans.

Last, it's worth noticing that to the best of our knowledge there is no previous work on Covid detection through FPGAs. Thus, we will compare some related projects on this problem domain which mainly involves hardware acceleration of CNNs targeting Pneumonia detection which is a fair comparison for our hardware implementation. For example, Chouhan et al. [15] developed a CNN model using the transfer learning approach from models in ImageNet. They reported an average inference computation time of 0.043s in an Nvidia GTX 1070 GPU card. Also, Azemin et al. [2] implemented a ResNet-101 CNN model architecture for Covid-19 detection and reported a speed of 453 images/min in CPU.

To conclude, a lot of work has been done using CNNs and Covid-19 detection. Our project presents a novel CNN with higher accuracy than previous known work but also an acceleration method for deployment in cloud FPGAs.

3   Software Implementation

In this study, we constructed several CNN topologies in order to classify the CXR images of the dataset. The best AI model was selected in terms of accuracy and efficiency in order to be deployed in the FPGA (described in next section). In this section, we focus on the analysis of the problem formulation, the dataset used, the training procedure and the hw-oriented optimizations that we did on the models in order to efficiently deploy them on the FPGA device.

3.1   Dataset

We developed the database of Covid-19 X-Ray images from the Italian Society of Medical and Interventional Radiology (SIRM) COVID-19 DATABASE [1,4]. The number of samples used to train and evaluate the AI models is comprised of a total of 2905 CXR images, split in 219 for Covid, 1345 for Viral Pneumonia and 1341 for Normal class. Although the dataset is relatively small and irregular, we managed to introduce several techniques to overcome this issue as we will describe next. The choice of this dataset was guided by the fact that it is open source and fully accessible to the research community and the general public, and as the datasets grow we will continue to develop and finetune the models accordingly. In the bar chart below, we show the CXR images distribution for each infection type split to train and test sets (test dataset set to 25%).

3.2   Model Topology

We propose three different topologies for this problem in order to have a better evaluation on the dataset and select the most suitable model for acceleration on the FPGA afterwards. We developed separate models that each has different prediction accuracy, architectural complexity (in terms of number of parameters) and computational complexity (in terms of number of MAC operations). A CustomCNN which is a classic convolution neural network, a lightResNet which is a ResNet50 variant and DenseNetX which is based on DenseNet architecture but it also includes the Bottleneck layers and Compression factor.

3.3 Training

Below we will analyze several techniques that we applied on the training procedure. These optimizations mainly had to do with the specific dataset characteristics but also include several hardware-aware optimizations on the model that helped us deploy and accelerate the CNNs in the FPGA more efficiently.

Class Weighting. Training with a dataset like ours with very few Covid-19 images as opposed to Normal or Viral Pneumonia images constitutes a class-imbalanced problem. This is a complexity that poses significant challenge to the converging of our models as CNNs are normally assume to be trained on identical distribution datasets. To overcome the class variance we imposed specific class weights (i.e. $6\times$ on Covid class) which applied to the model's loss for each sample and eventually helped the model learn from the imbalanced data.

HW-Aware Optimizations. The CNNs' topology needed some minor modifications in order to be compatible and efficient with Vitis AI quantizer and compiler. In particular, the order of the Batch Normalization (BN), Rectified Linear Unit (ReLU) activation and Convolution layers has been altered from $BN \Rightarrow ReLU \Rightarrow Conv$ to $Conv \Rightarrow BN \Rightarrow ReLU$. Also, another optimization that we did is in the case of GlobalAveragePooling2D, which we needed for example in DenseNetX and we replaced it with AveragePooling2D plus a Flatten layer. Last, softmax was implemented in the DPU and not in SW (proved to be more than 100 times faster) using an AXI master interface named `SFM_M_AXI` and an interrupt port named `sfm_interrupt`. The softmax module used `m_axi_dpu_aclk` as the AXI clock for `SFM_M_AXI` as well as for computation.

4 Hardware and System Design

In this section we will describe the process of quantizing, evaluating, compiling and at last running the AI models on the Alveo FPGA platform. Also, we analyze the full architecture of the FPGA design working in an heterogeneous system that allows efficient communication with the host processor. Last, we create a full end-to-end environment that anyone can use and test our project seamlessly through an FPGA-containerized application.

4.1 Acceleration Method

As our application can be used from millions of users across the globe, an efficient and fast solution is needed. We chose to use Vitis AI environment in order to deploy our CNN models in an Xilinx Alveo U50 FPGA and eventually create an application with high inference throughput and small memory footprint as well, an essential factor for cloud workloads.

Below, we analyze further the steps required for model quantization and evaluation and last the compilation of the model which creates the DPU instructions for utilizing the compute units (CUs) of the FPGA.

1. *Quantization*: First, before proceeding with the quantization process we converted our models to a Tensorflow compatible floating-point frozen graph. Next, we chose to quantize the trained weights of our CNNs with 8-bit precision as this has been proven to keep an acceptable accuracy at similar CNN applications. Last, we provided a sample set of the training data to calibrate the quantization process. The data performed a full forward pass through the model and the weights were calibrated according to the data range the application needs for inference.

2. *Evaluation of quantized model*: The conversion from a floating-point model where the values can have a very wide dynamic range to an 8-bit model where values can only have one of 256 values almost inevitably leads to a small loss of accuracy. Thus, the prior evaluation of the quantized graph on Tensorflow was essential before proceeding with the compilation of the model. Nevertheless, this technique most of the times gave almost identical accuracy results compared with the actual application tested on the board. Also, the quantized graph on the FPGA compared with the floating point graph on CPU had a small impact on the final accuracy (<0.5%).

3. *Model compilation*: In the final stage, we compiled the graph into a set of micro-instructions that were passed to the DPU in `.xmodel` file format. The Vitis AI compiler converted and optimized where possible the quantized deployment model and gave as output the final "executable" for CNN inference. The generated instructions were specific to the particular configuration of our DPU which in our case the **DPUCAHX8H** DPU IP was selected. We passed the DPU's parameters in a `.dcf` file for the target Alveo U50 board.

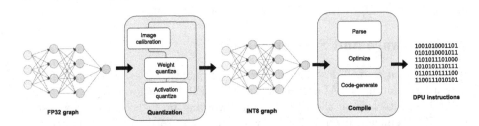

Fig. 1. CNN graph quantization and compilation for the FPGA DPU

5   Evaluation and Results

In this section we will evaluate and profile our application. We will start from the model performance of the neural networks in terms of validation loss, accuracy and several other classification metrics. Next, we will proceed with the performance evaluation of the hardware accelerator in terms of resource utilization, acceleration and power efficiency achieved over CPU and GPU. Last, we will present some qualitative results that help localizing areas in the X-Ray image most indicative of Covid or Viral Pneumonia.

5.1 Model Evaluation

In this study, experiments were ran with Tensorflow and Keras using the typical 224 × 224 image dimensions found in most CNNs. All the models have been trained with Adam optimizer along with EarlyStopping and best model callbacks. The classification models were optimized by minimizing the cross-entropy loss function. Also, several parameters and hyperparameters of each model were tuned during the training such as Learning Rate (LR) and epochs. Below, in Table 1 you can observe the major characteristics of each model in terms of training hyperparameters, model specifications and model evaluation.

Table 1. CNN model characteristics and performance

Model	Hyperparameters		Model specs		Evaluation	
	LR	Epochs	Params	FLOPs	Accuracy	Loss
CustomCNN	0.0001	70	2.033G	1.025G	96.2%	0.16
LightResNet	0.001	60	2.697G	2.814G	96.5%	0.408
DenseNetX	0.005	80	0.758G	1.722G	94.9%	0.264

5.2 Qualitative Analysis

In the previous tables we showed a variety of performance criteria that can be used to evaluate the performance of our classification models. Under certain circumstances we can select a different model with certain characteristics that satisfies our needs depending on the performance efficiency (FLOPs) or accuracy. For demonstration purposes and the FPGA implementation we selected the Custom-CNN model which has the most efficient performance as it achieves high accuracy (almost same as lightResNet) while having minimal compute requirements which is essential for compute workloads. Additionally, below we present several useful activation maps that were obtained for the last convolutional layer of CustomCNN network. These are very important because they give us an insight on the model's classifier capability as well as validate the regions of attention of the disease.

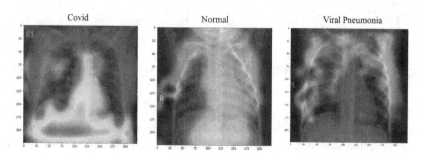

Fig. 2. X-Ray visualizations using attention heatmaps

5.3 System Performance

For the evaluation of the system design we first confirmed the resource utilization of the FPGA DPU. The hardware setup for the deployment was a Xilinx Alveo U50 Cloud FPGA with 8 GB HBM Memory Capacity and 316 GB/s total bandwidth. The device was installed on Gen4x8 PCI express running at a kernel clock of 300MHz. Table 2 shows the resource utilization of a DPUv3E kernel with five batch engines (our design used two kernels).

Table 2. Resource utilization of a single DPU kernel

Name	Utilization summary				
	BRAM	URAM	DSP	FF	LUT
Used	628	320	2600	310752	250290
Percentage	46.7%	50%	43.6%	21.2%	28.7%

Next, we evaluated inference with the CustomCNN model on other high performance systems, specifically an Nvidia V100 GPU and a 10-core Intel Xeon Silver 4210. The inference on the other devices was tested on Tensorflow with the default settings and choosing appropriate batch sizes. On the left side of Fig. 3 we can observe the maximum throughput each device achieves measured with X-Rays per second (FPGA: 3600, GPU: 1157, CPU: 204). Also, we annotated the latency (in ms) for single X-Ray image inference in each device. Additionally, on the right side of Fig. 3 we show the measurement for the power efficiency of each device in X-Rays/Sec/Watt (FPGA: 51.3, GPU: 11.1, CPU: 3.9).

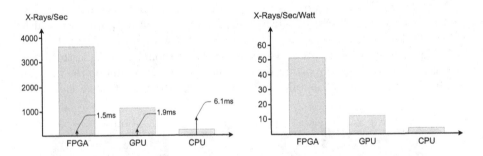

Fig. 3. Performance and Performance/Watt metrics across different architectures

The throughput metric is essential for cloud workloads that operate with large size of patient data while the latency metric is important for edge scenarios (i.e. mobile phones) which are time critical and an immediate response is needed.

It is evident from the quantitative comparison that the FPGA exhibits the highest inference speed for large batch size scenarios in the cloud achieving 3.1×

speed-up from GPU and 17.6× speed-up from CPU in throughput. It's worth mentioning that the 8-bit quantized CNN used on FPGA had less than 0.5% accuracy loss which was desired for the performance and power efficiency gains.

Last, the FPGA outperformed the other two devices in the power efficiency metric measured in X-Rays/Sec/Watt. Specifically, it achieved 4.6× speed-up from GPU and 13.1× speed-up from CPU. The 51.3 X-Ray/Sec/Watt metric of the FPGA means that in order to specify a disease in a single chest X-Ray image we would only need 0.019 s and 1 W of compute power. This is crucial for cloud providers which aim to reduce energy consumption in datacenters while maintaining the required performance for the needs of each application.

6 Conclusion

In this study, we introduced several AI models each with its own characteristics for the detection of COVID-19 cases from CXR images that are open source and available to the general public. We demonstrated significant improvement in accuracy and performance compared with the aforementioned related work. Moreover, we investigated how our model makes predictions using an attention heatmap method in an attempt to gain deeper insights into critical factors associated with COVID cases, which can aid clinicians in improved screening as well as improve trust and transparency when leveraging our CNN.

Moreover, we quantized, compiled and accelerated the AI model for deployment on an Alveo U50 FPGA with the aim to accelerate the computer-aided screening. The application was containerized and can be seamlessly ported in a cluster of FPGAs operating in the cloud with high performance and energy efficiency compared with other architectures.

By no means this is a production-ready solution intended for self-diagnosis. From a research point of view, we are focusing on boosting more the performance and adding further features in our AI Health framework as new data is collected such as risk stratification for survival analysis or predicting hospitalization durations. The spectrum of possible AI automated systems is vast but this work shed some light to the area with successful results aiming to make FPGAs contribute fundamentally into the computer-aided Medical Diagnosis.

Acknowledgements. This project was funded from the Xilinx University program and the Hellenic Foundation for Research and Innovation (HFRI) and the General Secretariat for Research and Technology (GSRT), under grant agreement No 2212-Hardware Acceleration of Machine Learning Applications in the Cloud.

References

1. COVID-19 DATABASE. https://www.sirm.org/category/senza-categoria/covid-19/. Accessed 30 Oct 2020
2. Azemin, M., Hassan, R., Mohd Tamrin, M.I., Ali, M.: Covid-19 deep learning prediction model using publicly available radiologist-adjudicated chest x-ray images as training data: preliminary findings. Int. J. Biomed. Imaging 1–7 (2020). https://doi.org/10.1155/2020/8828855

3. Channa, A., Popescu, N., Malik, N.U.R.: Robust technique to detect covid-19 using chest x-ray images 1–6 (2020). https://doi.org/10.1109/EHB50910.2020.9280216
4. Chowdhury, M., et al.: Can AI help in screening viral and covid-19 pneumonia? IEEE Access **8**, 132665–132676 (2020). https://doi.org/10.1109/ACCESS.2020.3010287
5. Danopoulos, D., Kachris, C., Soudris, D.: Acceleration of image classification with caffe framework using FPGA, pp. 1–4 (2018). https://doi.org/10.1109/MOCAST.2018.8376580
6. Danopoulos, D., Kachris, C., Soudris, D.: Automatic generation of FPGA kernels from open format CNN models, pp. 237–237 (2020). https://doi.org/10.1109/FCCM48280.2020.00070
7. Danopoulos, D., Kachris, C., Soudris, D.: Utilizing cloud FPGAs towards the open neural network standard. Sustain. Comput. Inf. Syst. **30** (2021). https://doi.org/10.1016/j.suscom.2021.100520. https://www.sciencedirect.com/science/article/pii/S2210537921000135
8. Dansana, D., et al.: Early diagnosis of covid-19-affected patients based on x-ray and computed tomography images using deep learning algorithm. Soft Comput. (2020). https://doi.org/10.1007/s00500-020-05275-y
9. Davies, H.D., Wang, E.E.L., Manson, D., Babyn, P., Shuckett, B.: Reliability of the chest radiograph in the diagnosis of lower respiratory infections in young children, the pediatric infectious disease journal. Pediatr. Infect. Diseas. J. **15**, 600–604 (1996)
10. Jain, R., Gupta, M., Taneja, S., Hemanth, D.J.: Deep learning based detection and analysis of covid-19 on chest x-ray images. Appl. Intell.1–11 (2020). https://doi.org/10.1007/s10489-020-01902-1
11. Mangal, A., et al.: CovidAID: Covid-19 detection using chest x-ray (2020)
12. Miranda Pereira, R., Bertolini, D., Teixeira, L., Silla, C., Costa, Y.: Covid-19 identification in chest x-ray images on flat and hierarchical classification scenarios. Comput. Methods Programs Biomed. **194**, 105532 (2020). https://doi.org/10.1016/j.cmpb.2020.105532
13. Neuman, M.I., et al.: Variability in the interpretation of chest radiographs for the diagnosis of pneumonia in children. J. Hosp. Med. **7**(4), 294–298 (2012)
14. Pham, T.: A comprehensive study on classification of covid-19 on computed tomography with pretrained convolutional neural networks. Sci. Rep. **10** (2020). https://doi.org/10.1038/s41598-020-74164-z
15. Singh, S., Khamparia, A., Gupta, D., Tiwari, P., Moreira, C., Damasevicius, R., Albuquerque, V.: A novel transfer learning based approach for pneumonia detection in chest x-ray images. Appl. Sci. **10**, 559 (2020). https://doi.org/10.3390/app10020559
16. Wang, L., Wong, A.: Covid-net: a tailored deep convolutional neural network design for detection of covid-19 cases from chest radiography images (2020)
17. Zhang, J., et al.: Viral pneumonia screening on chest x-rays using confidence-aware anomaly detection. IEEE Trans. Med. Imaging **PP**, 1 (2020). https://doi.org/10.1109/TMI.2020.3040950

Author Index

Printed in the United States
by Baker & Taylor Publisher Services